I0762824

Kentucky Horse Country

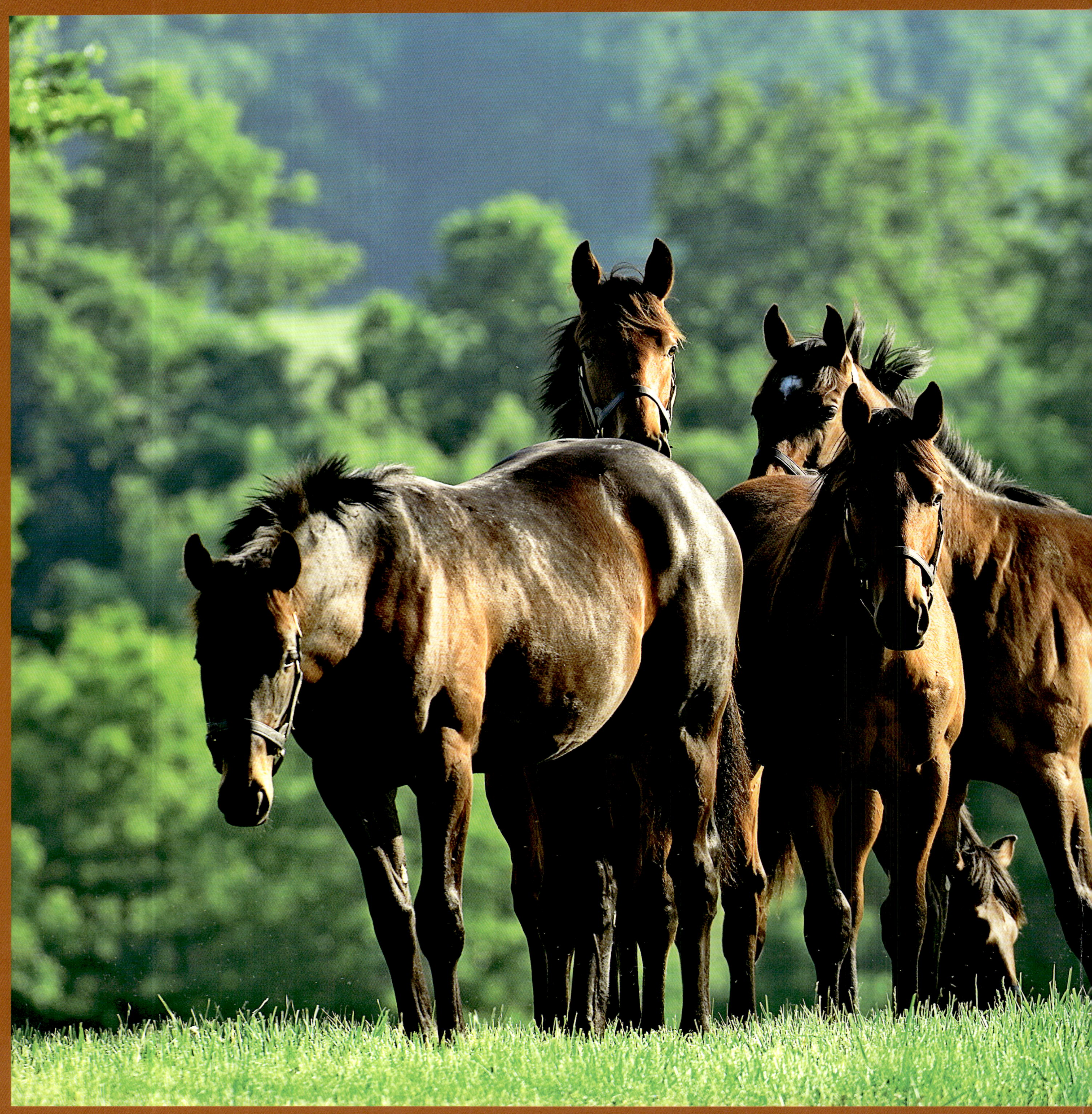

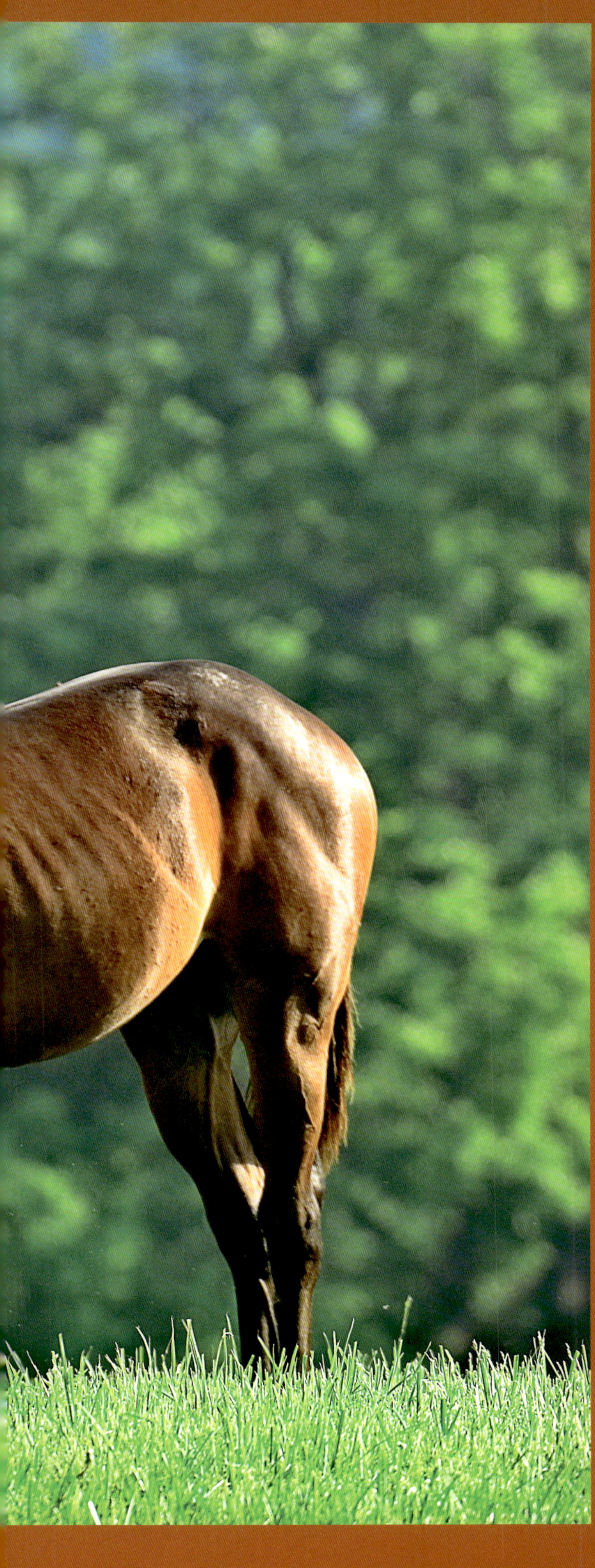

JAMES ARCHAMBEAULT

Kentucky Horse Country

IMAGES OF THE BLUEGRASS

The University Press of Kentucky

Frontispiece:

MARES ALONG MOORES MILL ROAD, SCOTT COUNTY

Having spent the night in a field, a group of mares gathers on a hilltop before being led to their stalls. Although most horse people will tell you that horses prefer being outside, the change of scene is probably welcome—along with some special attention, such as a rubdown or a breakfast of oats. Spring is breeding season, so these mares have already been bred or soon will be. The gestation period for horses is eleven months, so being bred in May means a new foal next April.

Publication of this volume was made possible in part by a grant from the National Endowment for the Humanities.

Scholarly publisher for the Commonwealth,
serving Bellarmine University, Berea College, Centre College of Kentucky, Eastern Kentucky University, The Filson Historical Society, Georgetown College, Kentucky Historical Society, Kentucky State University, Morehead State University, Murray State University, Northern Kentucky University, Transylvania University, University of Kentucky, University of Louisville, and Western Kentucky University.

Editorial and Sales Offices: The University Press of Kentucky
663 South Limestone Street, Lexington, Kentucky 40508-4008
www.kentuckypress.com

12 11 10 09 08 5 4 3 2 1

Library of Congress Cataloging-in-Publication Data
Archambeault, James.
Kentucky horse country : images of the bluegrass / James Archambeault.
p. cm.
ISBN 978-0-8131-2505-3 (hardcover : alk. paper) 1. Horses—Kentucky—Pictorial works. 2. Kentucky—Pictorial works. 3. Photography of horses. I. Title.
SF337.A73 2008
636.1'2097690222—dc22 2007052573

This book is printed on acid-free recycled paper meeting the requirements of the American National Standard for Permanence in Paper for Printed Library Materials.

Designed and typeset by Julie Allred, BW&A Books, Inc.
Manufactured in China

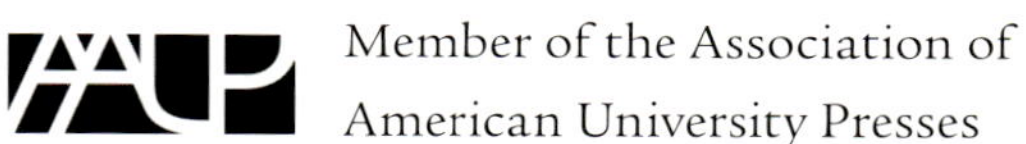
Member of the Association of American University Presses

For all who believe in and work for the preservation of the Bluegrass and its rich history and traditions

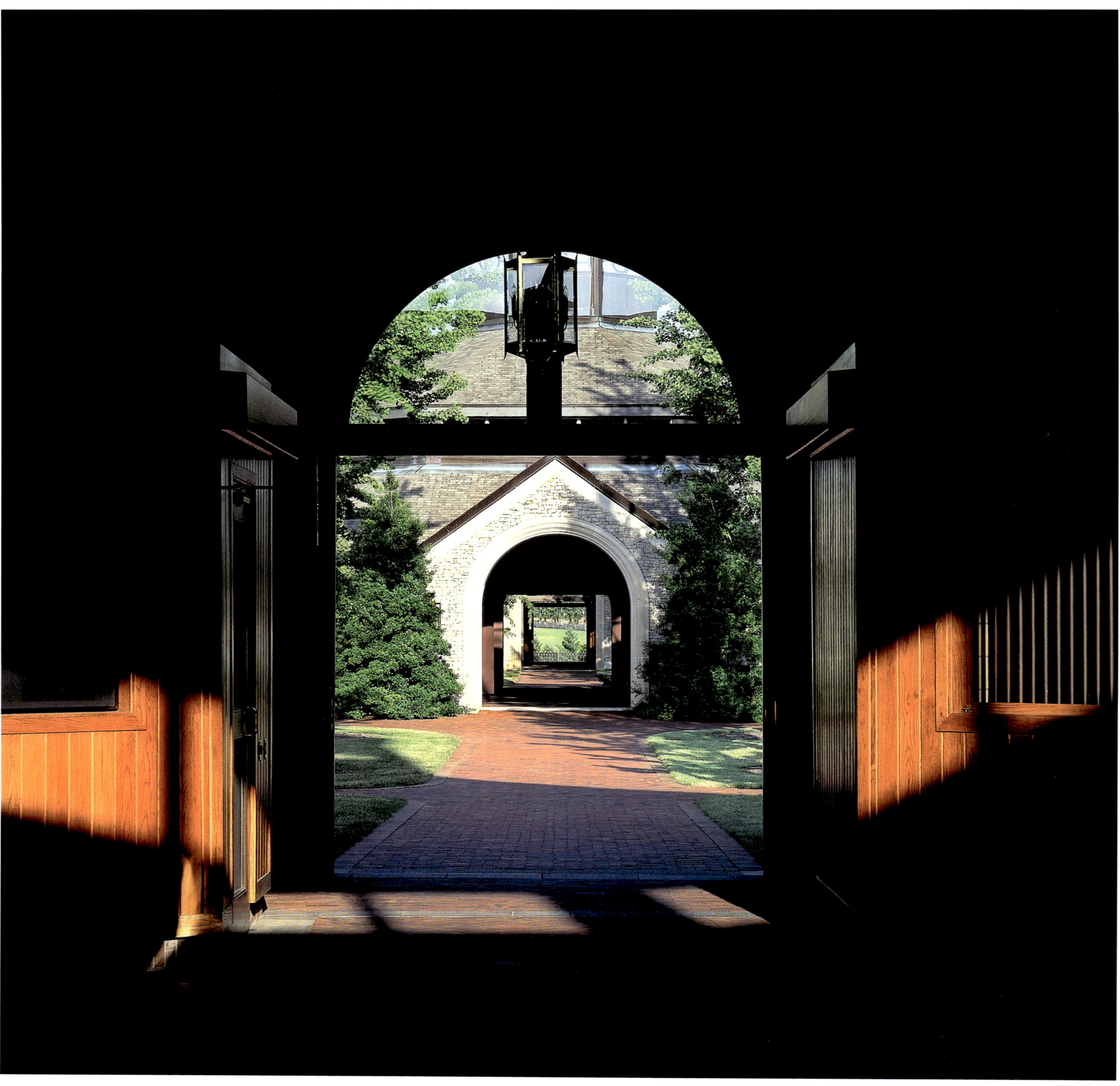

Contents

Facing: STALLION BARN, DARLEY'S GAINSBOROUGH FARM

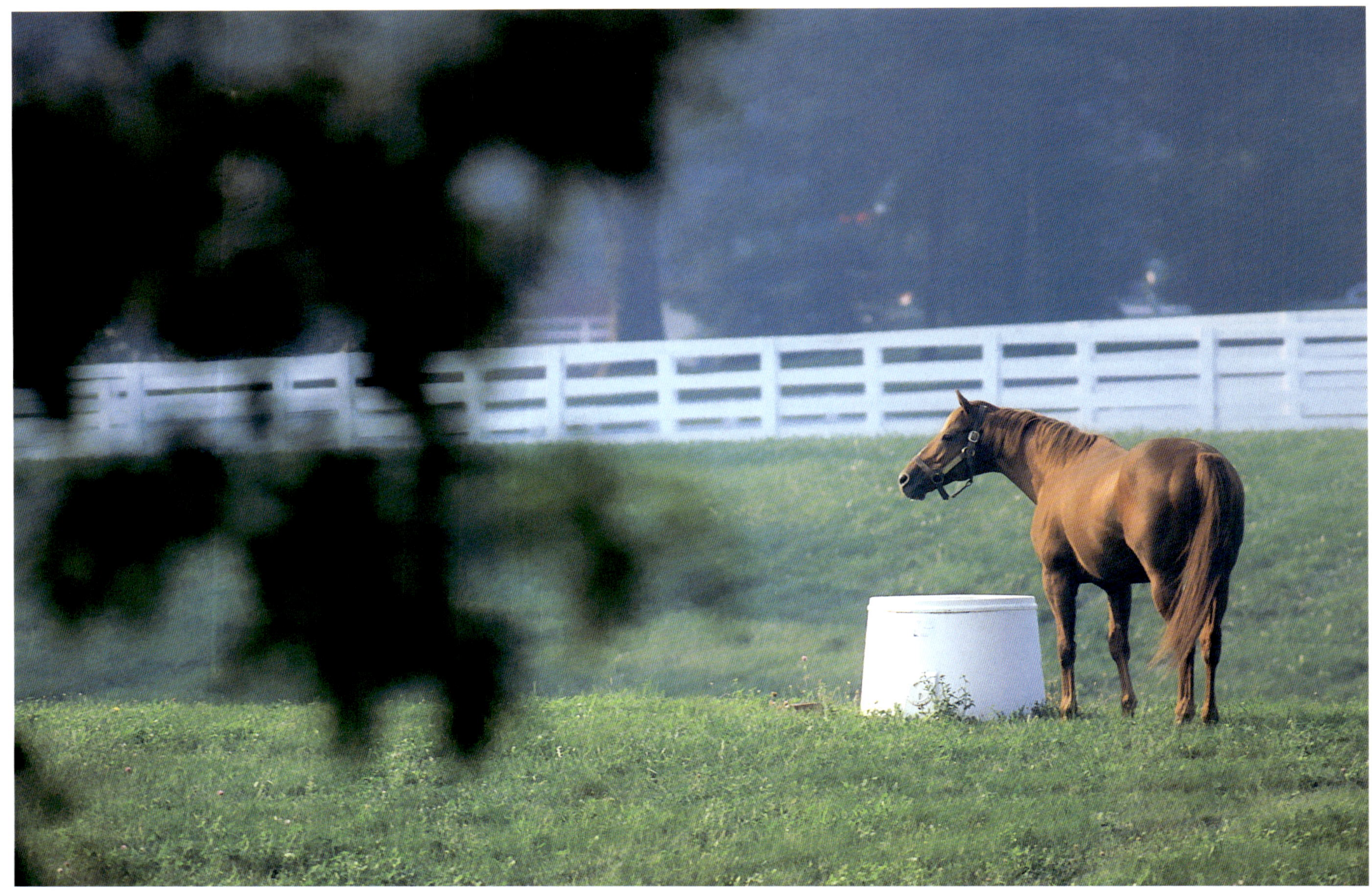

AFFIRMED, 1978 WINNER OF THE TRIPLE CROWN

In one of the most memorable Triple Crown series of all time, Affirmed defeated his rival, Alydar, in the Kentucky Derby, the Preakness, and the Belmont by a combined distance of less than two lengths. People still marvel at the performance of those two great competitors. The length of time that followed without another winner was even longer than the quarter-century interval between the Triple Crown wins by Citation and Secretariat.

Foreword

IN THE EARLY 1970S, a few years before my racing career began, James Archambeault started photographing the horses and landscapes of the Bluegrass region of Kentucky. Jim was fortunate to have captured on film some of the greatest horses of the time, including Secretariat, A. P. Indy, Storm Cat, Silver Charm, Charismatic, Seattle Slew, and many others, all of which are pictured in this excellent book. He also witnessed many of the greatest races of the era, including the classic Triple Crown duel between Affirmed and Alydar in 1978.

It is hard to believe that it has been thirty years since Affirmed and I entered racing history together. Since then, I have ridden overseas, traveled widely, and experienced many wonderful places. But no matter where I go, the Bluegrass State remains home. To those of us who love horses, there is no place on earth that is more special. Today, my family and I live on a farm in Kentucky, where I raise cattle and breed and train Thoroughbreds.

In this wonderful collection of photographs, James Archambeault perfectly captures the natural beauty of central Kentucky, in particular the unique landscape that serves as a backdrop to the horse industry. These photographs—ranging from mares and foals grazing alongside Kentucky's rolling hills to backstretch scenes of farriers and exercise riders to images of historic horse farms—are a celebration of Kentucky horses and the rich racing tradition that fans around the world associate with the Bluegrass State. I hope that you enjoy them.

STEVE CAUTHEN
Verona, Kentucky

In 1978, Steve Cauthen became the youngest jockey to win the Triple Crown, riding Affirmed. He is a recipient of three Eclipse Awards, Sports Illustrated*'s 1977 Sportsman of the Year Award, and the George Woolf Memorial Jockey Award and was inducted into the National Thoroughbred Racing Hall of Fame in 1994. The only jockey to win the Kentucky, Epsom, Irish, French, and Italian derbies, Cauthen retired from racing in 1992.*

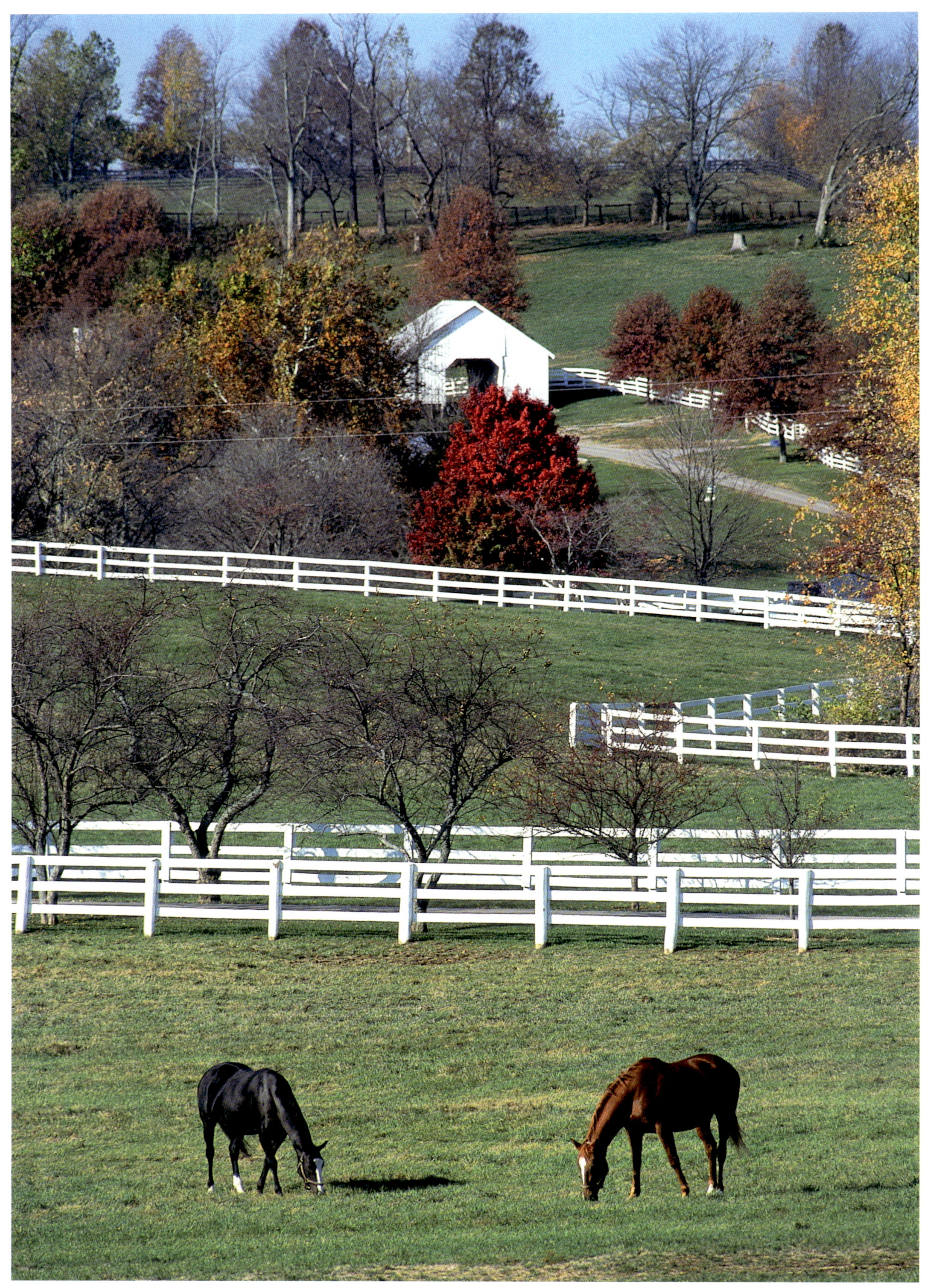

MARES GRAZING IN AUTUMN, VAN METER ROAD

Preface

THERE IS NO PLACE on earth comparable to the Bluegrass region of Kentucky. The 2,500 square miles surrounding the city of Lexington are covered with rich, brown, fertile soil that a simple hand spade cuts through like warm butter. Below this topsoil lies an ancient cap of limestone, fertilizing the land and creating a perfect environment for the raising of crops, livestock, and the beautiful animals we call horses.

In 2005, Kentucky's Bluegrass was named one of the most endangered cultural sites in the world by the International World Monument Fund, a designation that includes the Taj Mahal in India and the Great Wall of China. More than 1 million acres, encompassing seventeen counties, are threatened by environmental damage caused largely by poor local planning or overdevelopment. Like that of unique places the world over, the beauty of the Bluegrass is its Achilles' heel. After decades of being a closely held secret, the region has been discovered by the outside world and is now a "destination point." Without proper planning, love and greed will destroy the Bluegrass, forfeiting a legacy going back to the first western settlements in America.

Beginning in the mid- to late 1700s, early explorers to the western country called "Kentucke" included Daniel Boone, Simon Kenton, James Harrod, Dr. Thomas Walker, and many others. It was some of the richest land they had ever seen, with great savanna grasslands, huge trees (some of which survive today), and tens of thousands of wild game animals. Native American tribes in the area had agreed among themselves that the land could be used by all the tribes for hunting and trading, but no tribe would live on the land. As the Europeans began coming over the Appalachian Mountains through the Cumberland Gap or down the Ohio River in an attempt to settle the Bluegrass region, the Indians fought hard to keep them out. After many bloody encounters over the next twenty to thirty years, the settlers succeeded in pushing the Indians west and north, thus leaving the Bluegrass ripe for development in the cultural traditions of the early American colonists.

No time was wasted. The first settlements were established in Harrodstown in 1774 and Lexington in 1775. Only thirteen years later, on 16 February 1788, this ad appeared in the first newspaper west of the Appalachian Mountains, the *Kentucky Gazette:*

> The famous horse PILGARLICK of a beautiful chesnut colour, full fourteen hands, three inches high, rising ten years old, will stand the ensuing season on the head of salt river at capt. Abr. Irvins mercer county and will cover mares at the very low price of ten shillings a leap if the money is paid down, or fifteen at the expiration of the season: and twenty shillings the season in cash, or thirty shilling in good trade. Pilgarlick was got by the noted imported horse janus, his dam be old Silver-eye: And is the swiftest horse in the district of kentucke from one to six hundred yards.

And so began the Bluegrass legacy. In 1871, a horse named Lexington was foaled in Scott County and became the sire of sires. Many of the Thoroughbred horses today are of his lineage in some way. His skeletal remains are on display at the Smithsonian Institution in Washington, D.C. Other great horses raised in the Bluegrass include Man o' War, Leamington, Citation, Secretariat, Seattle Slew, and Alydar. There are now more than 500 horse farms in the Bluegrass region of Kentucky. On any given day, at least 40,000 horses are roaming the fields of the Bluegrass.

The horse is one of the most beautifully sculptured and beloved animals in the world and needs no photographic embellishment. All these photographs appear as they were taken in nature. Most were shot on medium-format or 35mm transparency film; a few were taken with a digital camera. All scans and digital imagery are true to the original photographs. Although every effort was made to secure accurate information for the captions, any errors in content are mine.

There are many people who offered their help and guidance, culminating in the creation of this book. Special thanks to my wife, Lee, for understanding my mission and putting up with my long absences and to my sister Kathy and her husband Bennett for their support and encouragement. I am also grateful to Dan Rosenberg and the staff of Three Chimneys Farm; Bob Brady and the staff of Kentuckiana Farm; Jim Williams and Fran Taylor of the Keeneland Race Course; Dan Silvestri of Impact Photography; Ed Bowen for his excellent introduction and insightful comments and suggestions; Joyce Fogleman of Lane's End Farm; Allen Kershaw, Mary Bourne, and the staff of Darley's Gainsborough Farm; Maryjean Wall, turf writer extraordinaire; the great jockey Steve Cauthen, for lending his name to these pages; and Laura Sutton, Melinda Wirkus, Steve Wrinn, and the entire staff of the University Press of Kentucky. It has been an honor to work with you all.

J. A.

The Bluegrass

VIGOR *amid* ELEGANCE

EDWARD L. BOWEN

WE SOMETIMES ASK much of words in the English language. The term *Bluegrass,* for instance, is well and heavily burdened, for it might be employed in one case to conjure natural wonders, whereas next being uttered to suggest a specific element of American culture. Further, it might be used to describe a relatively confined geographic locus, which is at odds with its role as a rather careless synonym for the whole state of Kentucky.

Each of these iterations evokes a loveliness scented with history. To the anthropologist, the Bluegrass can be a shorthand connoting an admixture of social customs ranging from rustic music to basketball to cultural refinement. To the historian, the Bluegrass might conjure rugged outdoorsmen and adventurers, risking life and fortune to migrate westward from the Atlantic coast to experience the massive continent in its entirety. In nature, with the help of humankind, the Bluegrass means north-central Kentucky, a land of pungent forests and voluptuous fields, many of which are the habitat of Thoroughbred horses.

Ah yes, the horses. Nothing equates with the Bluegrass, or Kentucky, more redolently than horses or their inseparable companion, the Kentucky Derby. Horses are probably more central to the core image of the Bluegrass and Kentucky than any other commodity or allusion. Specifically, it is the Thoroughbred that holds pride of place. Many distinguished show horses and high-flying Standardbreds have graced the history of Kentucky, but the Thoroughbred—the racing breed developed in England hundreds of years ago—has risen to preeminence.

The artistry of photographer James Archambeault is aimed at the visual realities and fantasies of this horse world and its environs as they exist today. Any enthralling *today,* of course, is the soufflé produced by the alliance and nuance of many a *yesterday.* The focus here is on the key ingredients, that combination of the designed and the happenstance that is the only true author of all history.

ACCIDENTAL NOMENCLATURE

That a society connected to horses would emerge as the predominant theme of the Bluegrass was not preordained by some cosmic force; however, a long-ago decision about the naming of Kentucky features might make it seem otherwise. In 1750, Dr. Thomas Walker set out to explore the 800,000 acres secured by the Loyal Land Company of Charlottesville, Virginia, in what was known as the district of Kentucke. To lead a party on such an assignment indicates that Walker was a man of daring and courage, but when it came to naming the features he discovered, his imagination was found wanting. When Walker discovered a gap through the mountains, he named it the Cumberland Gap, and he gave the mountains themselves the same name—the Cumberlands. Later, struck by the sight of an impressive waterfall, no other namesake came to mind.

Who was this Cumberland? According to the viewpoint of the teller, he was a military man, up one day and down the next; or a profligate gambler and hedonist who ate himself to death; or one of the most important figures on the turf. In the last context, he had the distinction of being the breeder of the most influential animal in the early development of the Thoroughbred as well as one of the other ancestors of the modern breed. These horses were, respectively, Eclipse and Herod.

The Duke of Cumberland was a son of England's King George II and had been commander in chief of the British army against the Scots at Culloden. After that battle earned him fame in England and enmity in Scotland, a defeat by the French at Hastenbeck in 1757 pushed him out of the war game and into another

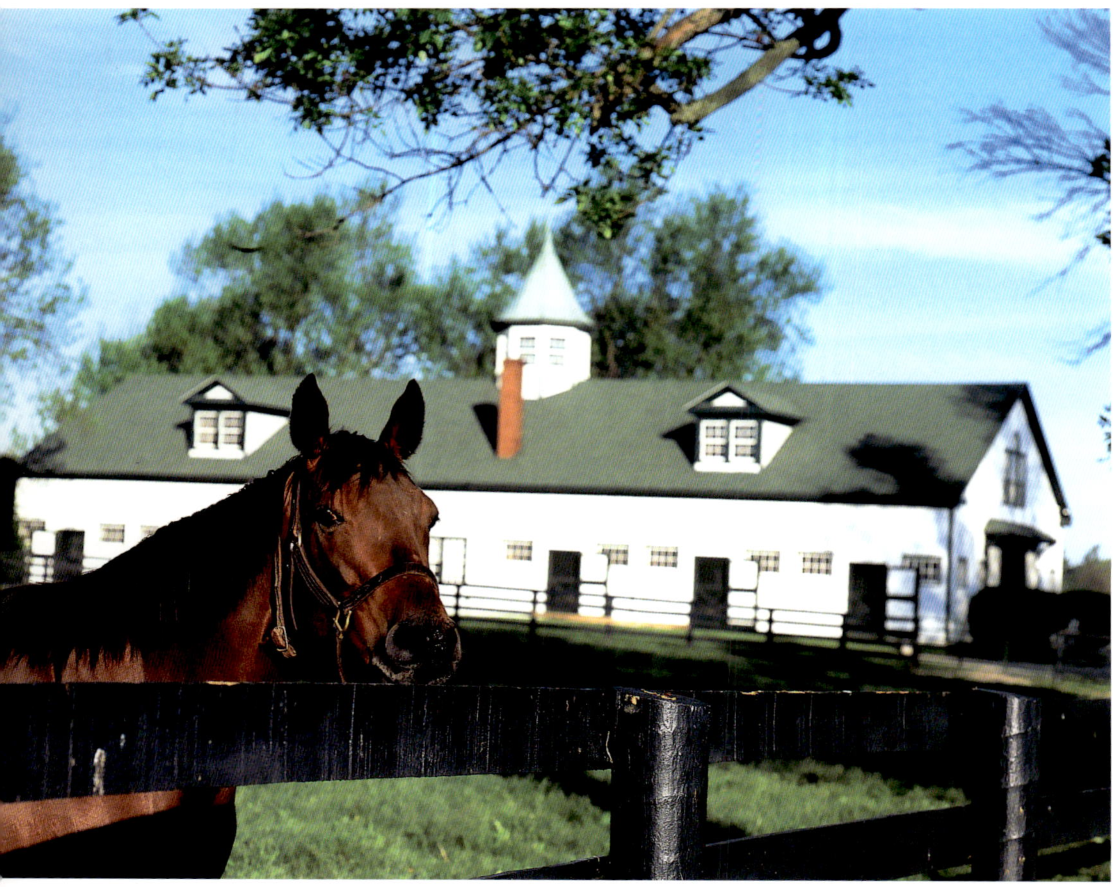

MARE AT DOMINO STUD

career. Thereafter, he waged his battles at the races. As one of the early members of England's Jockey Club, he was an avid breeder of horses and a gambler.

THE ORIGINS OF KENTUCKY HORSE RACING

Thus, by naming the key geographic and geologic features of Kentucky after a racing man, Walker inadvertently insinuated into its history a connection with the pastime that would prove to be its lasting identity. This identity took some time to develop, for those who first followed Walker into Kentucky were occupied primarily with clearing the land, growing crops, hunting, raising families, drinking, fighting Indians, and praying a good deal over all of the above. Daniel Boone spent enough time in Kentucky to be adopted as one of its image makers, giving that image a heroic slant.

Despite the rigors of their lives, these settlers soon discovered the diversion of racing their horses against their neighbors'. Horses were a necessity of life, but they were easily converted to a sporting use. Early horse racing was informal, consisting of short dashes with whatever stock was available. English Thoroughbred imports were rare. Nevertheless, the trappings of racing were being developed in Britain and would be mimicked in America. Despite the hostility during the War of Independence, Americans still felt an underlying sense of connection to what many considered the motherland.

Across the Atlantic, a combination of Asian imports, speedy little Irish horses, and some native stock had been nurtured by the British, leading to the breed that would become known as the Thoroughbred. As early as 1730, Bulle Rock was imported into Virginia—the first horse of the Thoroughbred style to reach these shores. In the era after the Revolution, racing became an autumn custom in Lexington and was popular in other towns as well. Dash races gave way to heat races, which might require a horse to run four miles three times in a single afternoon. That segue necessitated an improvement in the racing stock. In 1797, Benjamin Wharton advertised his horse Blaze, the first English stallion to find his way into Kentucky by way of Virginia. By then, the Thoroughbred was well established in England.

THOROUGHBRED BREEDING AND RACING IN THE BLUEGRASS

Early in the nineteenth century, a lengthy process began by which the Bluegrass would eventually separate itself from other racehorse-breeding areas and become synonymous with the Thoroughbred. This process involved part design, in the form of human visionaries and individual achievement, and part chance, dependent on the haphazard results of elements beyond human control.

Although the rough-and-ready pioneers certainly have their place in the story of the Bluegrass and the Thoroughbred, other characters played leading roles. One of these was Lexington physician Elisha Warfield, a transplanted Marylander who, in 1821, gave up his medical practice to pursue a number of business interests, including banking, real estate, and the hemp trade (which was legal at the time). He became one of the wealthiest men in Kentucky. The racing game has always been an attractive option for wealthy investors looking for excitement, and those who get involved in the horse world tend to be drawn into the management of the game and the protection of its better traditions. Warfield was no exception. His contributions included his involvement in the development of the Kentucky Association racetrack in Lexington, which opened in 1828 and operated for more than a century. That role, however, was secondary to his breeding of the horse named Lexington—proving that Americans were just as capable as their British counterparts in guiding the destiny of the noble Thoroughbred.

Lexington was a son of the renowned but aged Kentucky stallion Boston (named for the card game, not the city) and was foaled from the mare Alice Carneal. Boston was representative

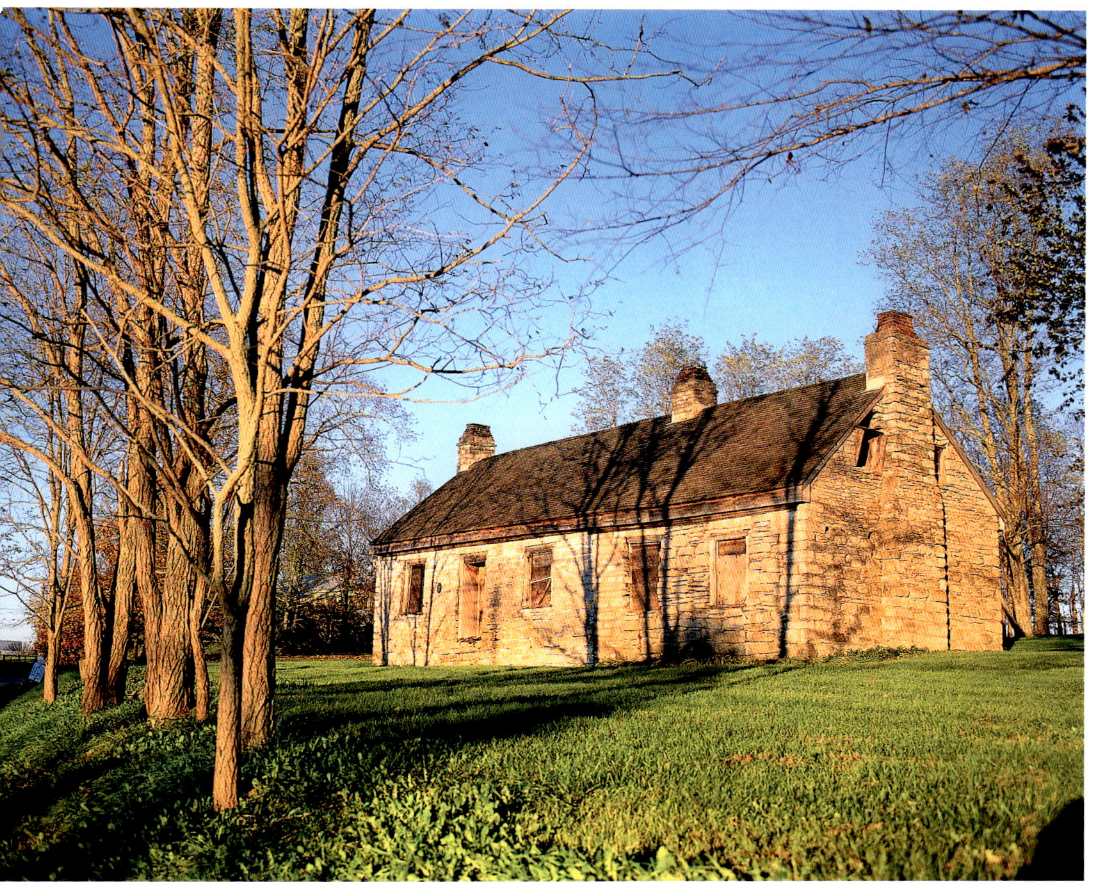

PIONEER STONE HOUSE, NEWTOWN PIKE

of the development of the American Thoroughbred from founding stock. His sire, Timoleon, was a son of Sir Archy, a stallion that gained prominence as a sire of racers in an earlier era. Sir Archy, in turn, was a son of Diomed, winner in 1780 of the first English Derby, a seminal event in Thoroughbred racing. Diomed had been declared a "proven poor foal getter" in England and had been sold off to the supposed bumpkins overseas, where he proved to be a sterling influence on the American branch of the breed.

The Boston-Alice Carneal colt was born on 17 March 1850 on the sprawling farm "The Meadows," which Warfield had developed near the racecourse in Lexington. Warfield originally named him Darley because the foal reminded him of John Sartorius's painting of the Darley Arabian. Sartorius was one of numerous artists who took advantage of sportsmen's urge to have their best animals memorialized in oil or bronze, and those who were sufficiently talented had successful careers. (It was said that a member of the sporting gentry would pay more for a portrait of his horse than for one of his wife.)

Then, as now, horses were ineligible to race until they were two years old, but Darley did not begin to compete until age three. Warfield was in his seventies by that time, and his wife and doctor had proclaimed that he should not subject himself to the excitements of racehorse ownership. Unwilling to detach himself from racing completely, Warfield came up with a plan: he would lease the colt to trainer Henry Brown (also known as Burbridge's Harry). However, because Brown was a black man, and because no black man—whether free or enslaved—was allowed to race a horse in his own name, Darley carried Warfield's registered silks. Warfield also put up half the entrance fee for Darley's first race.

Darley was so successful that he caught the eye of Richard Ten Broeck, who owned most of the stock in the Metairie Course down in New Orleans, one of several teeming sites of racing in the antebellum South. Ten Broeck was arranging an interregional horse race and worked a deal to have a small syndicate purchase Darley to represent Kentucky in the event. One condition of the deal was that Darley's name would be changed to Lexington, the better to identify his constituency.

To put into context the importance of the Great Post Stakes at Metairie, it is useful to heed Edward Hotaling's succinct description in *The Great Black Jockeys: The Lives and Times of the Men Who Dominated America's First National Sport* (1999):

> After the Revolution, puritan and anti-English sentiment combined to drive America's one organized sport out of the North. Horse racing was even banned in New York State, its previous northern stronghold, in 1802, on the admittedly accurate grounds that it was mostly gambling. The South, on the other hand, absolutely loved everything about it that the puritans hated—the gambling, the sport, the throwbacks to England's chivalric traditions. . . . Like the earlier quarter races, it [a South Carolina course] drew the mixed-up, almost democratic crowds that only sports could attract, a lesson lost on politicians then and on historians ever since. Women, for example, loved it. . . . As quarter racing [the short in-town dash]—with its backwoods sideshows of cock fighting, gouging contests, and bare-knuckle boxing—gave way to course racing in or near the cities, many jockey clubs found women turning out in force.

By the time Darley became Lexington, the sport had resumed in the North, and the Union Course in New York had been the innovator of the dirt oval concept since as early as 1821. Nevertheless, New York was among the states that did not come up with the $5,000 fee necessary to enter a favorite son in the Great Post Stakes. In fact, only Alabama, Mississippi, Louisiana, and Kentucky were represented before the crowd of 20,000 at Metairie. Lexington carried the Kentucky colors to glory, winning two consecutive four-mile heats.

As Hotaling noted, the turf appealed to all types of people, from backwoodsmen to the more sophisticated and educated

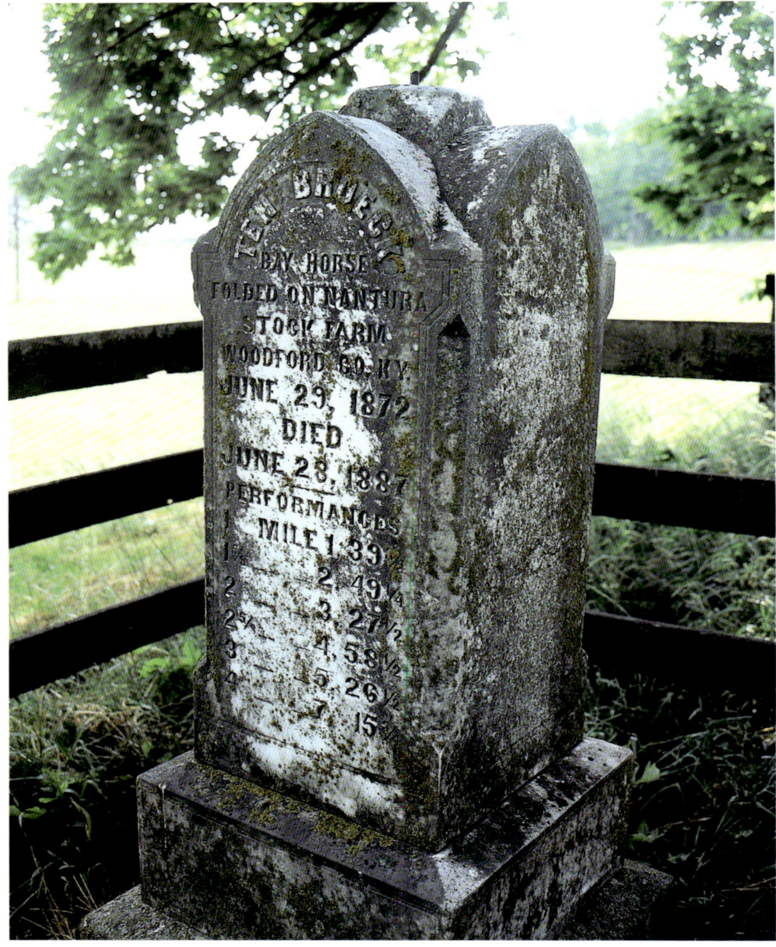

GRAVE OF TEN BROECK

On a hilltop in the middle of a Woodford County hay field, beneath a small oasis of giant trees, lies the grave of Ten Broeck, who established record after record in the 1870s, including the fastest four miles in history. Ten Broeck was foaled out of a daughter of the great sire Lexington, who stood at R. A. Alexander's famed Woodburn Farm in Woodford County, near where this monument stands. Ten Broeck was named after Richard Ten Broeck of New Orleans, who once owned and raced Lexington.

elements of society. Lexington's career would be touched by one of the latter: Robert Aitcheson Alexander. His impact on many aspects of the Bluegrass is difficult to exaggerate.

Robert Aitcheson Alexander was born in Kentucky in 1819. His grandfather, William, had visited Virginia and become so enamored of the colony that he decided to leave England and move there. William's son, also named Robert, had studied law in London and served as secretary to Benjamin Franklin in Paris. The elder Robert accompanied his father to America and settled farther west, purchasing land between Lexington and Frankfort. This would eventually become the famed Woodburn Stud, a bellwether of Kentucky's future as a horse capital. When young Robert was about thirteen, he became the heir of a rich bachelor uncle in Scotland and returned to Britain. After graduating from Cambridge, young Robert lived for several years in London before moving back to Kentucky and buying his siblings' interest in Woodburn.

Thus, one of the greatest horse breeders would be an effete Englishman who appeared in portraits as a high-collared dandy—left arm akimbo in classic style, with a hint of condescension in his countenance. Led by such a man of education and refinement, Woodburn would become a large enterprise that raised the finest of Ayrshire, Shorthorn, Durham, and Alderney cattle; Southdown sheep; and Standardbred and Thoroughbred horses.

WAR INTERCEDES

Robert Alexander did not become interested in Thoroughbreds until the mid-1850s. It is unclear how aware he was of the growing tensions between North and South, having spent so much of his life abroad. Nevertheless, he had been a horse breeder for only a few years before the outbreak of the Civil War, with its inevitable confiscation of animals by both warring parties. Before that happened, though, Alexander had struck his telling blow.

While en route to England to seek breeding stock, he mused in a letter to his brother that he was beginning to think that the American Thoroughbred was superior to the English insofar as the four-mile heat was concerned. English breeders, he felt, had concentrated too much on speed. Thus, when he chanced to meet Richard Ten Broeck, owner of the horse Lexington, he did not let his original plan to buy English stock stop him from purchasing a horse that was already in Kentucky. Ten Broeck had placed a high price on Lexington, who had been retired to stud with a great reputation, having won six of his seven matches. Alexander struck a deal for $15,000 and thus acquired Lexington for Woodburn.

Although nearly blind, Lexington proved to be a marvel. Statistically, he was the leading sire (measured by the racing success of his progeny) in America for fourteen consecutive years, plus an additional two years later. No other stallion in a major breeding or racing country has ever matched this record (although Sadler's Wells recently came close, reigning for thirteen years in England and Ireland).

Previously, the traditions of the turf had stressed sportsmen breeding horses to race for themselves. Woodburn, however, began producing annual catalogs and holding auctions of yearlings. This commercialization would give rise to a Bluegrass region where Thoroughbred farms operating as businesses—catering to a clientele of horse owners and yearling consignors—would exist side by side with farms of "private" horse breeders.

When the Civil War broke out, Alexander hoped to run the

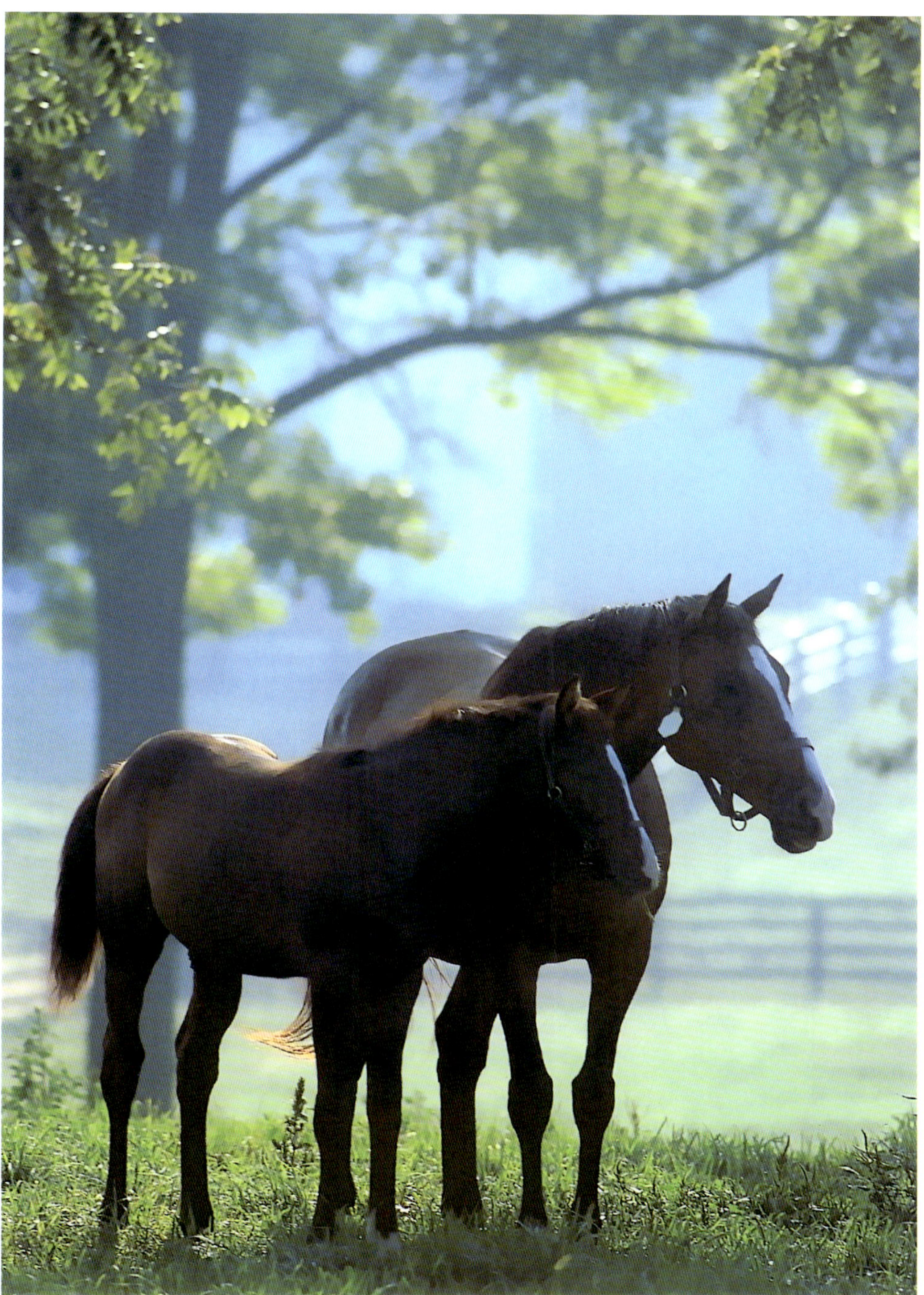

MARE AND FOAL IN SHADE

farm as normally as possible, but he eventually faced reality and, to avoid the confiscation of his stock, moved the stallions Lexington and Australian, along with a draft of some fifty horses, to another farm he owned in Montgomery, Illinois. At the end of the war, numerous tales allege, Alexander sent an agent to race some of his horses in the safety of Canada, and he returned with substantial winnings that saved Woodburn.

The Civil War interrupted many an agenda, and a sea change in the sport of horse racing was merely one of the many ripples caused by the war. As author Hotaling noted, the South had loved horse racing, but now this region was largely crumbled and impoverished. As racing historian Walter Vosburgh put it, "If the Turf were not, as an organization, to perish, its salvation lay with the victorious North."

The haphazard elements of history had come to the aid of Kentucky. For all its splendor, the antebellum Bluegrass had not established any definitive advantage over its neighbors to the east and south. Tennessee, for example, had enjoyed a lively breeding and racing program, and the state's crusty, resilient Andrew Jackson had once run a racecourse and later maintained a stable of runners on the grounds of the White House. As a border state, however, Kentucky had suffered less wartime devastation than more southerly states, and this circumstance proved pivotal in Kentucky's surpassing its neighbors to become the kingpin of the breeding industry.

RESPONSE TO THE NEW ERA

One of racing's most admirable traits is that it can transcend differences. In the fashionable racing center of Saratoga Springs in upstate New York, for example, the Alabama Stakes was inaugurated in 1872, less than a decade after the Civil War. The organizers of the race offered to name a race for William Cottrill, a native of Mobile, Alabama, who had served in the Confederate army. As described in Michael Veitch's *Foundations of Fame* (2004), a book on the history of Saratoga racing, Cottrill "suggested the race would be better served if named for his state. He was one of several southern sportsmen whose support was an important aspect of Saratoga racing during its first few decades." The Alabama Stakes survives today as the most important feature for three-year-old fillies at Saratoga and is one of the elite events for that age-gender division in America.

There was another connection between Kentucky and Saratoga: sons of Woodburn's great stallion Lexington won nine of the first fifteen runnings of the Travers Stakes at the New York venue. The Travers, which is still a major event today, had jumped ahead of any idea of postwar reconciliation. It was first run in

1864, before hostilities ceased, and was won by Lexington's son Kentucky.

The key ramification of the Civil War for Alexander, however, was that there were fewer racing opportunities in the South and far fewer customers. The economy was devastated, and several of the southern states had embraced the North's antigambling stance. Even today, parts of the Deep South have no legalized betting on horses, although some areas have surrendered to the siren song of modern riverboat casinos.

In 1867, Robert Aitcheson Alexander died at age forty-eight, and his brother, Alex, took charge of Woodburn. Alex lacked his brother's devotion to the farm and left many management aspects to his brother-in-law, Lucas Broadhead. Meanwhile, a former manager of Woodburn, Daniel Swigert, had gone out on his own and would become another of the industry's giants. Swigert established Elmendorf Farm and bred his own succession of Kentucky champions, including the Kentucky Derby winners Hindoo, Apollo, and Ben Ali, as well as the nationally acclaimed Firenze and Salvator.

Alex Alexander and Broadhead persevered with the farm operation for thirty years after Robert's death. By 1897, Alex was aging and weary, and in light of the national depression, the stock was sold at auction. To the end, Woodburn was a popular destination for the press and dignitaries, and the hospitality at the old home there elicited universal praise. (The main house had been built by Colonel William Buford, who owned a parcel of the farm at one time. Today, it has been renovated by a direct descendant of the Alexanders, Libby Jones. She and her husband—former Kentucky governor Brereton C. Jones—operate Airdrie Stud on an adjacent parcel of the old Woodburn estate.)

The destiny of the Bluegrass was constantly affected by happenings in the North. In 1866, Leonard Jerome, an occasional attendee at the Woodburn sales, had opened a new racetrack in New York. Jerome Park was at the cutting edge of opulence and helped usher in an era in which horse racing had a certain social cachet. In fact, a racetrack's list of subscribing investors might mirror the names in the *Social Register.* Jerome (the maternal grandfather of Sir Winston Churchill—a racing man himself, but not as his top priority) was considered the mogul who took racing to a new level. He and his ilk constituted a customer base for postwar Kentucky horse breeders.

Among Jerome's peer group was August Belmont I. Belmont had risen from a lowly role in the Rothschild Bank in France to the point where he could open his own bank in New York by 1837. He is thought to be the inspiration for the tycoon Beaufort in Edith Wharton's *The Age of Innocence.* Belmont began raising Thoroughbreds at Nursery Stud on Long Island, and if he had stayed there, the development of the Bluegrass might have followed a different path. In 1885, however, Belmont transferred his operation to Kentucky (but kept the name Nursery Stud), leasing some property near Georgetown. He apparently bought into the Bluegrass's reputation as a unique and salubrious location for the breeding of Thoroughbreds. Such claims for the 2,800-square-mile area around Lexington were originally based on natural phenomena—fertile soil covered by a lush, non-native strain of vegetation known as *bluegrass* (Latin name, *Poa pratensis*), owing to the fact that at certain stages of growth, it exhibits a bluish tinge. Beneath the pleasantly rolling hills and gentle valleys lies a form of Ordovician limestone that is rich in calcium and phosphorus, the residue of millions of shells and skeletons left behind when the area was underwater. The porous soil and the waters of Elkhorn Creek present these minerals to the animals that graze or drink there.

Belmont was not the only breeder lured to the Kentucky Bluegrass. The Whitneys, another key family of eastern racing, transferred their breeding operations from New Jersey to Lexington, along the Paris Pike. Likewise, the crafty Wall Street entrepreneur James R. Keene developed Castleton Farm on Iron Works Pike. (Today, Belmont's Nursery Stud is only a memory, and the barn where Man o' War was foaled, in the era when August Belmont II operated the place, has disappeared. The Whitney property is still populated by Thoroughbreds, however, under the names Payson Stud and Gainesway Farm. Keene's farm is now called Castleton Lyons, having been returned to Thoroughbred operations by the late Captain Tommy Ryan after many years as a Standardbred farm.)

Decisions by powerful businessmen and sportsmen from the East to center their breeding operations in Kentucky gave rise to a clan of local farm managers who possessed a high degree of horsemanship and were themselves community and industry leaders. The breeders paid these locals for their services, relying on them to take care of their mares, breed them to the proper stallions, and raise their foals until it was time to send them to the racetrack. As early as the 1850s, a forerunner of this combination horseman-entrepreneur-service provider had begun to appear. Major Barak Thomas, educated as an attorney at Indiana University and Transylvania College, retired from assorted Lexington business ventures to raise horses full time. Until then, raising Thoroughbreds had been a sideline, one of many agricultural pursuits and areas of expertise embraced by one individual. Thomas was distinguished as the breeder of the famed racehorse Domino, which was sent from Kentucky and sold as a yearling in New York.

These all-around horsemen became known as *hardboots.* Originally used to designate Kentuckians, based on their legendary preference for a certain type of rawhide boot that hardened in the rain, the term was gradually extended to denote a kind of rugged but worldly individualism. The hardboot was—and is—a hands-on agriculturalist as well as a keen businessman, comfortable in the foaling barn, the boardroom, or the country club. Kentucky hardboots became the allies of northern moguls. A hardboot could be the employee who cared for the businessman's horses, his friend and adviser, and the guy who sold him those horses in the first place. A few of these men were more colorful wheeler-dealers than upstanding citizens, but many became admired bulwarks of the multifaceted sport and business of Thoroughbreds.

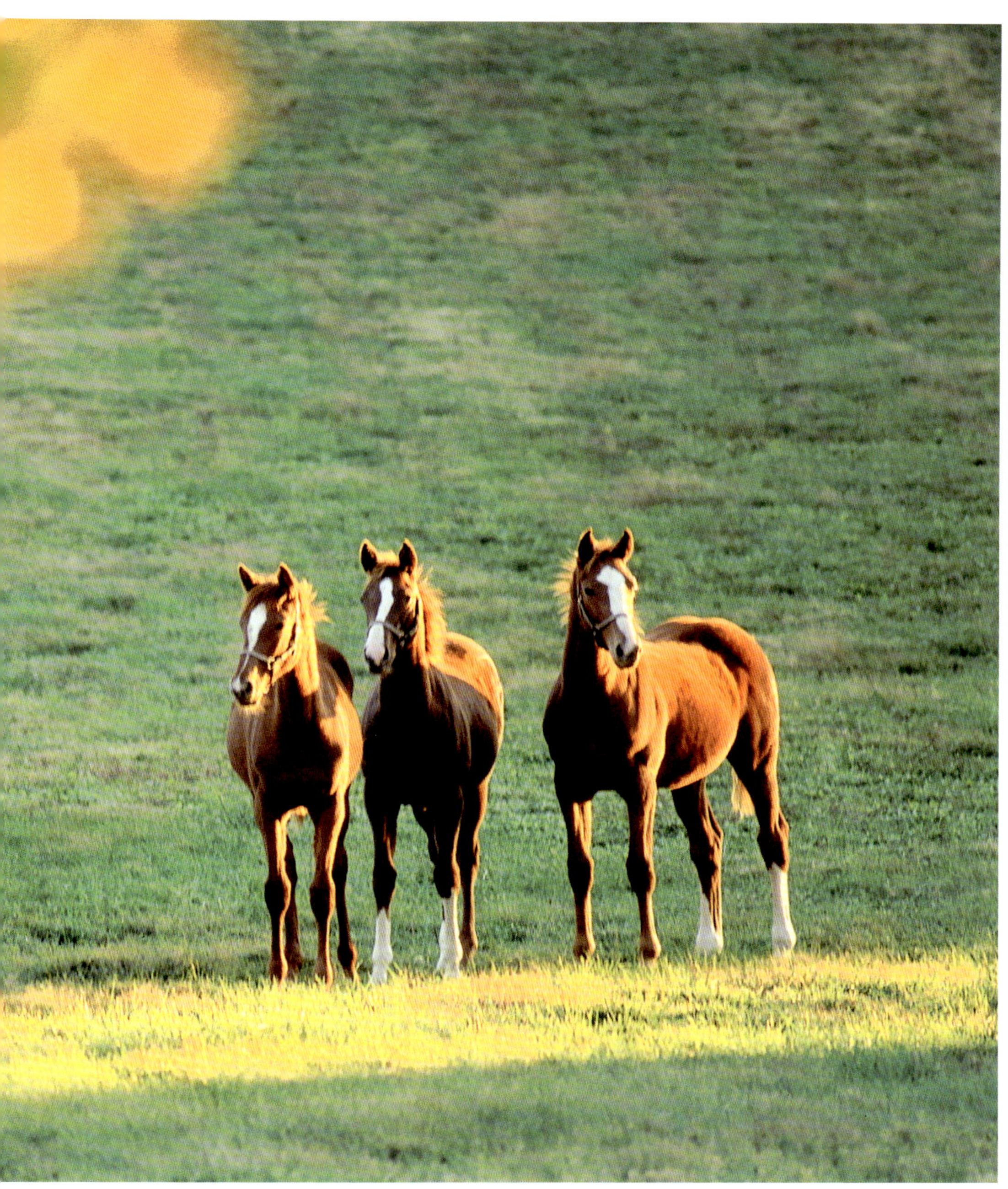

YEARLINGS IN AUTUMN PASTURE

DRAMATIS PERSONAE

In 1915, Harry Payne Whitney declared that his filly Regret had won the "greatest" race in America, referring to her victory in the Kentucky Derby. Today, that might seem to be stating the obvious, but back in those days, Kentucky and Chicago were still considered the West, and the top races and stables were concentrated in New York and New Jersey.

The Kentucky Derby was founded at Churchill Downs in Louisville in 1875. Although Louisville is outside the Bluegrass in a strictly geographic sense, all of Kentucky is, of course, the Bluegrass State. For Bluegrass horsemen, the advantages of operating within seventy-five miles or so of America's premier racing venue were difficult to quantify.

Racing in Lexington itself was declining. Five years after Regret's Kentucky Derby win, a newcomer to the Bluegrass, Colonel E. R. Bradley, publicly decried the declining quality of the facilities at the old Kentucky Association track. That year, the great Kentucky-bred champion Man o' War was exhibited at the track before retiring and going to stud. It was a contrast of images for such a heroic champion to have such a shabby stage.

When the track was forced to close in the early 1930s, Lexington's horsemen and some of its other businessmen recognized that the lack of racing in the center of the Bluegrass was an economically dangerous anomaly. A gathering of interested parties launched a bold plan that flew in the face of the Great Depression: a total of $400,000 would be raised to purchase a tract of land and create a new racetrack. Hal Price Headley, the son and grandson of Kentucky horsemen, was named to spearhead the drive. Against considerable odds, the plan was a success. The organization purchased 147 acres from Jack Keene, a dreamy horseman who had raced as far afield as Russia and Japan and had already built many of the features of the racetrack he envisioned. The new track, Keeneland, opened in 1936.

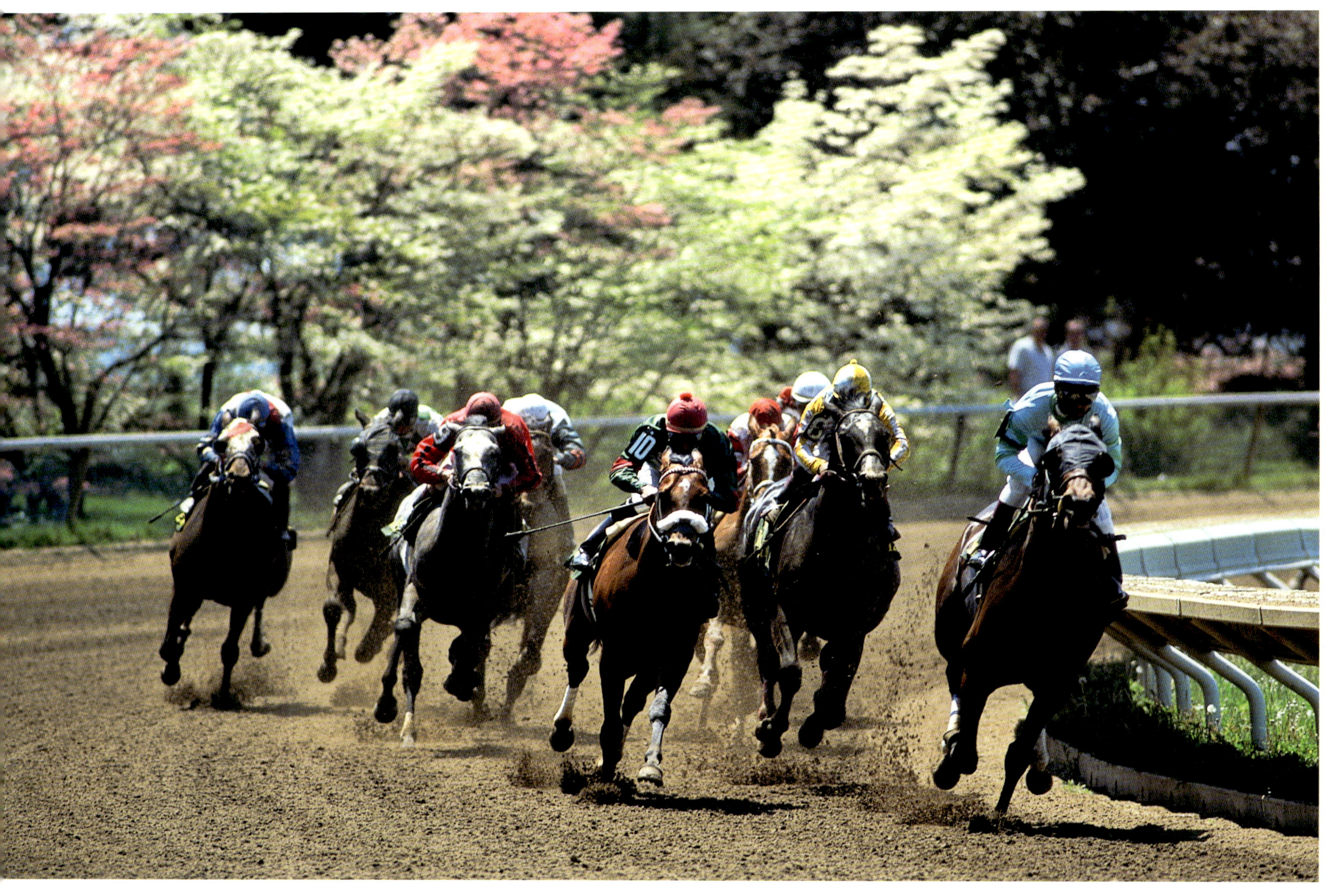

TURNING FOR HOME AT KEENELAND

The famed Keeneland Race Course was opened in 1936 along Versailles Road, west of Lexington. Over the years, the track has expanded and improved its facilities to state-of-the-art status while maintaining an intimate, welcoming atmosphere. Keeneland has often been a leader in innovation, including the replacement of its dirt track with Polytrack in the fall of 2006. In addition to its spring and fall racing meets, Keeneland hosts several annual horse sales, including the September yearling sale, the November breeding stock sale, the January sale (horses of all ages), and the April sale of two-year-olds in training.

Headley might be considered the Robert Alexander of his day, although he lacked the advantage of a rich uncle. Headley benefited for a time from his association with a well-heeled partner, William Baldwin Miller, but for the most part, his development of La Belle and Beaumont farms depended on his own agricultural and business acumen. Headley was just a young man when he became a guiding force in the organization of the Kentucky Thoroughbred Breeders Association, and he was instrumental in developing the pipeline for Kentucky's yearling purveyors—the Fasig-Tipton Company auctions in Saratoga. Later, as one of the masterminds of Keeneland, he set in motion a sequence of events that not only returned top-class racing to Lexington but also led to the most prestigious Thoroughbred auctions in the world. Less than fifty years after $400,000 created Keeneland, the offerings at one summer yearling sale *averaged* more than $500,000.

Many other individuals and institutions helped shape Thoroughbred breeding and racing in the Bluegrass. Here are just a few examples from a possible list of hundreds:

Colonel E. R. Bradley, an owner of posh casinos, was advised by his physician to participate in some fresh-air activities. Bradley developed Idle Hour Stock Farm, won four Kentucky Derbies, charmed Lexington society with his one-day races for the benefit of orphans, and imported a mare (La Troienne) whose descendants are prized even today.

Calumet Farm was originated by Chicagoans Warren Wright and his father. They commercialized the farm by giving it the name of their baking powder business, but it became entrenched in the hearts of Lexingtonians for producing a succession of great horses, including Triple Crown winners Whirlaway and Citation. The enterprise was carried on for years by the owner's beloved widow, Mrs. Lucille (Wright) Markey.

The Hancock family was led by transplanted Virginian A. B. Hancock Sr., followed by his son, Bull Hancock, and then by grandson Seth Hancock. In succession, they created and nurtured Claiborne Farm, home of the leading stallion for twenty-eight years, while ministering to the needs of such powerful clients as William Woodward Sr. (Belair Stud) and the Phipps family. The Hancocks also bred their own horses, including Kentucky Derby winner Swale. Bull Hancock's other son, Arthur III, established his own Derby-winning tradition at Stone Farm.

James Ben Ali Haggin, a Kentucky-born wanderer, returned home after amassing a fortune as an international minerals mogul and established a vast breeding operation at Elmendorf Farm. The Haggin family is still deeply involved with the management of sales and racing at Keeneland.

Hamburg Place was launched early in the twentieth century by the upward-striving, one-time Pennsylvania roughneck John E. Madden. Known as the "Wizard of the Turf," Madden was the breeder of five Kentucky Derby winners. His grandson, Preston Madden, bred Derby winner Alysheba and, with his wife Anita, hosted glamorous Kentucky Derby parties.

John D. Hertz, the Chicago-based founder of Yellow Cab and Hertz car rental, established Stoner Creek Stud in Paris, Kentucky, and bred 1943 Triple Crown winner Count Fleet.

Whitney cousins Jock and C. V. Whitney, partners in producing *Gone with the Wind,* carried on the tradition of their ancestors by pursuing the classiest of approaches to the turf. The Whitney family's roll of champions has been lengthened in recent years by world-renowned hostess Marylou Whitney, whose Birdstone won the Belmont Stakes. Another section of the Whitney property, Virginia Kraft Payson's Payson Stud, bred champion Vindication.

Edward Simms, a Kentucky native, prospered in the nascent oil industry and returned to Kentucky by 1897 to establish the productive and beautiful Xalapa Farm. It was still run by his descendants more than a century later.

Samuel D. Riddle, a crusty, aristocratic Pennsylvania fox and raccoon hunter, purchased and raced the great Man o' War. Riddle's Faraway Farm employee Will Harbut served many years as the sonorous interpreter of the stallion's wonders to the world's tourists. Mrs. Riddle's relatives, the Jeffords family, still have a hand in racing.

Runnymede Farm is the oldest family-owned Thoroughbred operation extant in Kentucky. It was originated by Catesby Woodford and Ezekiel Clay, who bred the likes of 1880s legend Hanover. Hanover's descendant, Catesby Clay, presides over the Paris farm today.

Darby Dan Farm occupies the site of the old Idle Hour. It was launched by Columbus, Ohio, real estate developer John W. Galbreath. Darby Dan Farm, the home of international stallions Ribot, Roberto, and Sea-Bird II, is flourishing today under the management of grandson John W. Phillips.

Elizabeth Arden (Graham), the cosmetics queen, purchased and raced Kentucky Derby winner Jet Pilot and established her own Maine Chance Farm, the producer of major homebred winners.

Spendthrift Farm, an echo of the nineteenth century, was launched by Leslie Combs II and named in honor of Spendthrift, a horse bred by his ancestor Daniel Swigert. Swigert was also the originator of the modern yearling consignment, a master recruiter of high-ticket investors, and a groundbreaking syndicator of million-dollar-plus stallions.

King Ranch was run from the 1930s to the 1970s by mastermind Robert Kleberg Jr., who organized a Kentucky Thoroughbred division of the famed Texas ranch and owned Triple

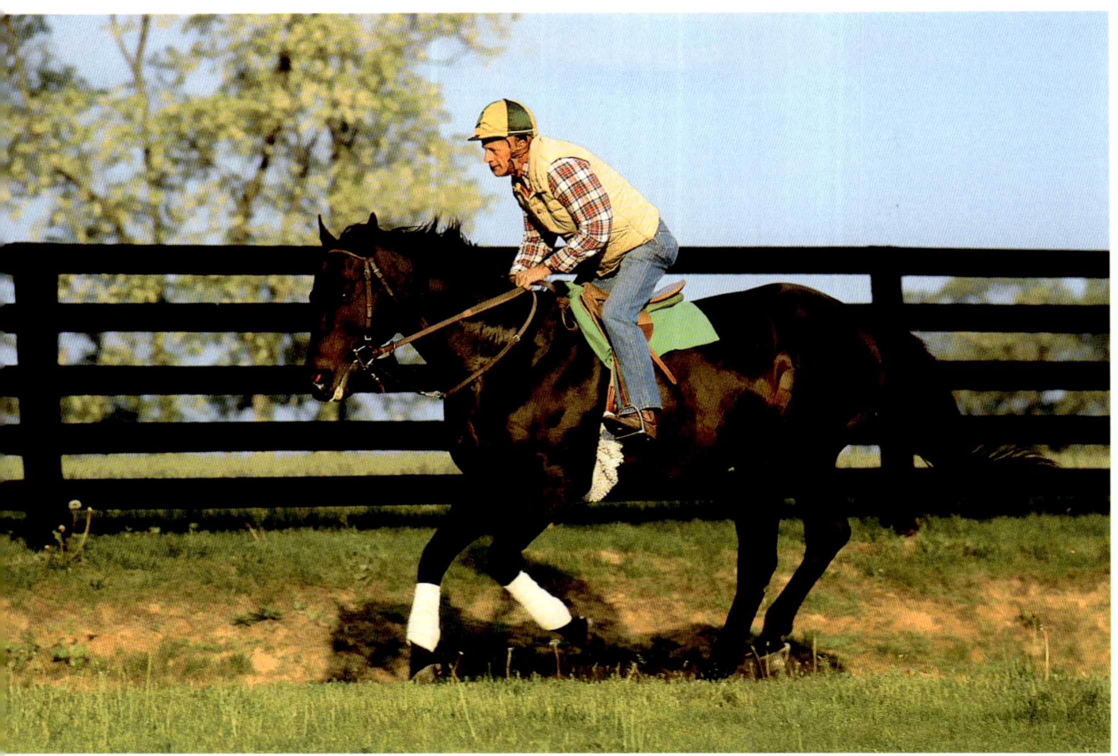

SEATTLE SLEW AT THREE CHIMNEYS FARM, CIRCA 1985
Seattle Slew was one of the greatest racehorses of all time. Purchased at a yearling sale for just $17,500, "Slew," as he would be called, didn't let that inauspicious beginning give him an inferiority complex. In 1977, he became the first and only horse to win racing's Triple Crown while still undefeated. After leaving the track, Slew continued to leave his mark, becoming one of the most prodigious sires of all time. His offspring broke record after record while winning millions for their owners. His bloodline will continue for decades. Seattle Slew died in 2002 at the age of twenty-eight.

Crown winner Assault. Kleberg left management of the ranch to a granddaughter, Helen Alexander, who now owns Middlebrook Farm in Lexington.

William T. Young, Lexington native and entrepreneur, established the elegant Overbrook Farm with proceeds from his peanut butter company and other ventures. Young bred, raced, and stood the major stallion Storm Cat. His family continues to run the farm today.

John R. Gaines, intellectual and sophisticate, facilitated the creation of the Breeders' Cup series in the 1980s. His father had raced Standardbreds. Gaines's Gainesway Farm stallion barn (Vaguely Noble, Lyphard, Riverman, Blushing Groom) once dominated Europe from Lexington. Graham Beck of South Africa purchased the farm and continues to run it today.

Alice Chandler, daughter of Keeneland founder Hal Price Headley, is the keeper of traditions. She is the breeder of Sir Ivor —Kentucky-bred winner of the Epsom Derby—and head of an international stallion operation at her Mill Ridge Farm.

Nelson Bunker Hunt, a Texas-based internationalist, paid tribute to his love of Kentucky by naming his Lexington farm Bluegrass Farm. He bred and raced a succession of champions of England, Ireland, and North America while also sending fashionable consignments to the yearling sales.

Three Chimneys Farm was established by Robert Clay, son of politically influential Kentucky agriculturalist Albert Clay. It was the home of Triple Crown winner Seattle Slew and public hero Smarty Jones. Three Chimneys is an example of an upscale twenty-first-century farm, embracing a modern management philosophy.

John A. Bell III could easily be seen as the archetypal Kentucky hardboot, but in fact, he was a transplanted Princeton geology major from Pittsburgh who fell in love with Kentucky. Bell raised Epsom Derby winner Never Say Die for client Robert Sterling Clark and launched a family-run farm, Jonabell. The farm was purchased in the twenty-first century by the ruler of Dubai.

William S. Farish, scion of the Standard Oil family and former U.S. ambassador to Great Britain, has made Lane's End Farm in Woodford County his home. It is also home to internationally acclaimed stallions and a vacation destination of Her Majesty Queen Elizabeth II.

Keeneland has evolved from a modest breeders' cooperative into the destination of the most affluent and influential purchasers from around the world. Individuals have spent as much as $13 million plus for a single horse, but Keeneland's products also include the $8,000 King of the Roxy, a major 2006 stakes winner bred by a bail bondswoman in Ohio.

Fasig-Tipton Company was long associated with the sale of Man o' War in Saratoga. Its modern Kentucky division turned out Triple Crown winner Seattle Slew and filly Derby winner Genuine Risk, among others, to establish its own lasting presence in the Bluegrass.

As the preceding list illustrates, the relationship between Kentucky farms and outside investors continues to be a theme. In the middle of the twentieth century, one of the most compelling tales of this sort involved a yearling sold for $700 to northerner Albert Sabbath by quintessential Kentucky gentleman-agriculturalist Thomas Piatt. Sabbath named the colt for himself—calling him Alsab—and raced him to championship honors in 1942.

Among more modern examples, one of the most compelling began when Kentucky hardboot Robert Courtney, founder and owner of Crestfield Farm, sold a colt at Saratoga to longtime friend MacKenzie Miller, a Versailles native and a prominent trainer working for philanthropist and sportsman Paul Mellon of Virginia. Mellon, who had helped fill the National Gallery of Art (founded by his father, Andrew Mellon) by donating his own art treasures, named the colt Fit to Fight and enjoyed watching Miller guide him to victories in the Metropolitan, Suburban, and

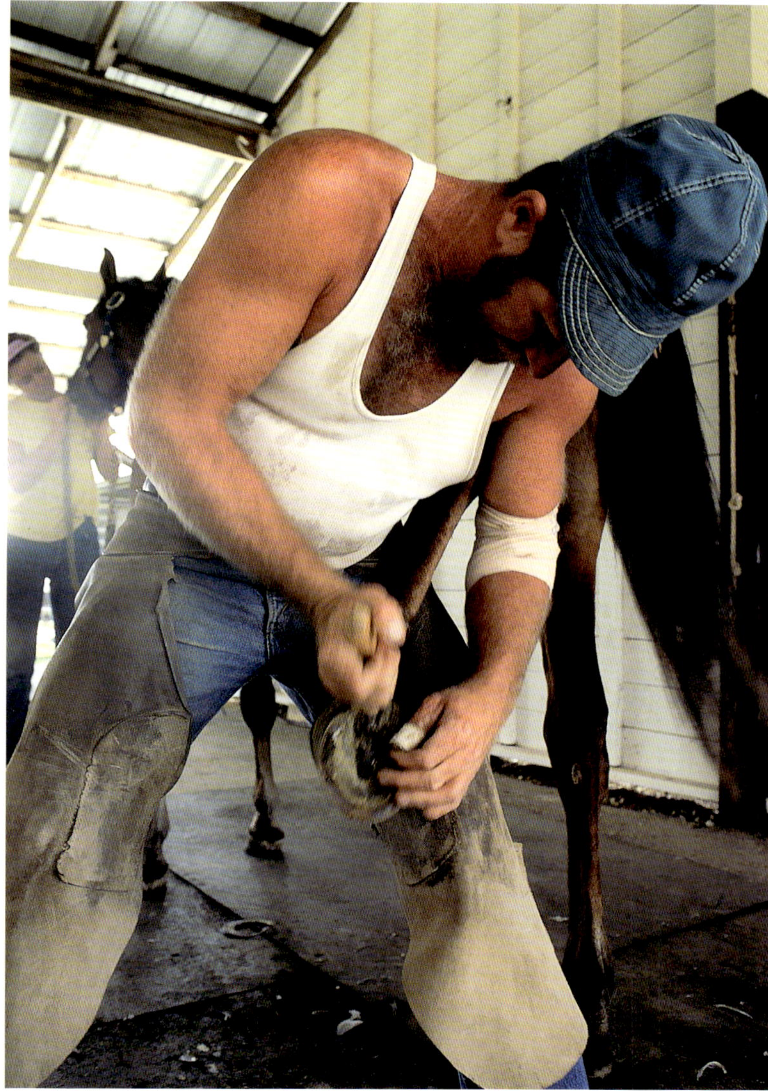

THE FARRIER
The farrier's job is an often overlooked but important part of the daily business of horses. Here in a Keeneland barn, a farrier plies his trade of horseshoeing—fitting and nailing metal U-shaped plates to a horse's hooves to protect them. Hooves grow like human fingernails and must be trimmed by the farrier every couple of months. Farriers often work out of their vehicles, traveling from barn to barn or farm to farm as needed.

Brooklyn handicaps. Underlining the ongoing interdependence between Kentucky breeding and New York racing, this series of races was for years revered as the New York Handicap Triple Crown and has been swept by only three other horses.

American businesspeople who own Kentucky farms today (or have in recent years) include the late Allen Paulson, founder of Gulfstream Jet; international auto-parts manufacturer Frank Stronach; oil industry representatives Jack Oxley and Josephine Abercrombie; Chicago journalist Jim Squires; and NFL franchise owner Robert McNair. Underlining the ecumenical aspect of the Bluegrass, each one of this small sample has bred or owned a Kentucky Derby winner or Horse of the Year or managed the sire of one. Similarly, other powerful businesspeople are deeply involved in the Bluegrass but prefer to invest in Kentucky bloodstock and rely on local horsemen to run their enterprises for them.

AN INTERNATIONAL AGE

One of the most striking features of the Bluegrass in the last thirty years has been its impressive cast from around the world. Elsewhere, national, religious, and cultural differences are often the cause of conflict, but on the turf, disparate cultures come together in harmony. The sense of competition is strong, but the lure of the game—and mutual respect for the horses—creates an arena where, by and large, differences can be put aside.

There was a period during the 1970s when Japanese purchasers dominated the headlines at Keeneland sales. The Japanese remain important clients, but back home, they have populated their breeding industry with international-class sires and dams and are more self-sufficient than they once were.

Since the 1980s, the ruling family of Dubai has brought an exotic air to the Keeneland sales, their impressive jets with elegantly inscrutable logos looming at nearby Blue Grass Airport. The Maktoum brothers, Sheikhs Mohammed, Hamdan, and the late Maktoum al bin Rashid al Maktoum, have spent billions buying world-class racing and breeding prospects that have been deployed to Europe, Dubai, and Australia, as well as the United States. Meanwhile, they have also purchased some 6,000 acres of prime Bluegrass property and, under the names Darley, Gainsborough, and Shadwell, have proved to be immensely generous and respectful stewards of the land. Their handsome barns and immaculate pastures have spawned international racing champions.

During the same era, Prince Khalid Abdullah of Saudi Arabia created at Juddmonte Farm a virtual throwback to an earlier day, when farms such as Calumet, Greentree, and C. V. Whitney bred almost exclusively to race their own stock and turned out a procession of classic and other major winners. With the assistance of Dr. John Chandler (whose wife, Alice Chandler, owns Mill Ridge Farm), Juddmonte has bred and raised a modern parade of European classic winners, as well as American stars such as Belmont Stakes winner Empire Maker and Breeders' Cup race winners Banks Hill and Intercontinental.

In terms of international influences, England and Ireland have been known as horse country since before the Bluegrass was the Bluegrass. Today, the impressive Irish-based conglomerate known as Coolmore has a major Kentucky presence at Ashford Stud, led by John Magnier.

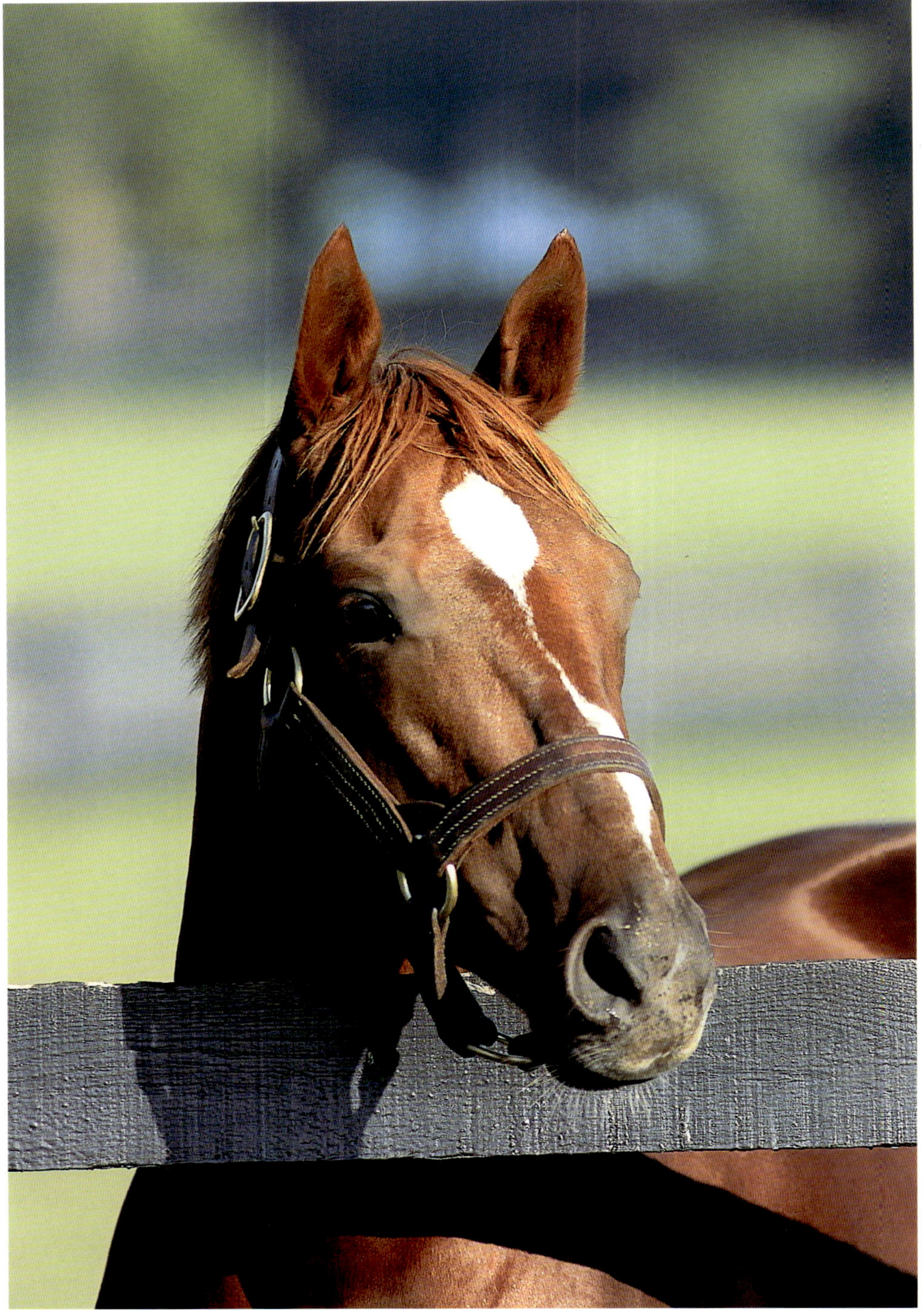

CHARISMATIC

It seemed that everyone was cheering for Charismatic to win the 1999 Belmont and become the first colt since Affirmed (1978) to win the Triple Crown. But after taking the Kentucky Derby and the Preakness, the big chestnut was pulled up lame by jockey Chris Antley near the finish of the Belmont and had to be taken from the track by ambulance. Fortunately, Charismatic's injury was not life threatening, and he was retired to stud at Lane's End Farm in Woodford County.

The Bluegrass also supports an array of other professions and entrepreneurial offshoots: large veterinary complexes, as well as one-person practices; feed and tack suppliers; equine research labs; specialist equine advertising agencies; trade periodicals and their printers; bloodstock agents; equine acupuncturists and other health specialists; blacksmiths; sign painters; auctioneers; van drivers; association executives and staffs; real estate agents; caterers; broadcast talent; Web site managers; pedigree and race information suppliers; and artists and sculptors. The list is lengthy year-round, and when the races are on at Keeneland, numerous other jobs can be added: trainers and grooms; jockeys and exercise riders; pari-mutuel clerks; security and shop personnel; and chefs and wait staff.

In addition to the Thoroughbred segment of the horse world, there are many other elements at work. At Lexington's Kentucky Horse Park, an assortment of breeds and equine disciplines have their home offices. The park itself teems with diversity. For instance, the annual Rolex Three-Day Event brings top-class horses and riders to participate in dressage, stadium jumping, and cross-country competitions. This event is considered a run-up to the World Equestrian Games, which Kentucky Horse Park will host for the first time in 2010. Meanwhile, riding for the handicapped, horse retirement efforts, steeplechase races, horse shows, trail rides, polo, hunts, pony clubs, and plain old companionship with a beloved animal have their proper place in the Bluegrass's tapestry of relationships between humankind and the horse.

It is a special place where the ruler of Dubai and a stable groom have something in common; the queen of England can admire a leathery old jockey; a philanthropist and a veterinary professor have the same goals; a hustling yearling seller benefits from the graciousness of an elegant hostess; and a $2 bettor celebrates at the same moment that a corporate CEO grits his teeth in disappointment.

Multiple pieces fit together to create the jigsaw puzzle that is the Bluegrass, but ever present—as a bit of background or center stage—are the delicate ear and glistening eye, arching neck and graceful loin, sinewy leg and cadenced hoof. Ah yes, the horse.

The Photographs

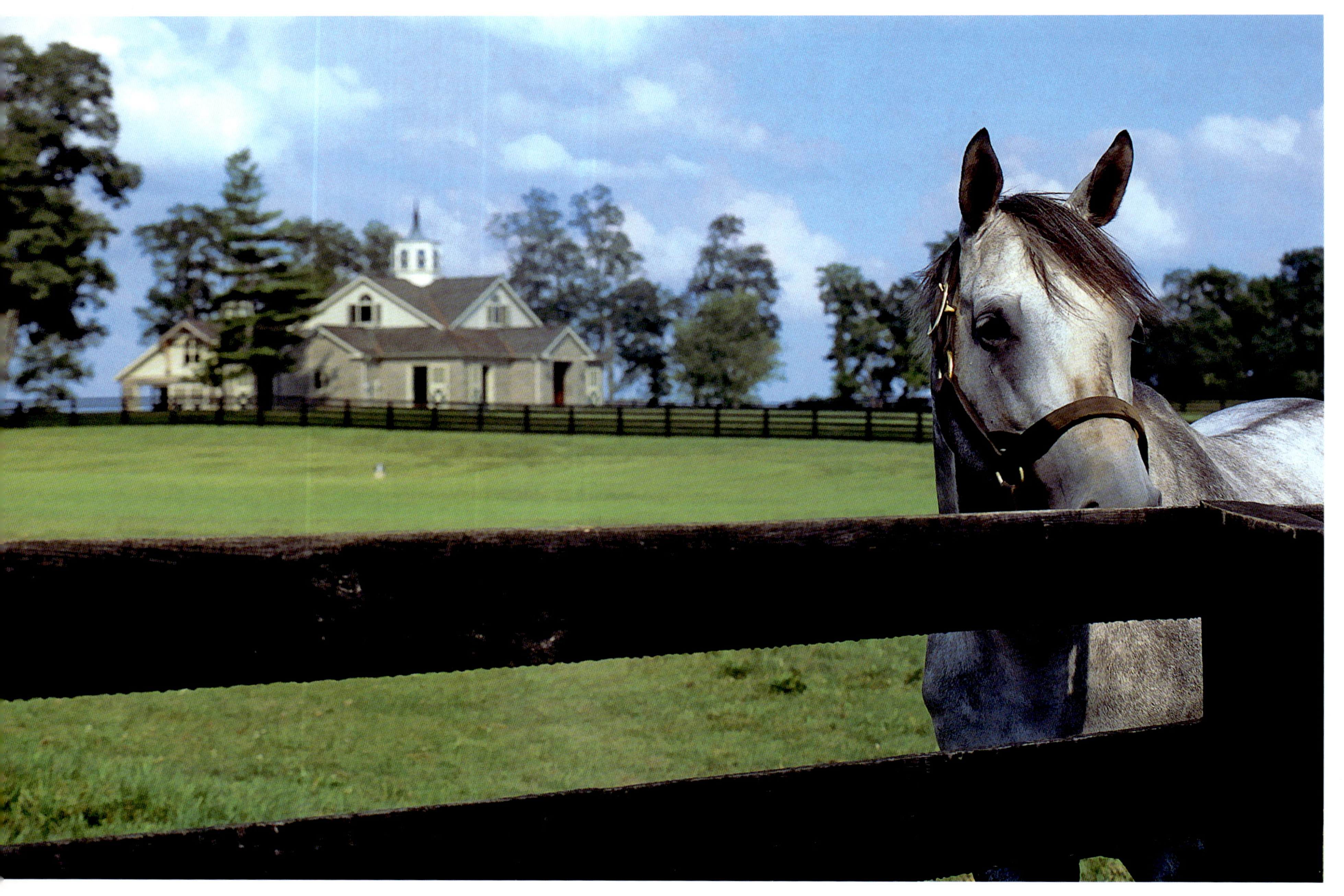

KENTUCKY DERBY WINNER SILVER CHARM AT THREE CHIMNEYS FARM

In 1997, Silver Charm won the Kentucky Derby and the Preakness before losing to Touch Gold by three-quarters of a length at the Belmont. The gray thus joined many who almost made it to Triple Crown glory. Along with his colorful trainer Bob Baffert, Silver Charm became a fan favorite, winning twelve of twenty-four starts and amassing nearly $7 million in winnings during his career. He was named to the National Thoroughbred Racing Hall of Fame in 2007.

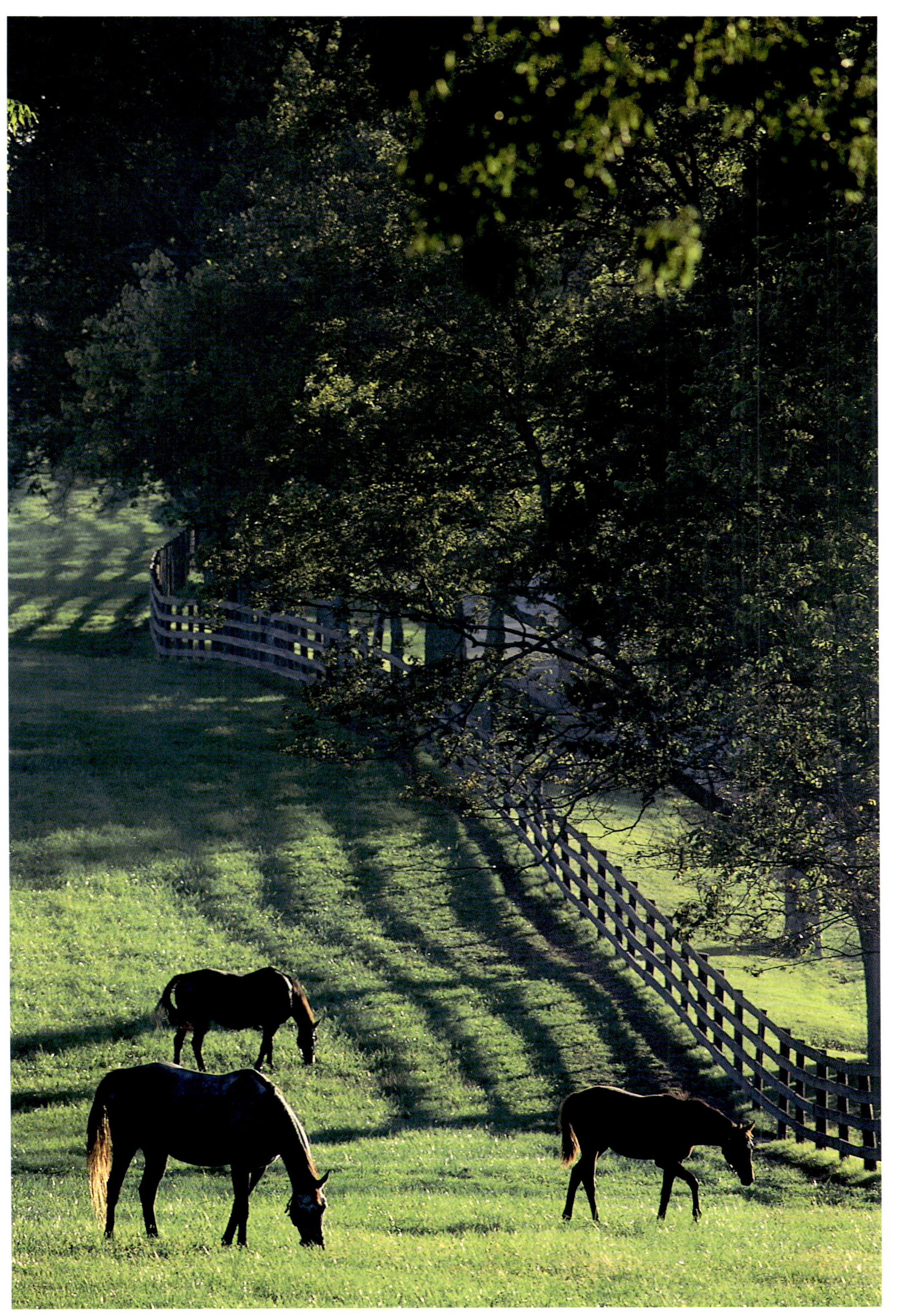

THOROUGHBRED MARES AND FOAL AT STONE FARM NEAR PARIS

Foals are weaned from their mothers when they are four to six months old and placed with others of their age. As yearlings, they bond with their peers, running free in the fields and paddocks, before beginning the rigors and discipline of training to race, the reason for which they were bred.

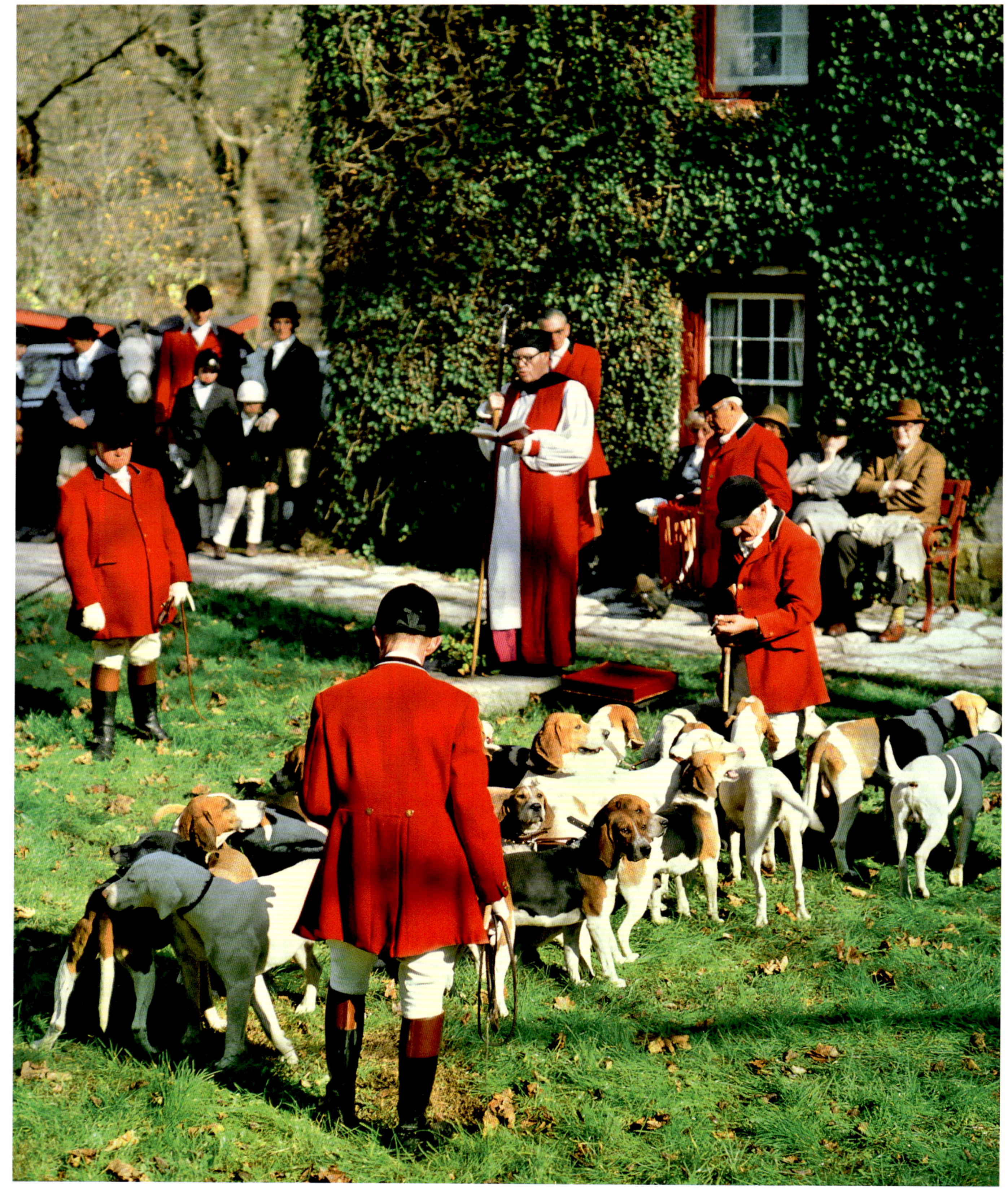

BLESSING OF THE HOUNDS, IROQUOIS HUNT CLUB, FAYETTE COUNTY

Each October, hundreds of horses and riders from all over the Bluegrass and beyond gather at the historic Iroquois Hunt Club for the annual Blessing of the Hounds and the daylong hunt that follows. The hills, pastures, woodlots, rock walls, streams, and valleys of the surrounding area provide the ideal conditions for chasing the fox—if one can be found. Here, an Episcopal priest blesses the gathering while the Master of the Foxhounds looks on.

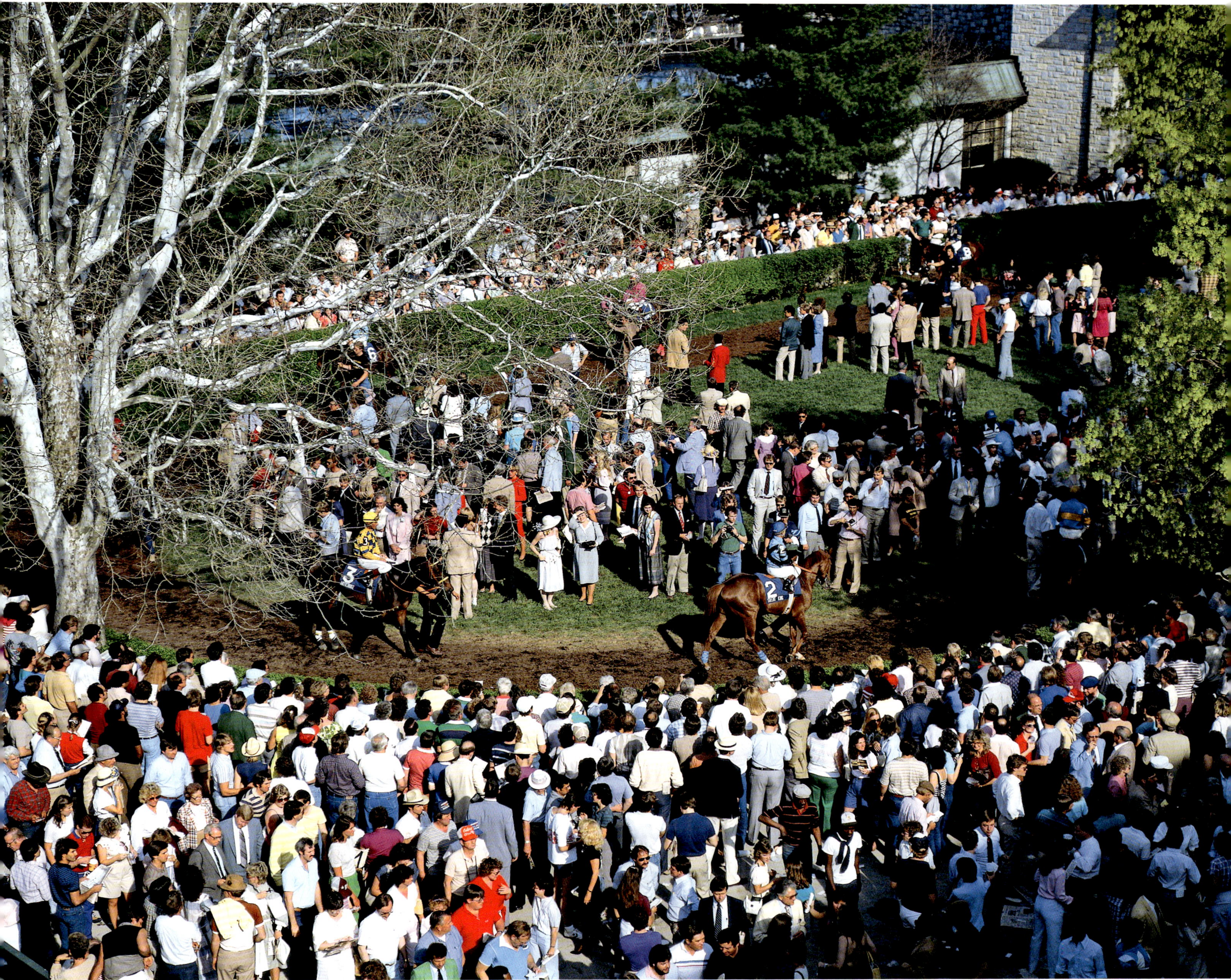

PADDOCK AT KEENELAND RACE COURSE BEFORE THE BLUE GRASS STAKES, 1984

Veteran jockey Willie Shoemaker sits atop No. 2, Silent King, prior to the running of the Grade I Blue Grass Stakes at Keeneland Race Course. The April event draws record crowds to the famous Lexington track. Shoemaker's mount ran second, behind Taylor's Special. One of the top jockeys of all time, Shoemaker retired in 1990 with 8,833 wins, including 11 Triple Crown races, earning him an honored place in the National Thoroughbred Racing Hall of Fame.

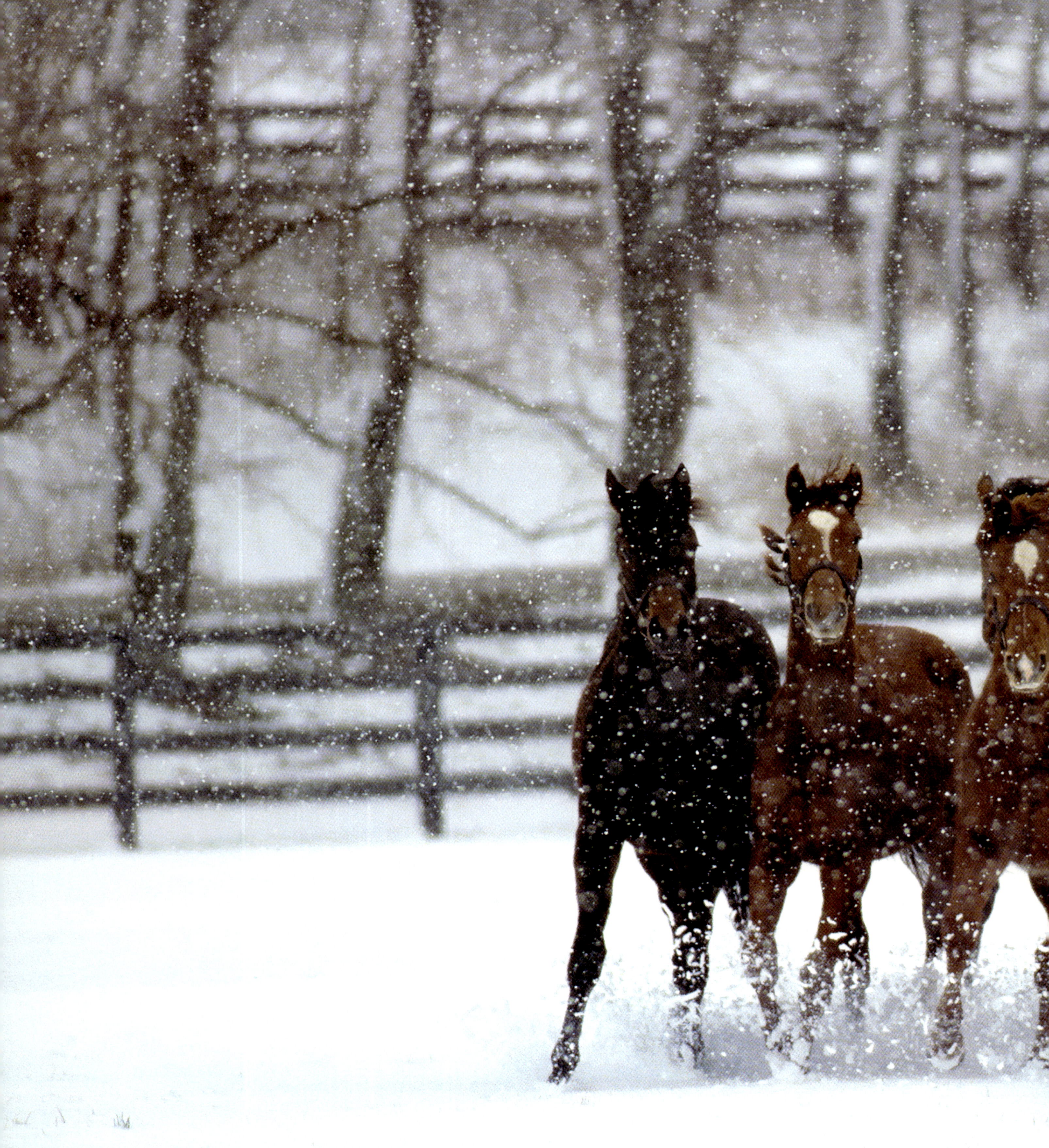

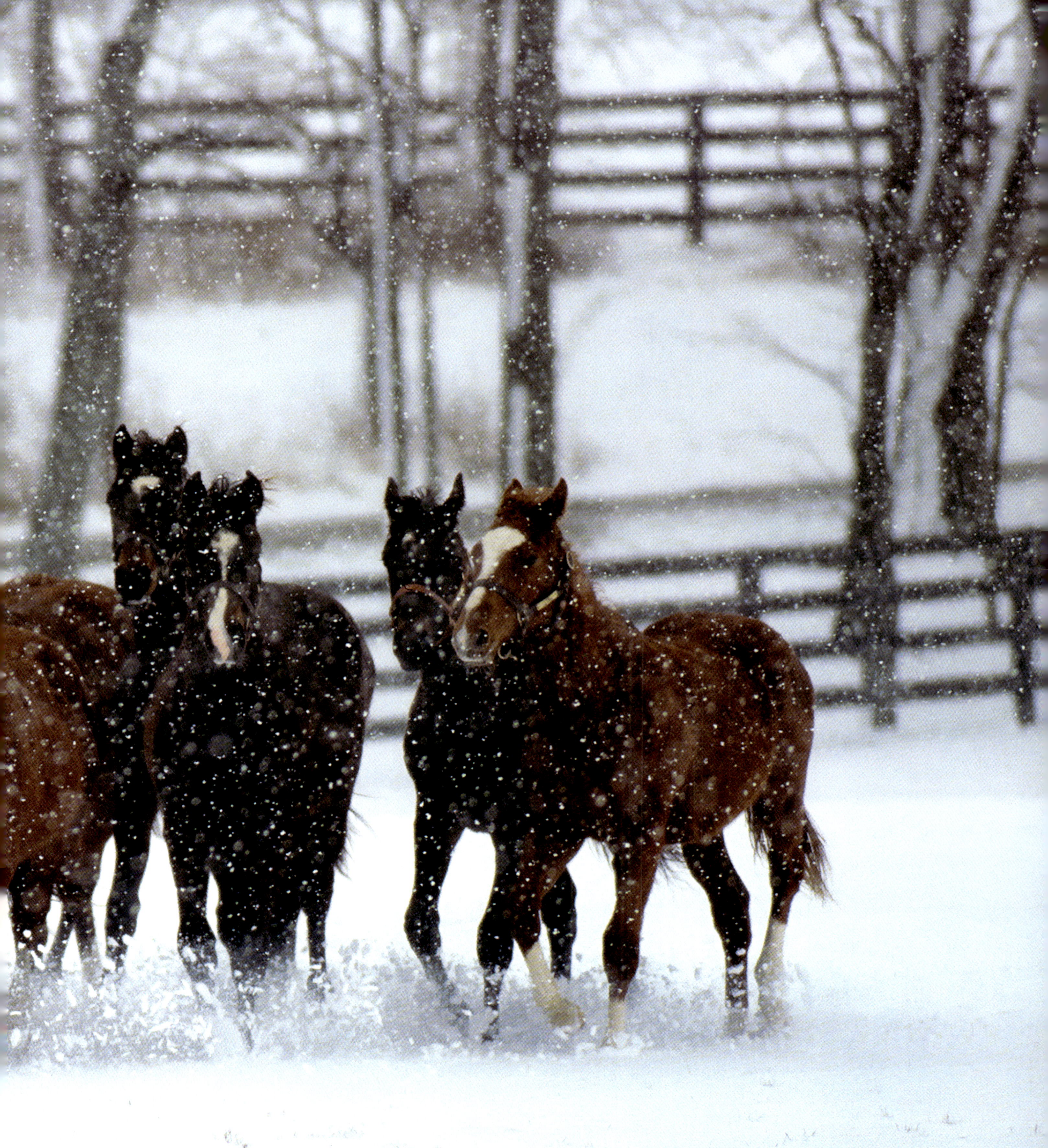

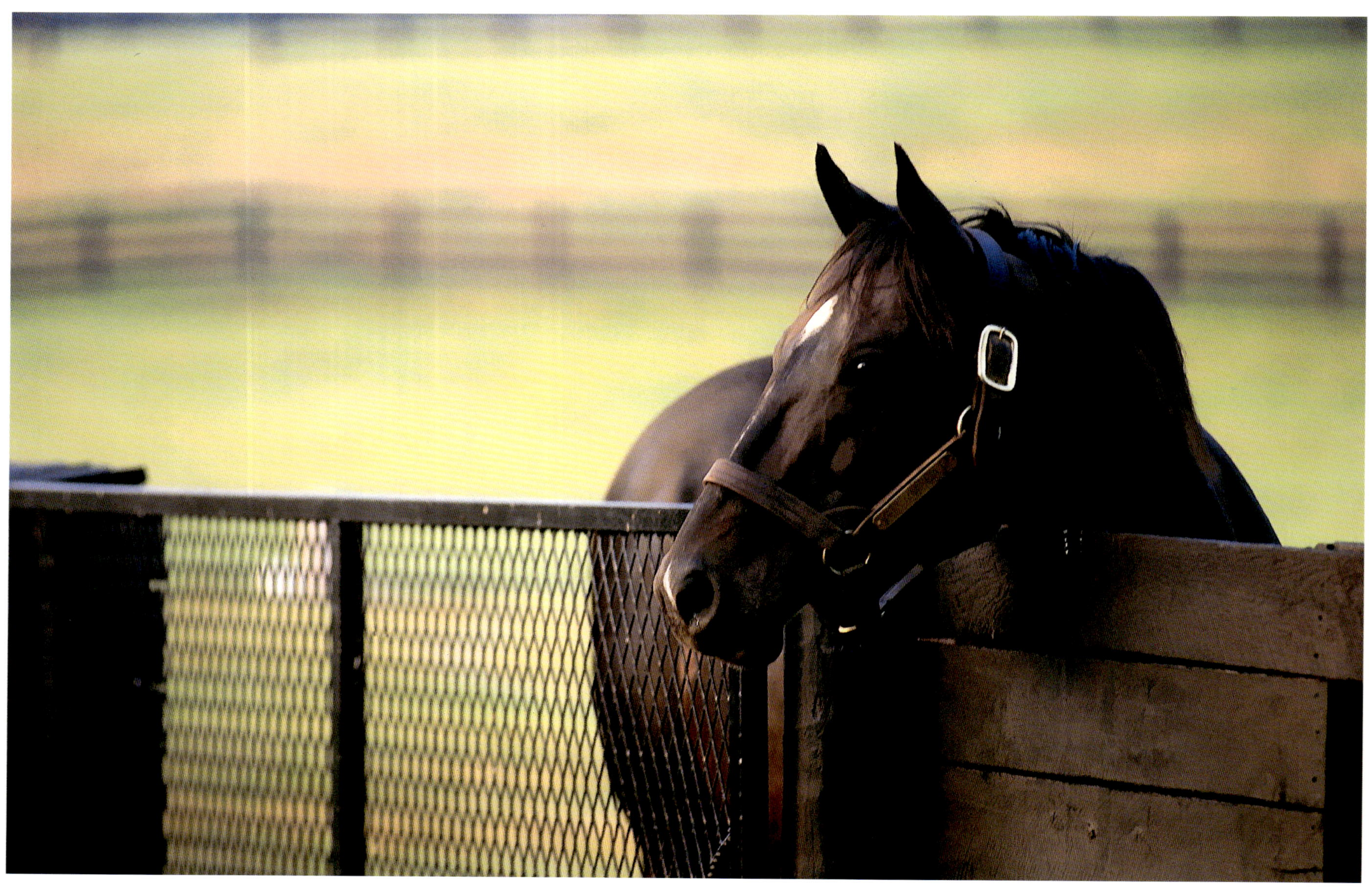

Previous spread:

YEARLINGS IN FIRST SNOW

In early winter, nature unleashes a frozen surprise for these young horses. Like children, they relish playing in the powdery snow. These Thoroughbred yearlings acknowledge the photographer as they race across their paddock in Woodford County.

CHAMPION SIRE STORM CAT IN HIS PADDOCK AT OVERBROOK FARM

Although a few horses earn huge incomes from racing, breeding is where the money is. It takes several seasons to determine which studs are producing champion racers. After a brief career on the track, Storm Cat was retired to become one of the most productive sires in history. The stallion commanded large stud fees and produced offspring whose combined winnings totaled millions of dollars. In 2008, he was retired as a breeder.

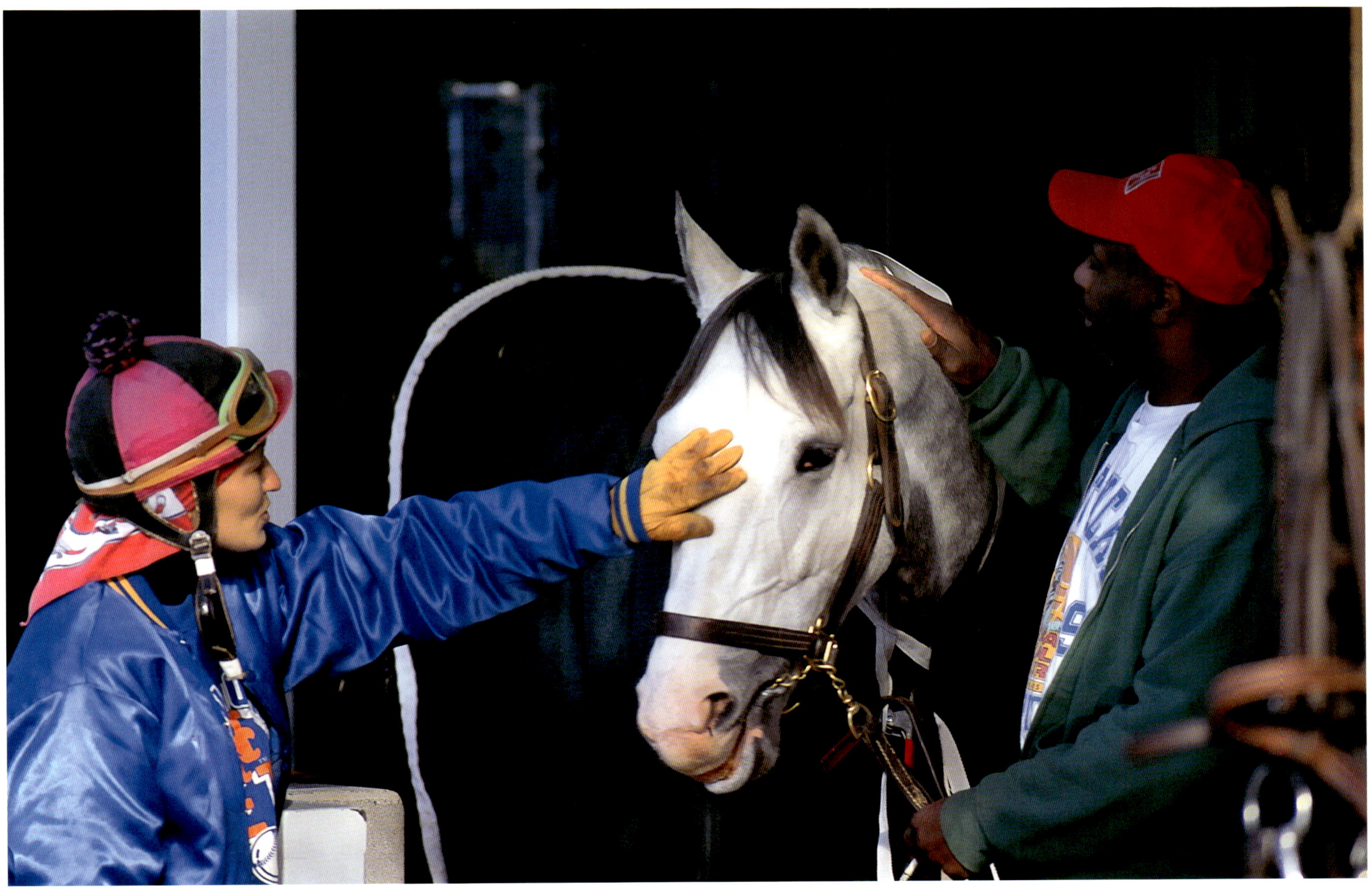

MORNING AT THE BARNS, KEENELAND RACE COURSE

The love of exciting and beautiful animals is what drives many people to pursue careers in the horse business. In Kentucky's Bluegrass, thousands of people are employed in some capacity in the equine industry. In Keeneland's stable area, an exercise rider and a groom share an intimate moment with one of their charges.

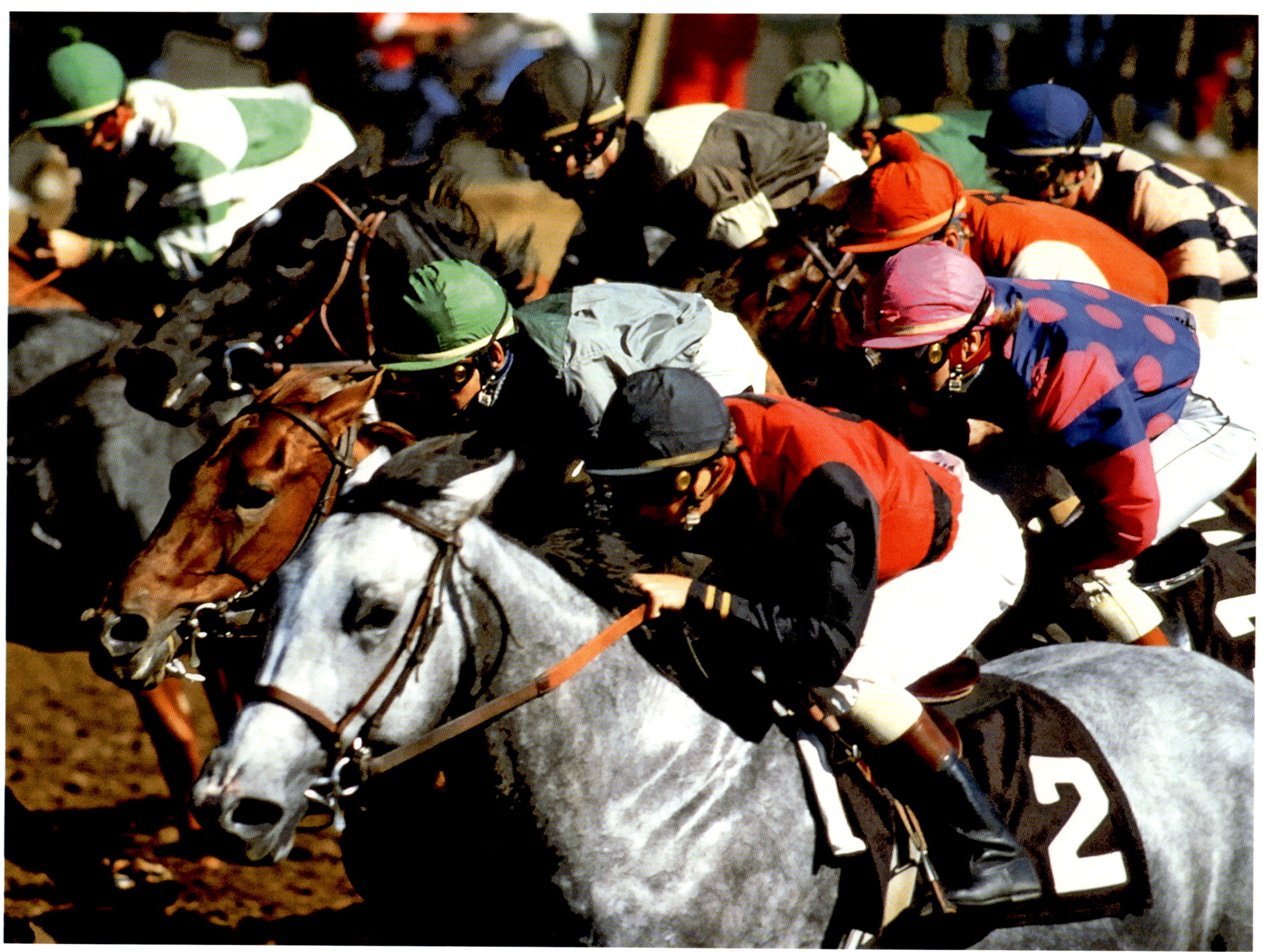

FIRST TURN AT KEENELAND

How to position the horse early in a race is one of the most important decisions a jockey has to make. Here, at the first turn, riders and horses cluster together before settling into a place that, to a large extent, will determine their strategy for the rest of the race. From here to the finish, a mixed brew of luck, rider's skill, and horse's heart determines the winner.

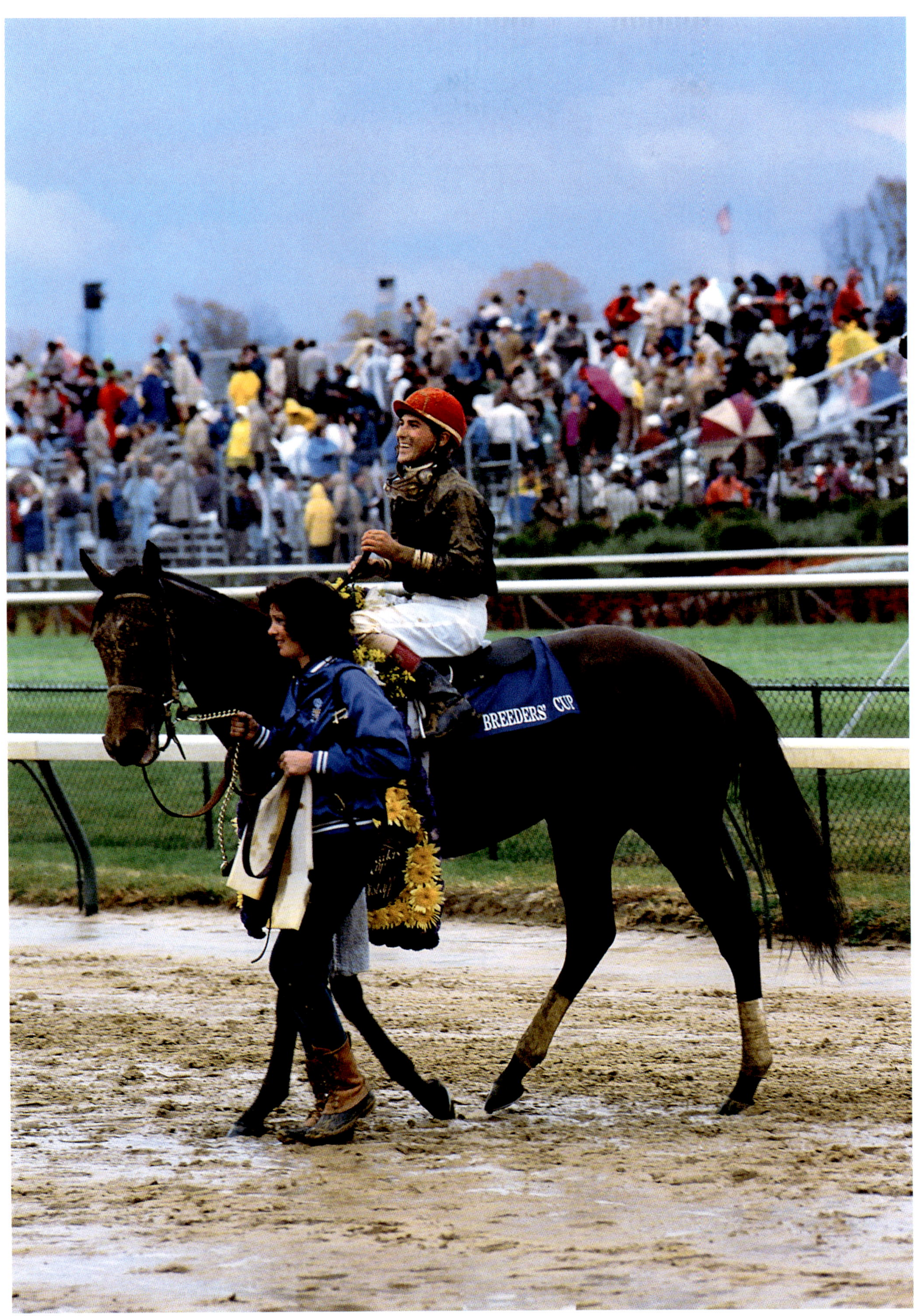

PERSONAL ENSIGN RETIRES UNDEFEATED

It was a race for the ages: undefeated Personal Ensign going head-to-head with Kentucky Derby winner Winning Colors in the 1988 Breeders' Cup Distaff at Churchill Downs in Louisville. As they came to the wire, Winning Colors seemed to have an insurmountable lead, but Personal Ensign gained on her rival and put her nose in front at the finish. Personal Ensign retired after that race, undefeated in thirteen starts. She went on to foal several major winners.

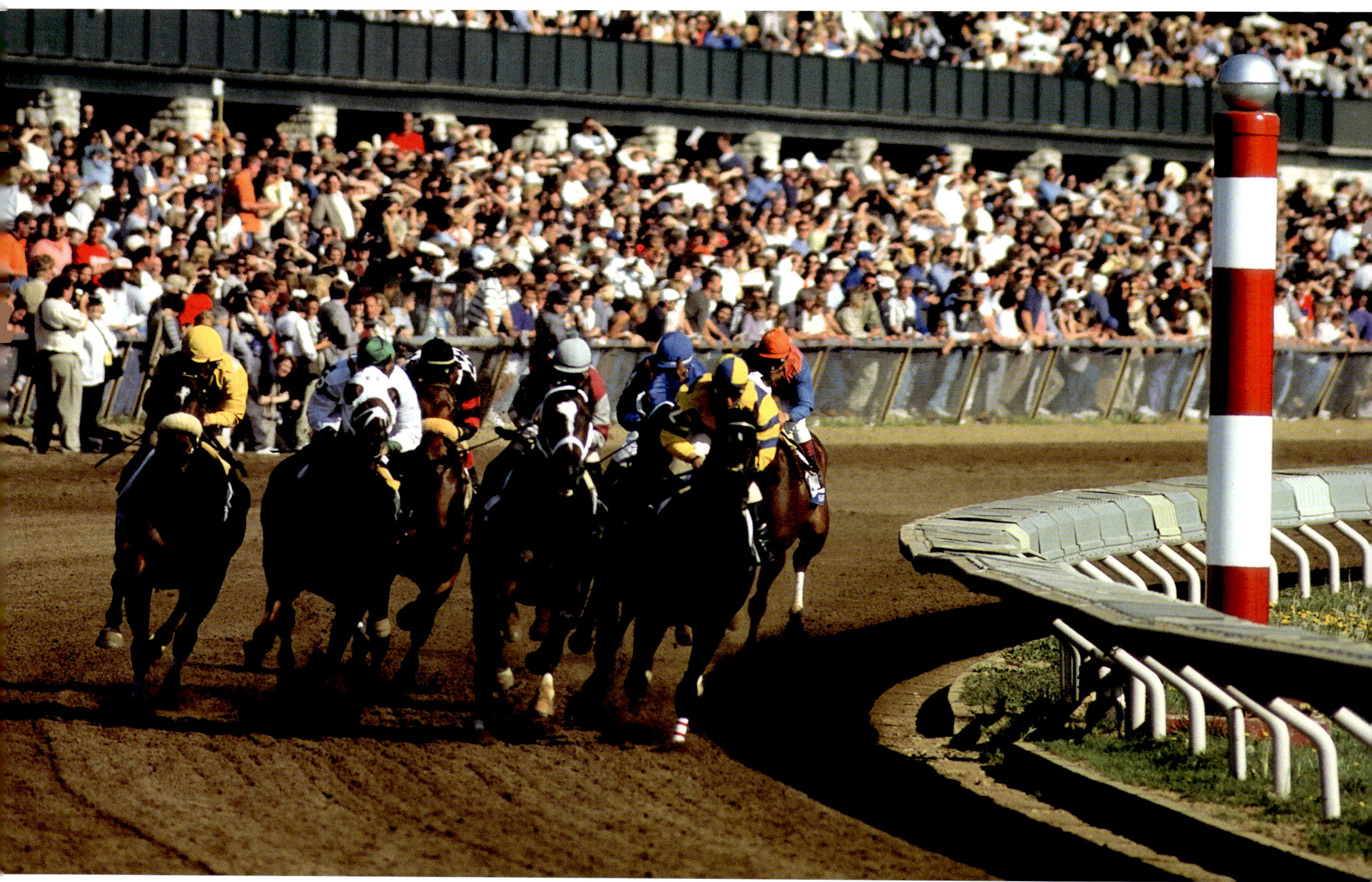

BLUE GRASS STAKES AT KEENELAND

In April, the Blue Grass Stakes at Keeneland Race Course is one of the top races leading up to the Kentucky Derby on the first Saturday in May. A number of winners of the Blue Grass Stakes have gone on to win the Run for the Roses, which Kentuckians consider the most prestigious horse race in the world. In the best of weather, more than 30,000 race fans fill Keeneland's grounds to witness the Grade 1 event.

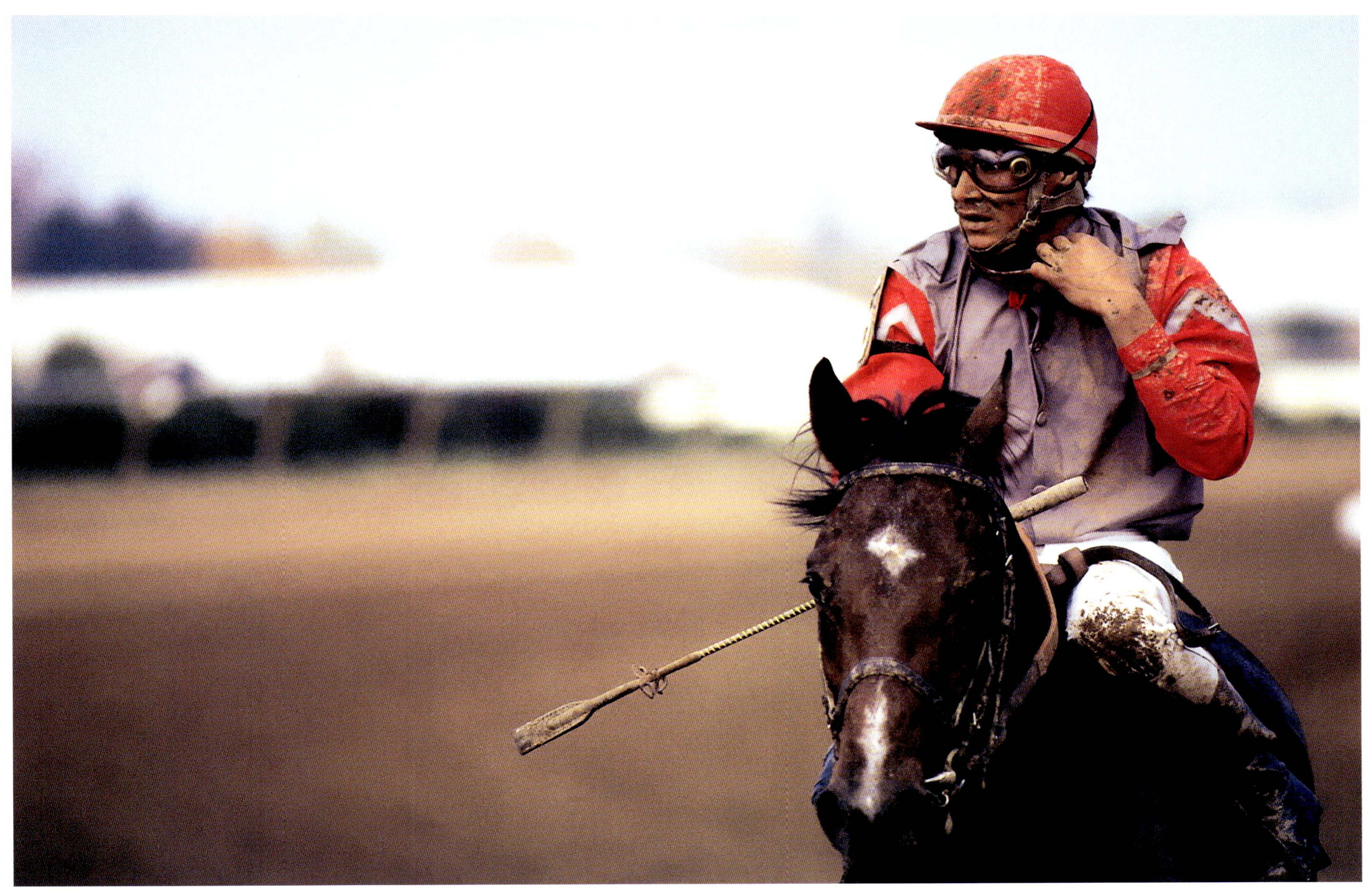

BACK OF THE PACK, KEENELAND RACE COURSE

A jockey pulls dirt from his collar after finishing well off the pace on a sloppy track at Keeneland. He will return to the jockey room, clean up, put on new silks, and be ready for the next race.

ALYDAR

This photograph was taken just before Alydar's death in 1990, when he suffered a broken cannon bone in his stall while standing at stud at Calumet Farm in Lexington. The strong-willed colt was a favorite of many fans and will always be remembered as the horse that fought Affirmed to the wire, only to finish second in each of the Triple Crown races in 1978. Alydar's prowess at stud vindicated him, and his offspring, including Alysheba, Easy Goer, and Strike the Gold, became members of racing's elite.

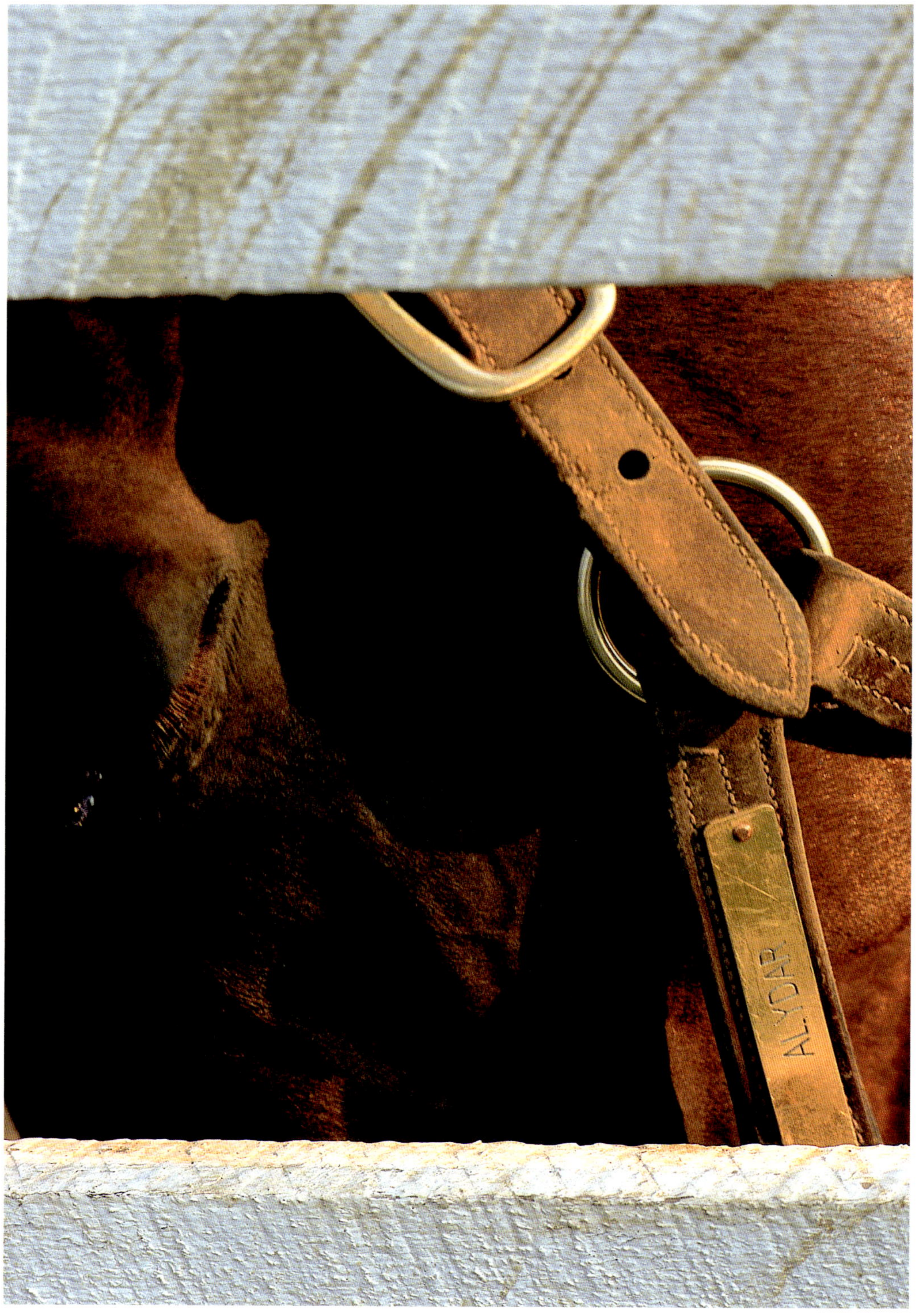

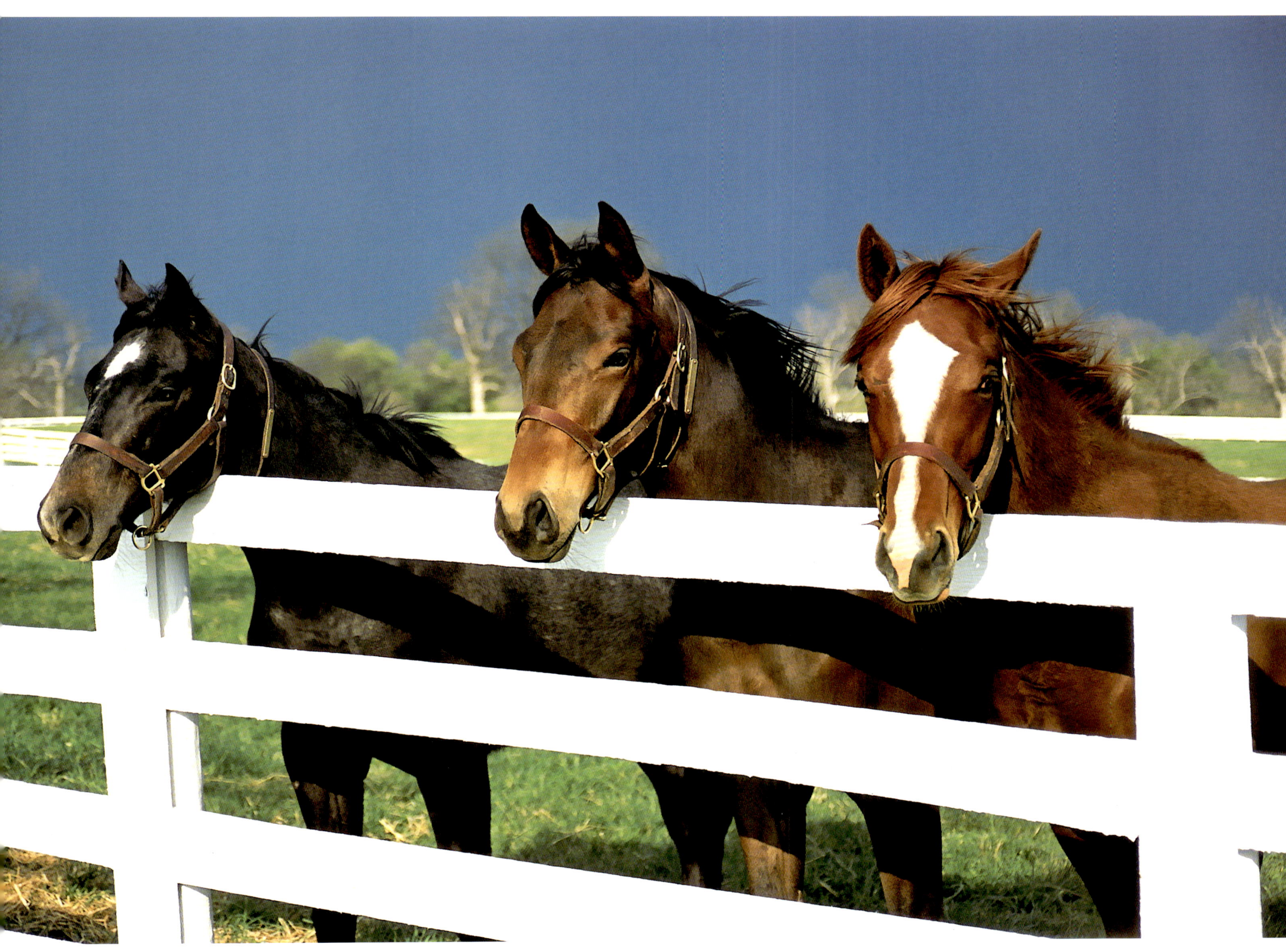

THOROUGHBRED YEARLINGS ON OLD FRANKFORT PIKE

Hundreds of miles of rural roads run along manicured fields filled with horses all year long. Curious by nature, mares, foals, and yearlings often amble over to the fence to be petted or to have their picture taken.

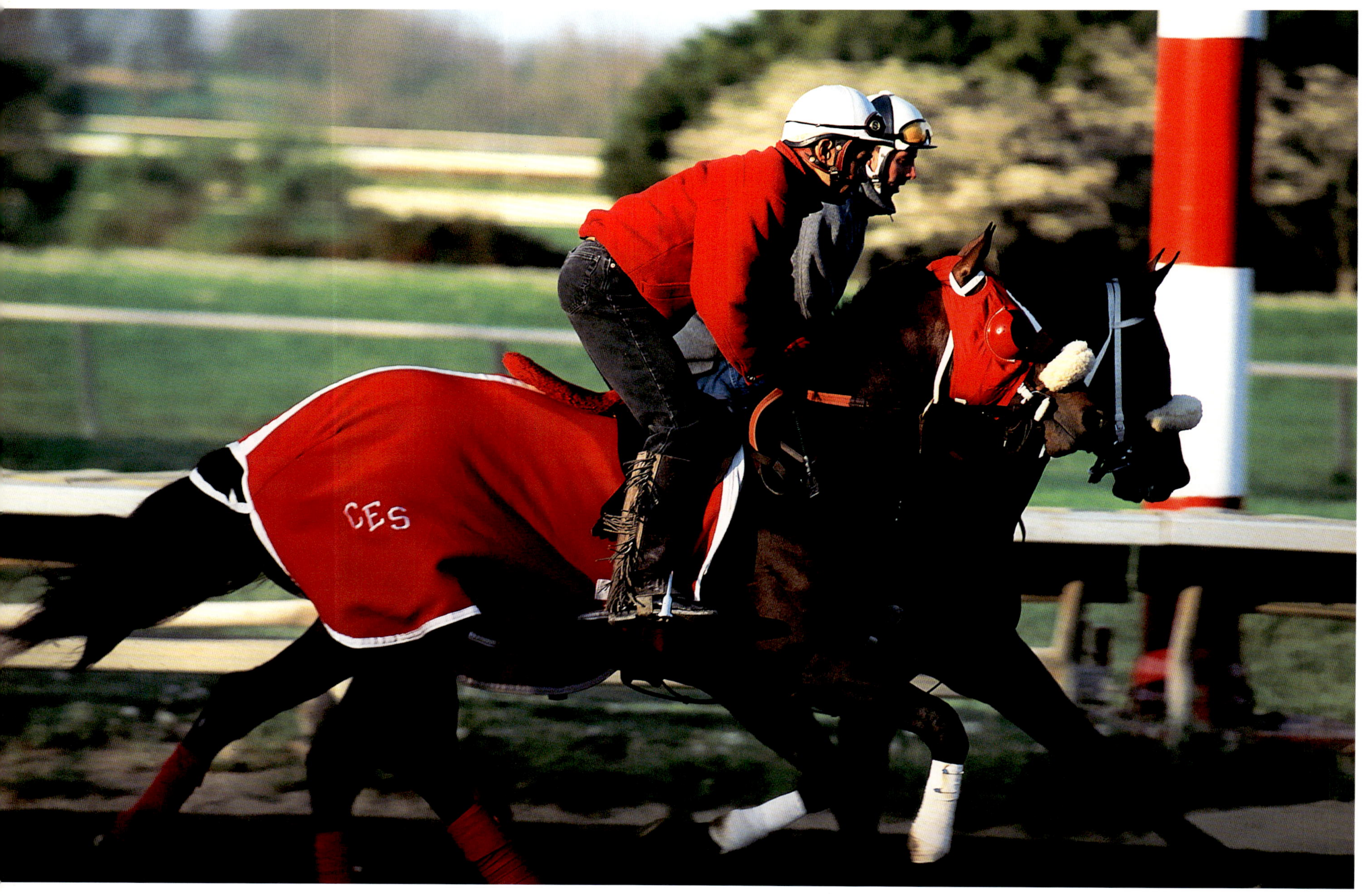

MORNING BREEZE

The game of horse racing is a 24-hour-a-day, 365-day-a-year kind of madness, both loved and cursed by those involved. Every morning, most racehorses are saddled and ridden a number of times around the track—sometimes slowly, sometimes at full gallop, depending on the stage of their careers and the will of the trainer. The goal is to keep the horses sharp and ready for the next call to the post.

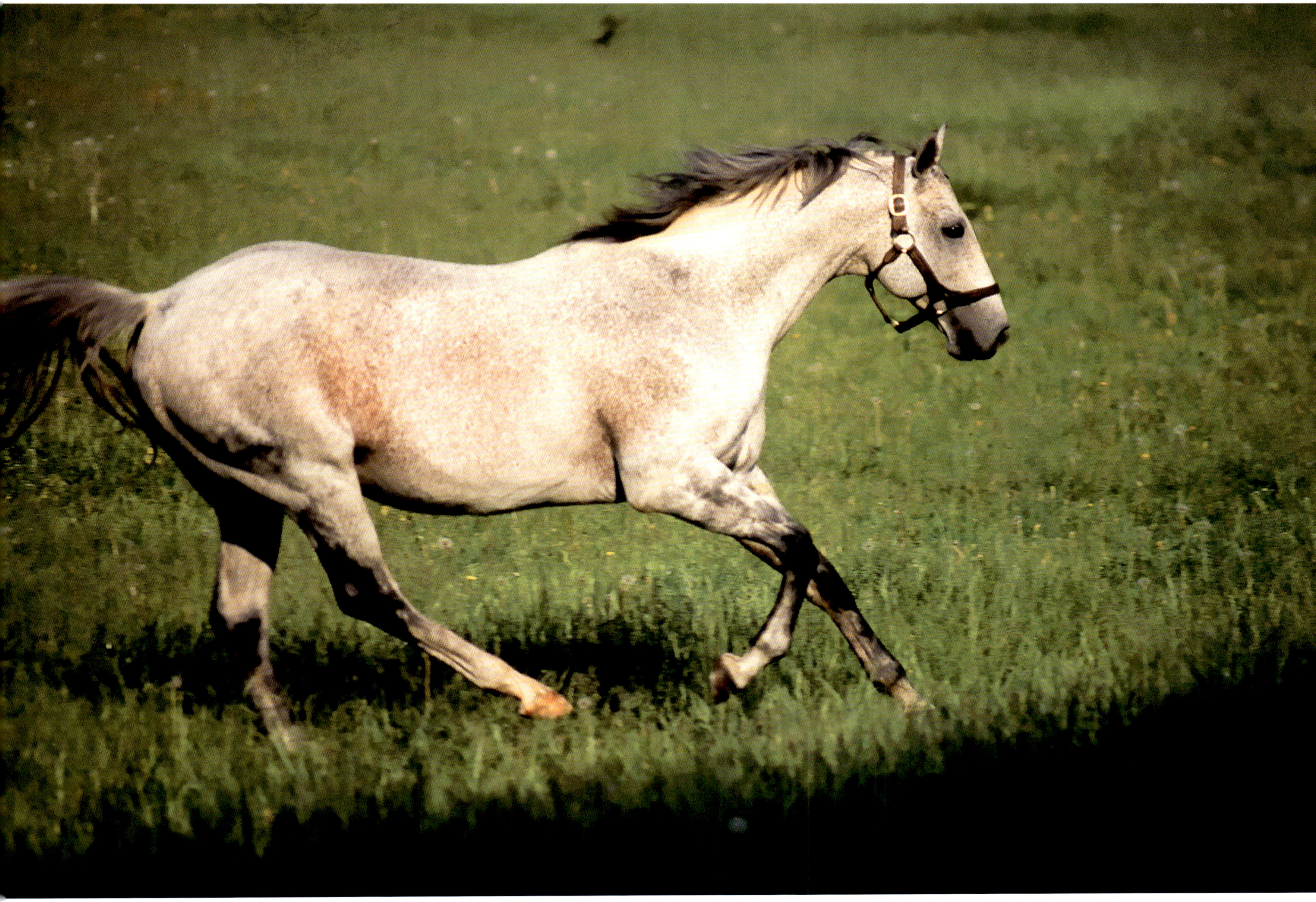

SPECTACULAR BID AT CLAIBORNE FARM, NEAR PARIS

The tough gray Kentucky-bred horse (stabled in Maryland) seemed to have a lock on the Triple Crown in 1979. As a two-year-old, he demolished most of his competitors, winning seven times in nine starts. However, after winning the Kentucky Derby and the Preakness, Spectacular Bid lost the Belmont after a safety pin was found in and removed from his hoof just prior to the race. In spite of this defeat, the horse went on to compile a lifetime record of twenty-six wins in thirty starts while breaking numerous track records—an accomplishment almost unsurpassed in racing history. Spectacular Bid retired from racing to stand at stud in Kentucky.

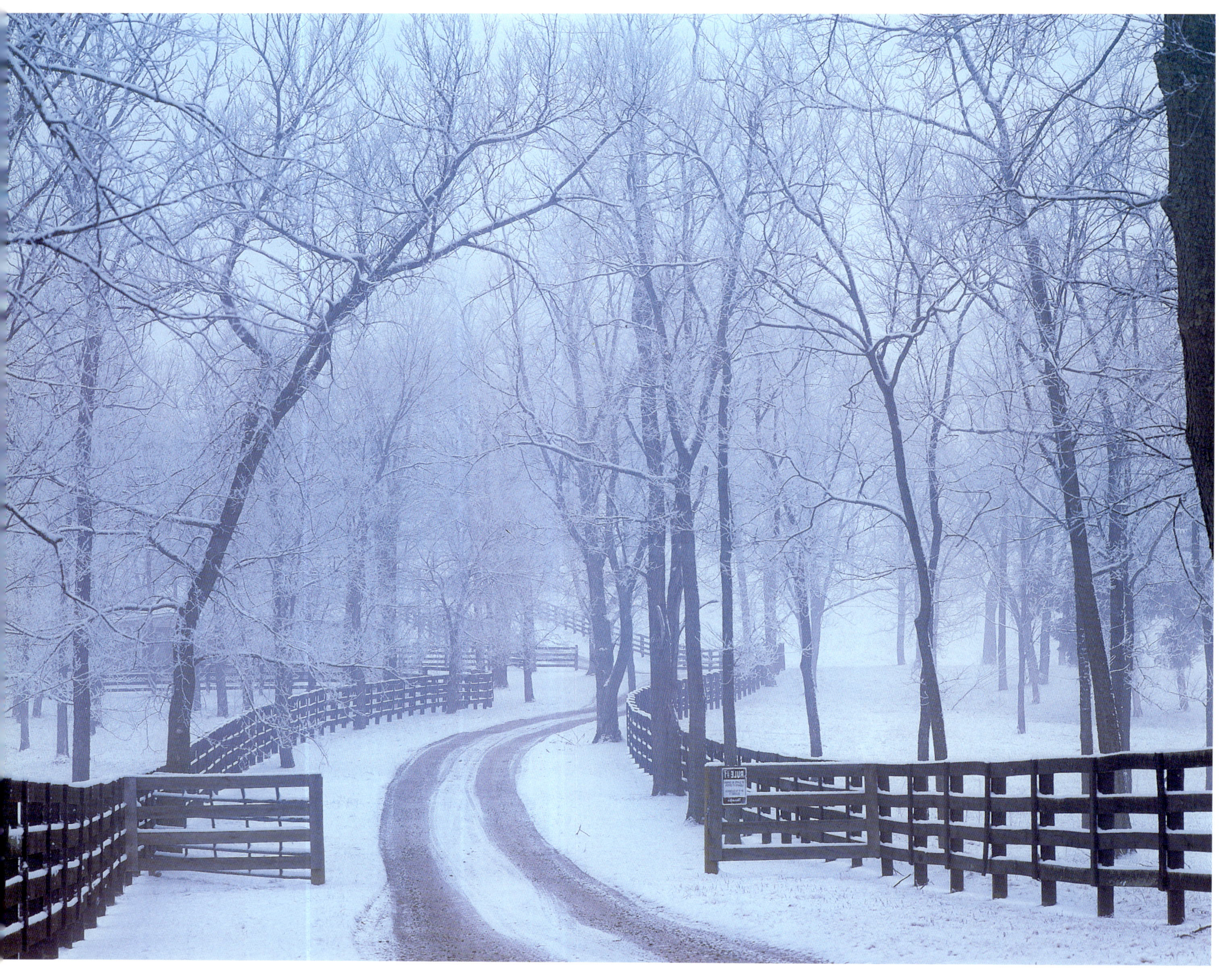

FARM ENTRANCE IN WINTER

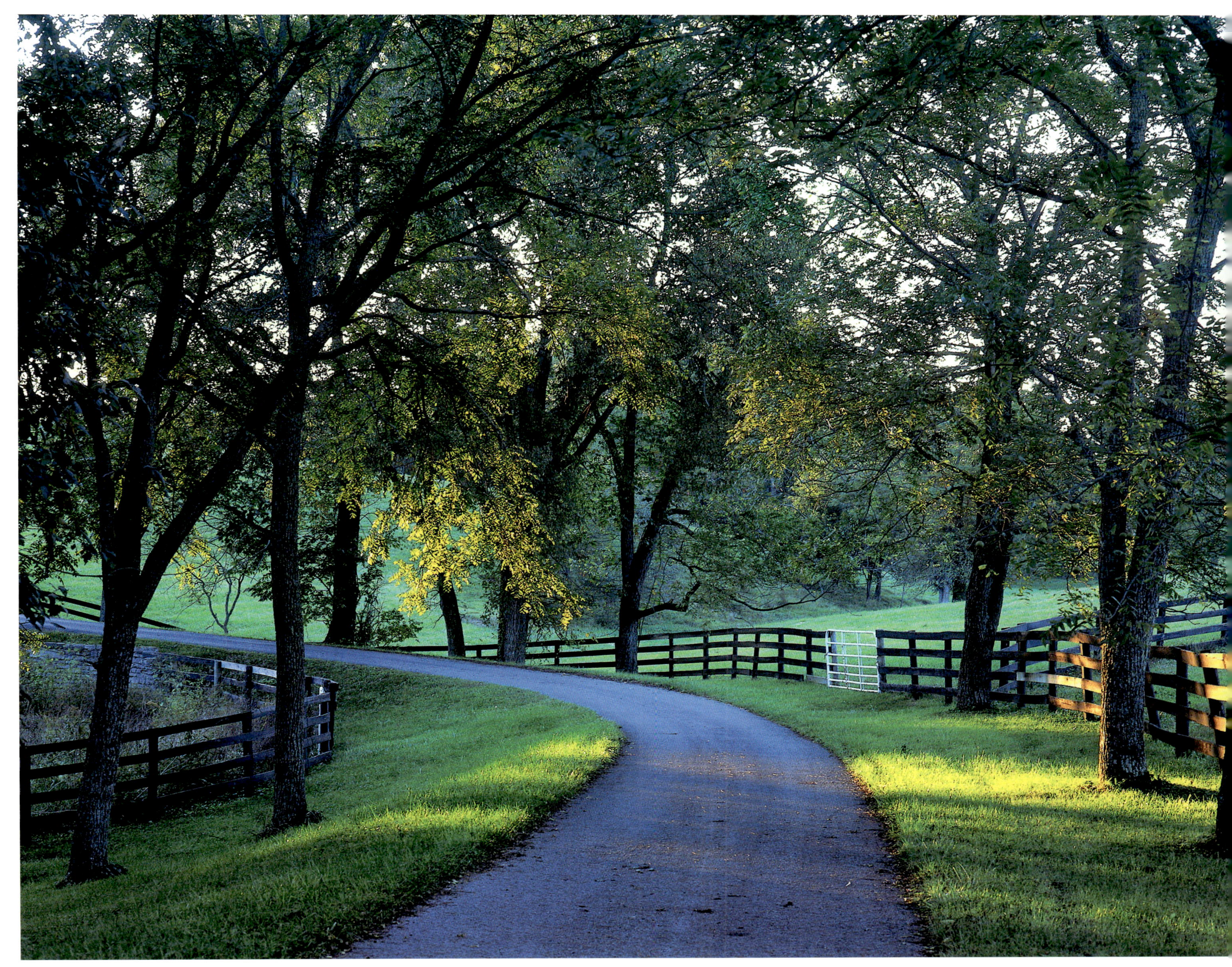

EVENING ON XALAPA FARM, BOURBON COUNTY

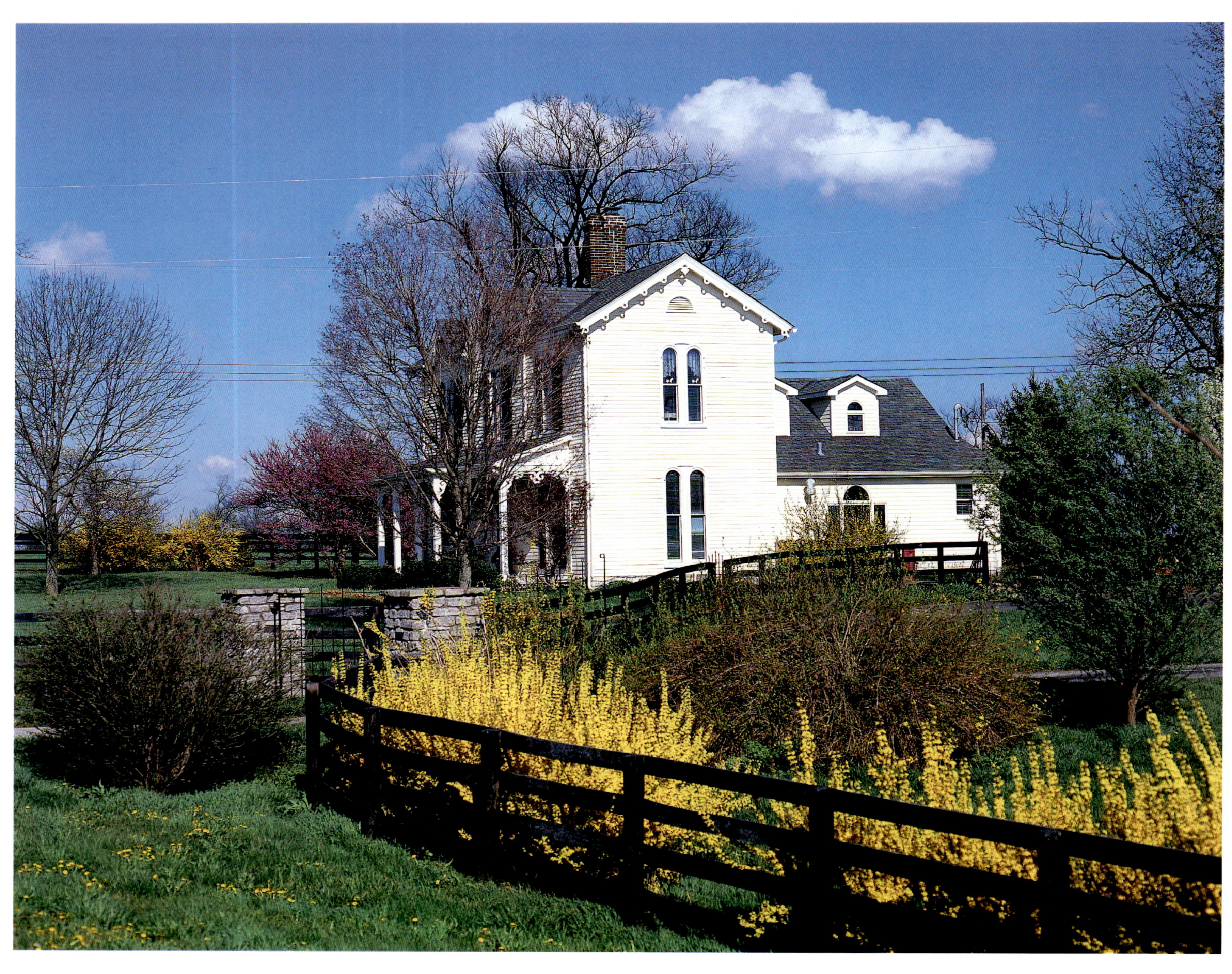

FORSYTHIA AND FARMHOUSE, PARIS PIKE

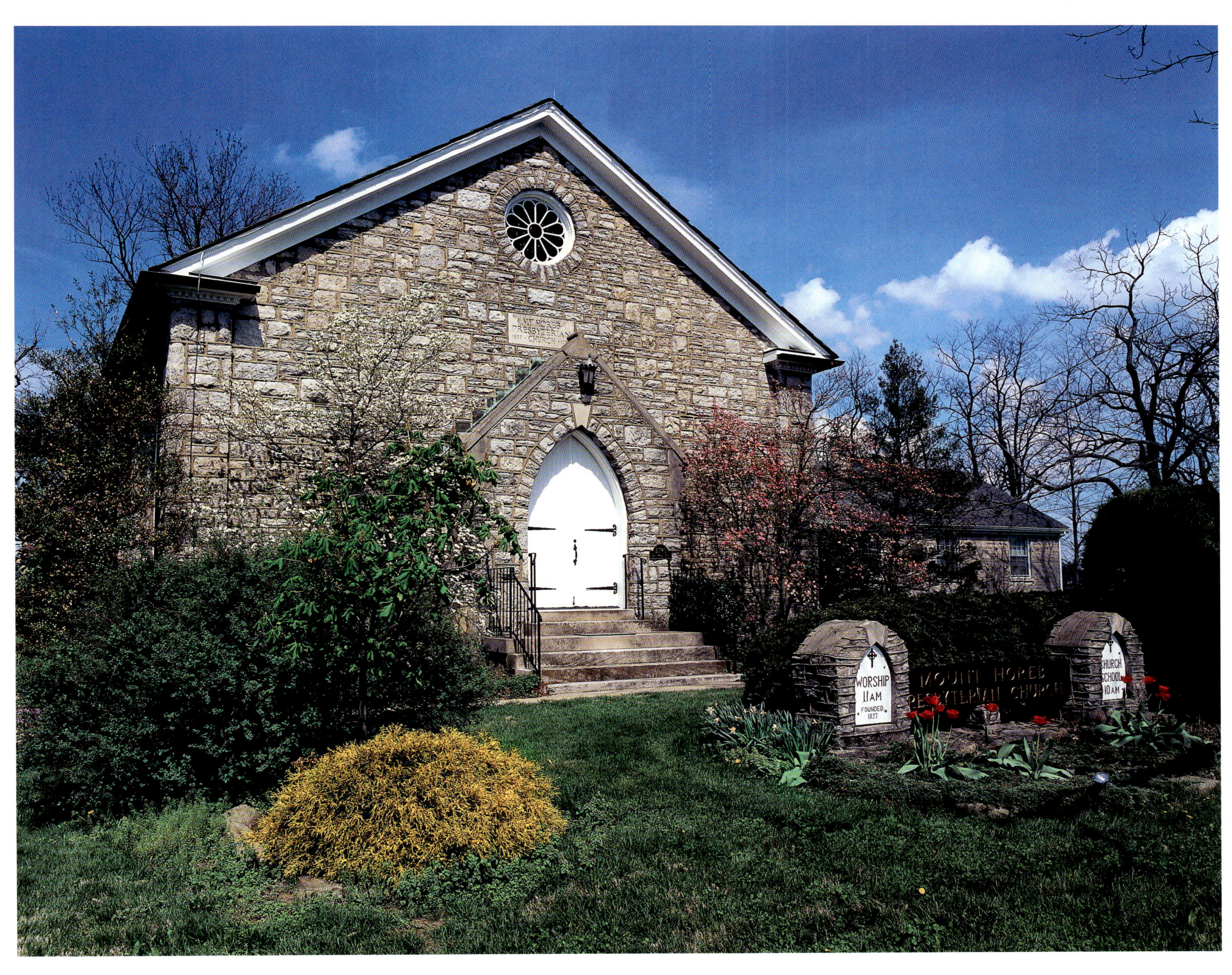

MT. HOREB PRESBYTERIAN CHURCH, IRON WORKS PIKE

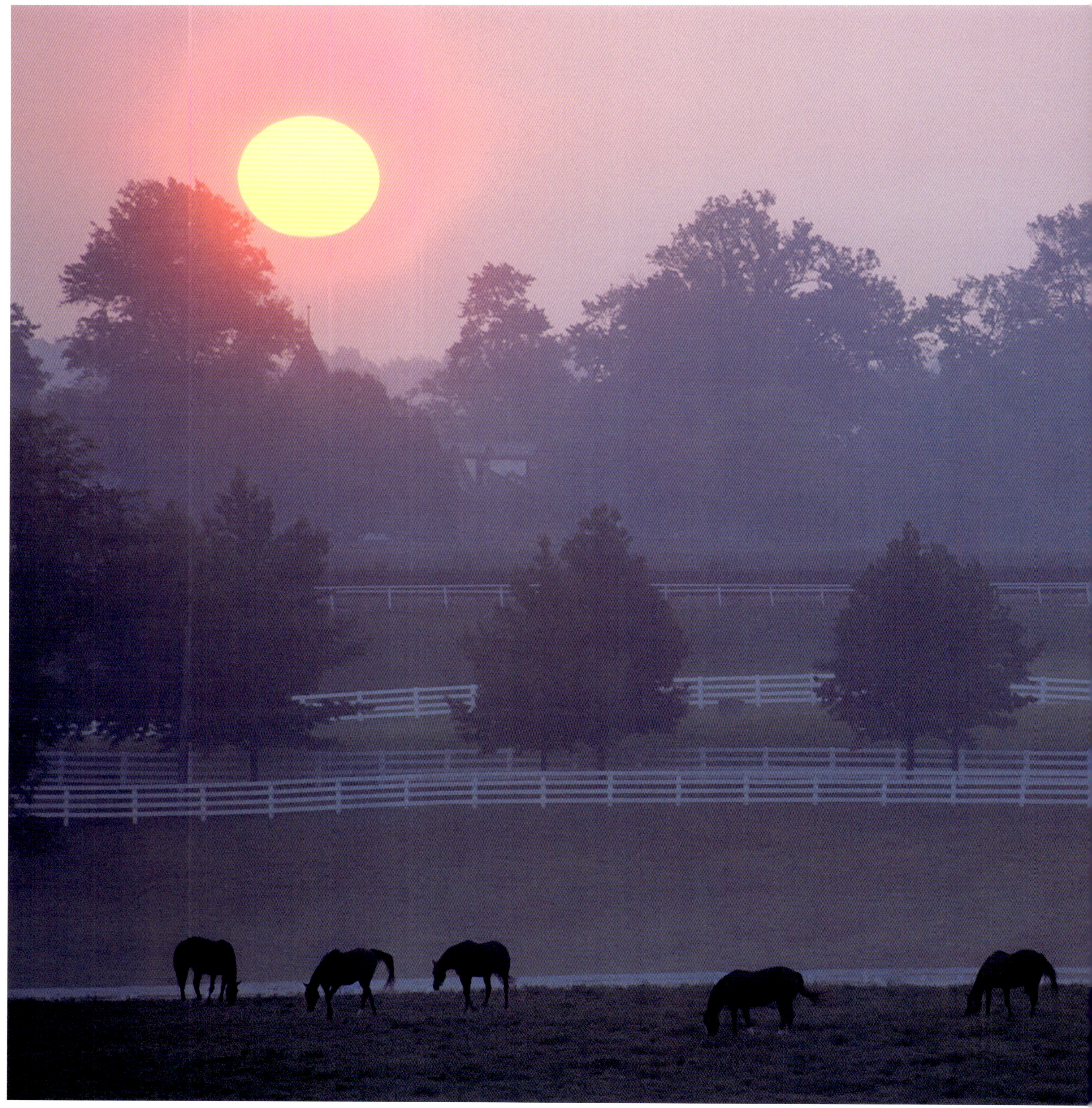

SUMMER SUNSET, CALUMET FARM

Van Meter Road affords stunning views of Calumet, Manchester, and Fares farms, all practically within sight of downtown Lexington. These working farms are among the elite of the hundreds of equine operations in the Bluegrass. Urban sprawl in the form of residential subdivisions and light industrial development is standing at their doorstep, but so far, the will of the owners and agricultural zoning have kept development at bay.

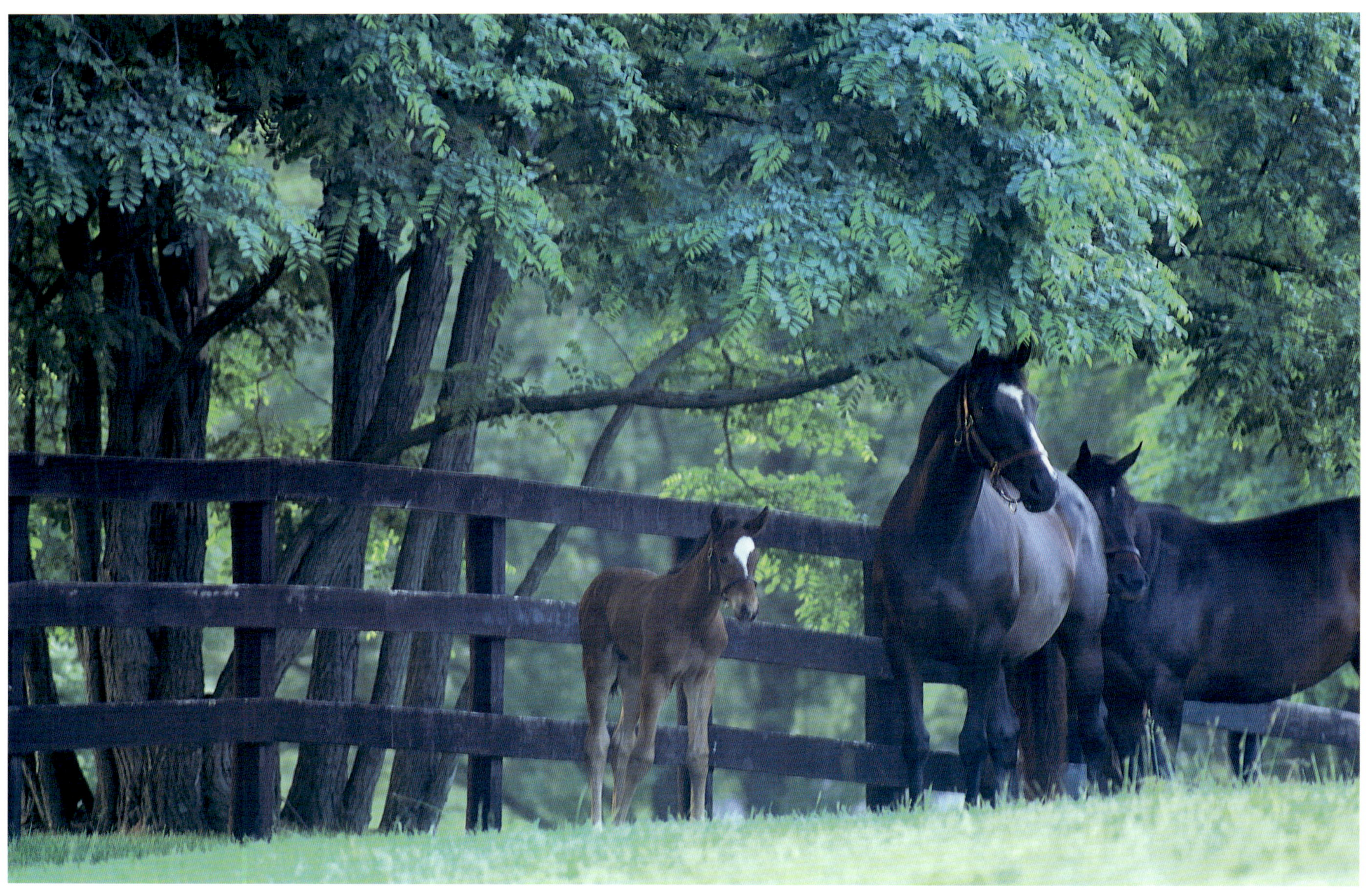

A BLUEGRASS SUMMER MORNING

Framed by a cluster of locust trees, a mare and her foal stand in their paddock on the Patchen Wilkes Farm in Fayette County. Like other horse farms just outside the Lexington city limits, Patchen Wilkes has capitulated to development pressures and is being subdivided. The struggle to protect Bluegrass farms and their scenic enrichment of central Kentucky is a top priority among preservationists in both the public and private sectors.

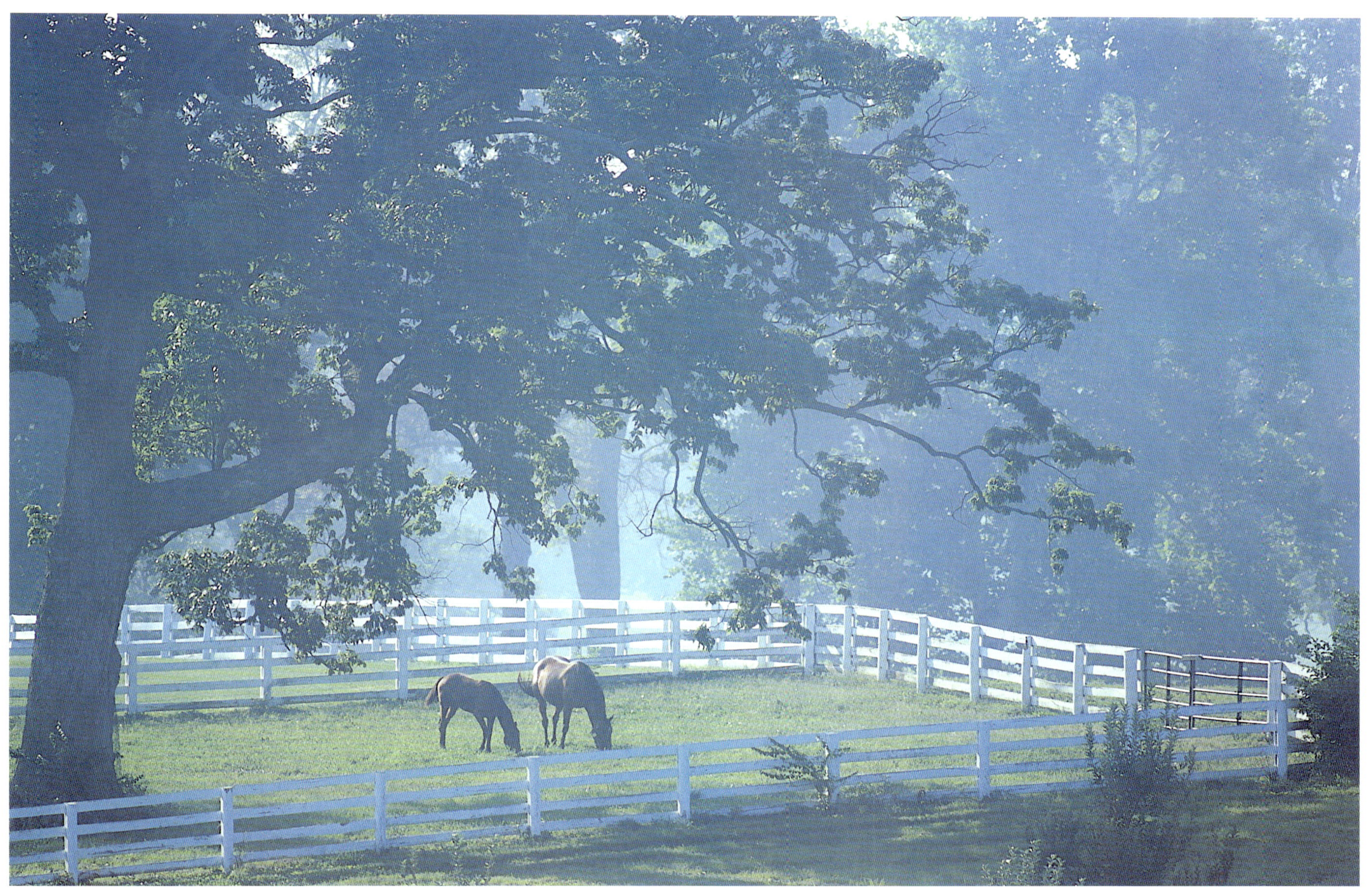

MARE AND FOAL IN SUMMER PADDOCK

Early fog gives way to hazy sunshine on a June morning at Fayette County's Darby Dan Farm. Although often overused, the term *idyllic* seems to fit life in Kentucky's Bluegrass region. Its thousands of acres of emerald pastures and neat plank fencing are often interspersed with trees that predate European settlement.

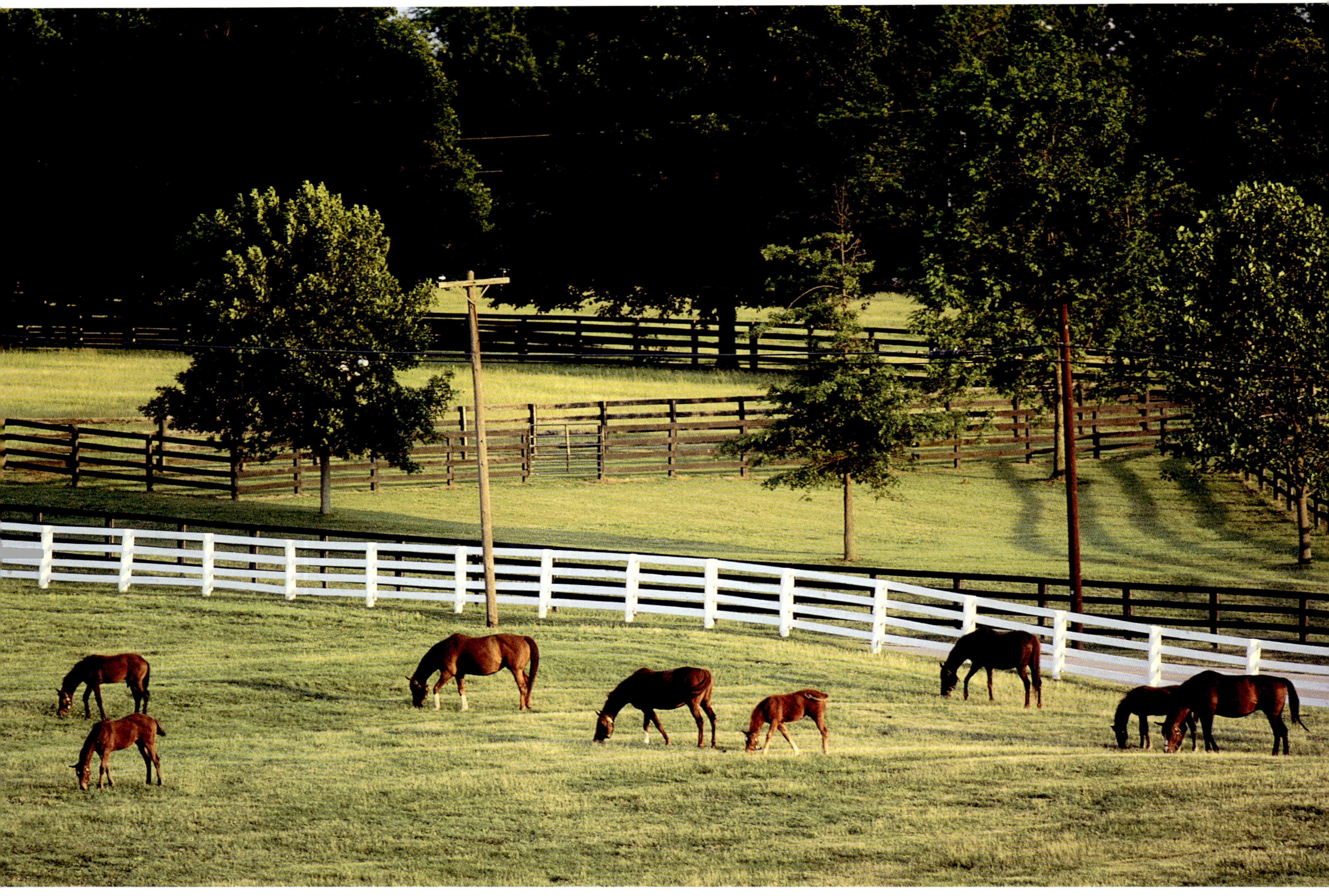

MARES AND FOALS ALONG OLD FRANKFORT PIKE

In any given year, around 10,000 foals are born in the Bluegrass State. Only a few will go on to greatness. Many others will end up roaming the backside of second- and third-class racetracks, and some will never run a race due to injury or inability. As in any endeavor, there are only a few big winners.

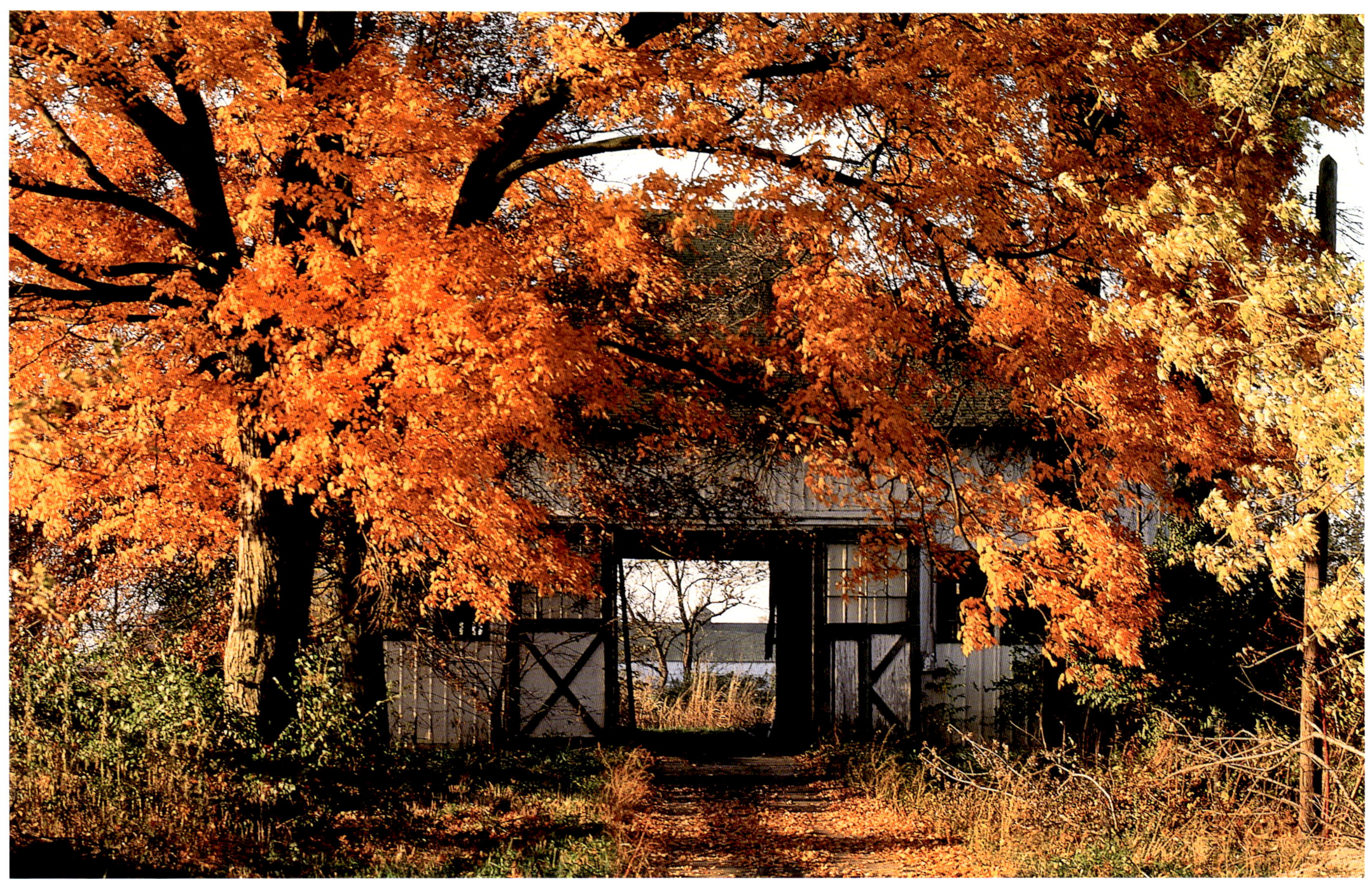

MAN O' WAR'S BARN AT FARAWAY FARM

The great racehorse Man o' War lived out his days at stud in this barn on Faraway Farm, north of Lexington. Man o' War was an icon that captured the imagination of the racing public during the 1920s and then won fame as a prepotent sire during the hard economic times of the 1930s. Winning all but one of his twenty-one races, "Big Red" became a hero to his fans, and as many as 2,000 people attended his funeral in 1947. His full body was buried in a tomb on the farm, but he now rests below a larger than life-size bronze statue at the Kentucky Horse Park in Lexington. Ironically, the great horse, loved by all Kentuckians, never raced in the state. The barn has been renovated, and the site is now part of Mt. Brilliant Farm.

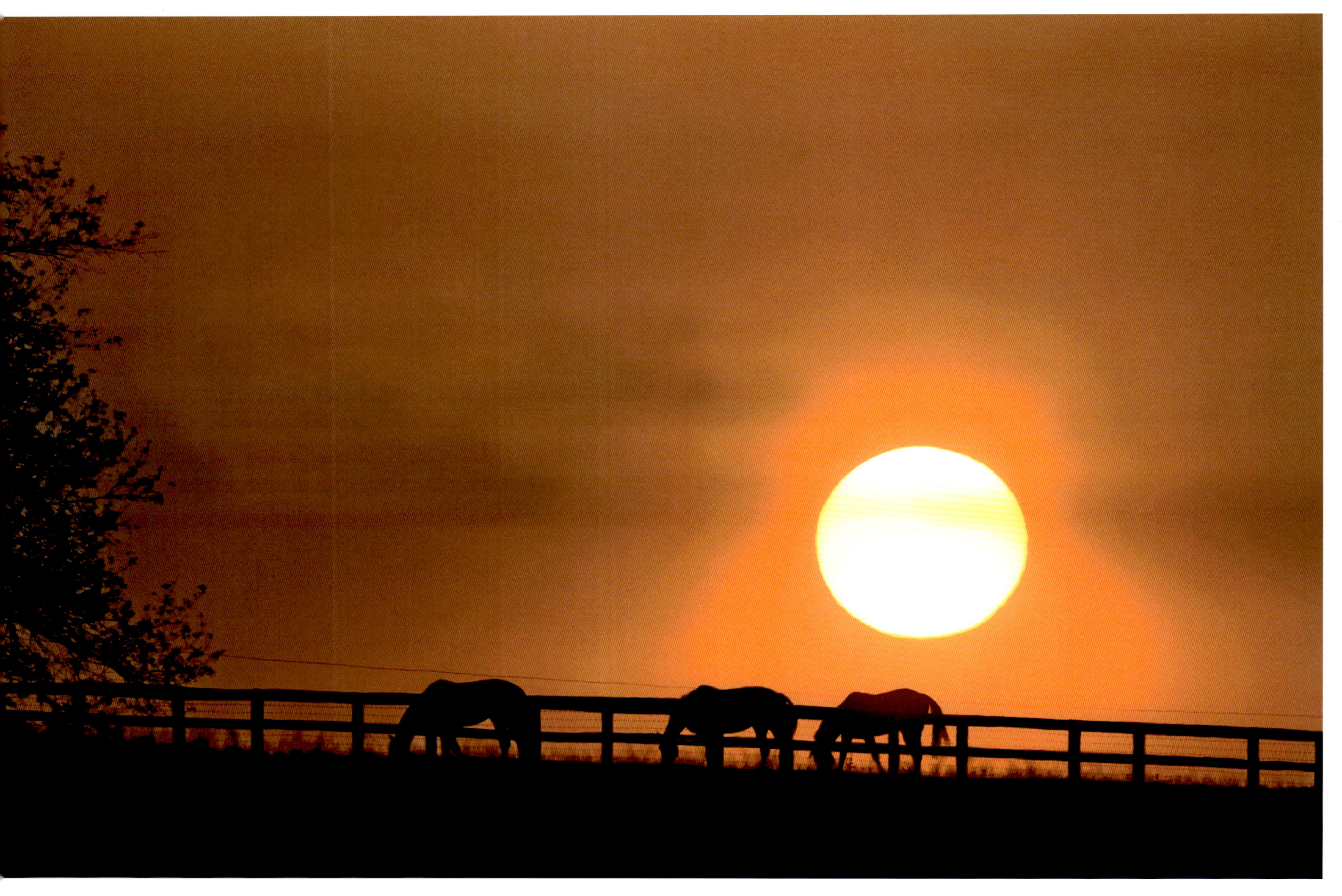

JESSAMINE COUNTY SUNSET ALONG MCCAULEY ROAD

Just south of McCauley Road, not far from the tiny village of Keene and the small town of Wilmore, the Kentucky River gorge forms a natural boundary, cutting through central Kentucky like the blade of a jagged knife. North of the river lie most of the major horse farms in Kentucky; south of the river, the fertile soil gives way to hills, forested knobs, and the foothills of the Appalachian Mountains.

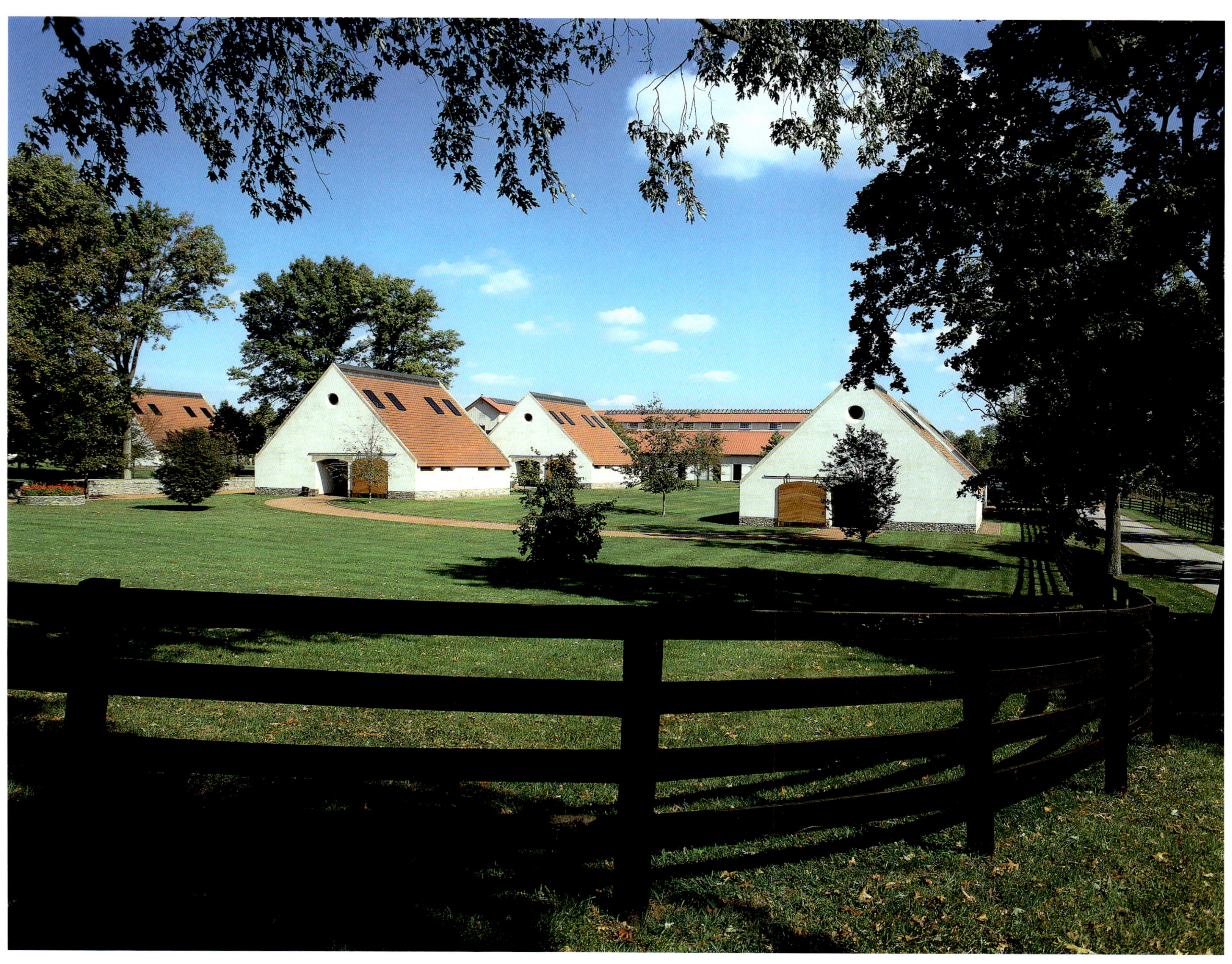

BARNS AT GAINESWAY FARM

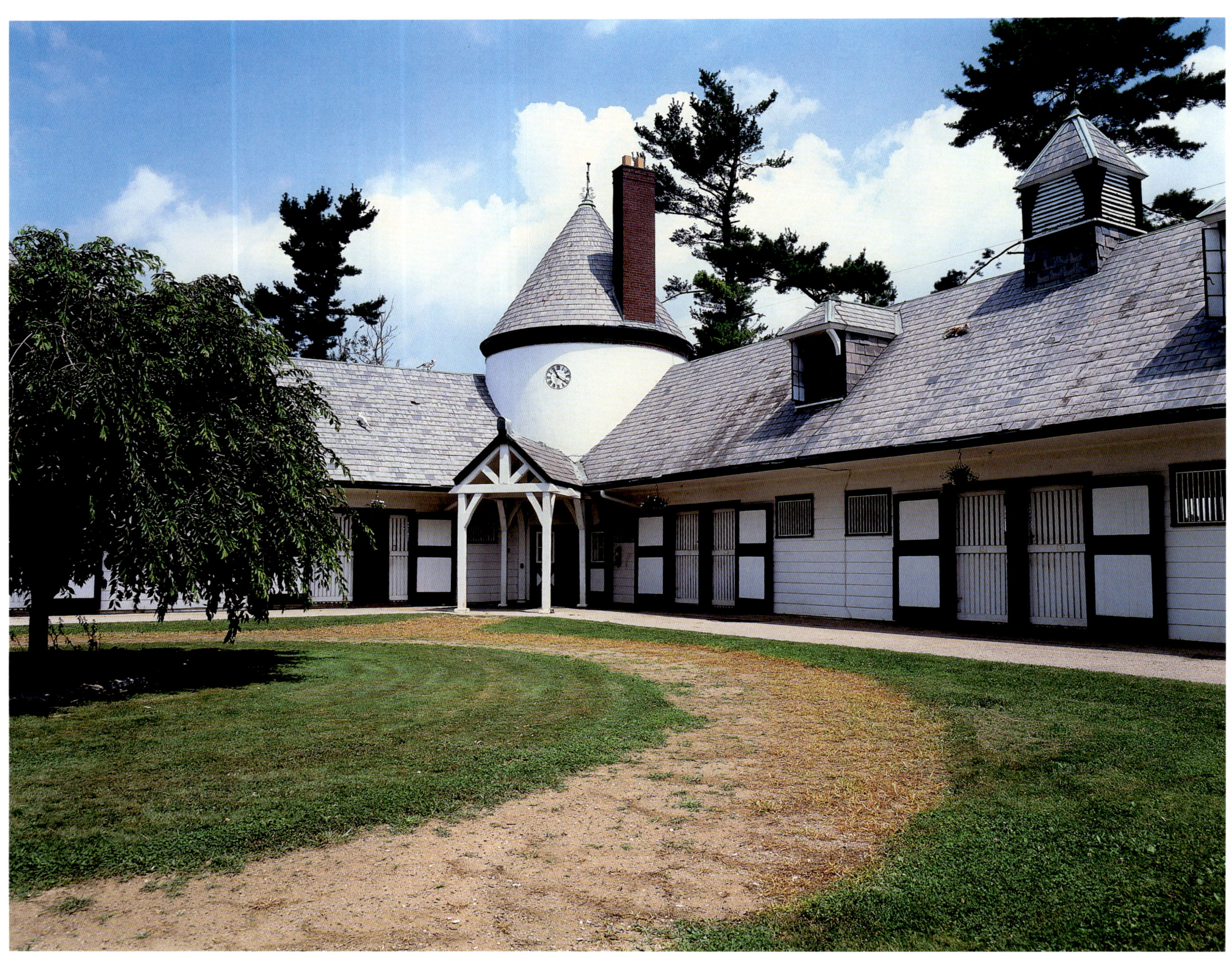

BARN AT NORMANDY FARM, PARIS PIKE

The Normandy Farm along the Paris Pike was formerly part of the famed Elmendorf Farm. The design of this barn, commissioned in 1933 by Elmendorf owner Joseph E. Widener, is based on those in the Normandy region of France. The L-shaped barn is anchored by a brick clock tower. Superstition dictates the placement of ceramic animals on the roof, apparently to ward off evil spirits. The barn is a tourist destination and has been depicted in several movies, most recently *Seabiscuit.* Normandy Farm is the site of the graves of Man o' War's sire and dam, Fair Play and Mahubah.

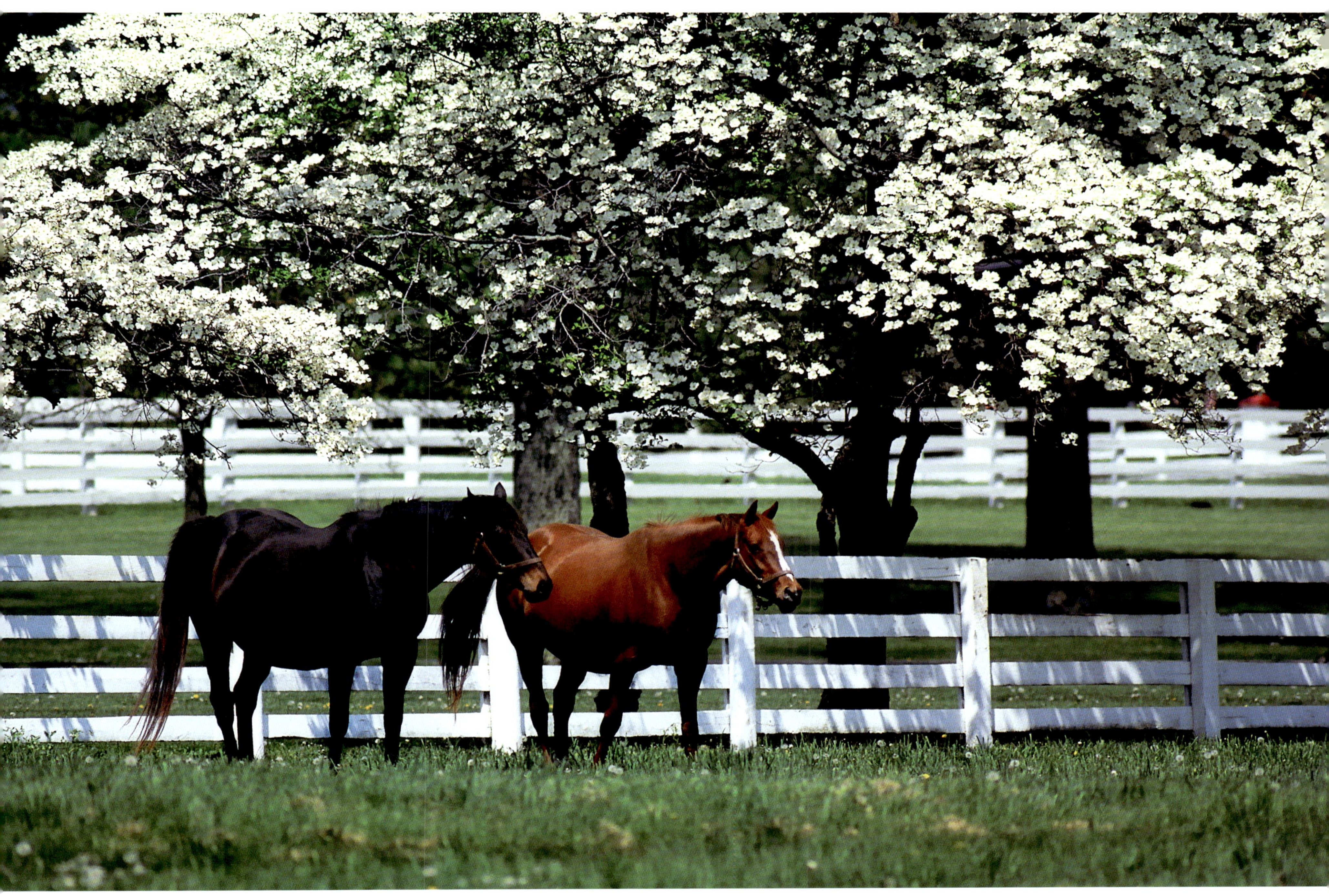

MARES AND DOGWOODS

Spring in Kentucky is a welcome blessing after the sometimes harsh winter months. Kentucky lies in a geologic middle ground of seasons and temperatures, providing perfect conditions for flowering trees and plants native to both the North and the South. Kentuckians rejoice in the warmth of gentle spring days that provide a feast of color for the eye.

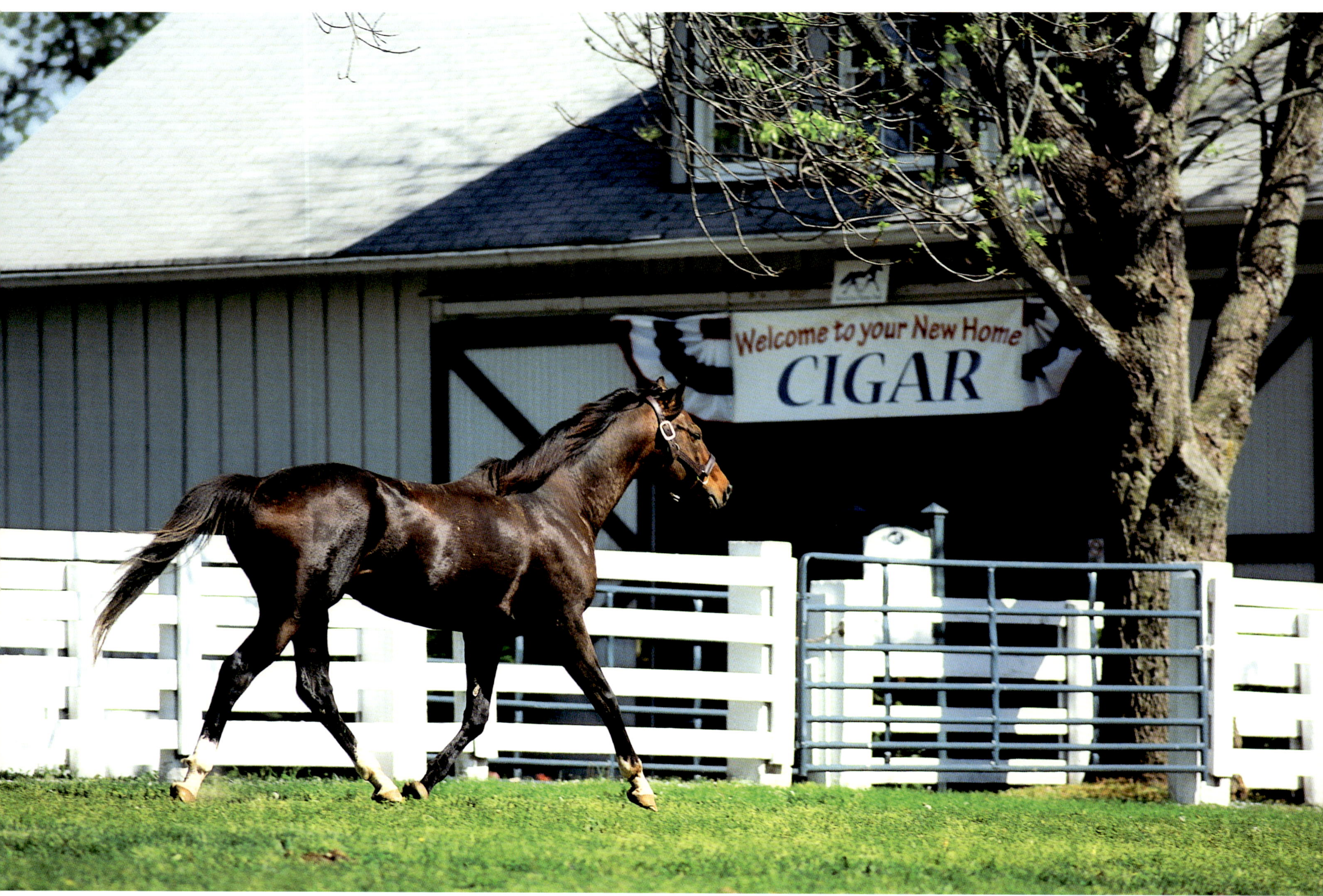

CIGAR, WINNER OF SIXTEEN CONSECUTIVE RACES

In the mid-1990s, Cigar captured the imagination of the racing world by winning sixteen straight races—a feat rarely repeated in modern history (Citation and Hallowed Dreams did it as well). Cigar's family tree includes Northern Dancer and Seattle Slew. His career earnings of nearly $10 million were the most of any racehorse in the twentieth century. After his career on the track, Cigar was found to be sterile, and he is now retired at the Kentucky Horse Park in Lexington.

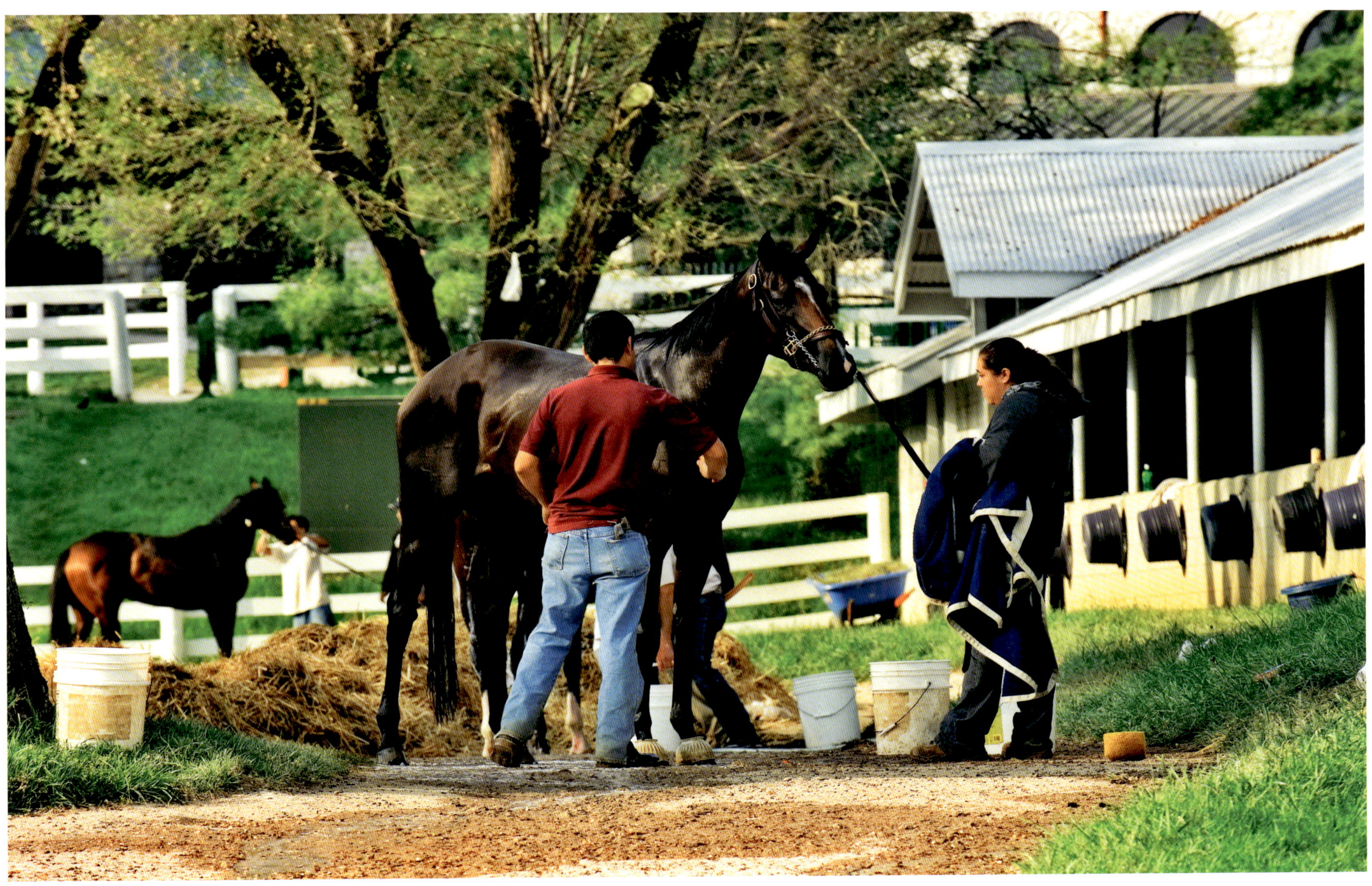

MORNING TRADITION AT KEENELAND

During the spring and fall racing meets, the barn area at Keeneland Race Course resembles a small city. In early morning, hundreds of workers bustle about, caring for the few hundred prize Thoroughbreds stabled there. With so much seemingly chaotic activity, one could easily be run down by a hot-walking, 1,200-pound animal. Photographing a soothing bath presents little danger, however, provided one's peripheral vision is on high alert.

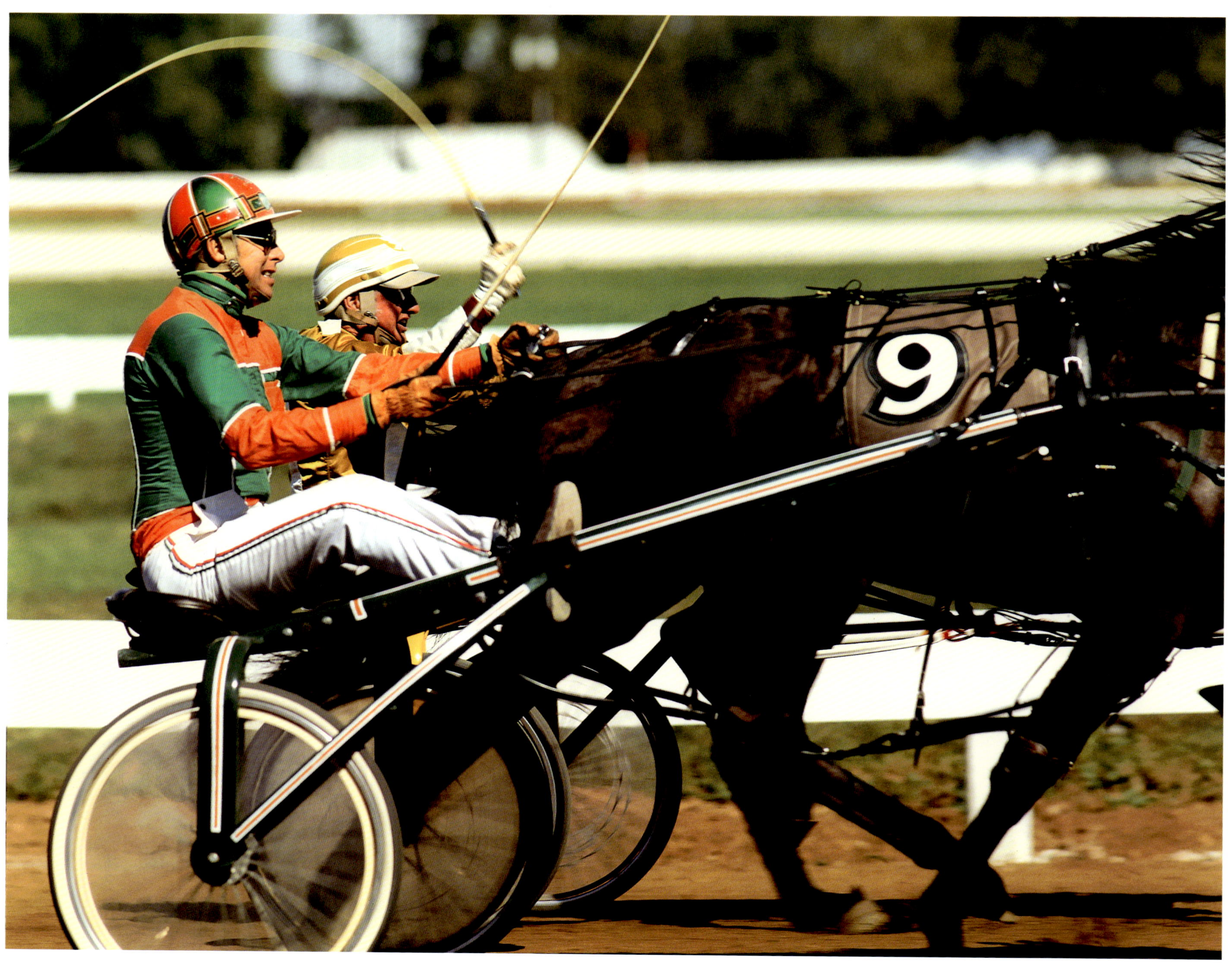

RED MILE TROTTING TRACK, LEXINGTON

The Red Mile in Lexington is often called the world's fastest harness track. Grand Circuit meets draw the best horses in the country and thousands of harness racing fans each year. Trotters and pacers are Standardbreds, and the best and greatest of them are raised in the Bluegrass. The Red Mile hosts the Kentucky Futurity, first run in 1893, making it the oldest stakes in harness racing. The Kentucky Futurity is one of the four Grand Slam races of trotting, along with the Hambletonian, the Yonkers Futurity, and the Dexter Futurity. Among the hundreds of famous racers to have walked in Bluegrass fields are George Wilkes, Bay Chief, Alexander's Abdallah, and Nancy Hanks.

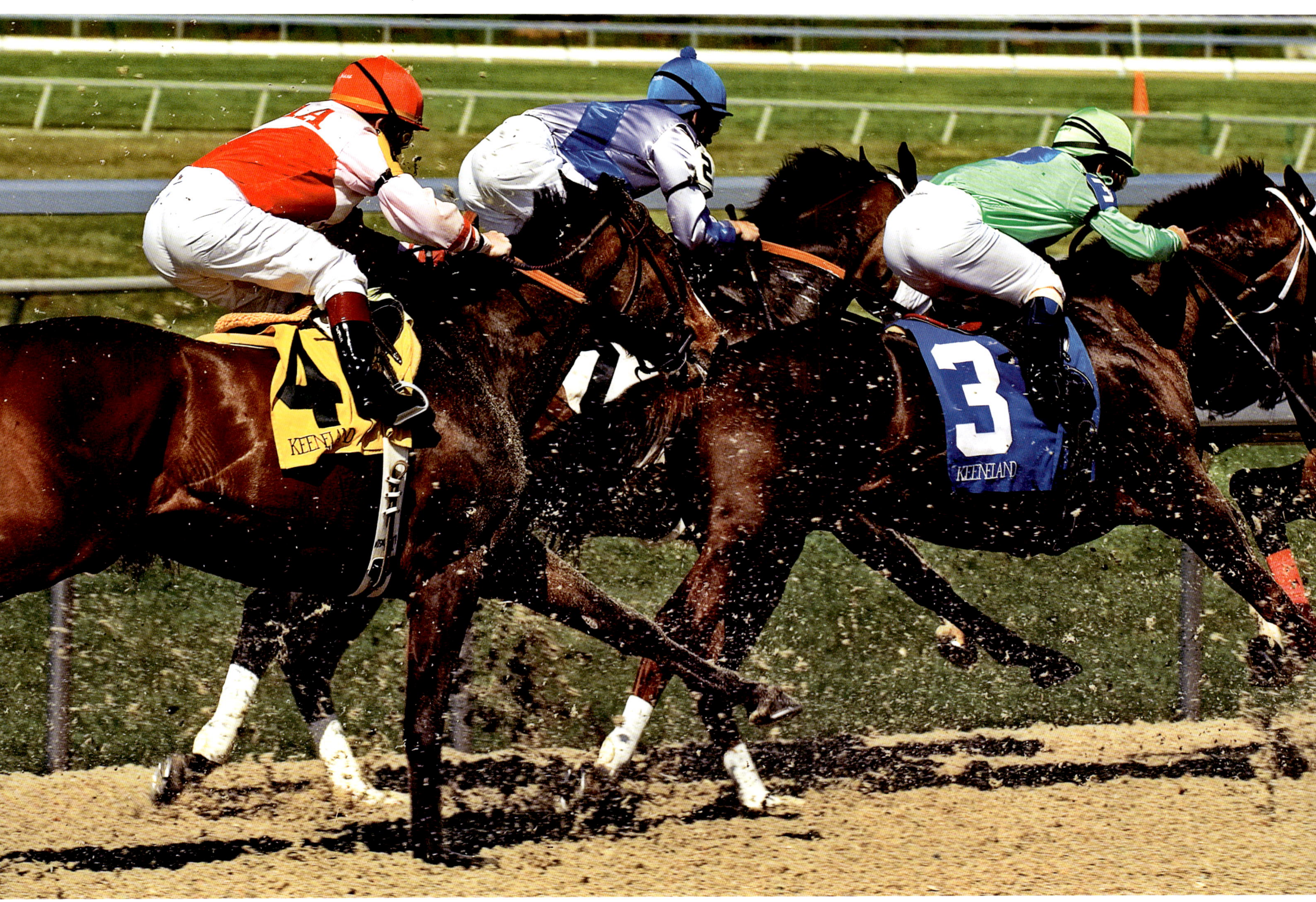

NEAR THE RAIL AT KEENELAND

If you've ever stood at the rail at Keeneland or any other racetrack, you're familiar with the phrase "pounding hoofbeats." The teeth-jarring sound of several 1,200-pound animals blinking by at thirty-five miles per hour makes one appreciate the danger of riding one of these beautiful beasts for a living. Adequate health insurance for jockeys has only recently been addressed by the horse industry.

SECRETARIAT

When Secretariat won racing's Triple Crown in 1973, he became the new darling of Thoroughbred lovers everywhere. Although no horse could duplicate the mystique of Man o' War, Secretariat came close in the opinion of many. Were it not for a malfunctioning clock at the Preakness, Secretariat would be credited with breaking every time record in the Triple Crown races. In one of the most astonishing performances in racing history, Secretariat won the Belmont by thirty-one lengths. He died in 1989 at age nineteen of complications from laminitis, a chronic disease of the hoof.

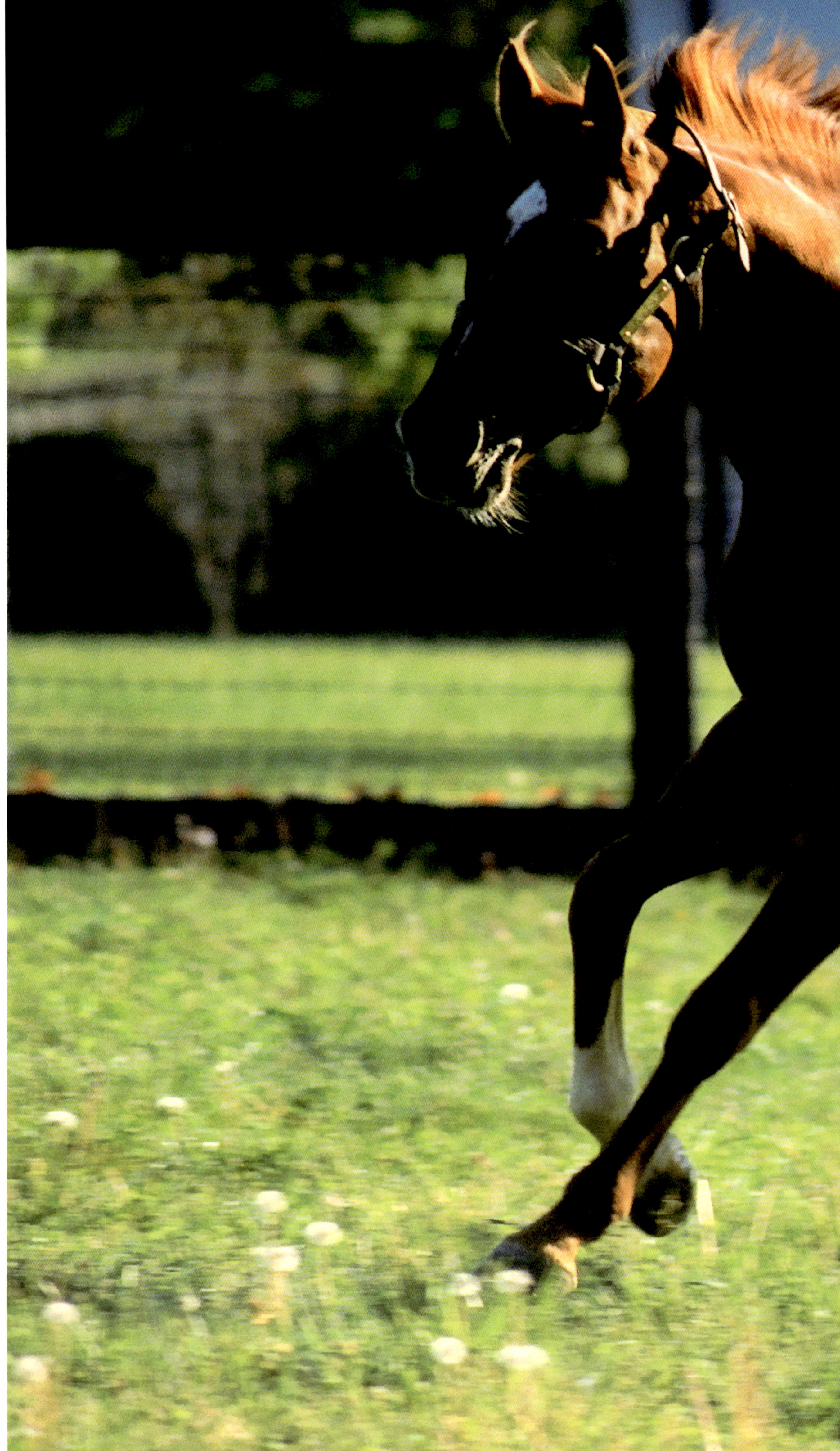

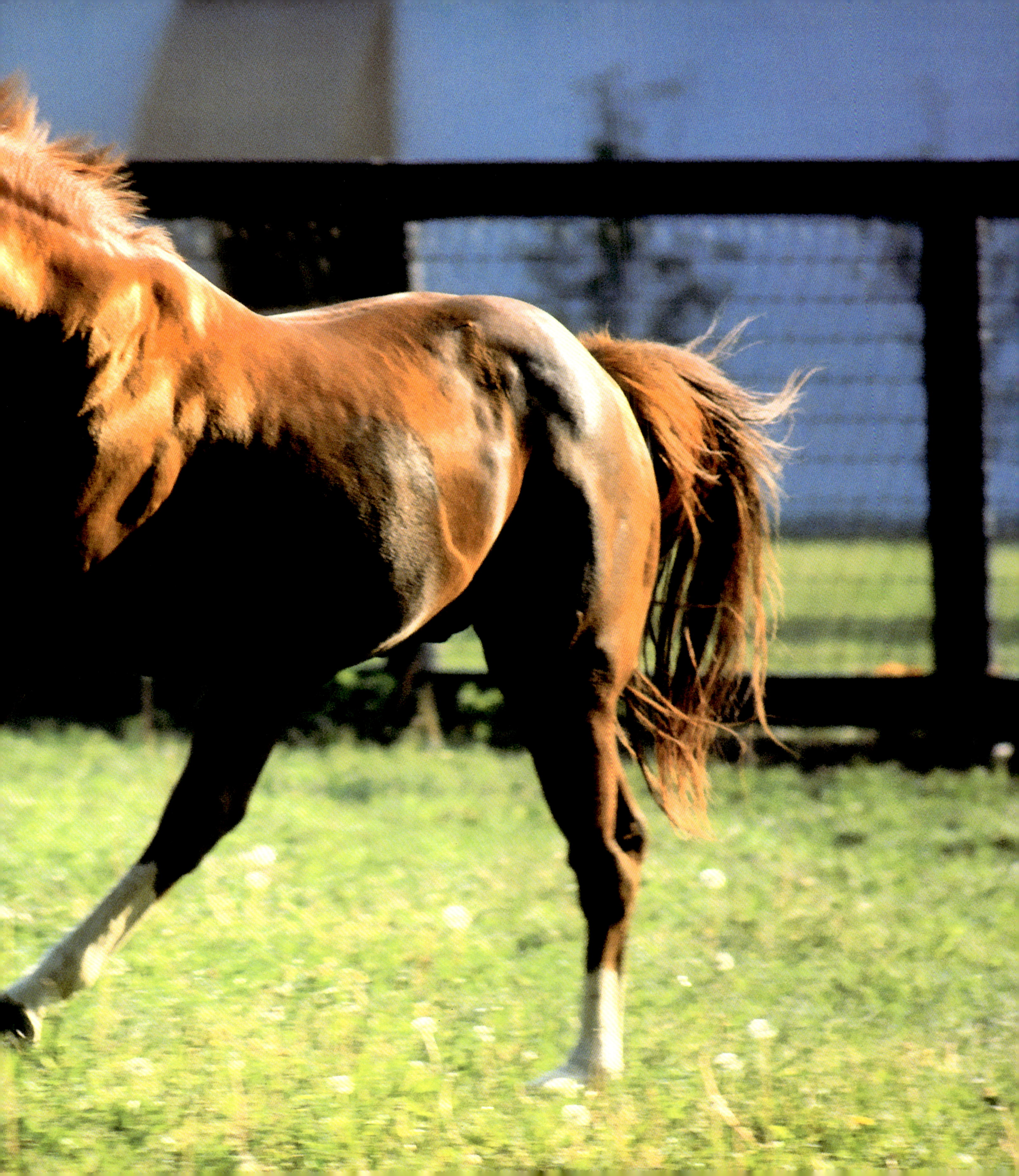

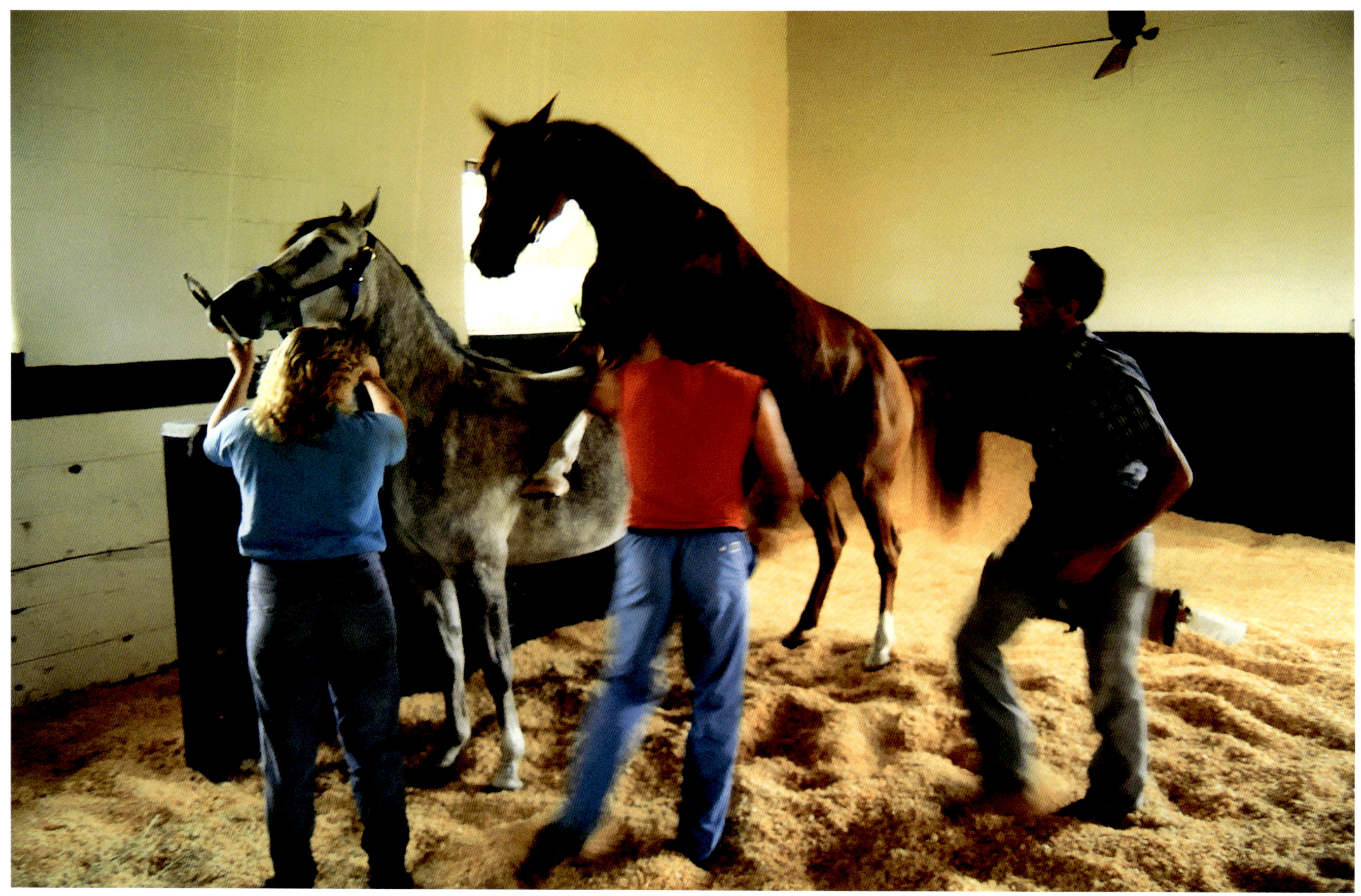

IN THE BREEDING SHED

The breeding shed is no place for the faint of heart. Several experienced persons are required to bring a stallion and a mare together to ensure conception of a healthy foal. Breeding is a multimillion-dollar industry, so little is left to chance. Bloodlines of horses are much more closely monitored than those of people. No artificial insemination is permitted in Thoroughbred breeding. A good stallion can cover 100 to 150 mares in a season.

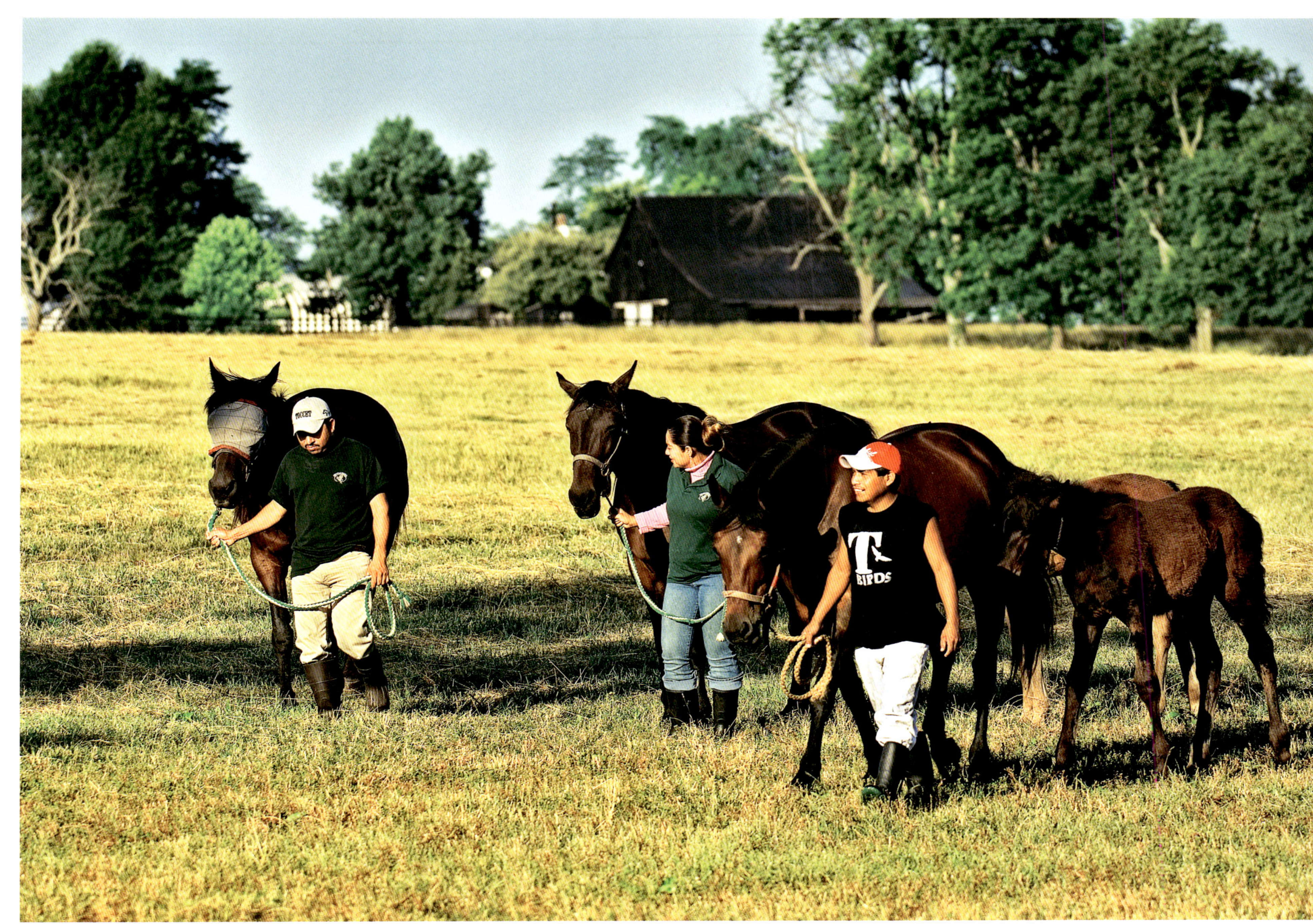

BRINGING IN THE MARES AND FOALS, KENTUCKIANA FARM, SCOTT COUNTY

Most horse farms in Kentucky depend on immigrant labor, particularly from Mexico and other Latin American countries, to maintain their successful operations. This dependence on immigrant workers exists throughout Kentucky and the United States. Through hard work and experience, many rise to managerial positions in the equine industry.

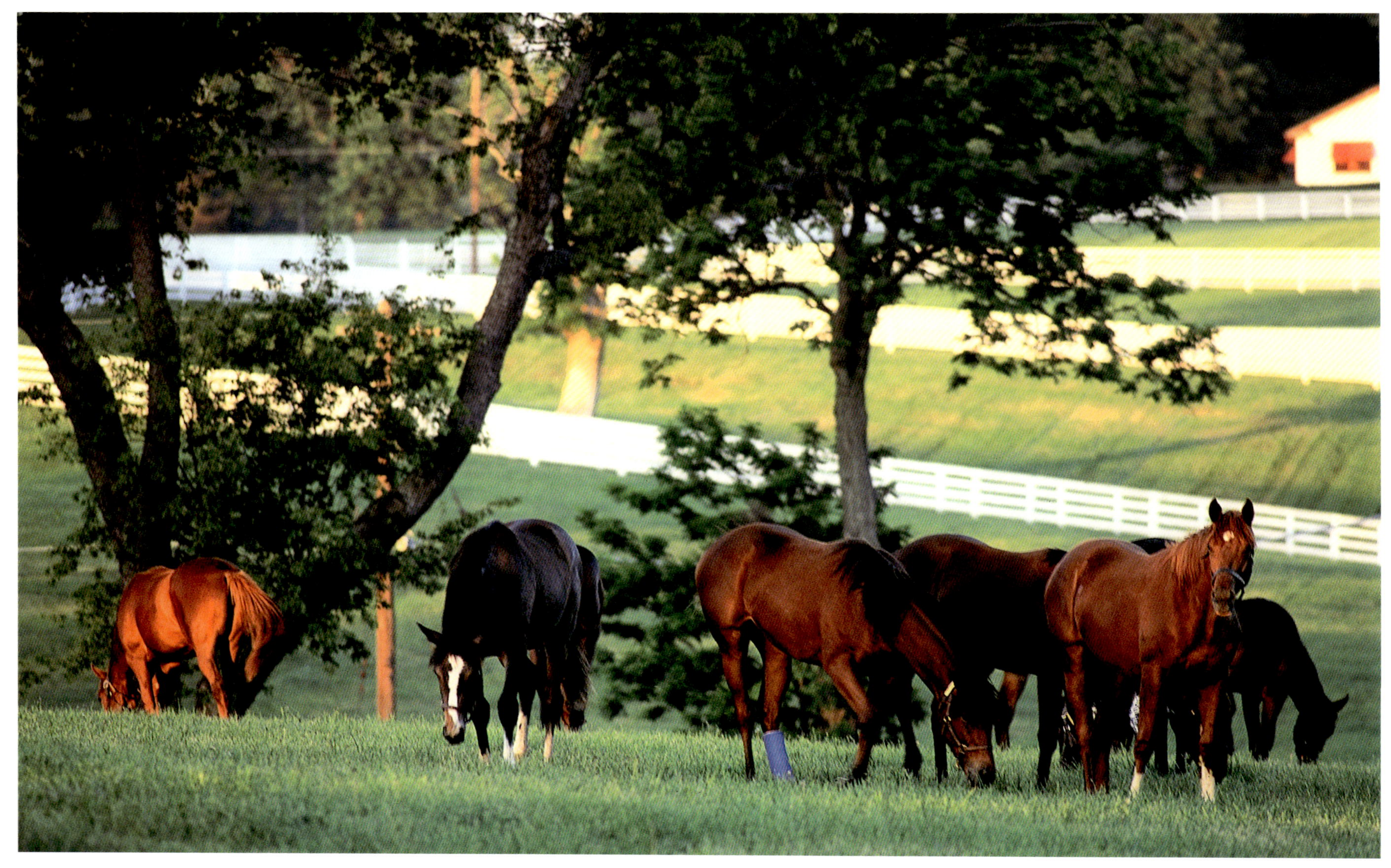

MARES GRAZING AT EVENING

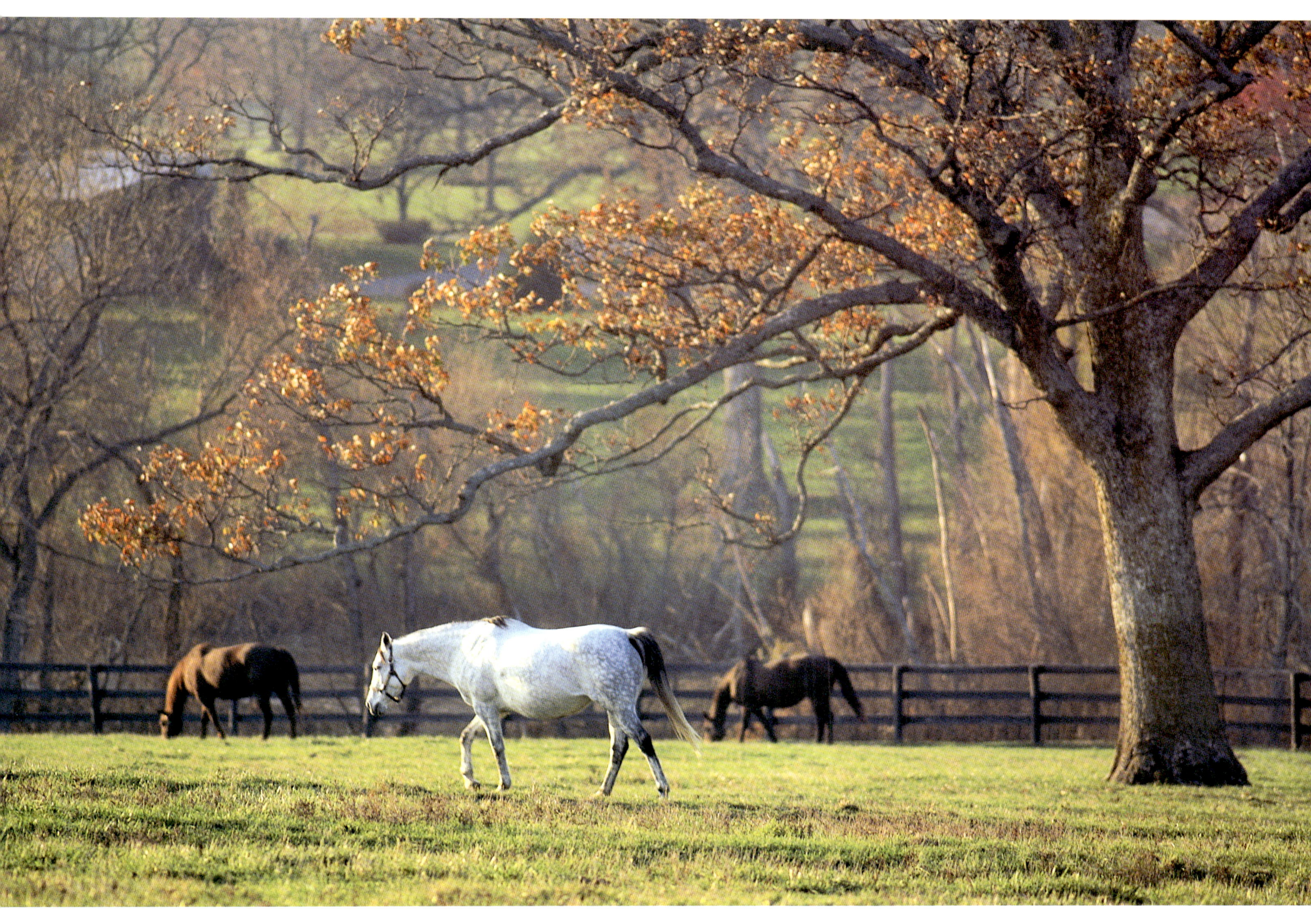

GRAY MARE IN AUTUMN, MT. HOREB PIKE

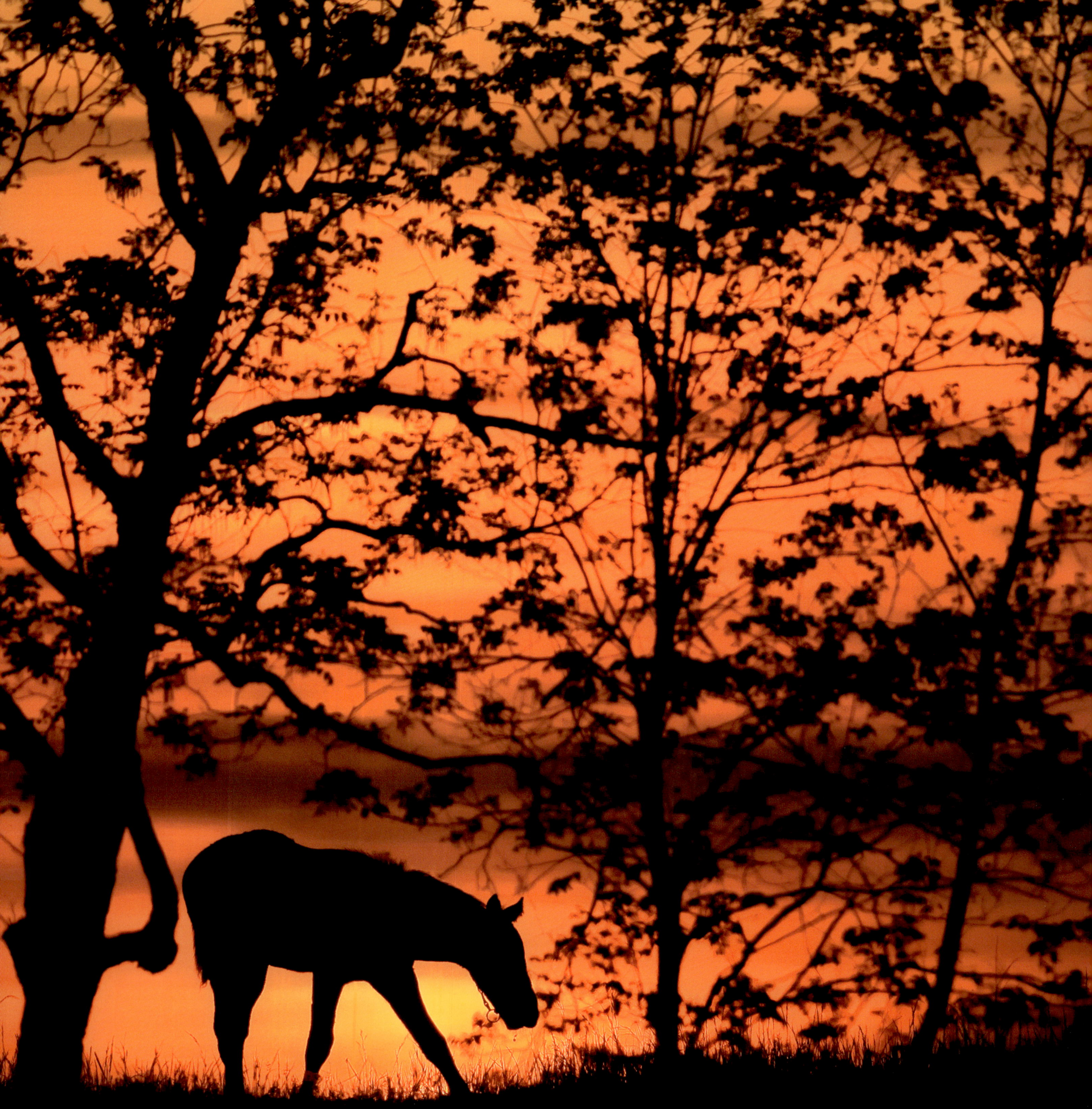

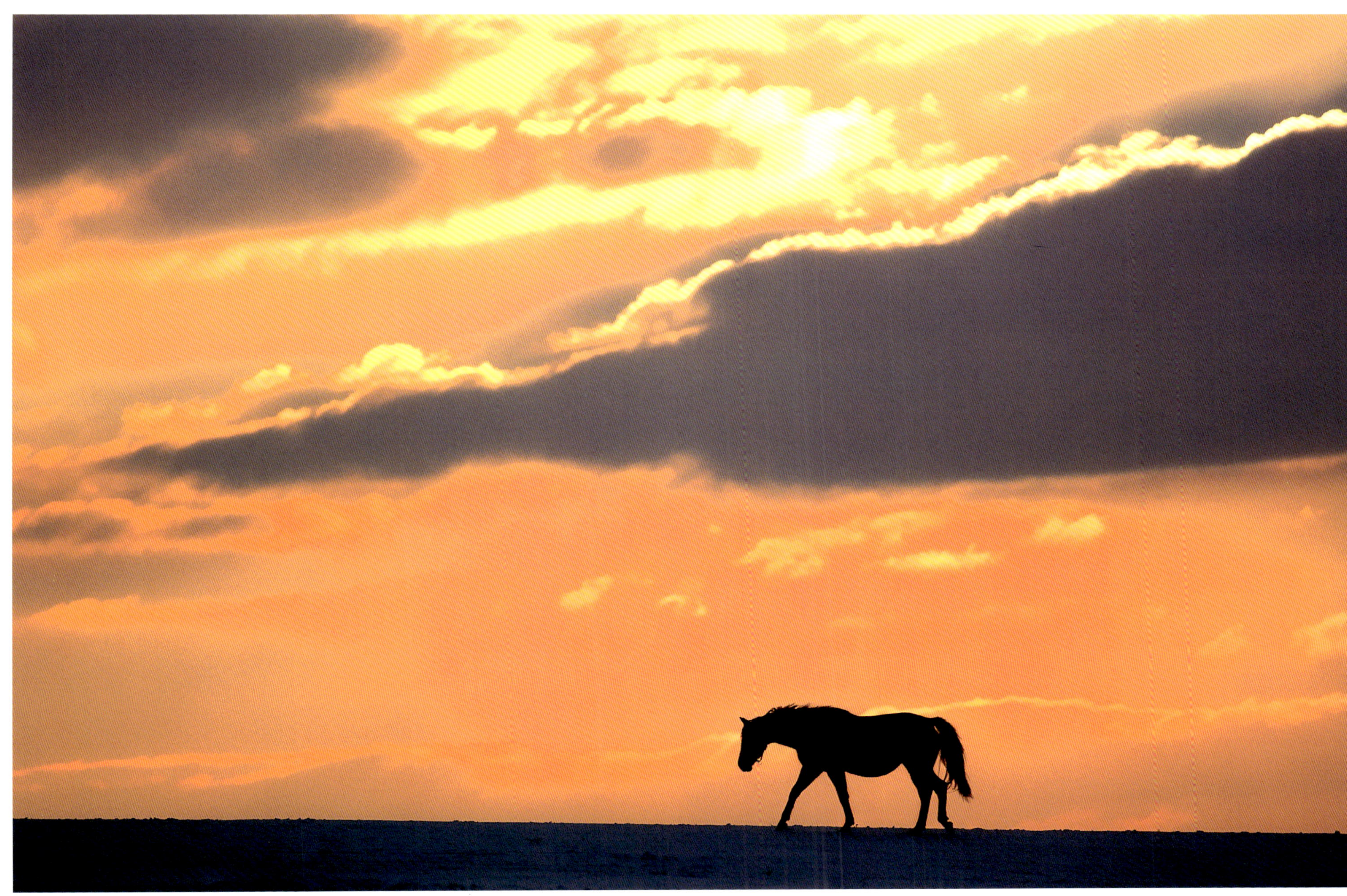

Above: THOROUGHBRED MARE AT EVENING

Facing: FOAL AT SUNSET ALONG HUME BEDFORD PIKE, FAYETTE COUNTY

This foal serendipitously moved itself squarely in front of a Bluegrass sunset on a hilltop in northern Fayette County. Thousands of foals roam Bluegrass pastures each spring, but this kind of setting is not easily created, let alone recorded.

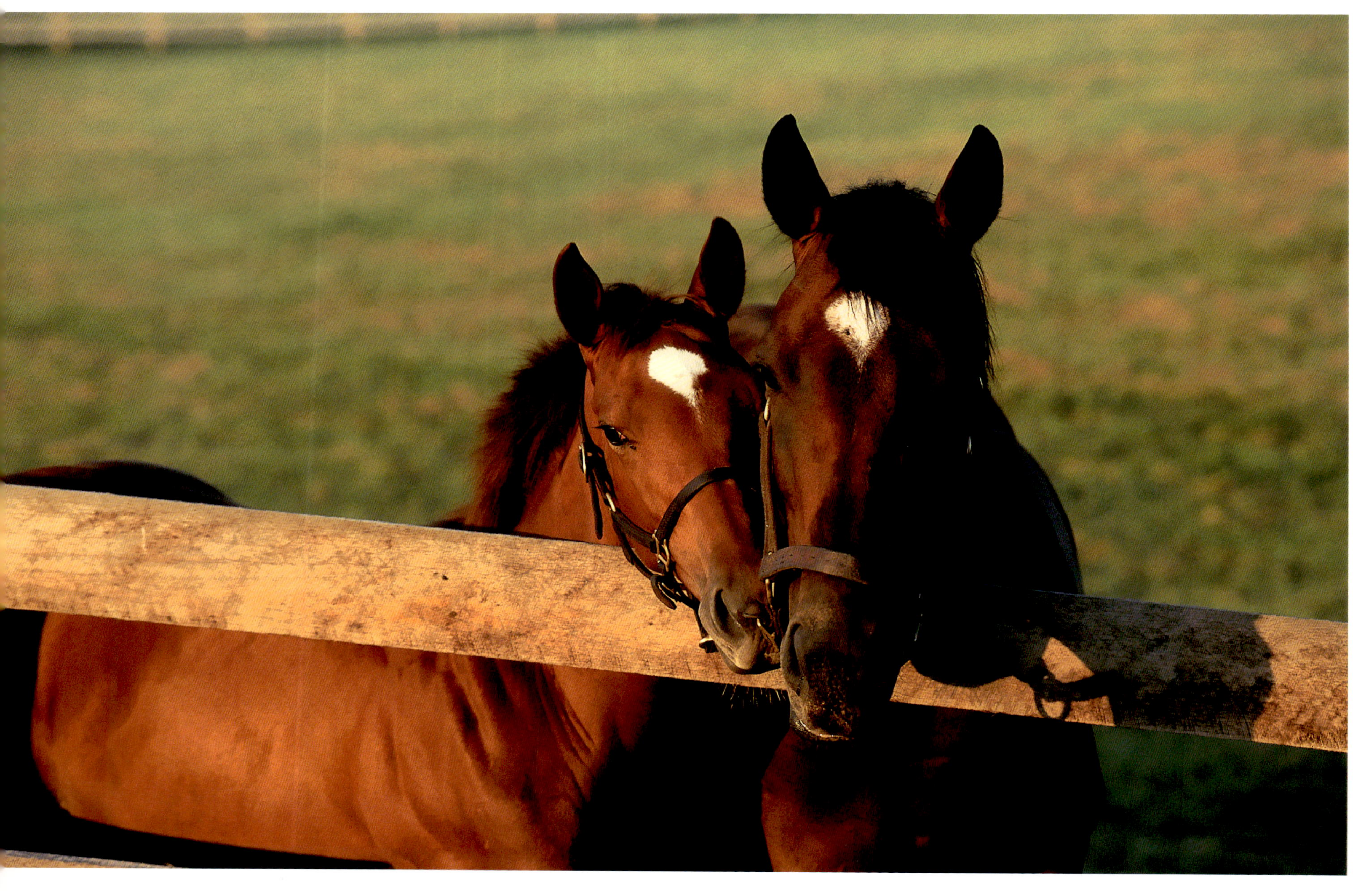

MARE AND FOAL AT FENCE

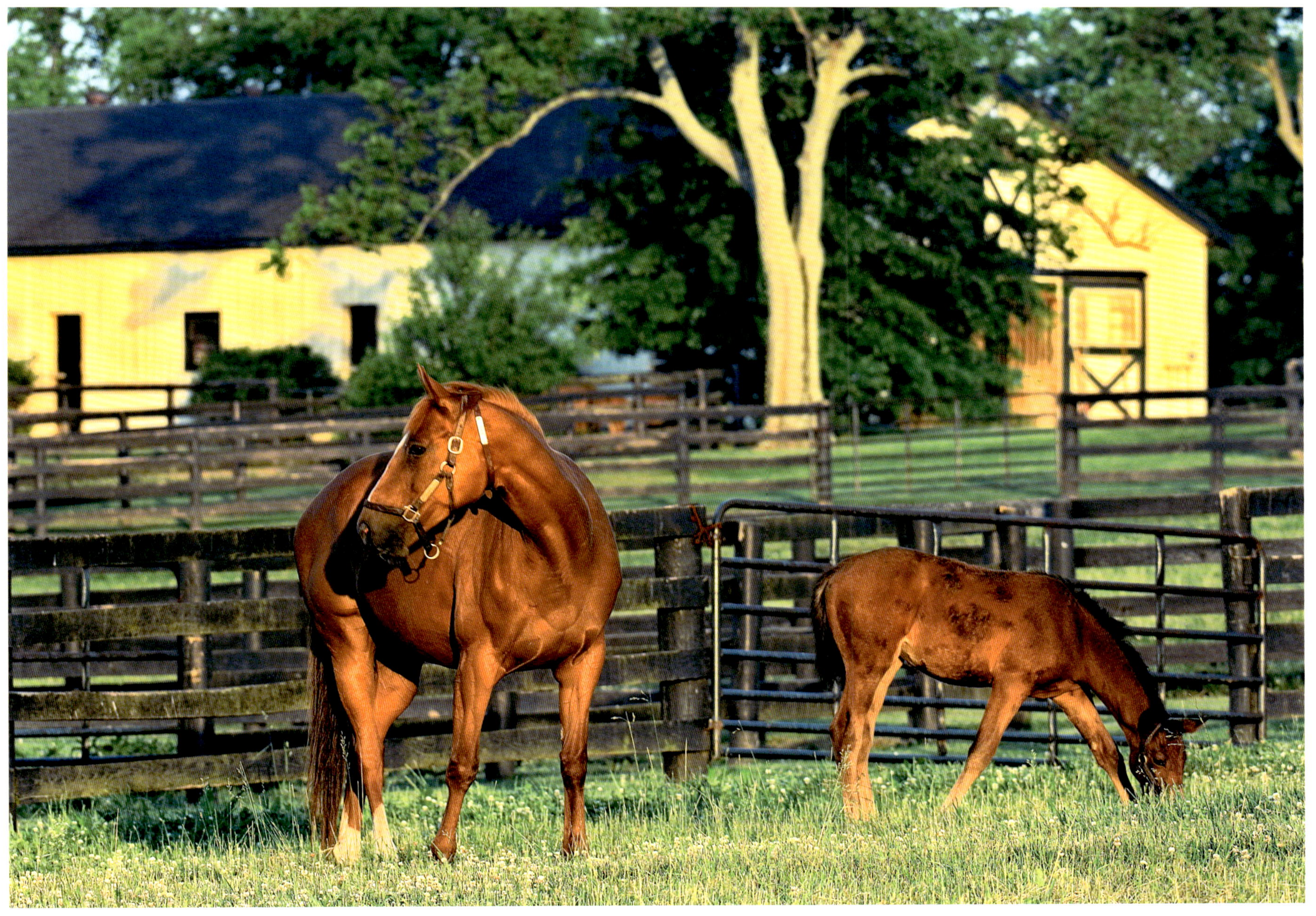

MARE AND FOAL ALONG U.S. HIGHWAY 62, SCOTT COUNTY

On a May morning, this mother keeps close tabs on her surroundings and her foal. Within yards of the paddock, rush hour is in full swing as hundreds of vehicles spill onto U.S. Highway 62 from Interstate 64, their occupants heading to jobs in Lexington or Georgetown. Central Kentucky's moderate climate, lush landscape, and low unemployment rate make it a desirable place to live, putting further development pressures on the beautiful land that attracted people in the first place.

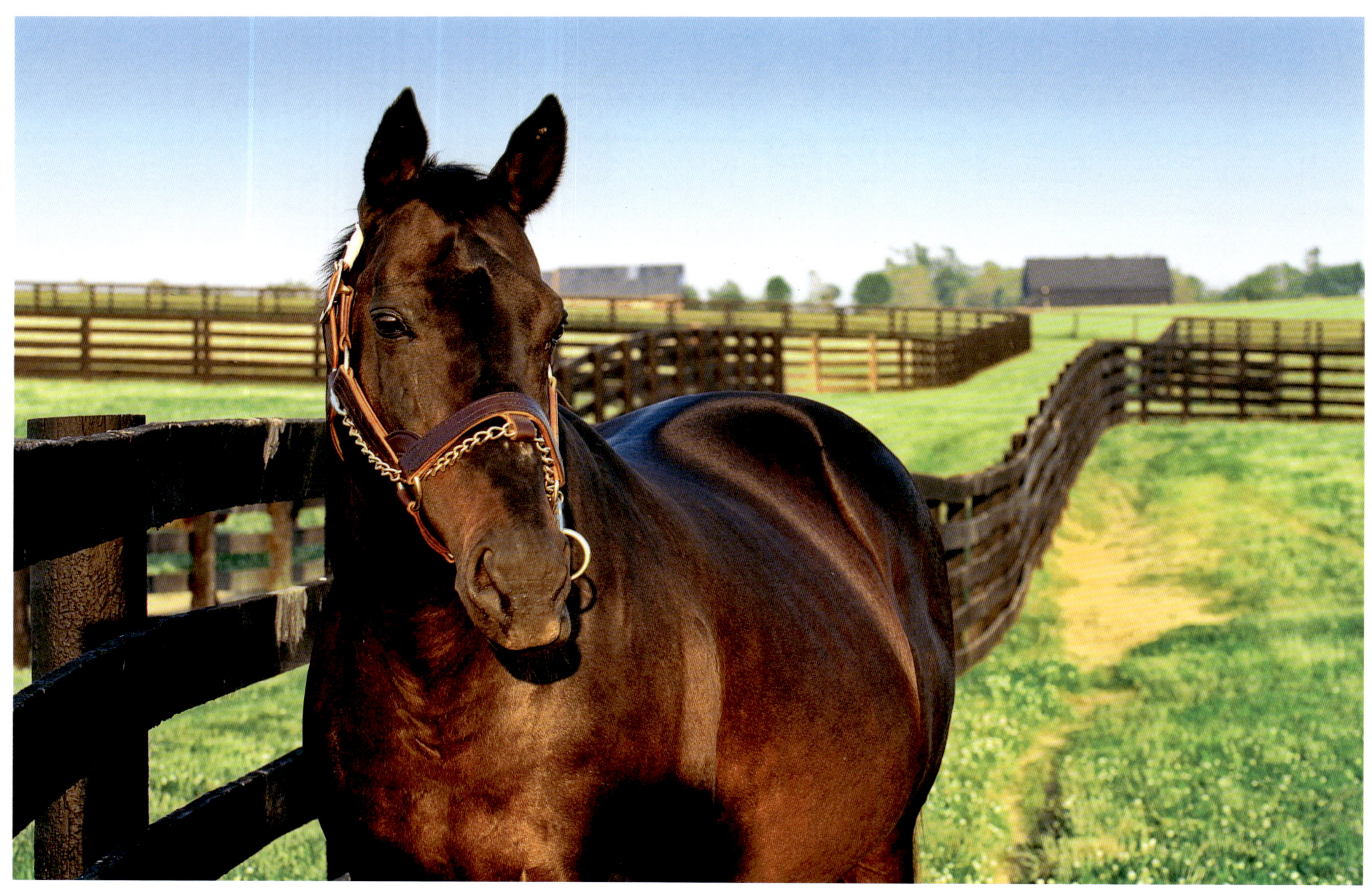

DYNAFORMER, SIRE OF BARBARO, THREE CHIMNEYS FARM, WOODFORD COUNTY

Dynaformer, a son of Roberto, was America's second leading sire in 2006. Dynaformer retired from the track at age four in 1989, and his offspring have earned nearly $70 million. His son Barbaro won the 2006 Kentucky Derby by six lengths, only to shatter his right rear foot at the start of the Preakness. A team of equine physicians from the University of Pennsylvania patched the bones together as best they could, and a worldwide vigil began. Even people with no prior interest in horses or racing prayed for Barbaro. Unfortunately, after nine months of on-and-off hope, the colt developed laminitis in his left rear foot, forcing the owners to euthanize him. Thus, a promising career on the track came to an end, but a legend was born.

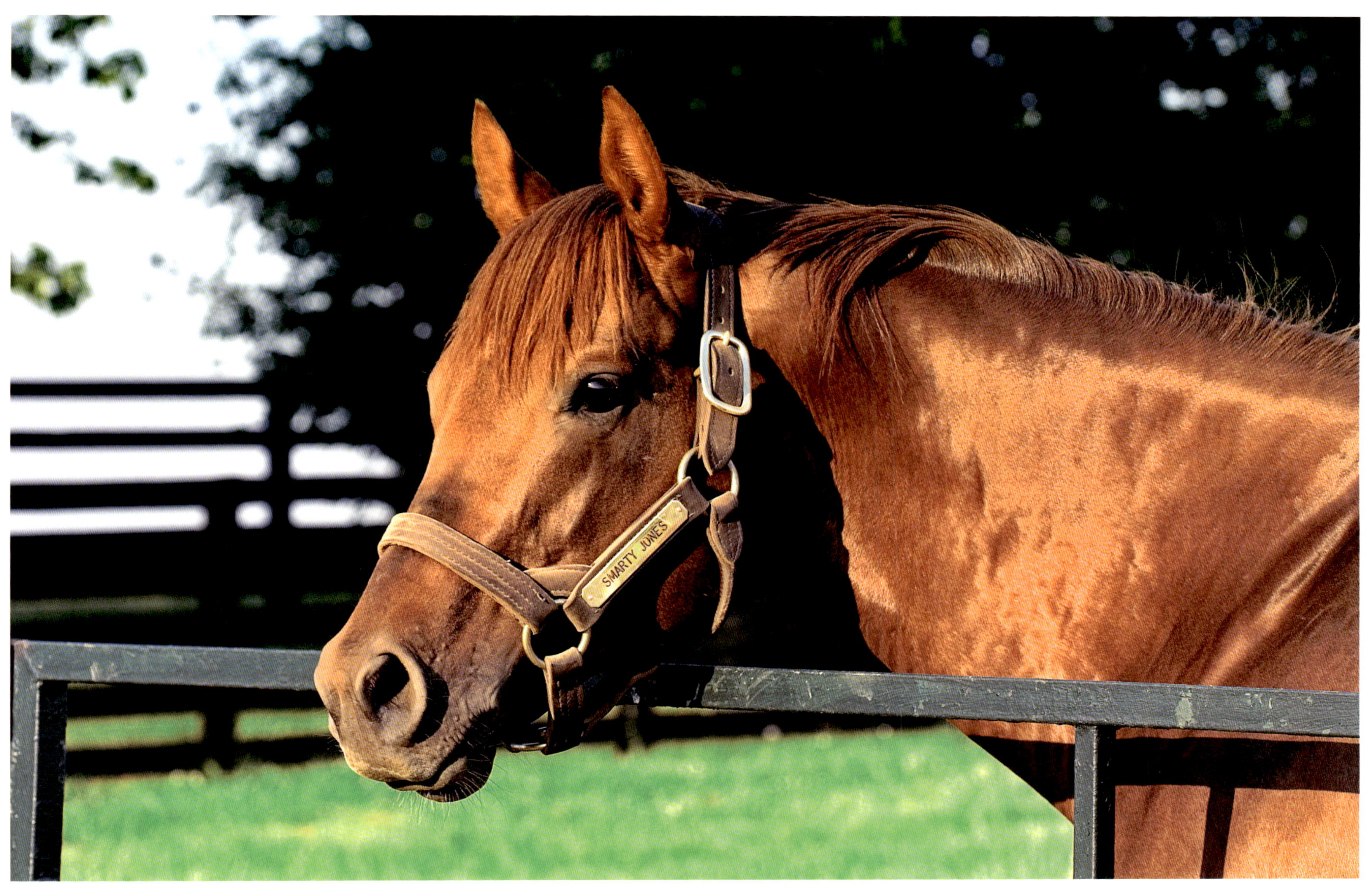

SMARTY JONES, THREE CHIMNEYS FARM, WOODFORD COUNTY

Racehorses' names can sometimes be a bit wacky, but just hearing the name Smarty Jones brings a little smile to one's face. That smile likely turned to a grin for those who bet on this colt in the 2004 Kentucky Derby and Preakness, which he won handily while still undefeated. The son of stallion Elusive Quality, Smarty was beaten by a length at the Belmont and then retired to stud, amassing a record of eight wins in nine starts and becoming the fifth-richest American Thoroughbred in history. This should come as no surprise with the likes of Foolish Pleasure, Mr. Prospector, and Gone West in his breeding.

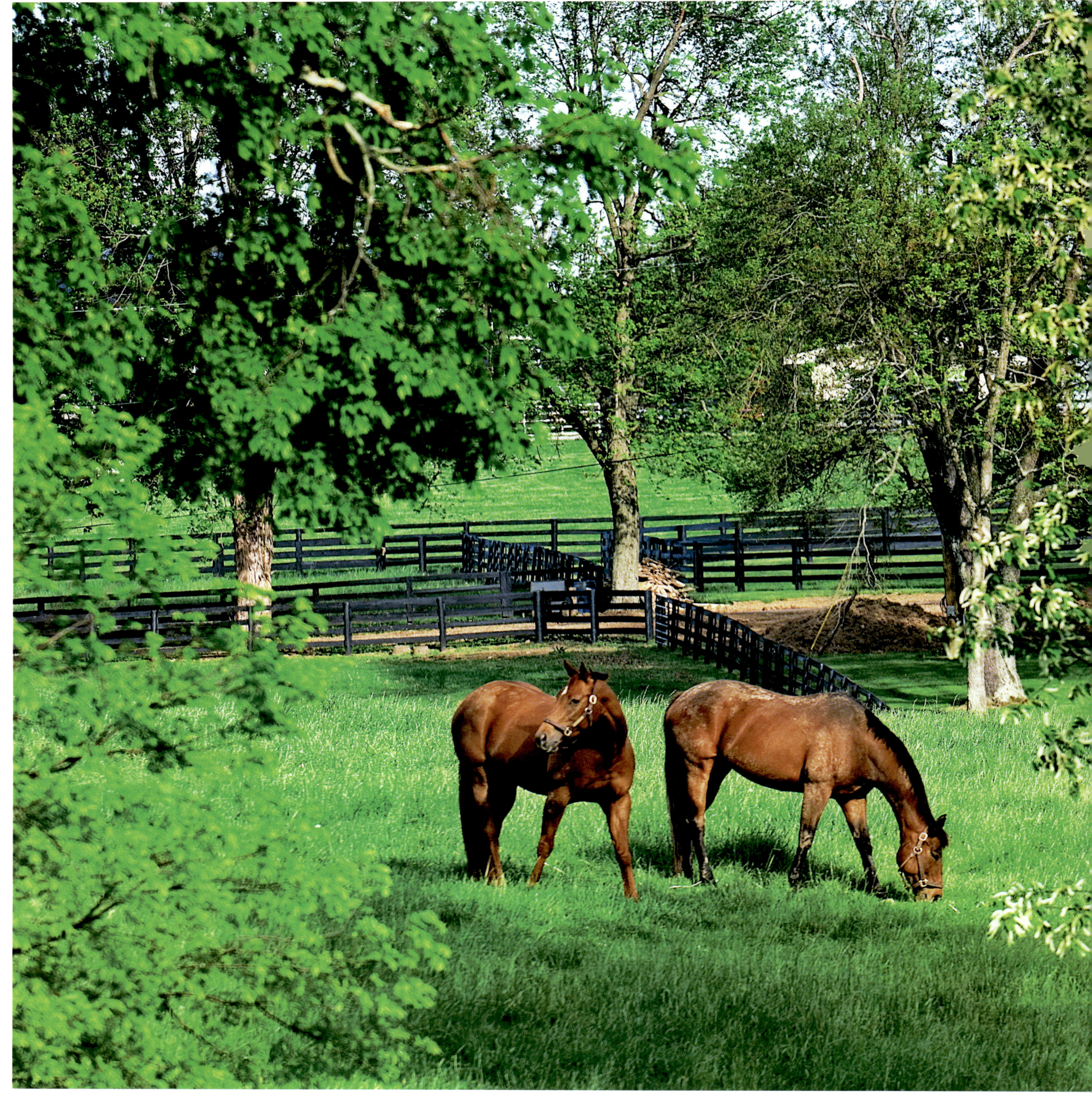

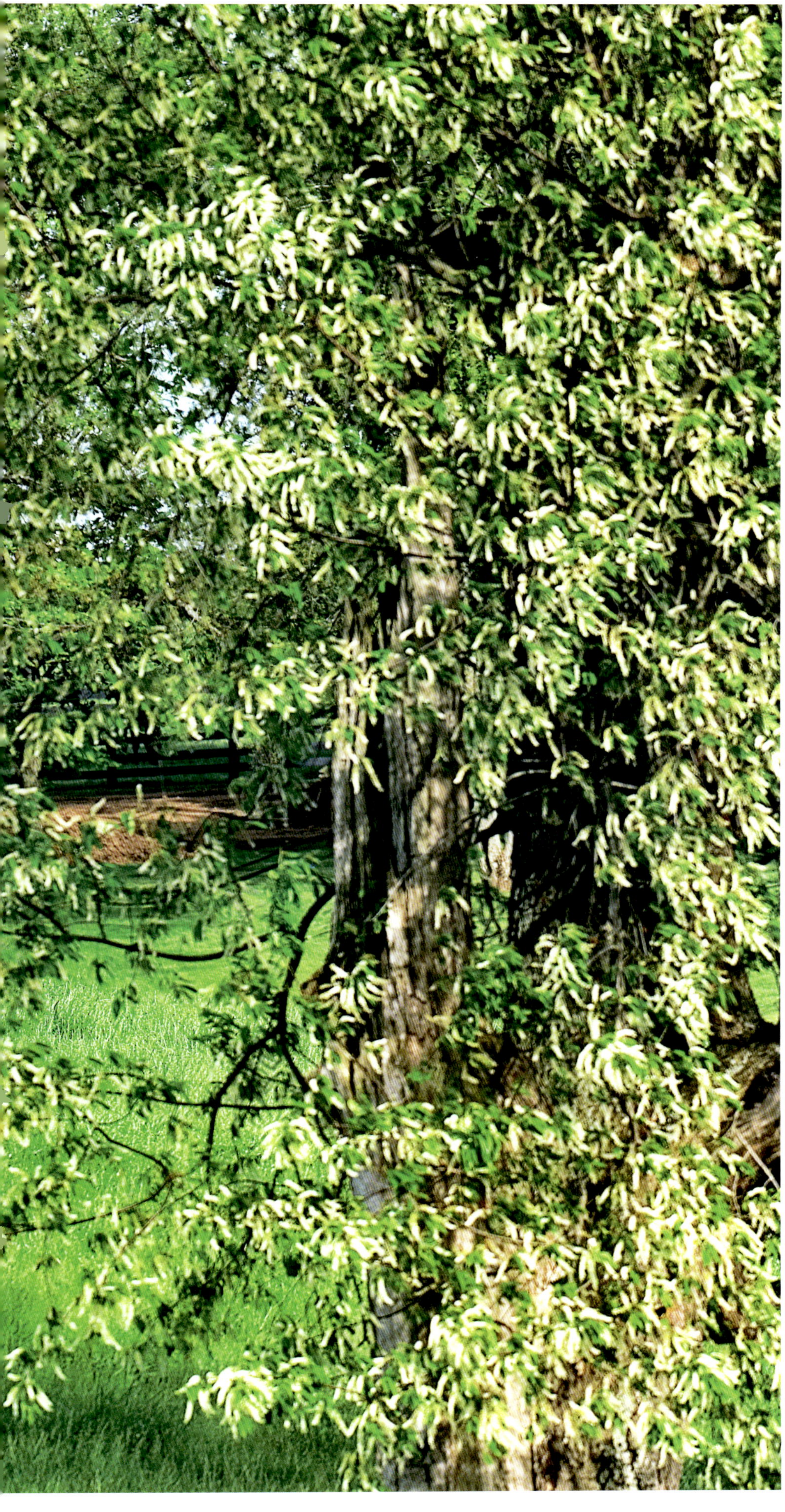

MARES AND BLOOMING LOCUSTS

Spring evenings bring calmness to the landscape. Framed by an early-blooming locust, these mares feast on bluegrass. On the bigger farms, large groups of mares can be seen roaming the fields. However, mares often pair off, spending most of the day together like a couple of girlfriends.

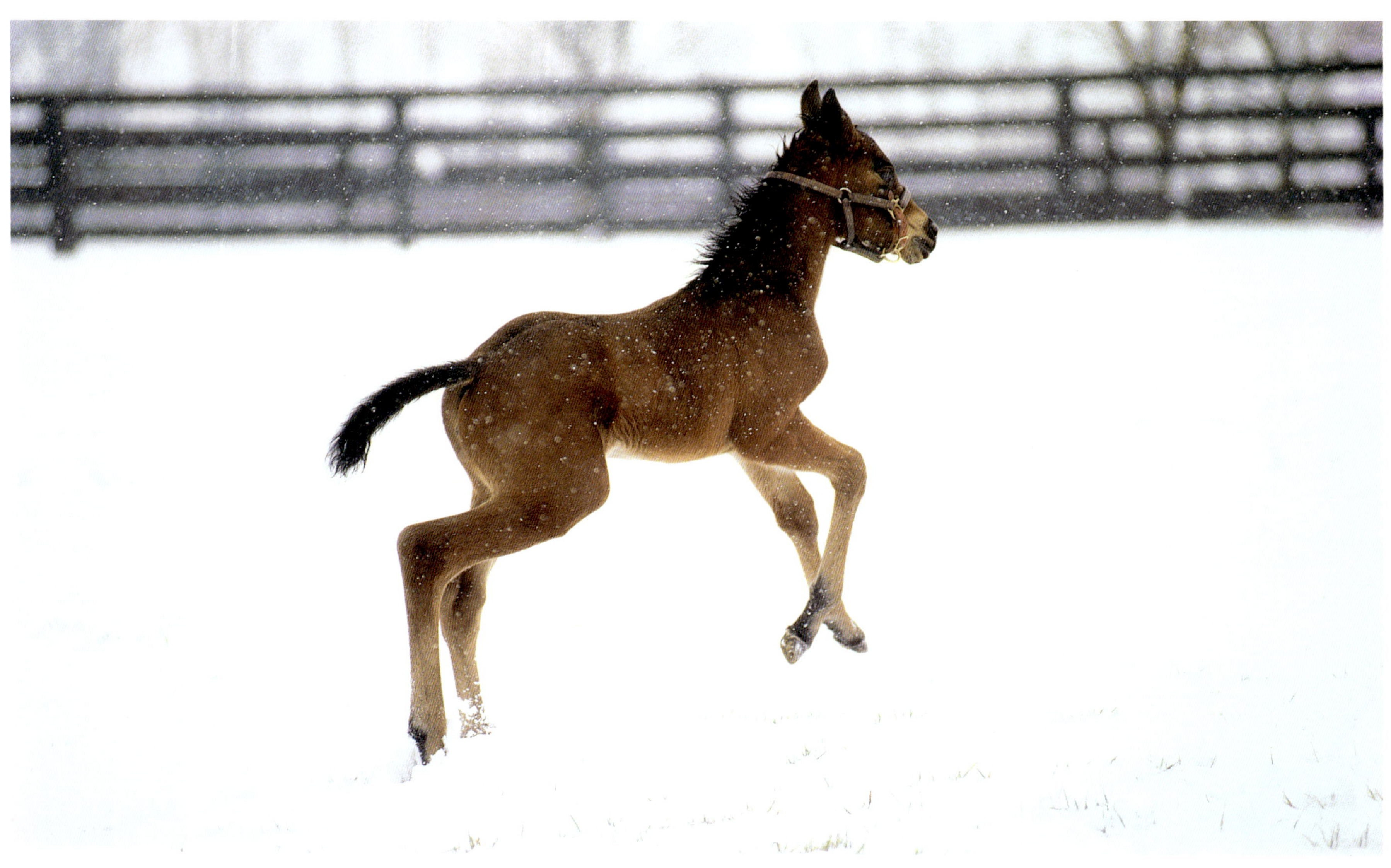

DANCING FOAL IN WINTER

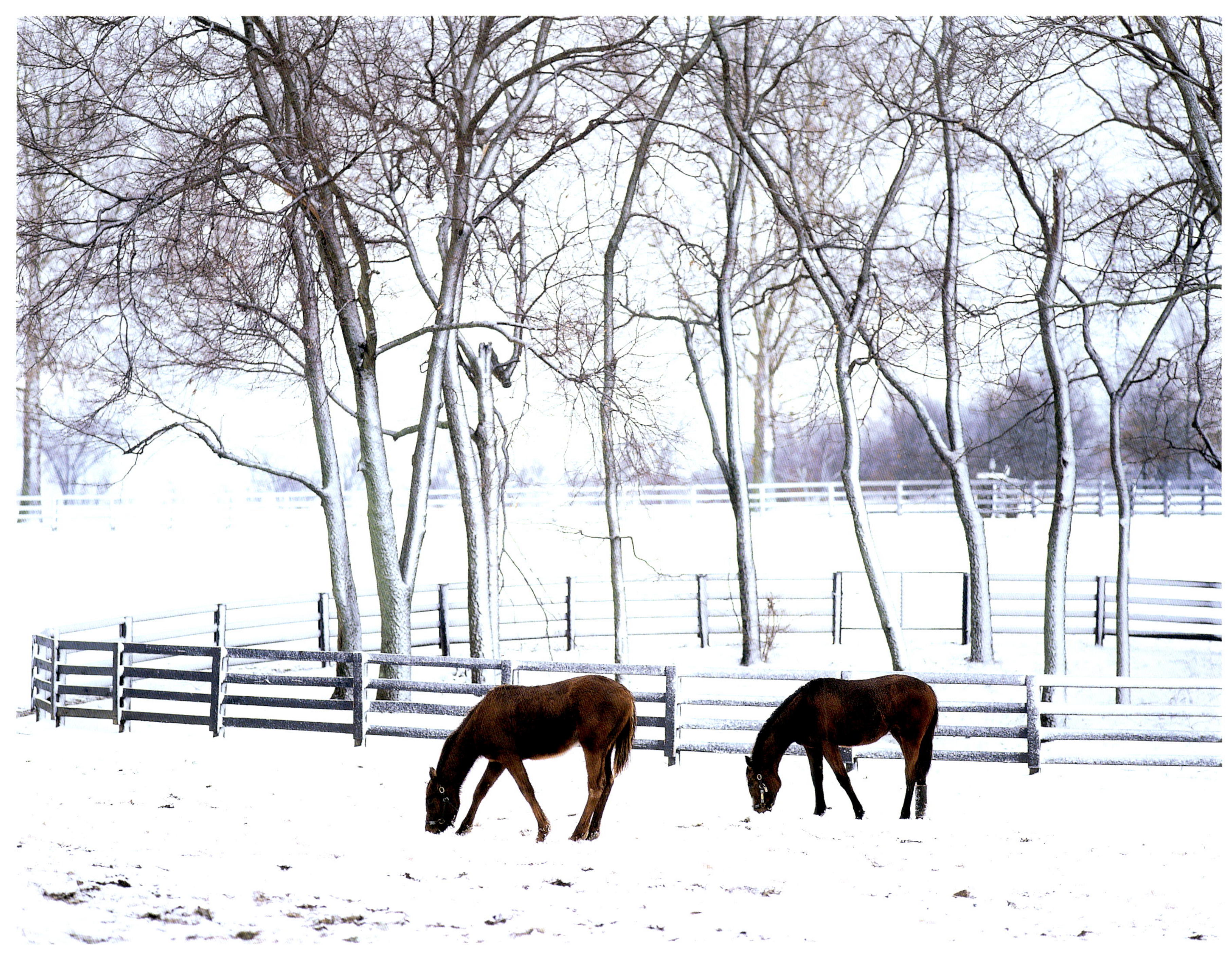

YEARLINGS IN WINTER PADDOCK

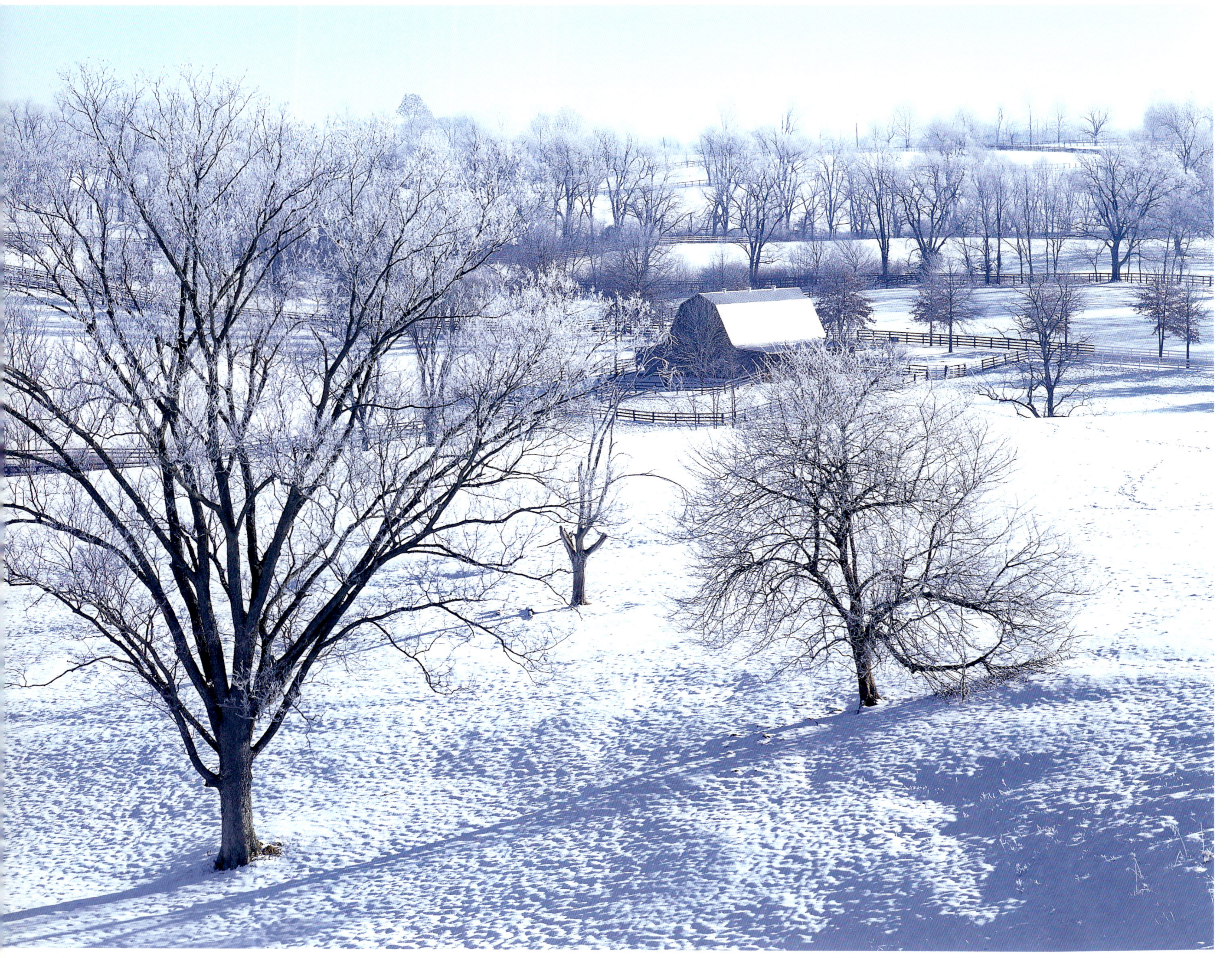

FARM ALONG BOSWORTH LANE

A Bluegrass farm lies hushed in silence following an overnight snow. Broodmares will soon fill these fields, located just west of the Keeneland Race Course complex. Because of its proximity to Keeneland and to prominent farms in the area, this valley is unlikely to be developed anytime soon, if ever. Saving Bluegrass farmland for future generations is near the top of the political agenda, and many nonprofit agencies have been formed to help preserve the land and the natural beauty of the area. Successful ongoing programs include the outright purchase of future development rights and the acquisition of permanent conservation easements.

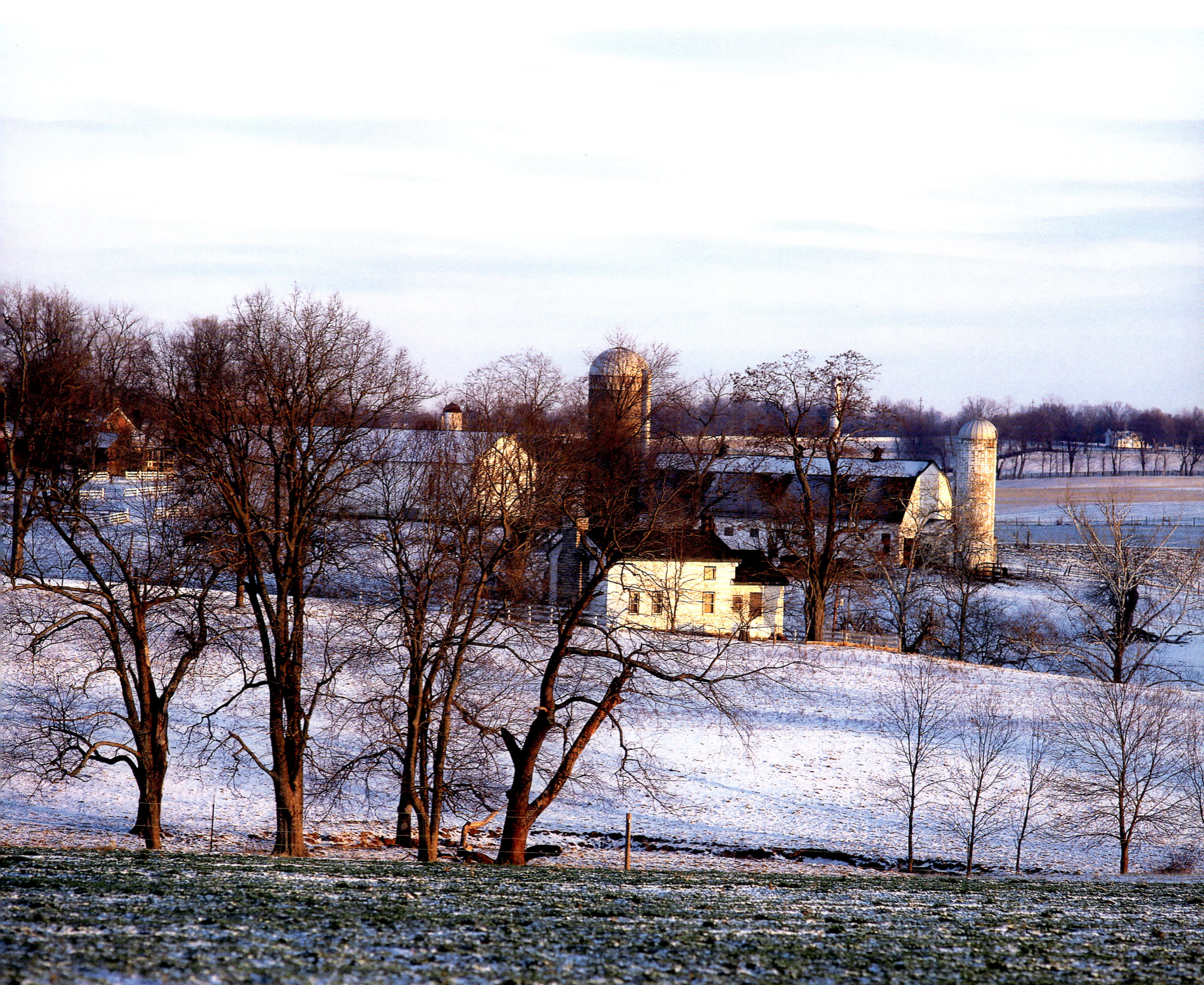

FARM ALONG STEELE ROAD, WOODFORD COUNTY

Not all Bluegrass farms are strictly related to the breeding and raising of horses. Many farms within what is called the "inner Bluegrass," or prime horse country, can be classified as traditional farming operations growing corn, soybeans, and other crops and raising livestock, primarily cattle, hogs, sheep, and goats. Burley tobacco is still grown widely, but with the end of price supports, most small farmers have slowly switched to other income-producing crops. Some farms have been bought by local and overseas interests and developed into equine operations.

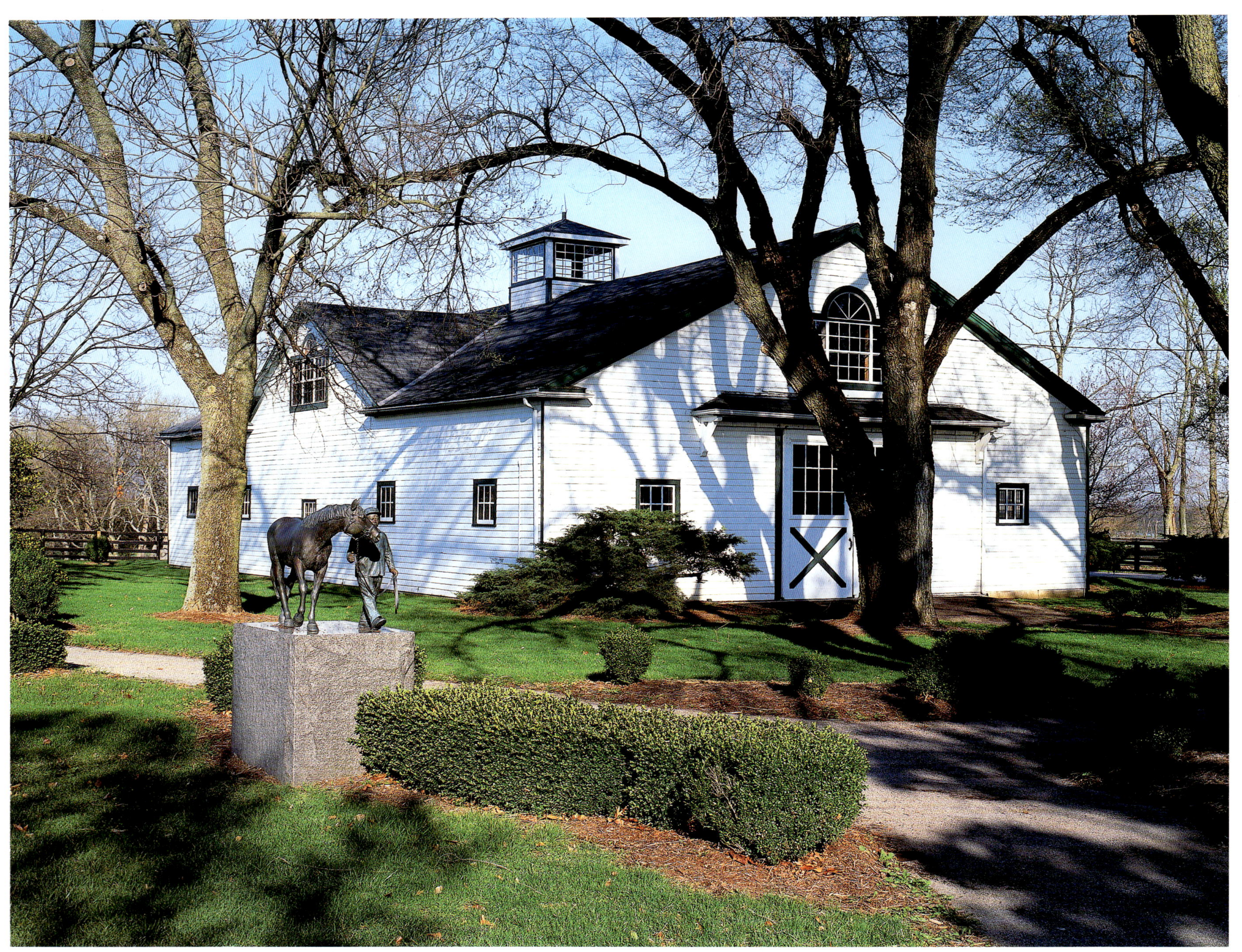

STABLE OF NASHUA, SPENDTHRIFT FARM

With the advent of televised racing in the early 1950s, the great horse Nashua became an instant hero to millions of Americans. Trained by the venerable Sunny Jim Fitzsimmons and ridden by Eddie Arcaro, Nashua won twenty-two of thirty lifetime starts, including the Preakness, Belmont, Dwyer, Arlington Classic, and two-mile Jockey Club Gold Cup (twice). As a three-year-old, Nashua was named Horse of the Year. He is best known for his turf battles with another great horse, Swaps, who beat him in the 1955 Kentucky Derby. At age four, Nashua retired to become a Kentucky tourist attraction while siring seventy-seven stakes winners.

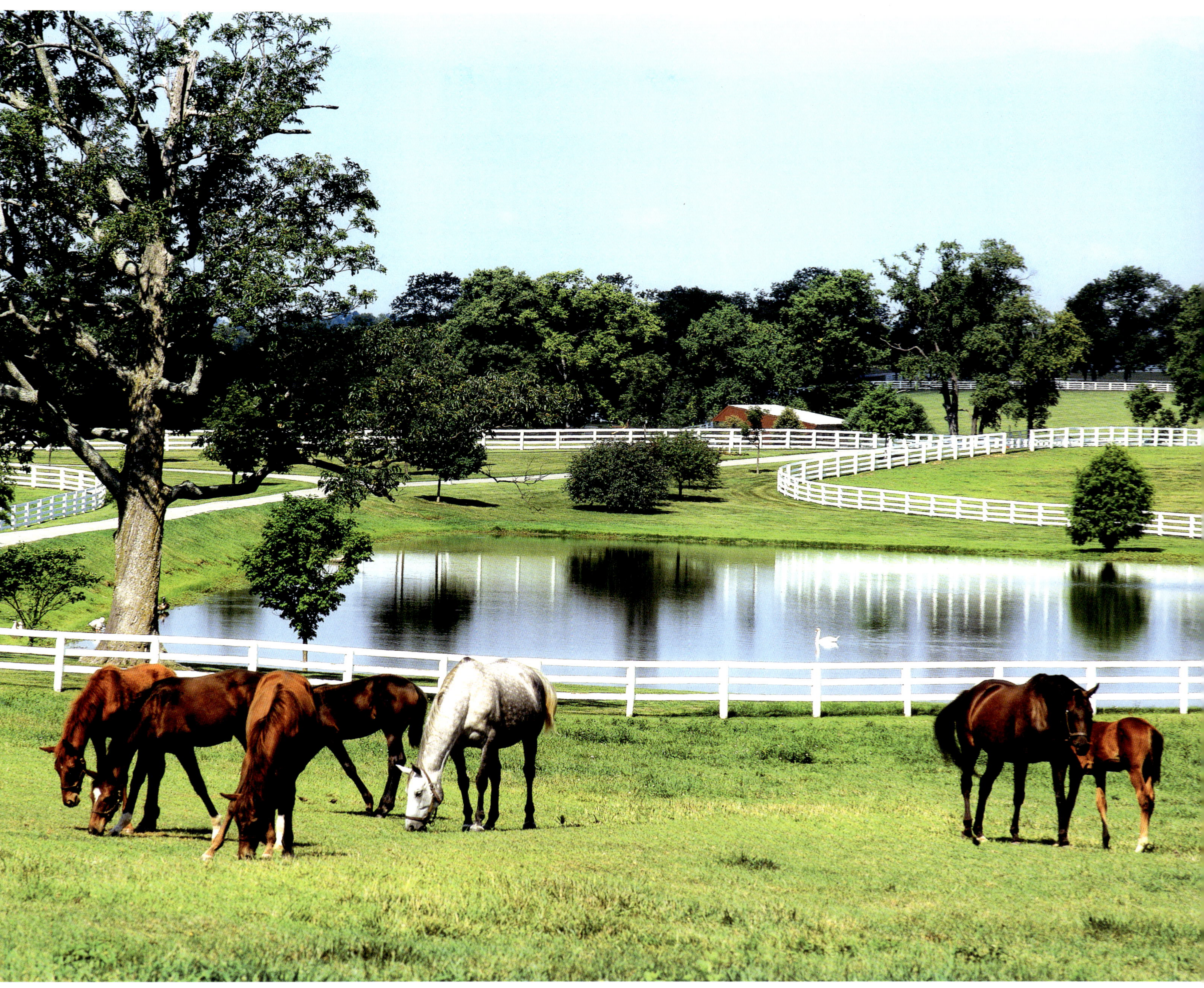

MARES AND FOALS IN SUMMER PASTURE

Horses are generally uncooperative when you attempt to photograph them in their natural setting, so you have to be ready to take the shot when it presents itself. Once these mares and foals were successfully "arranged," one of the resident swans filled in nicely in a supporting role along Mt. Horeb Pike in Scott County.

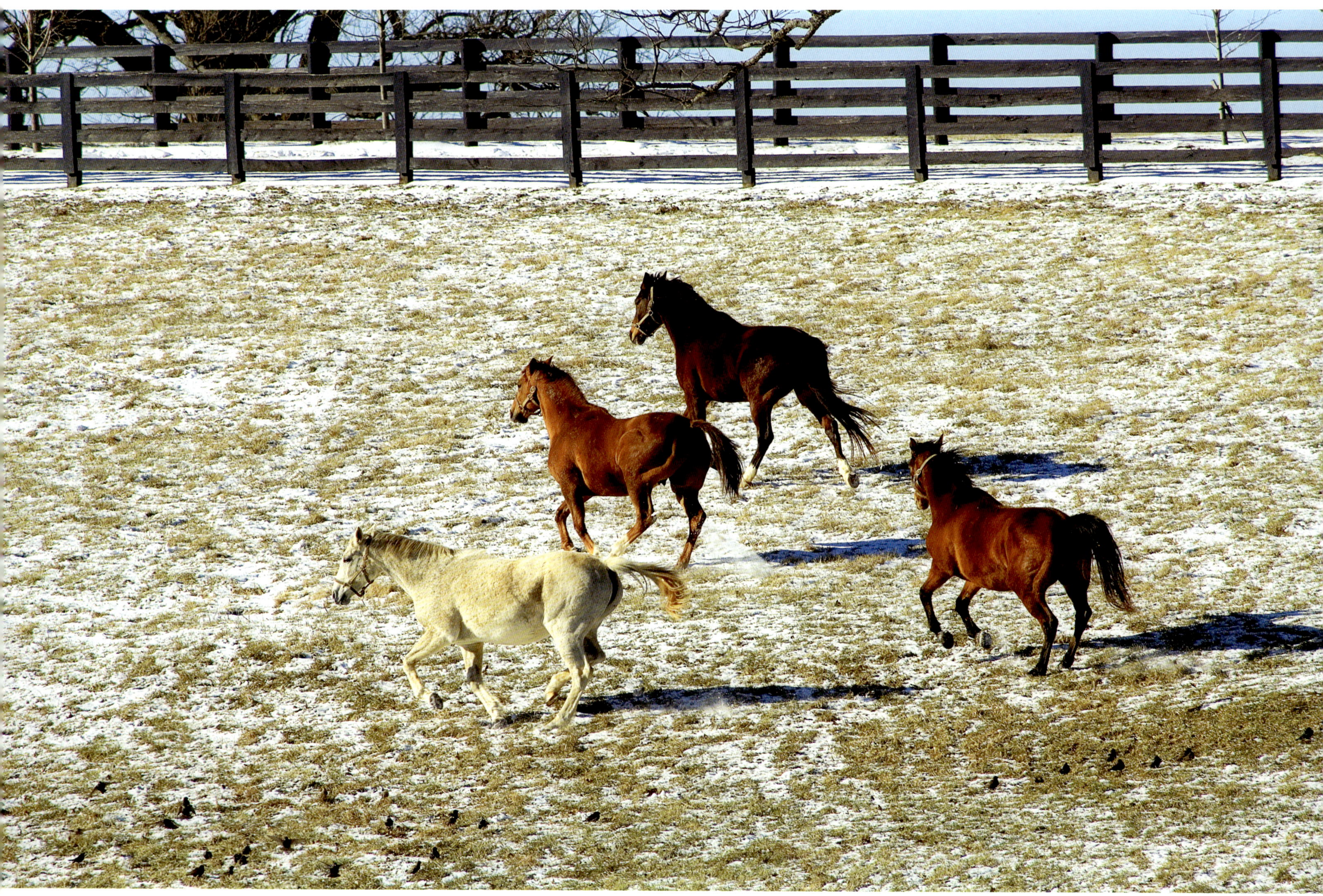

WINTER GALLOP

There is no telling what makes a horse start to run. These Thoroughbreds just took off galloping for no apparent reason. Maybe they wanted to warm up their hooves after standing around on the frozen field. For a photographer, anticipating the action and putting oneself in the right position increase the chances of capturing the interesting and the unusual.

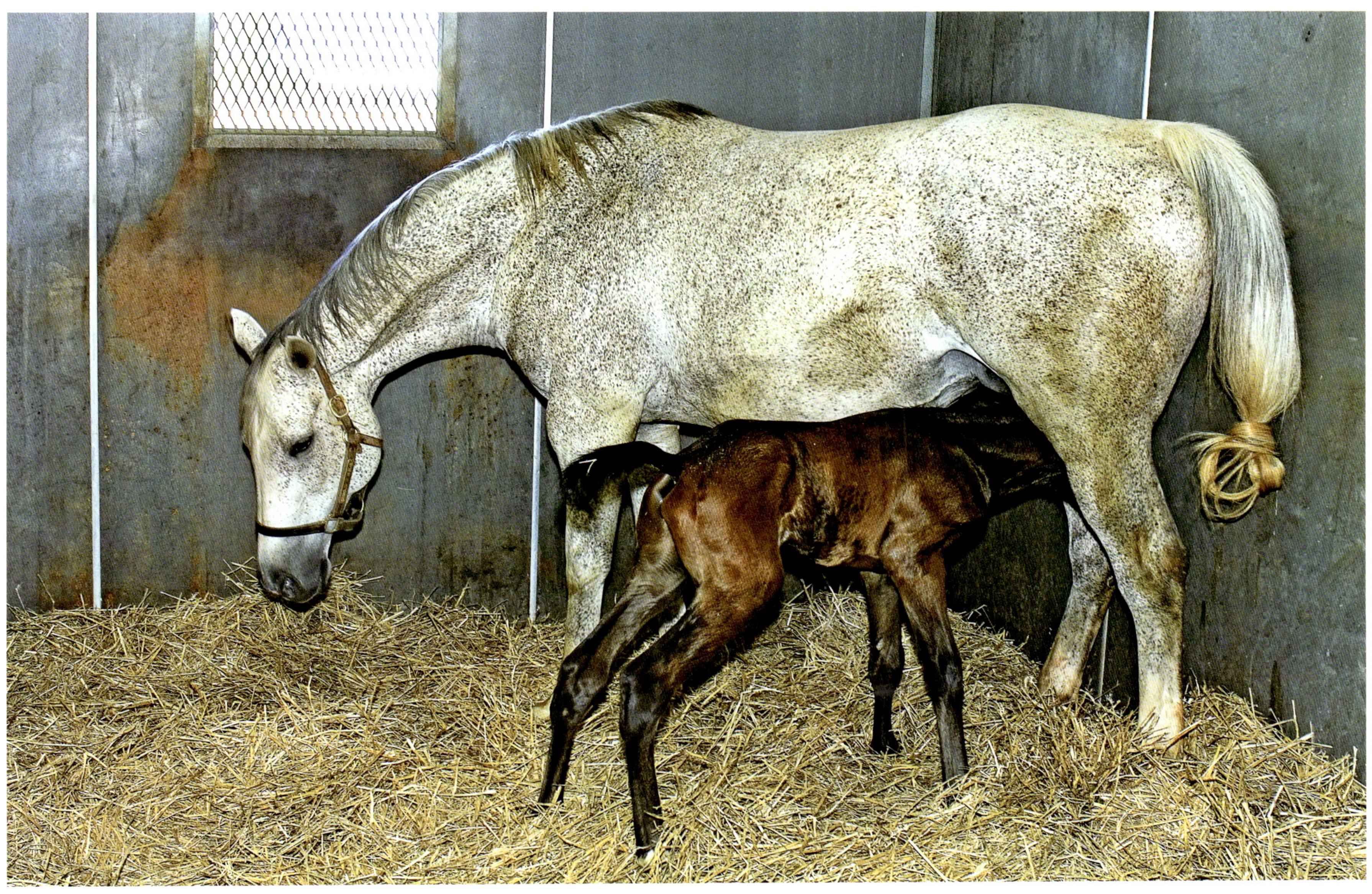

FIRST NURSING

After taking a quick look around, a foal's first instinct is to stand up, find its mother's teat, and begin nursing. Foaled at Three Chimneys Farm in Woodford County, this dark bay colt is by Elusive Quality, the sire of Kentucky Derby and Preakness winner Smarty Jones. The patient mother is Tangled Up in Blue by Phone Trick.

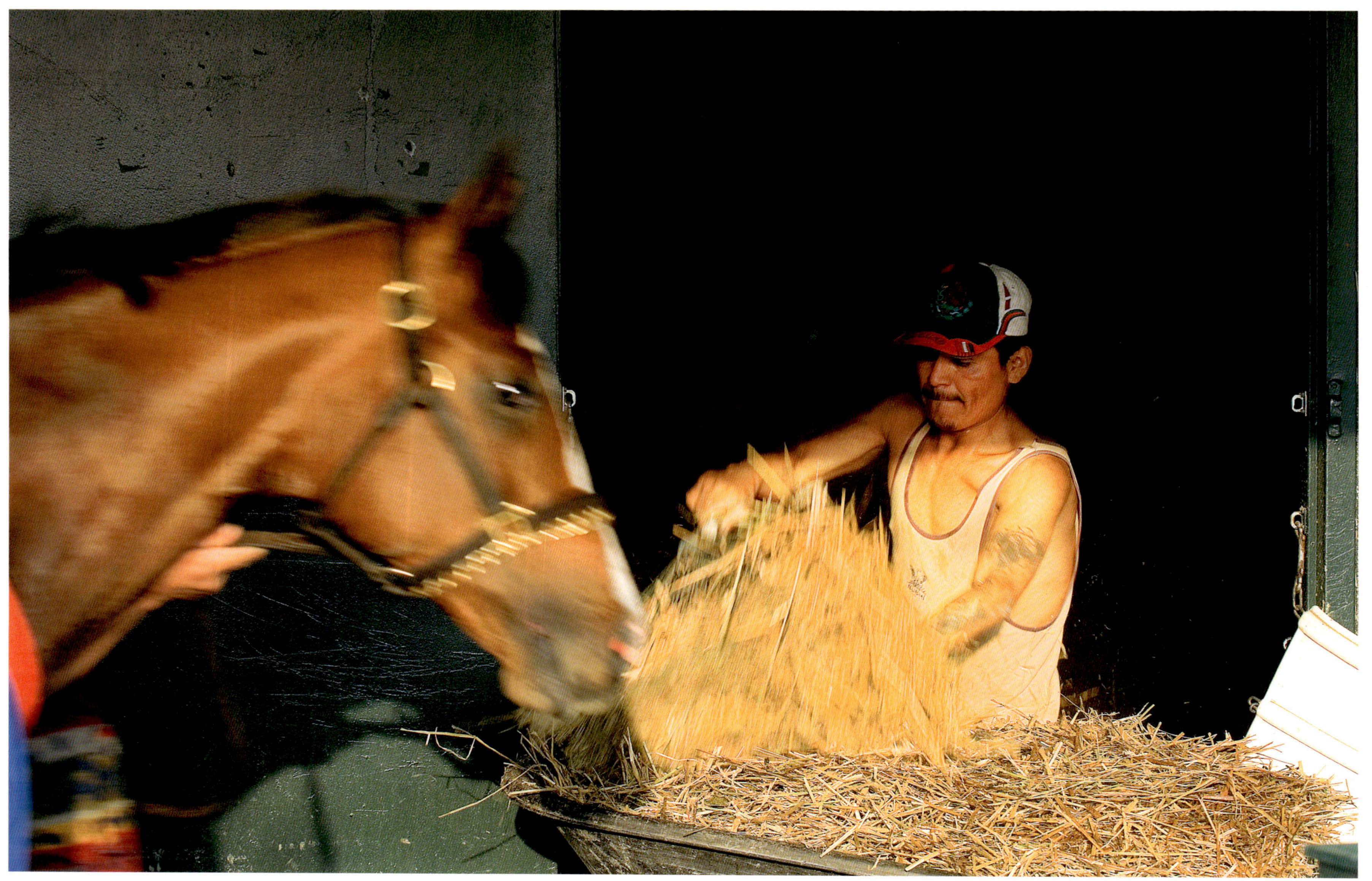

CLEANING STALLS AT KEENELAND

The cleaning of horse stalls is not the most desirable job in the equine industry, but it's a necessary one. Each day, the old straw must be removed and new straw put down. This worker is performing that chore in the barn area behind Keeneland, while a racehorse is cooled down after a morning workout.

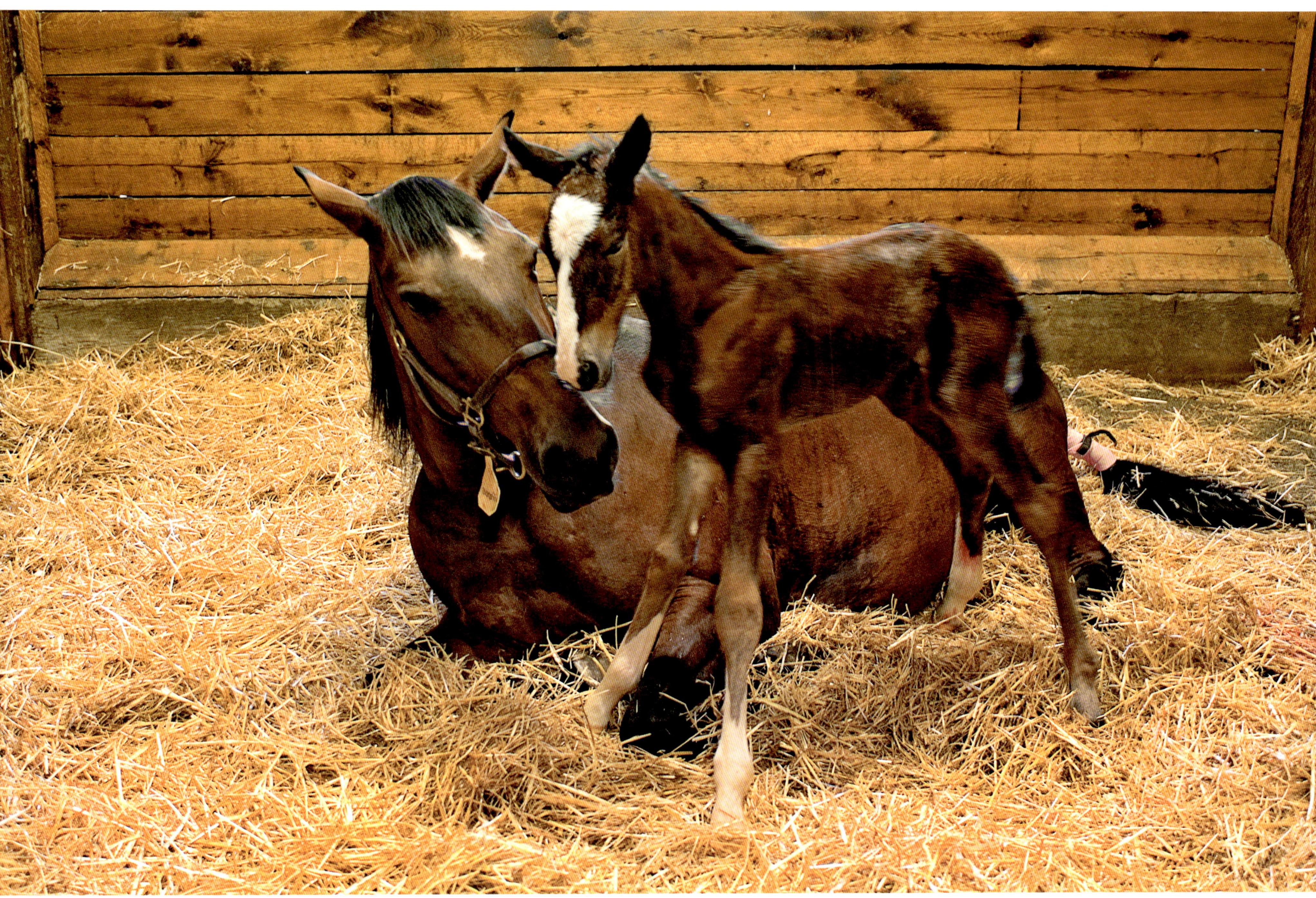

PROUD MOMENT

Most foals check out their legs within minutes of birth. After a few staggering steps and spills in the straw, babies are ready to go on to the next big thing: nursing. The mare is of some help in directing these early activities, but most foals learn quickly on their own, driven by intuition and hunger. Seeing her foal standing just ten minutes after birth is a proud moment for this Standardbred mare.

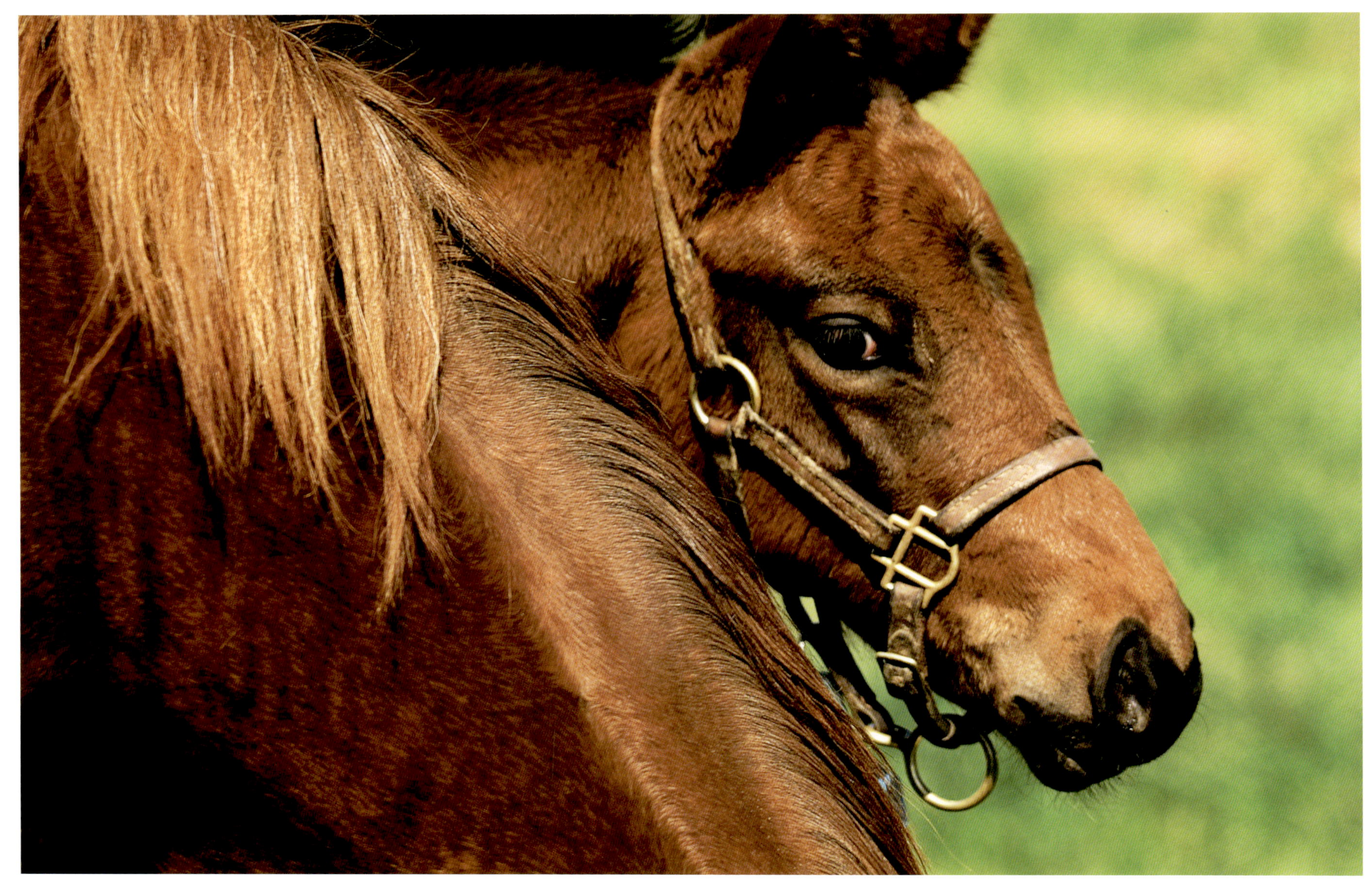

FOAL AT MOTHER'S MANE

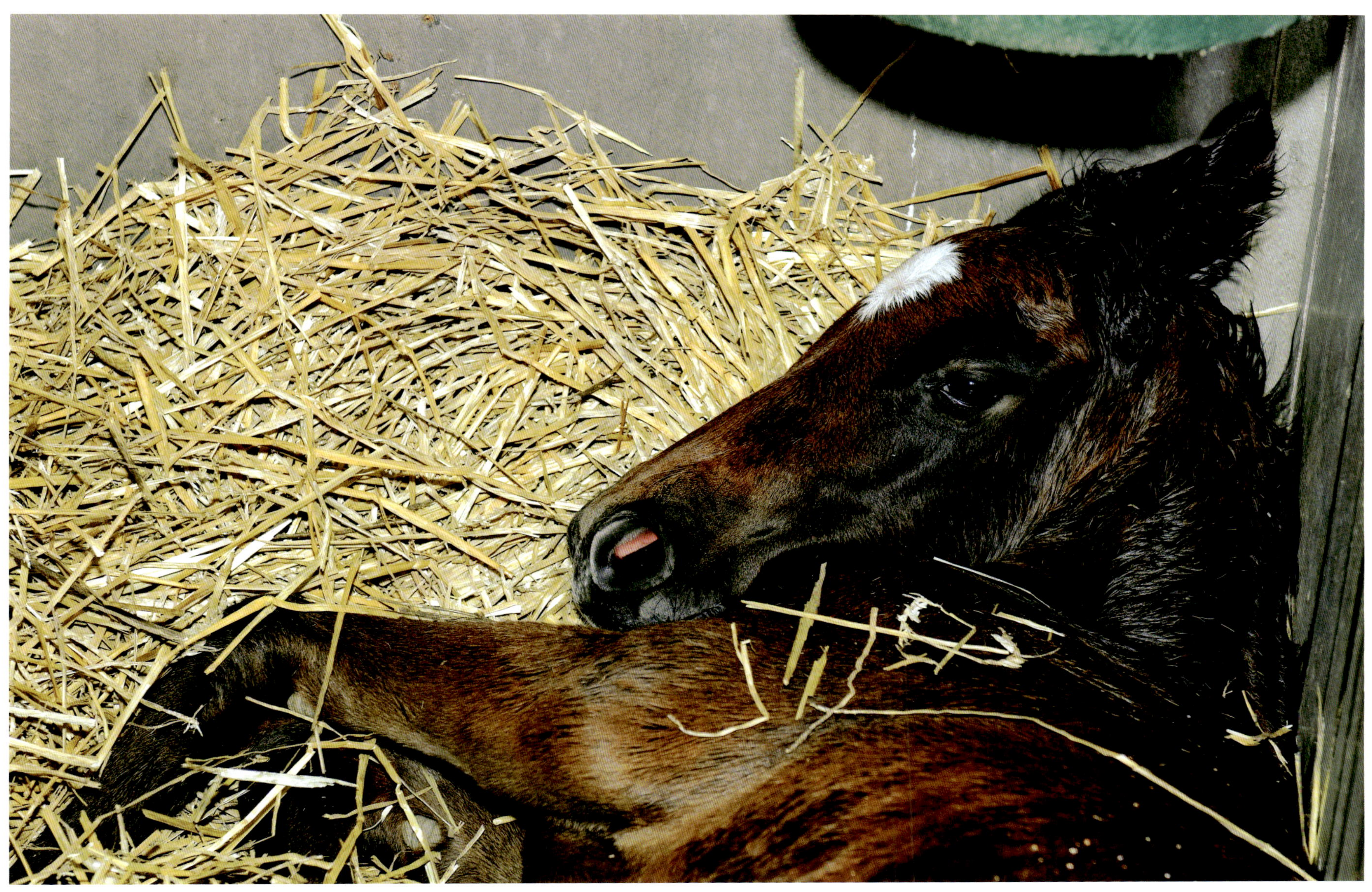

NEWBORN FOAL AT REST, MINUTES AFTER BIRTH

Overleaf: CORRECTIVE SURGERY ON A THOROUGHBRED FOAL

Equine veterinary medicine is big business in the Bluegrass. Just like people, horses get sick or injured or require specialized surgery to correct physical imperfections. At the start of the Preakness, 2006 Kentucky Derby winner Barbaro shattered his leg, and the world watched as veterinarians made a valiant attempt to save his life. Although the nine-month effort would ultimately be unsuccessful, it thrust the profession of equine medicine into public consciousness. Here, Dr. Rolf M. Embertson of Rood and Riddle Equine Hospital in Lexington inserts a stainless steel pin into the leg of a foal in an effort to correct an angular limb deformity. Other equine hospitals in the Bluegrass include Hagyard Equine Medical Institute in Lexington and the Woodford Veterinary Clinic in Versailles. Many smaller clinics and independent veterinarians provide health care to horses throughout the Bluegrass.

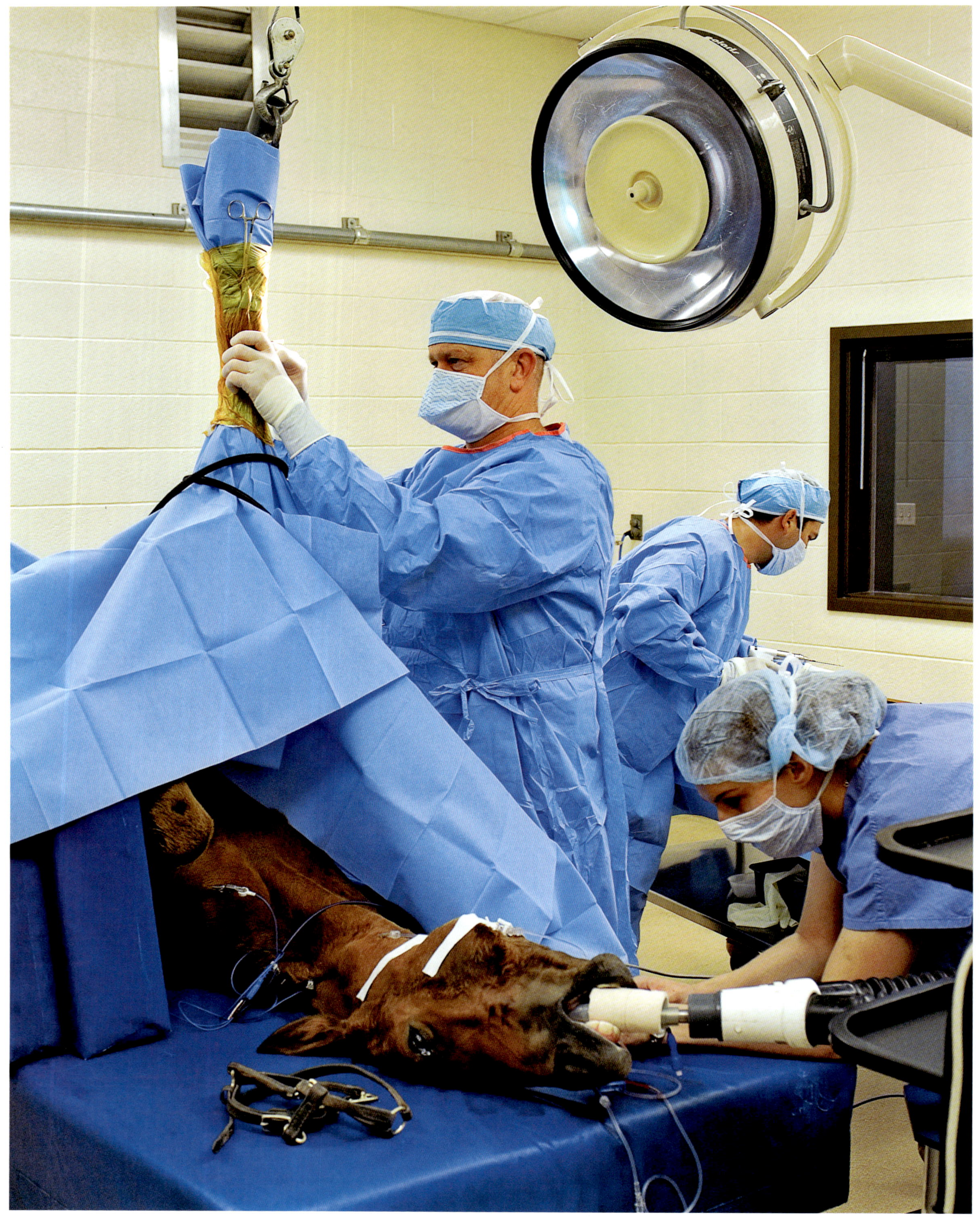

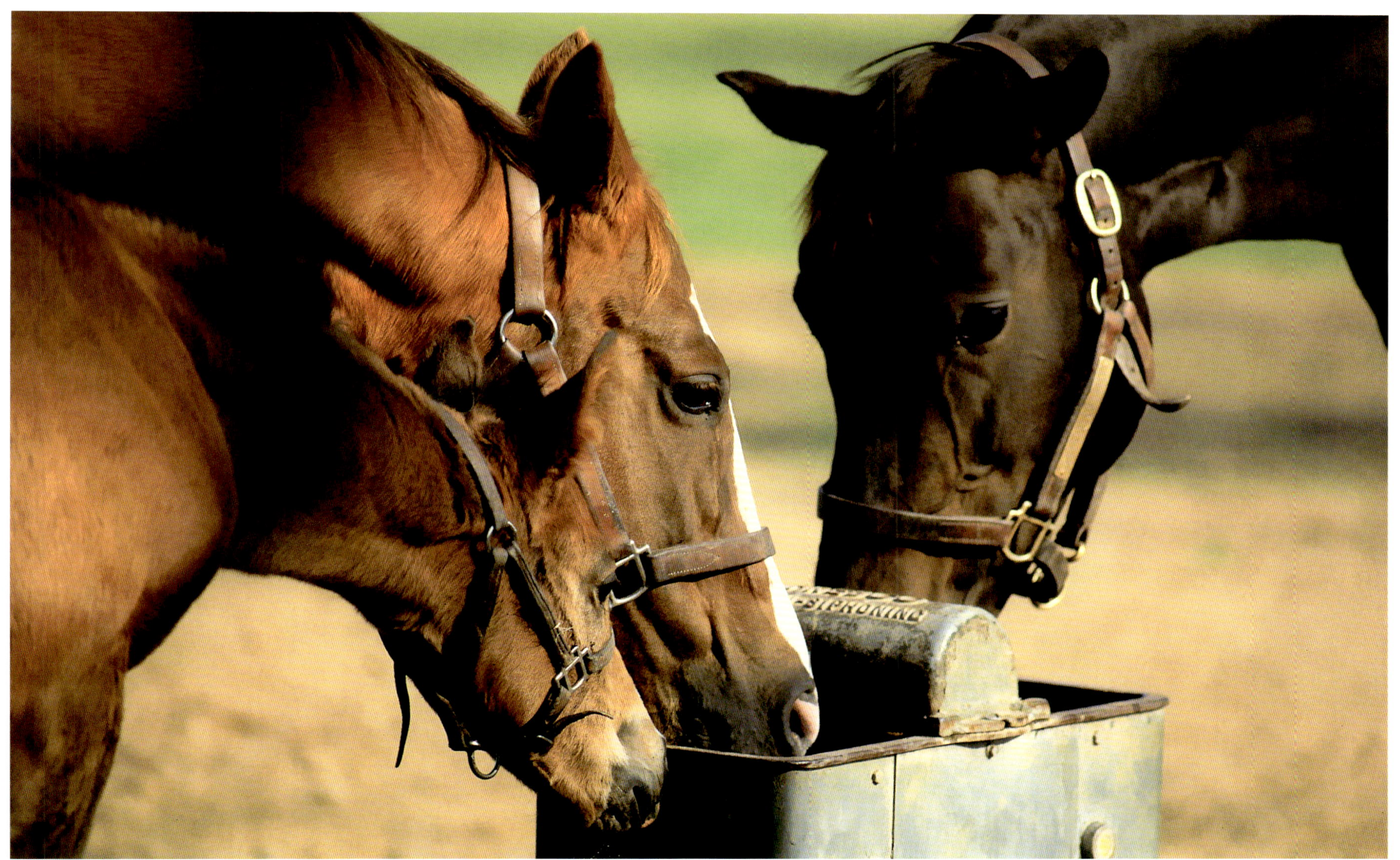

MARES AND FOAL WATERING

Large animals require lots of water to survive. Although ponds and streams are abundant in the Bluegrass, they are problematic when it comes to watering expensive racehorses. Ponds and streams are usually fenced off from these prized animals, lest they drink tainted water. Often, pure limestone well water is piped directly to the pastures, where the horses' thirst can be quenched, risk free, twenty-four hours a day.

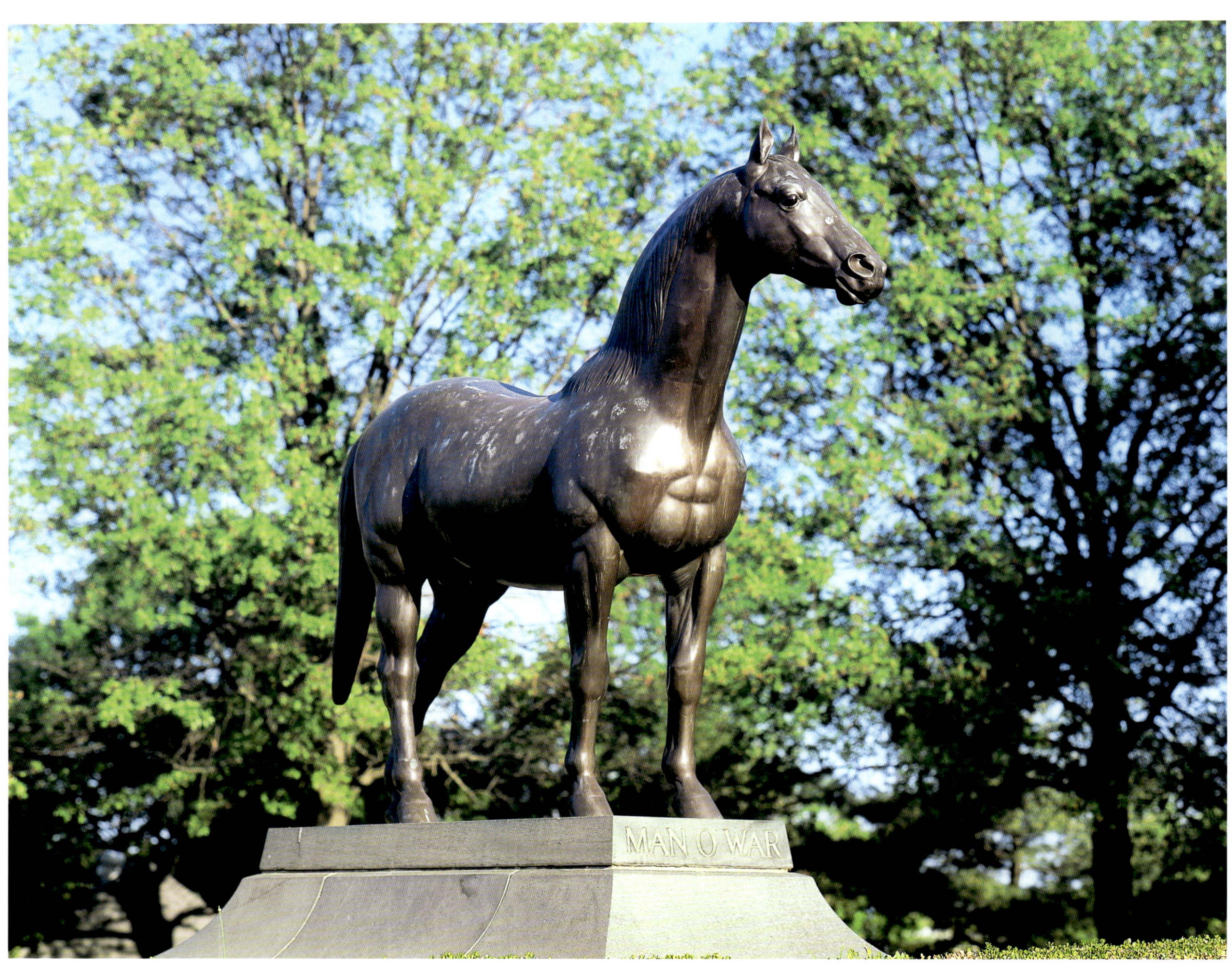

MAN O' WAR STATUE, KENTUCKY HORSE PARK, LEXINGTON

When the great racehorse and sire Man o' War died in 1947 at age thirty, his body was embalmed, placed in an oak casket, and buried on Faraway Farm, where he had stood at stud after retiring from racing. His burial service was broadcast on the radio and was attended by up to 2,000 people. In the 1970s, the remains were moved to the Kentucky Horse Park to rest below this bronze statue at the park's main entrance.

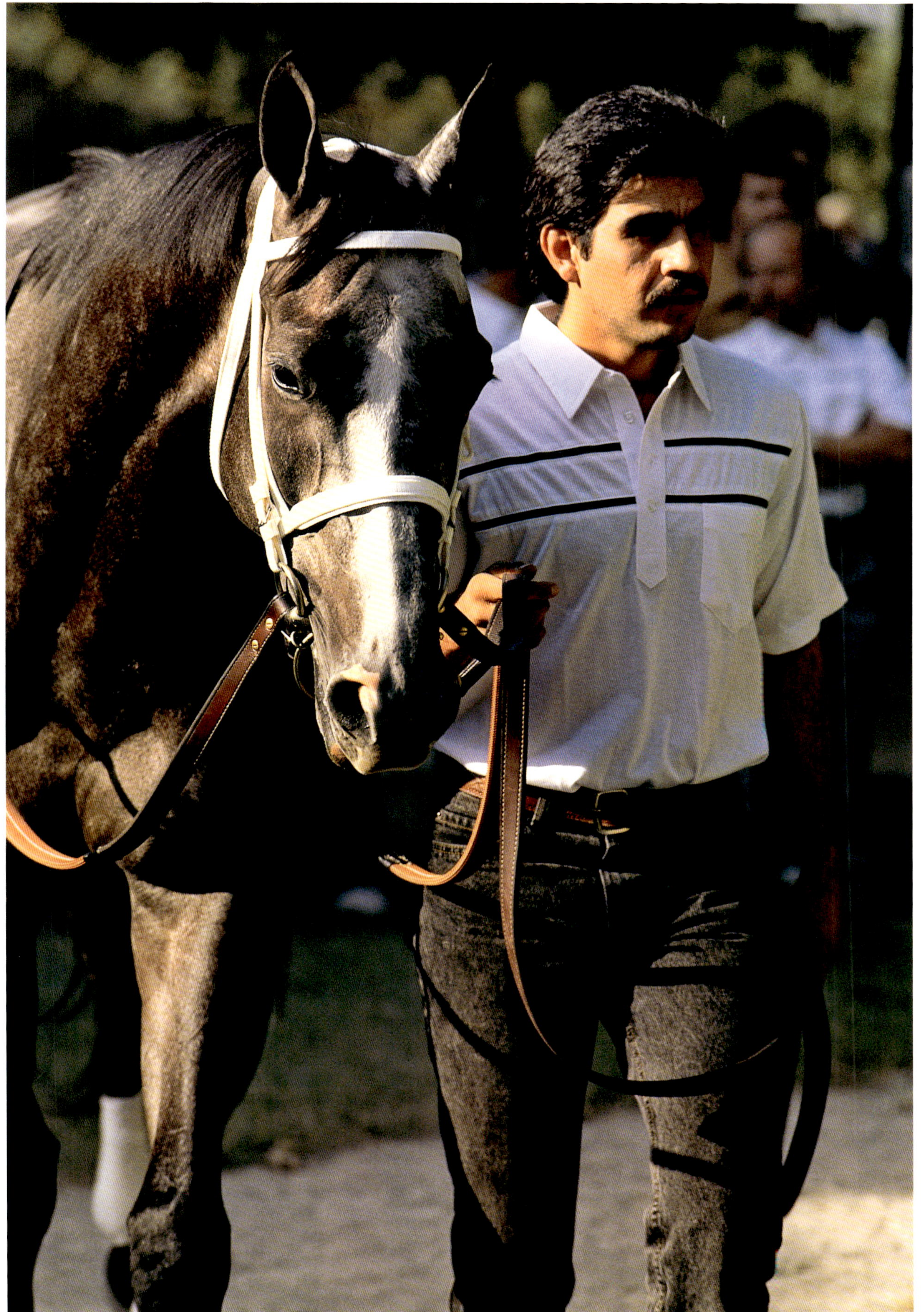

WINNING COLORS AT KEENELAND

In 1988, with Gary Stevens riding, Winning Colors became only the third filly to win the Kentucky Derby. The gray Thoroughbred led wire to wire and outlasted hard-driving Forty-niner by a neck. Other fillies to win the prestigious race were Regret in 1915 and Genuine Risk in 1980. Winning Colors' only appearance at Keeneland came in October 1988, when she finished fourth in the Spinster Stakes. She returned to Churchill Downs in November of that year and lost to the great filly Personal Ensign by a nose in the Breeders' Cup Distaff. Winning Colors retired from racing in 1989 and died in 2008.

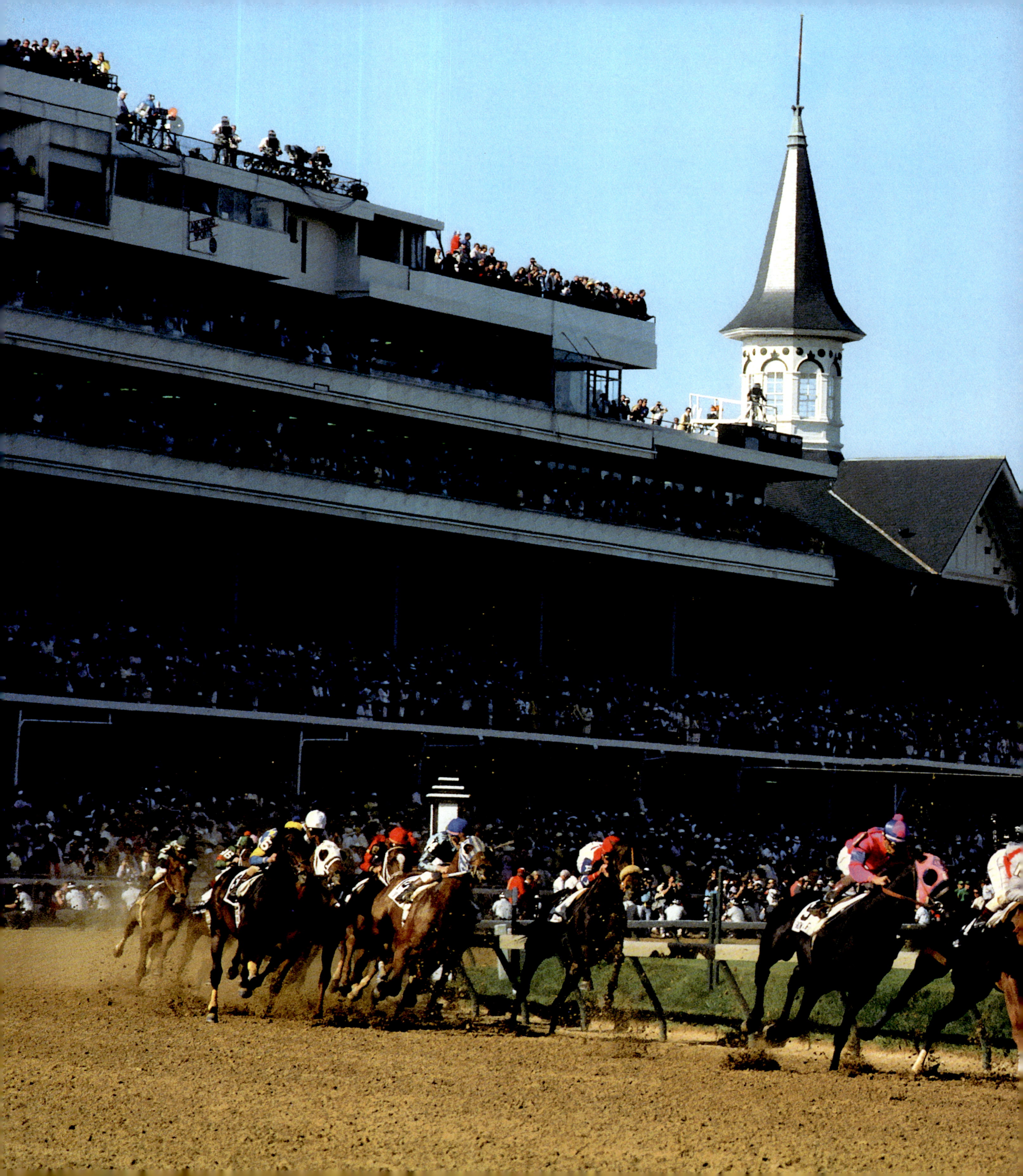

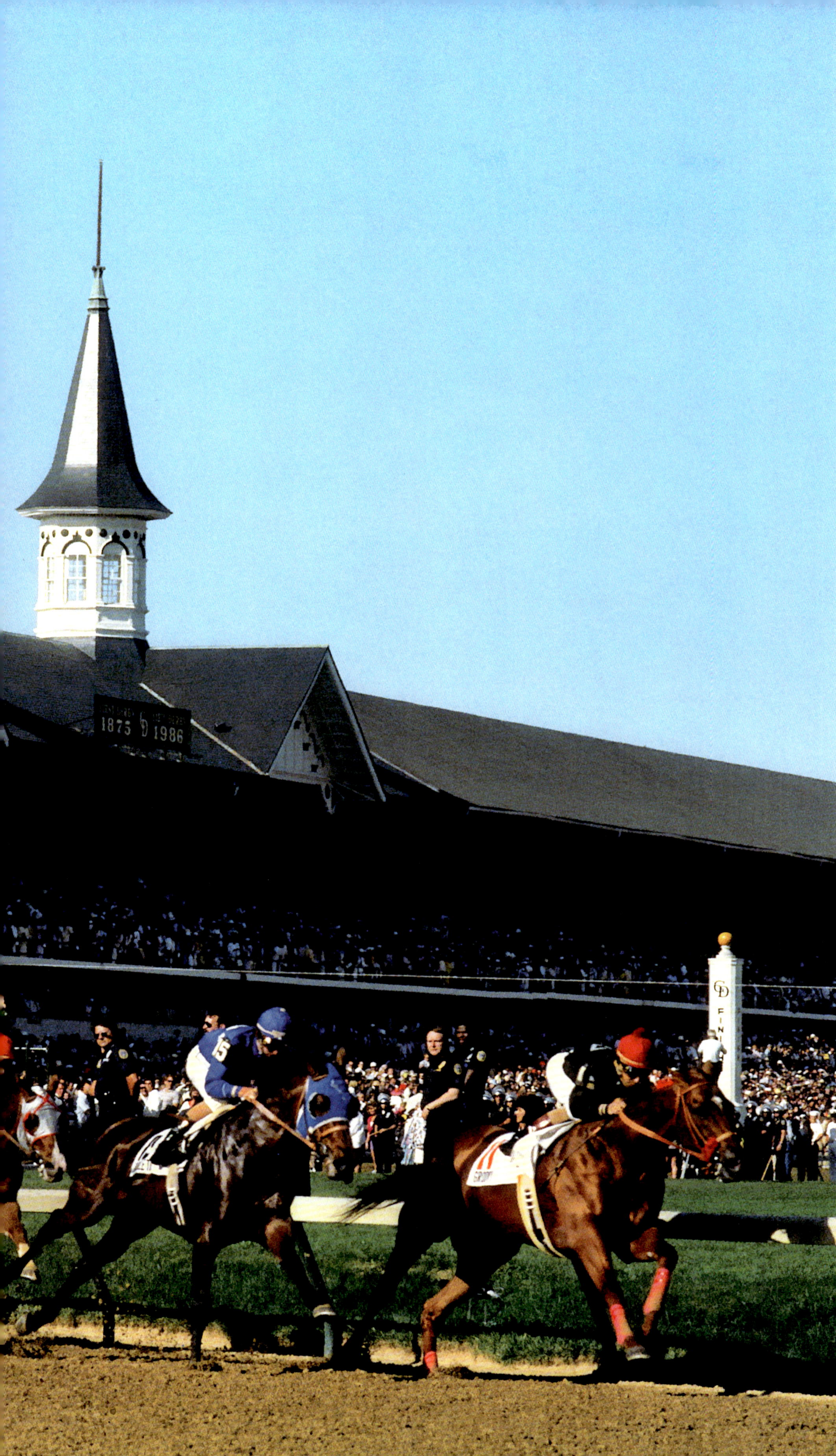

FIRST TURN AT THE KENTUCKY DERBY, CHURCHILL DOWNS, LOUISVILLE

On 17 May 1875, a horse named Aristides, with black jockey Oliver Lewis riding, romped to victory in the first running of the Kentucky Derby. The race was held at the brand-new Louisville Jockey Club grandstand and track, built on land owned by the Churchill brothers—thus the name Churchill Downs. The first of what would be called the Run for the Roses carded a field of fifteen, including future champion Ten Broeck, who finished fifth. Through the years, the Kentucky Derby has become the most famous and prestigious horse race in North America. For owners and trainers of Bluegrass-raised horses, it is a dream come true to have a horse good enough to run in the Derby.

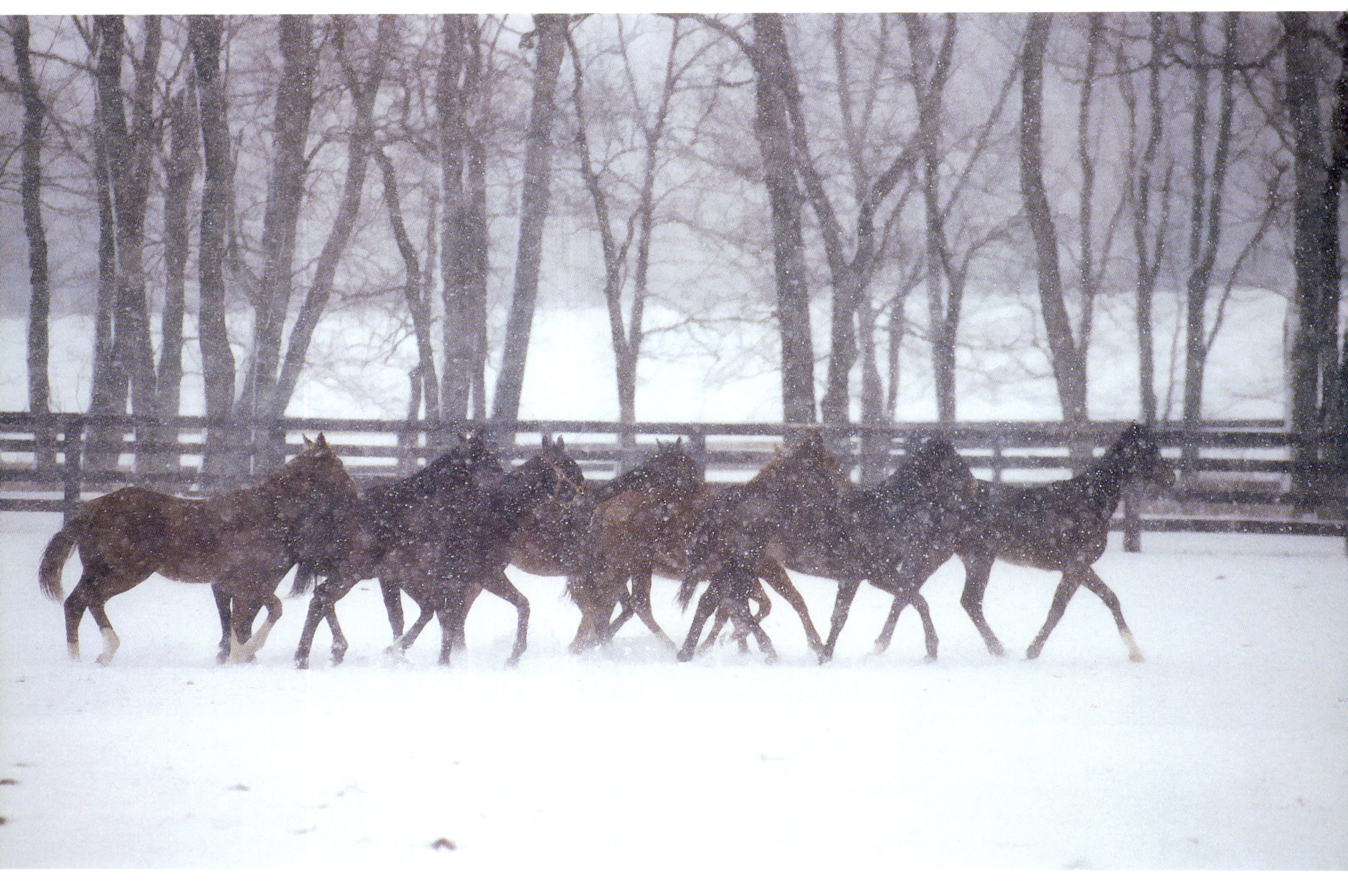

YEARLINGS IN SNOW

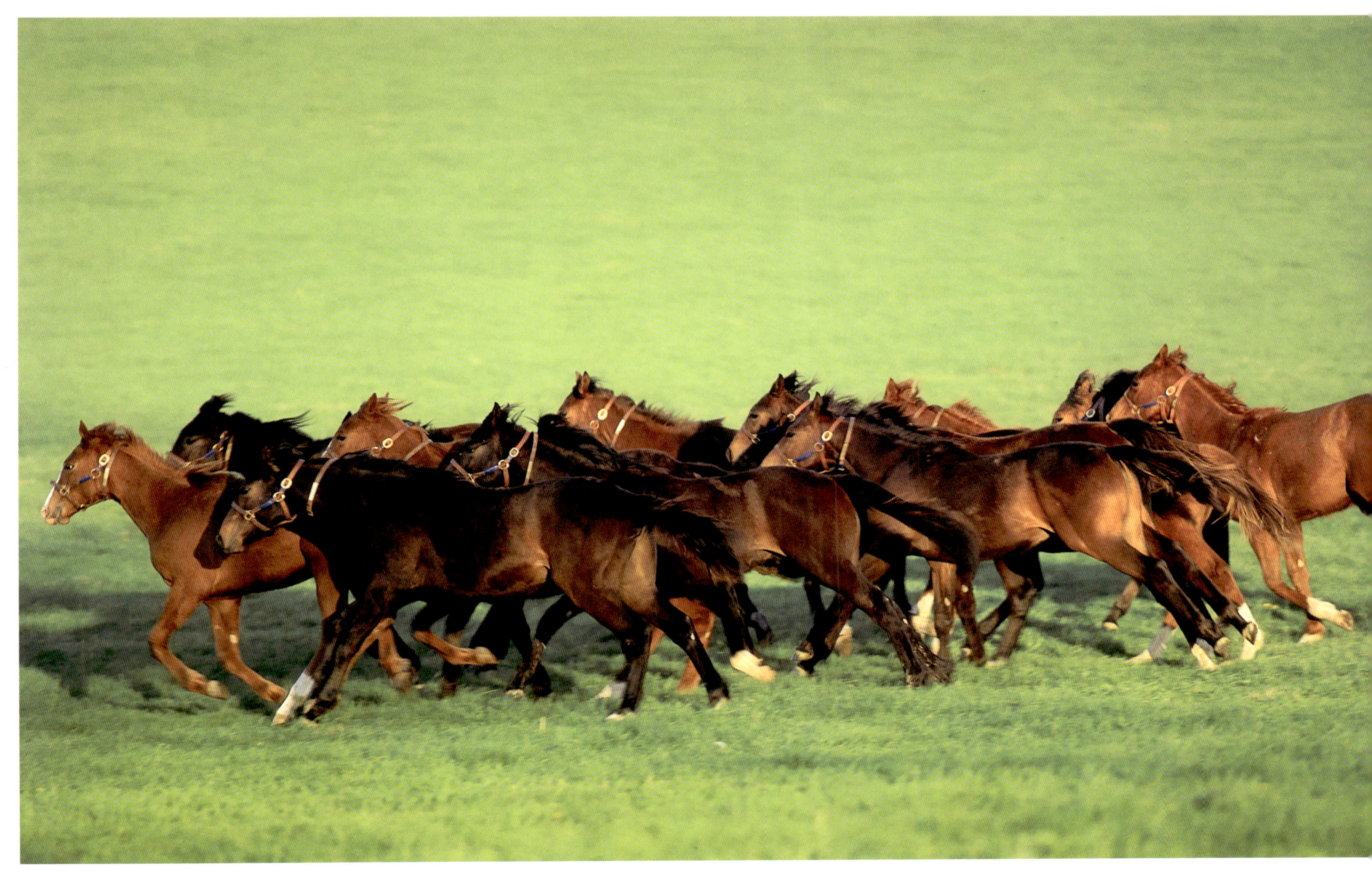

YEARLINGS IN SUMMER

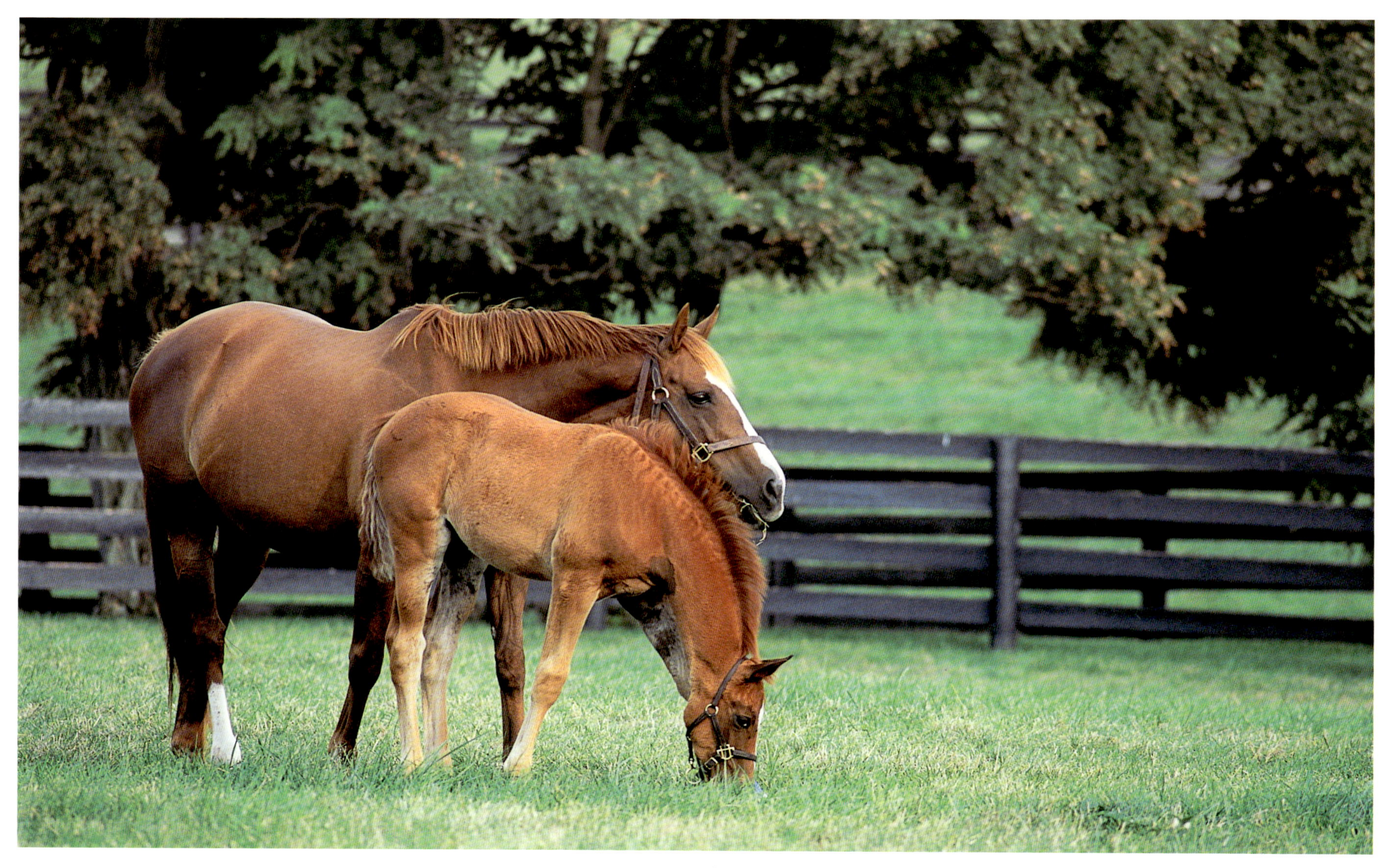

MARE AND FOAL ALONG DELANEY FERRY ROAD

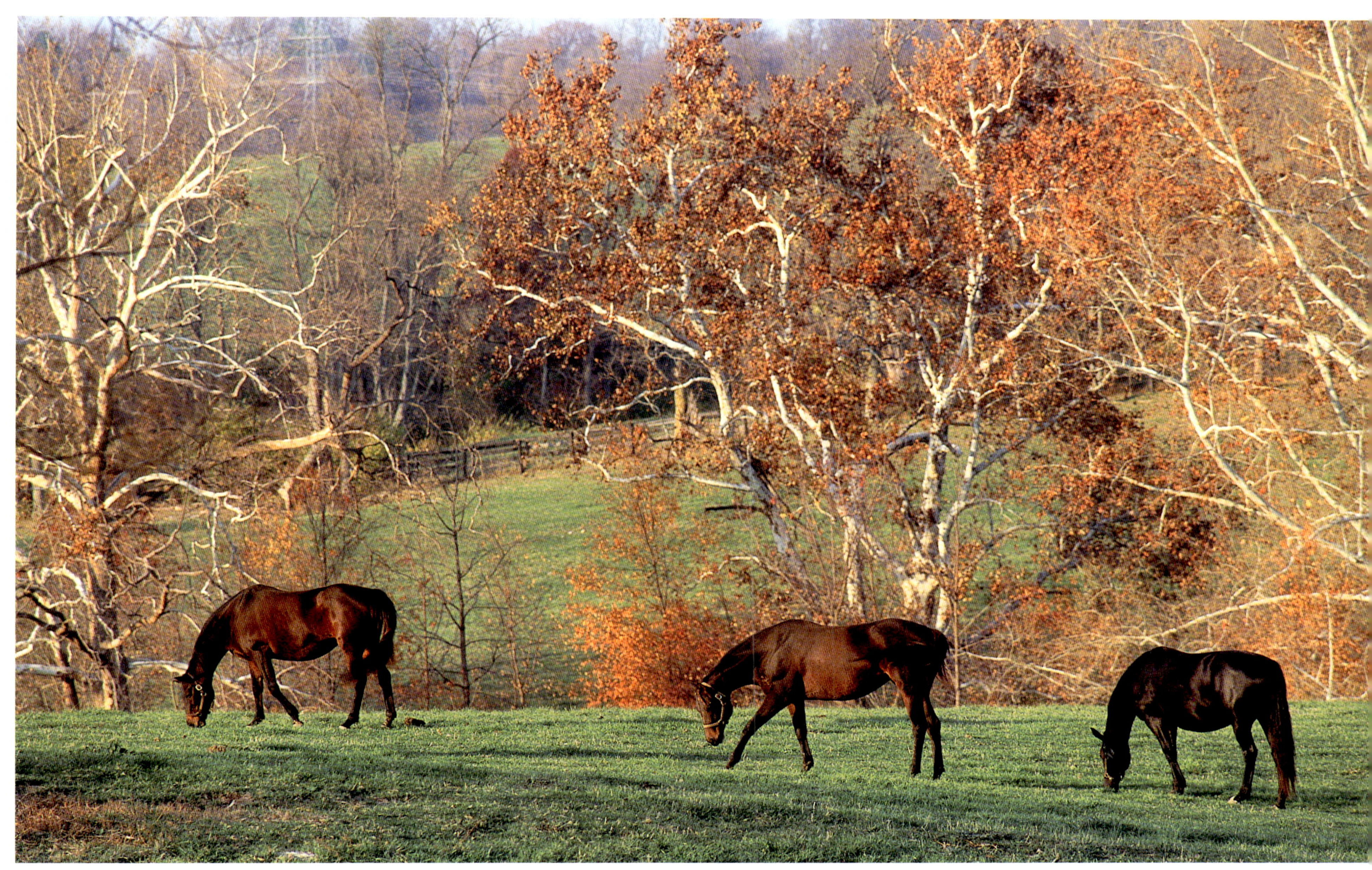

MARES WITH SYCAMORE IN AUTUMN, BOSWORTH LANE, FAYETTE COUNTY

On a late autumn afternoon, three mares graze on a hillside off Bosworth Lane, just outside Lexington. The white-barked sycamores are one of the dominant trees in the Bluegrass, and they usually thrive along streams. Because they grow a little apart from one another rather than in close clusters, they have room to expand, with lower trunk diameters often reaching four to six feet. This also allows their limbs to express their individuality.

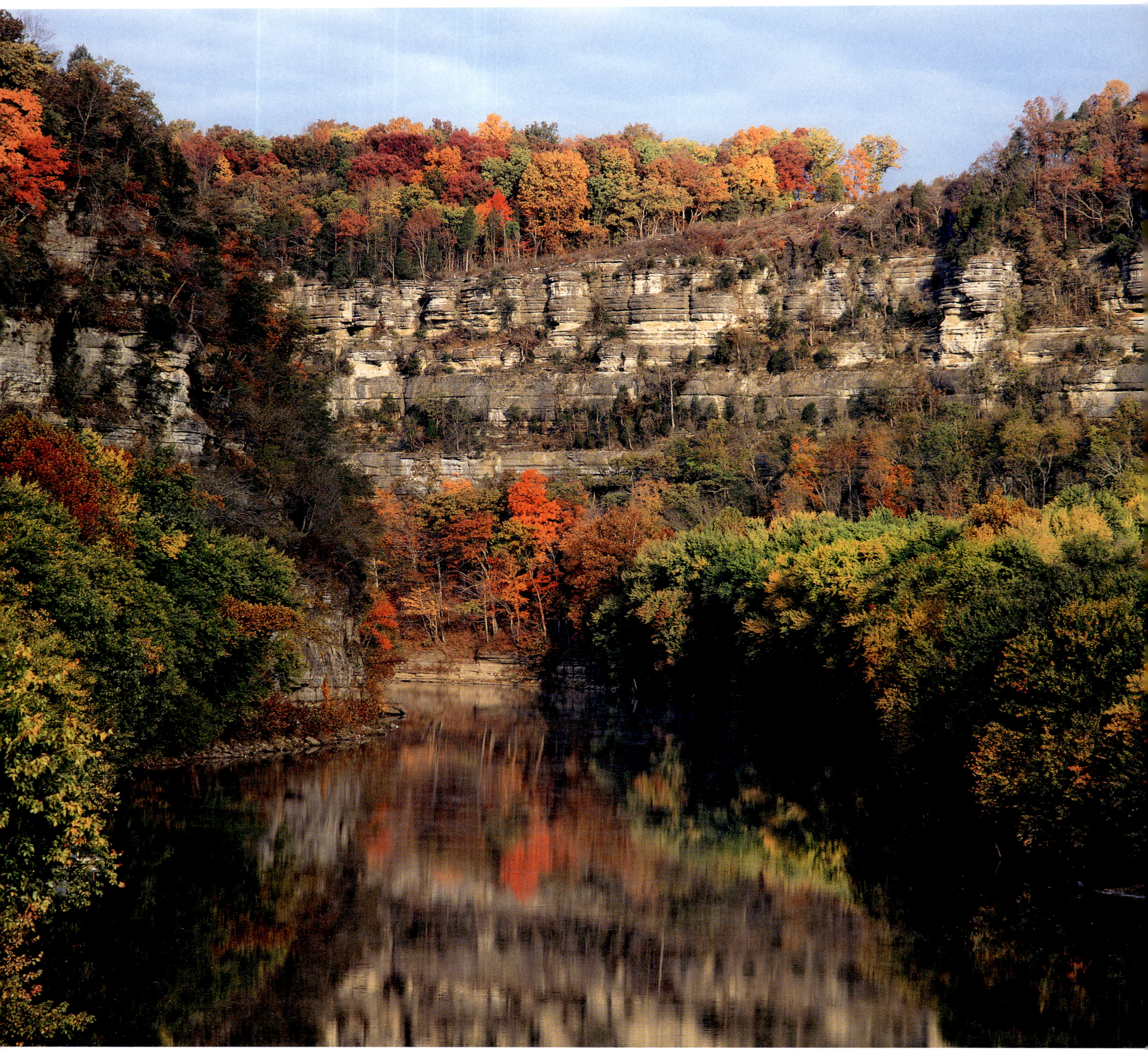

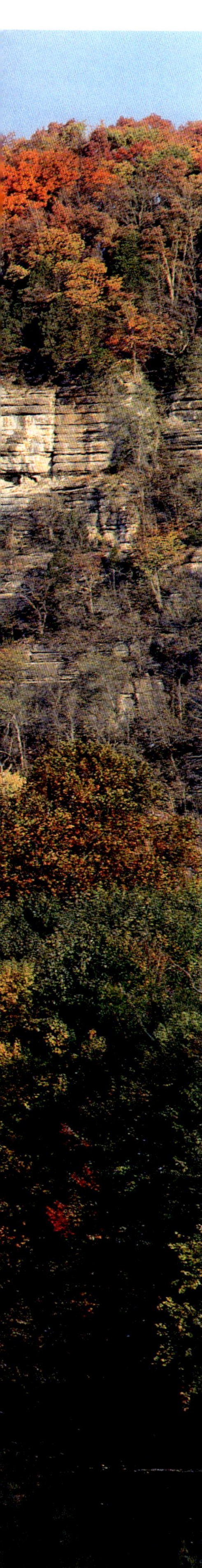

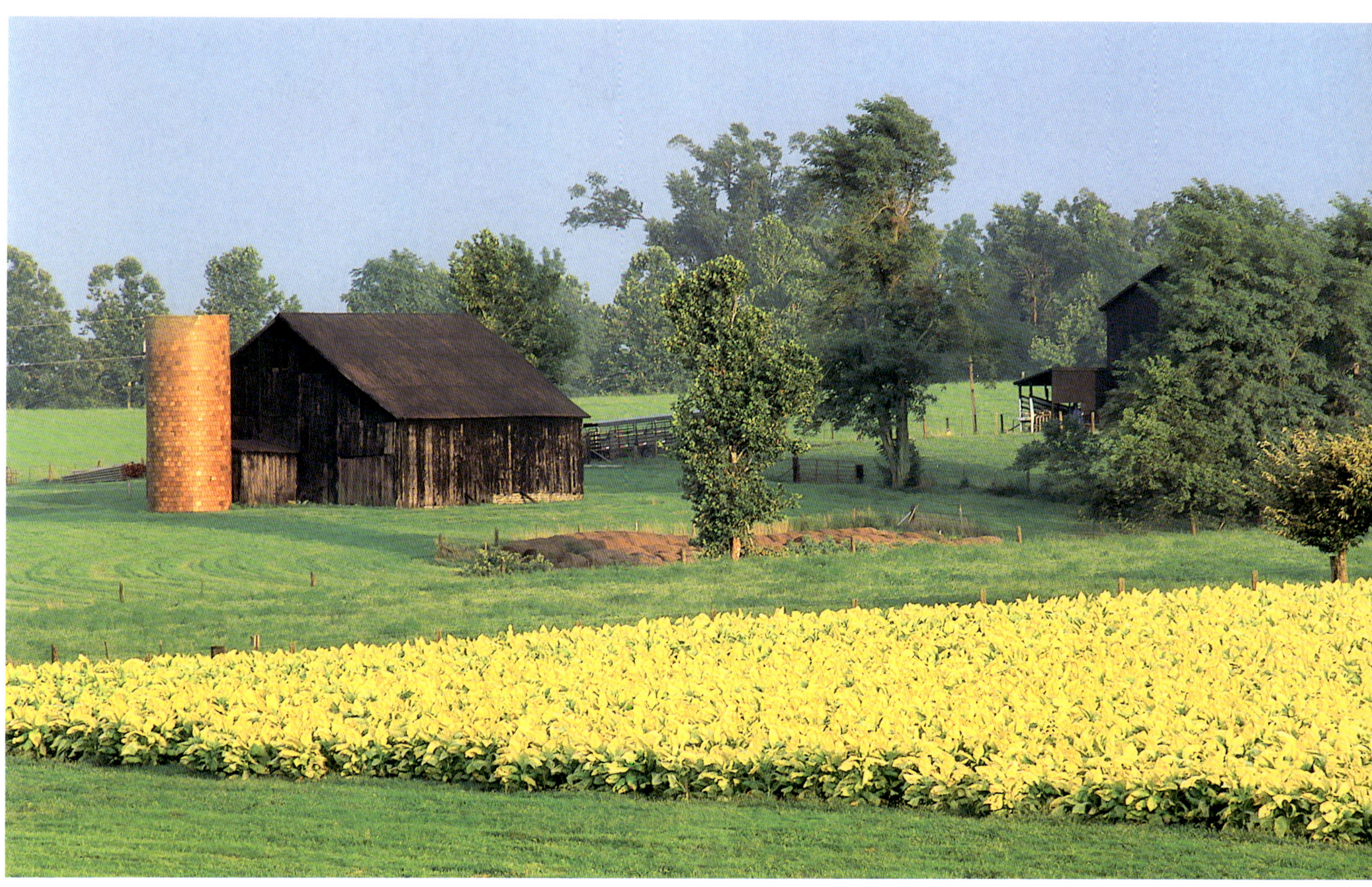

Above: BURLEY TOBACCO FIELD

Although its financial influence is waning, particularly for small farmers, burley tobacco still ranks high in the agricultural economy of the Bluegrass. On a Woodford County farm, this field of golden burley is ready for harvesting. With the elimination of price supports, tobacco is now sold by large growers to cigarette companies under contract. Small producers have virtually vanished.

Facing: KENTUCKY RIVER PALISADES

Over the millennia, the Kentucky River has cut a deep gorge through the southern Bluegrass region. Along a 100-mile stretch, rock palisades as high as 500 feet rise straight up from the river. The palisades are accessible only by boat or on foot. Thus, the area remains largely undisturbed and contains many rare native plants. Its ruggedness has created a unique ecosystem, preserved for study and enjoyment.

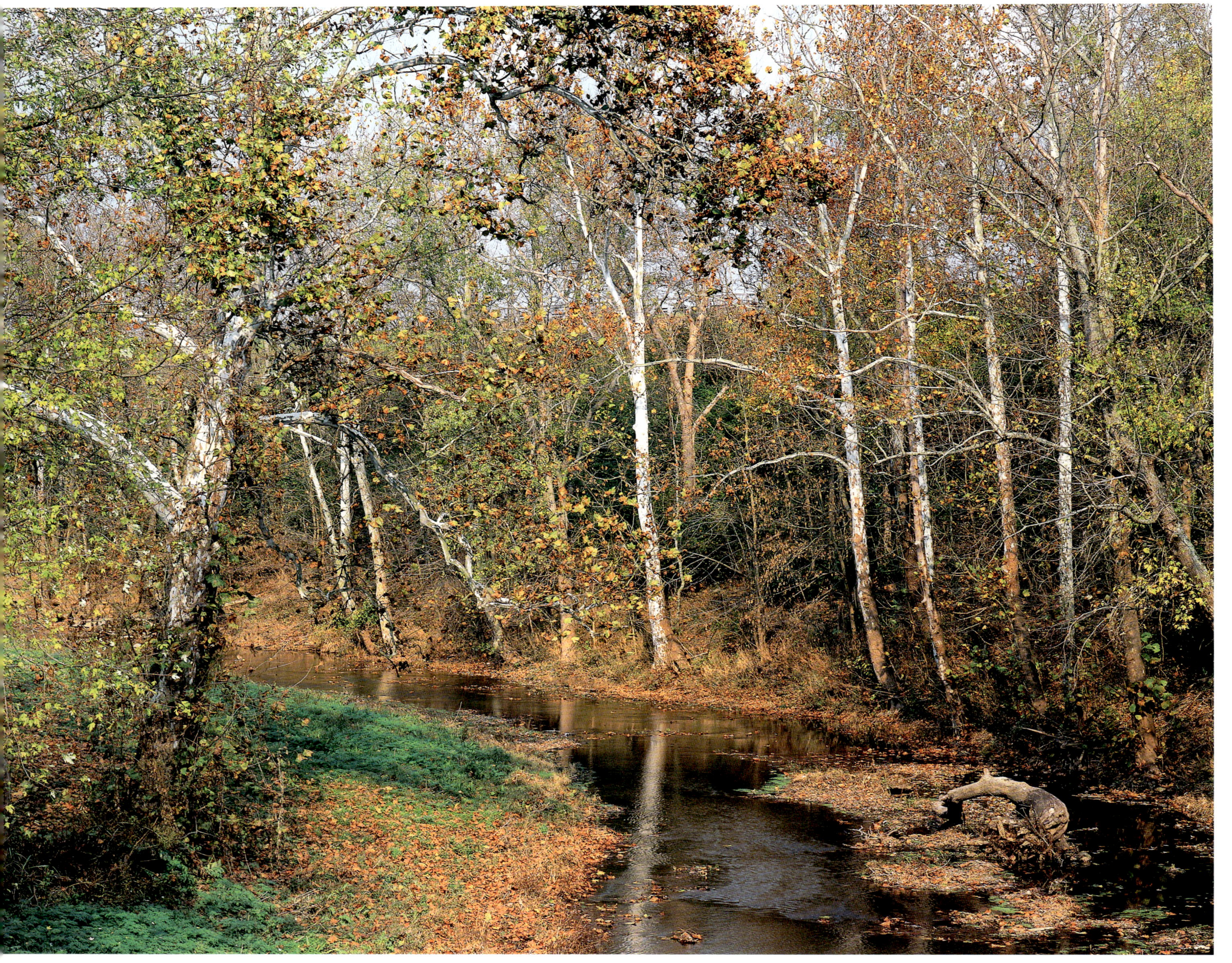

AUTUMN ON NORTH ELKHORN CREEK, SCOTT COUNTY

The North Elkhorn Creek cuts a twisting channel through the heart of Bluegrass horse country north and west of Lexington. Many of the area's most famous farms lie along its banks, and its limestone bottom offers some of Kentucky's best largemouth and smallmouth bass fishing. The earliest pioneers in the area, including Daniel Boone and Simon Kenton, laid claim to portions of the creek, recognizing its potential for development as future settlers came seeking fertile land. Because of its dependable flow of water, numerous gristmills were built along the banks of the North Elkhorn, serving local agricultural producers through the early twentieth century.

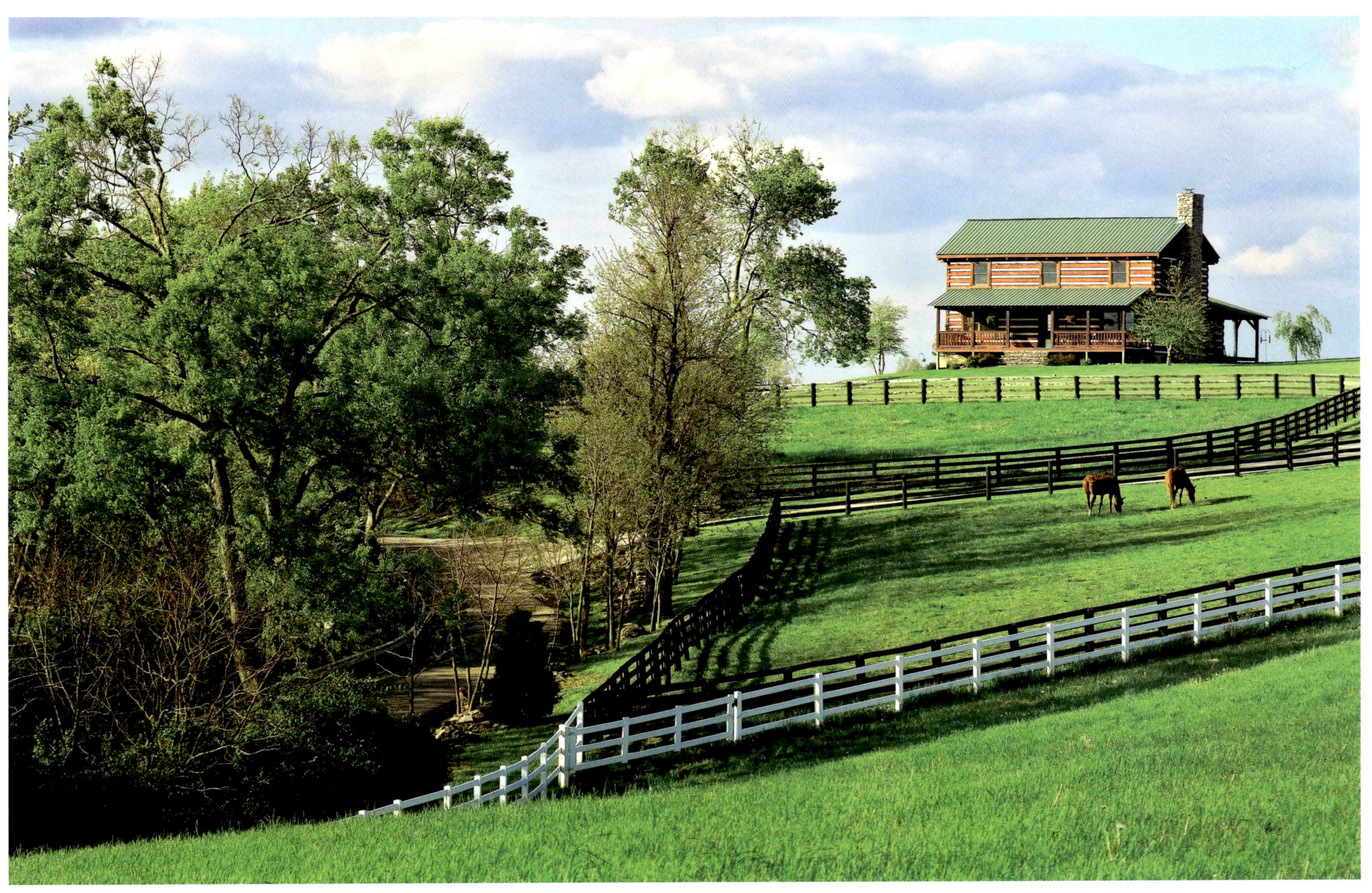

FARM ALONG NORTH ELKHORN CREEK, SCOTT COUNTY

In this idyllic setting along the North Elkhorn Creek in Scott County, two mares graze in their paddock below a Kentucky farmhouse. The Bluegrass region affords many views such as this. Attracted by fertile land and plentiful water, early settlers streamed into central Kentucky, as modern-day tourists do now.

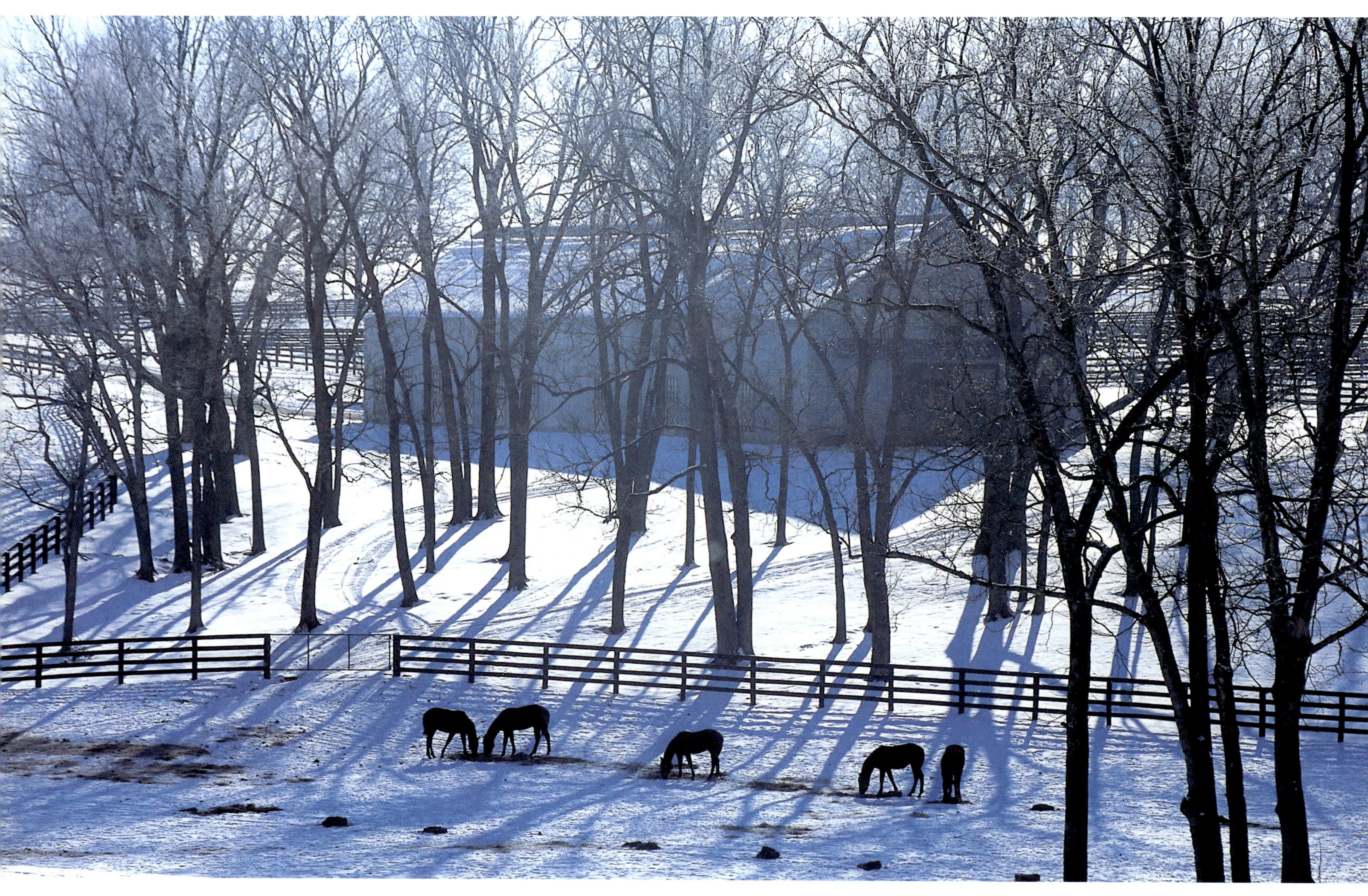

HOPEWELL FARM IN WINTER

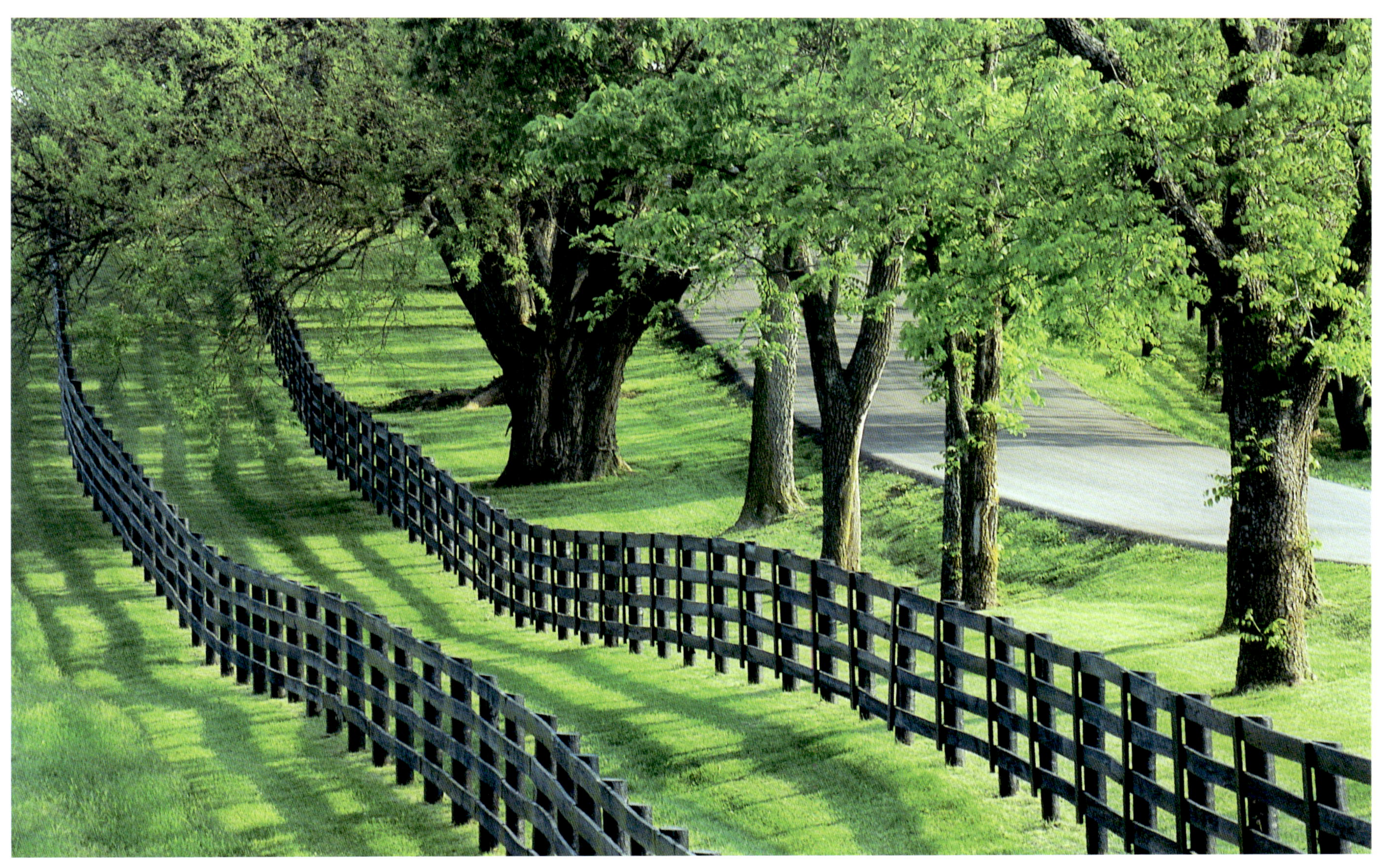

FENCE AND TREES ALONG PISGAH PIKE

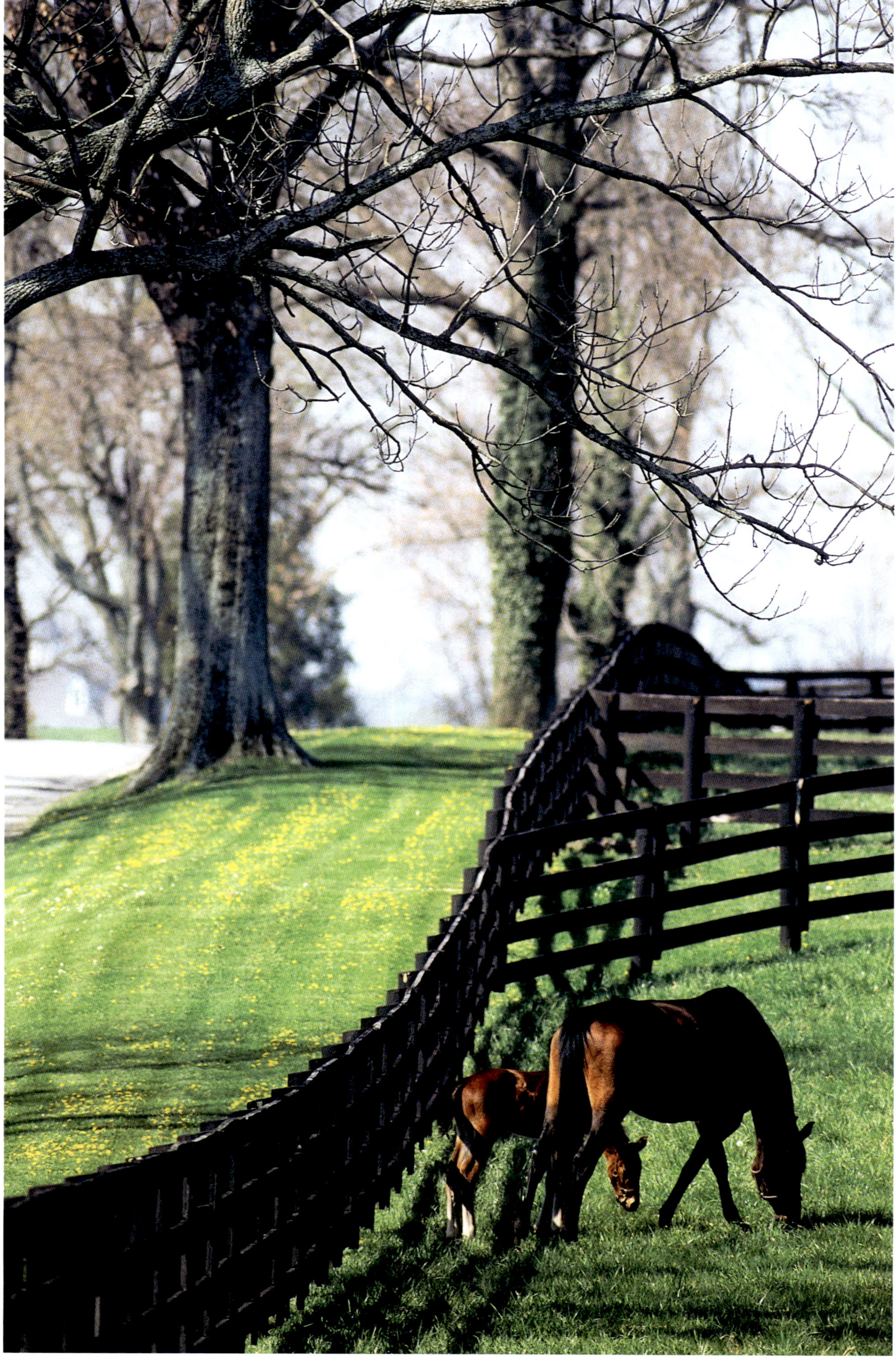

MARE AND FOAL ALONG GRASSY SPRINGS ROAD, WOODFORD COUNTY

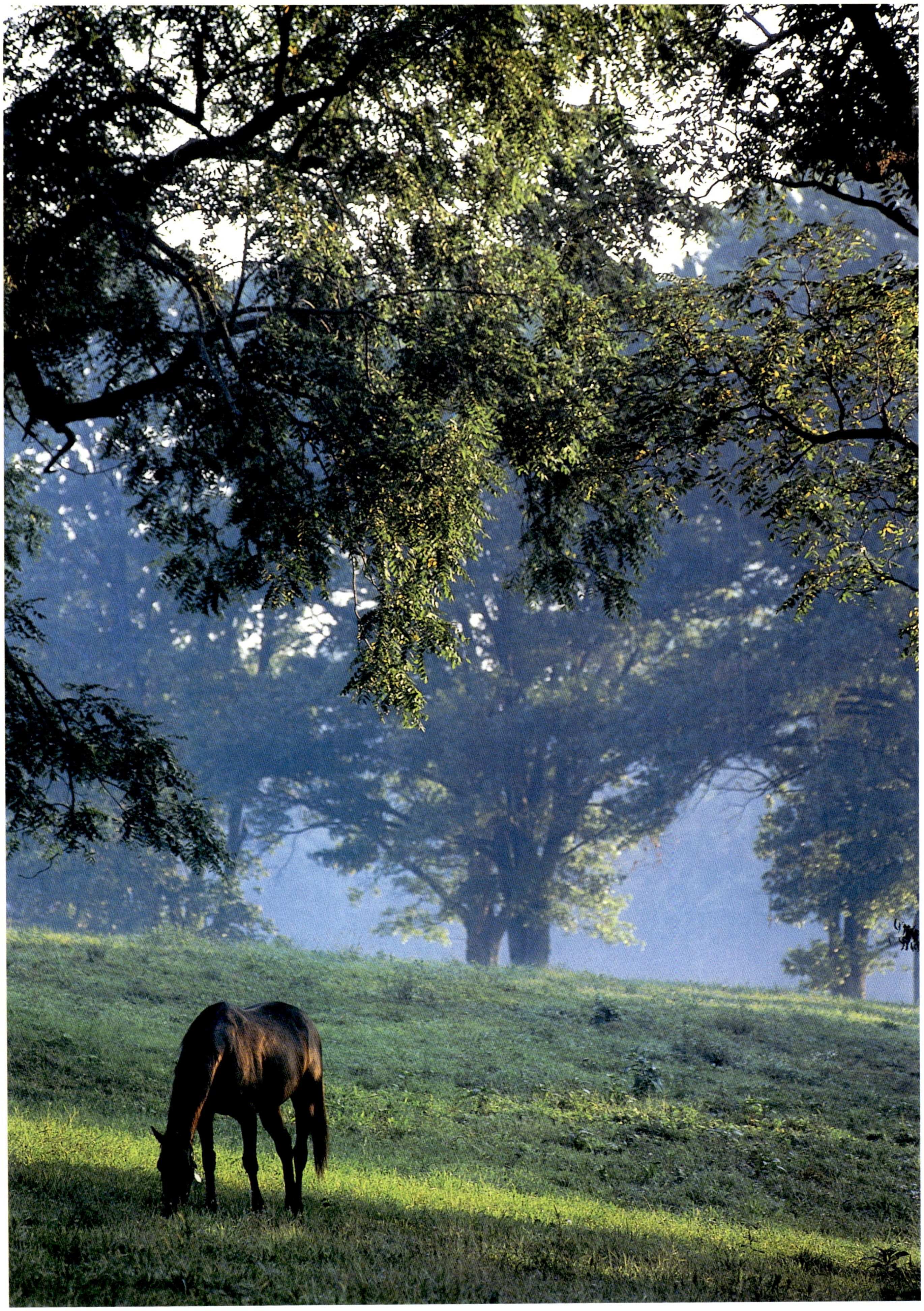

MARE IN GROVE OF TREES, BOURBON COUNTY

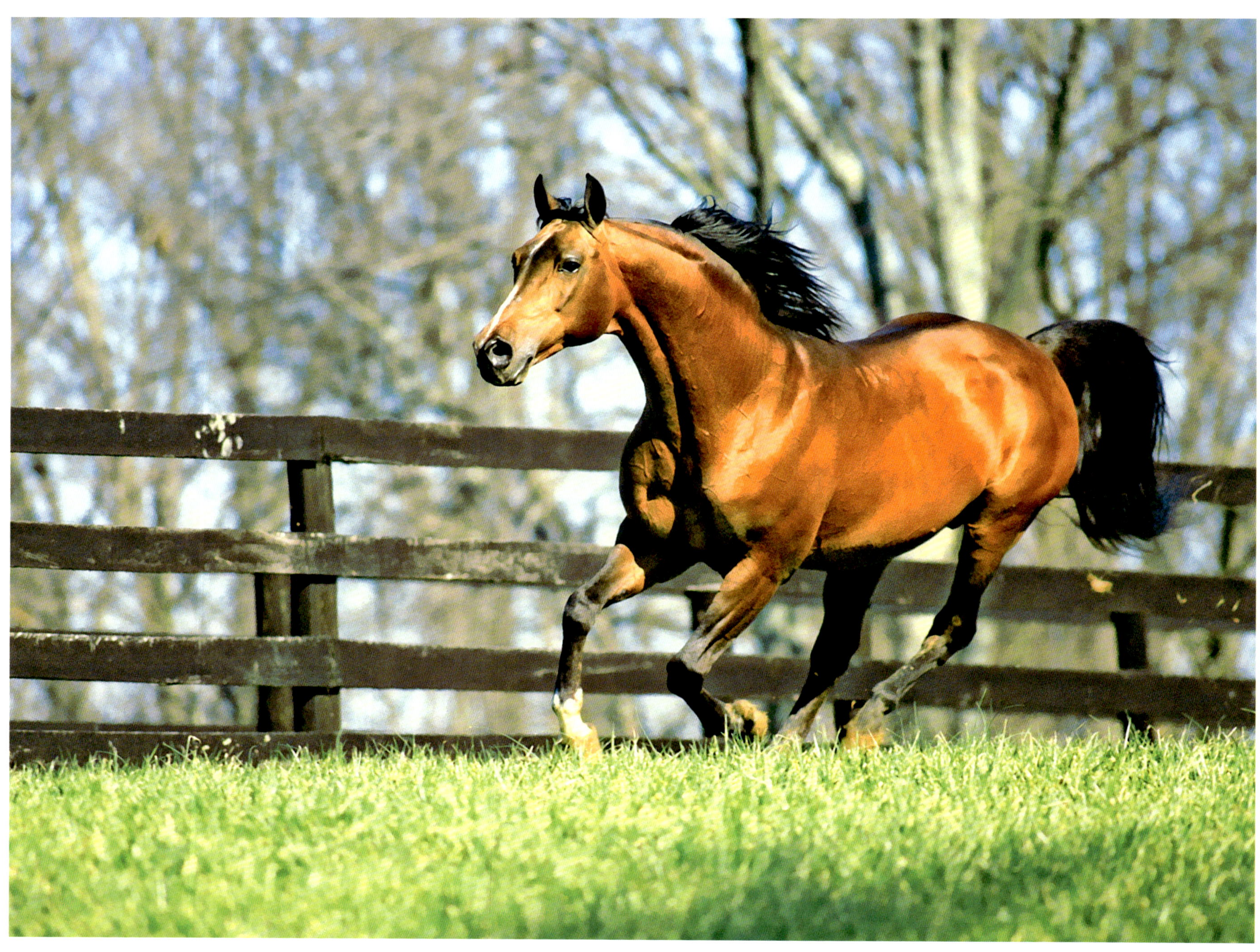

ARABIAN STALLION

Arabians have been bred in North Africa and the Middle East for centuries. This strong, adaptable, fine-featured horse contributed to the ancestry of Thoroughbred, Standardbred, and Saddlebred horses, among others. Stallions with partial Arabian ancestry, known as Turks or Barbs, were originally imported to England from Arabia several centuries ago. The Thoroughbred was created by breeding these horses, and the occasional pure Arabian smuggled in, with English mares. By 1730, a horse named Bulle Rock was brought to the colonies and is regarded as the first Thoroughbred in America. Today, Arabians are raised principally as show horses and for pleasure riding.

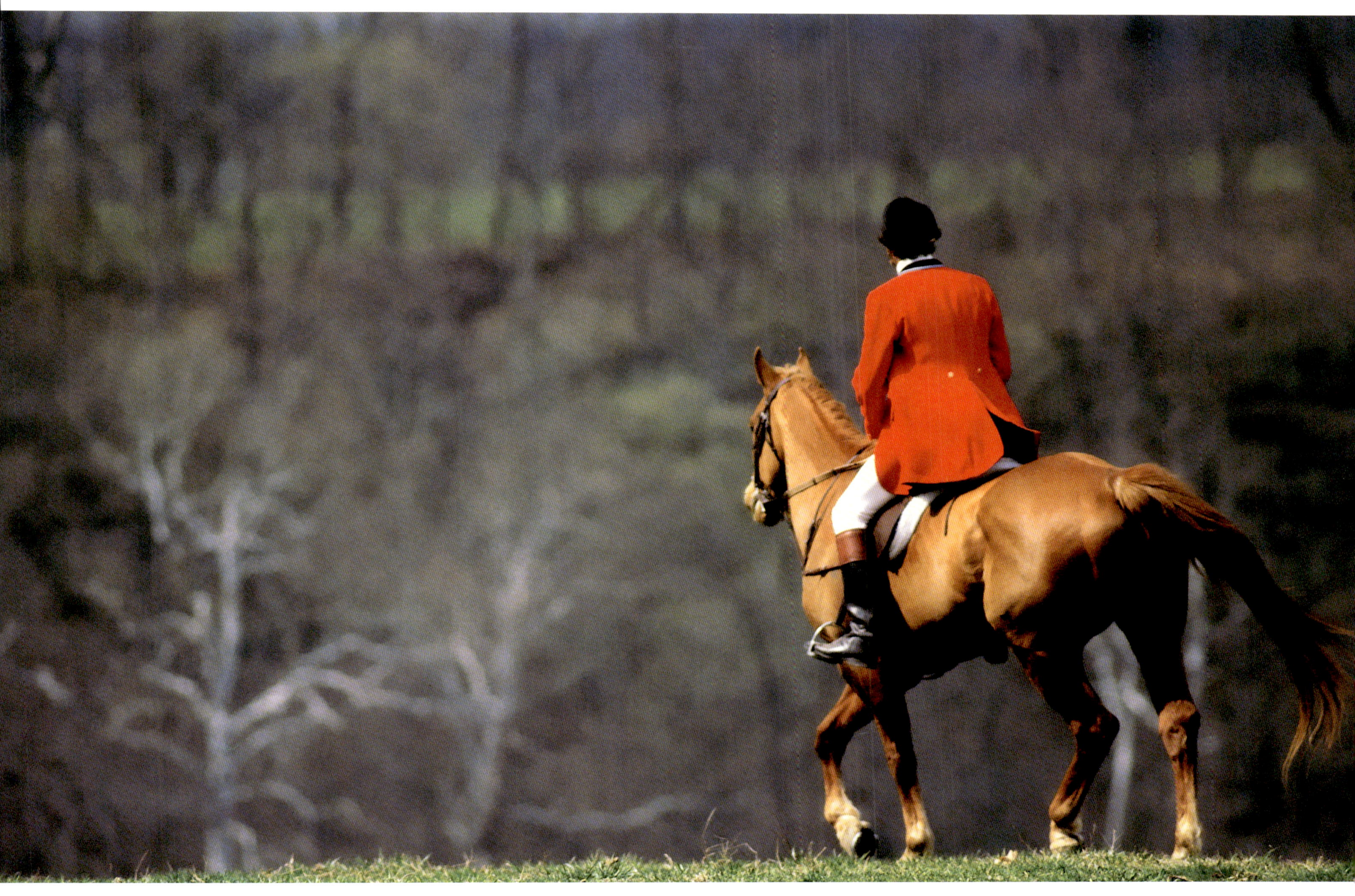

OFFICIAL AT IROQUOIS HUNT CLUB

On a Bluegrass hilltop, an official of the Iroquois Hunt Club looks out over the Clark County countryside. Dressed in traditional fashion, he is watching over the riders as they compete in the annual cross-country competition sponsored by the famed club.

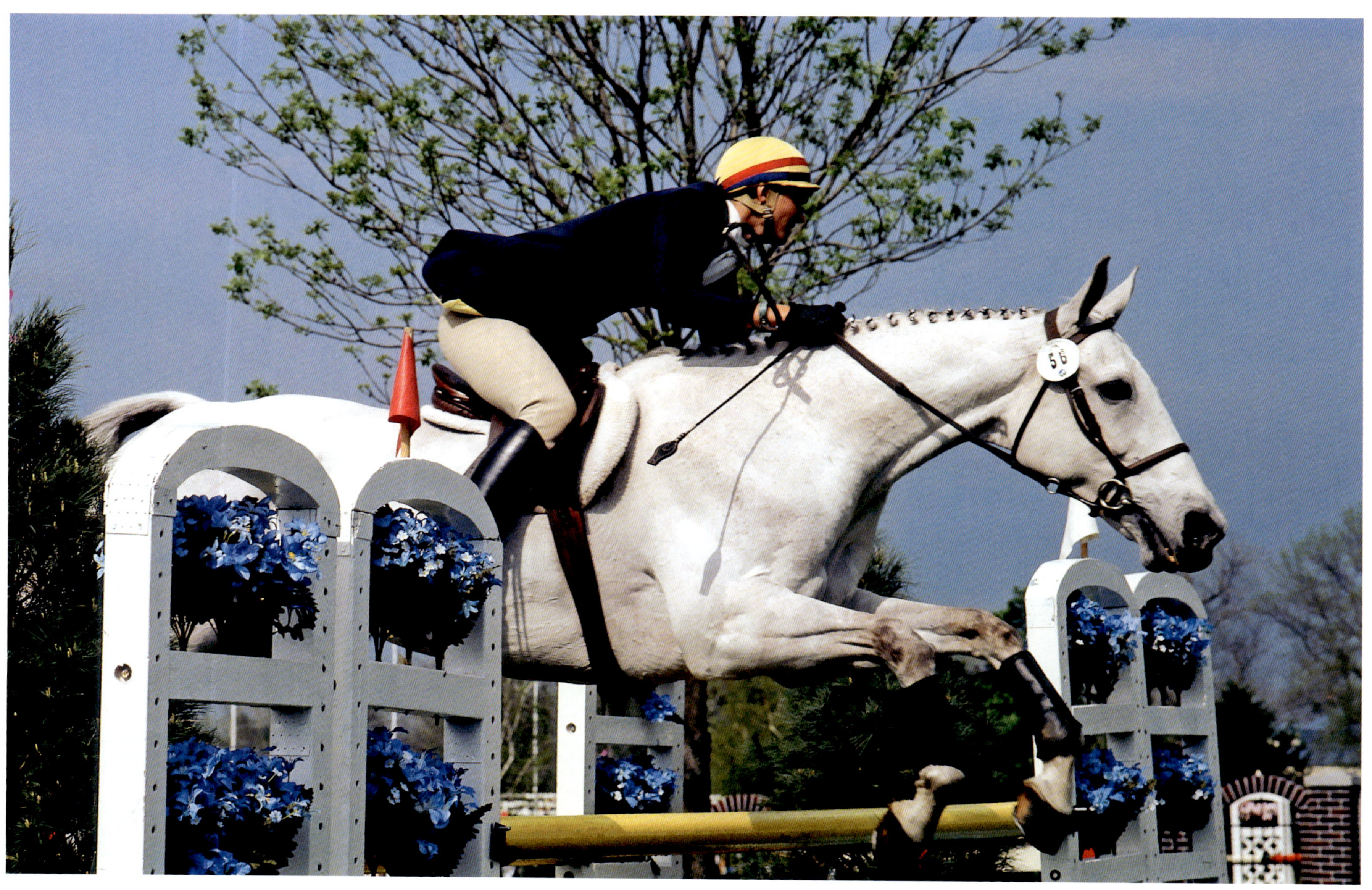

STADIUM JUMPING, ROLEX THREE-DAY EVENT, KENTUCKY HORSE PARK

Each spring, the Kentucky Horse Park in Lexington hosts the Rolex Three-Day Event. Many of the world's best horses and riders participate in dressage, stadium jumping, and the grueling cross-country competition, considered one of the most difficult courses in the world. The event is a major stepping-stone to the World Equestrian Games, traditionally held in Europe every four years. The United States will host the world games for the first time in 2010 at the Kentucky Horse Park.

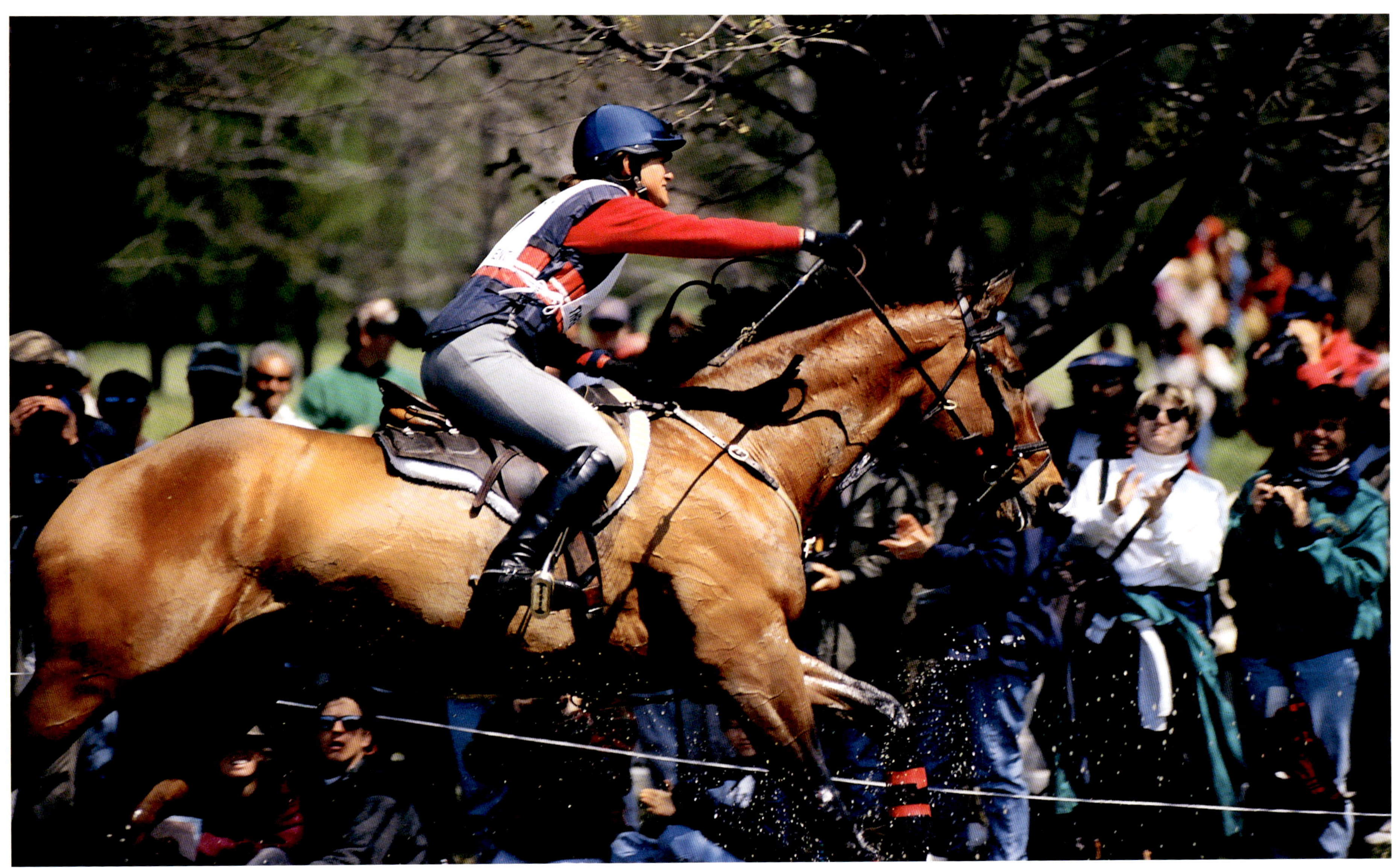

COMPLETING THE WATER JUMP, ROLEX THREE-DAY EVENT, KENTUCKY HORSE PARK

A rider and horse successfully complete the water jump, probably the most difficult obstacle on the long cross-country steeplechase course at the Kentucky Horse Park in Lexington. Although some horses balk and a few falls take place, most riders make the jump and advance through the course. Fine execution at this jump is greeted with hearty applause from the spectators in the gallery.

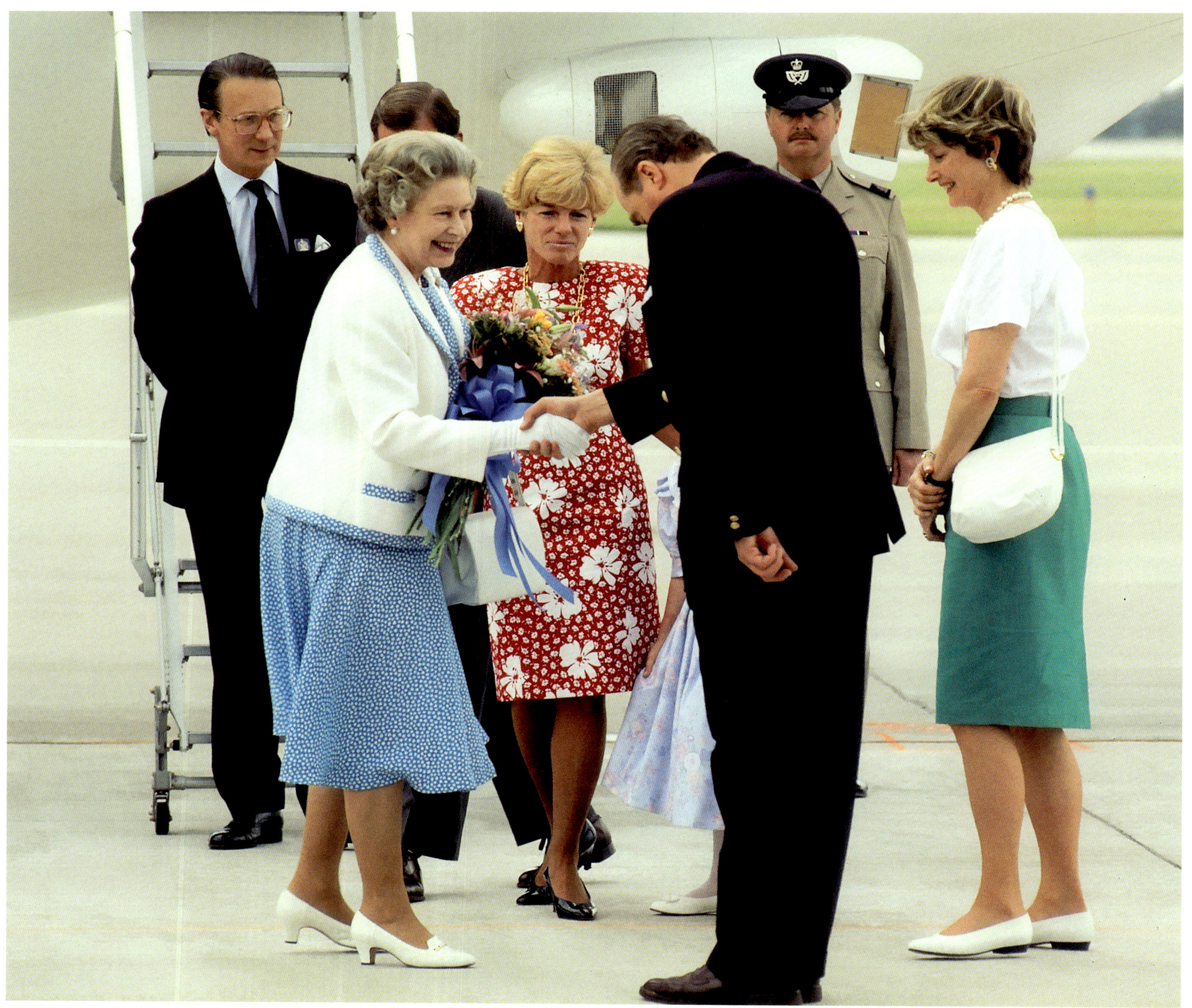

QUEEN ELIZABETH VISITS LEXINGTON

The English monarch is a racing enthusiast and occasionally visits the Bluegrass to indulge her equine interests in America. Queen Elizabeth has attended the races at Keeneland, and in 1984, the annual running of the Queen Elizabeth Challenge Cup stakes was established. The queen visited Lexington again in 2007 and attended her first Kentucky Derby at Churchill Downs in Louisville.

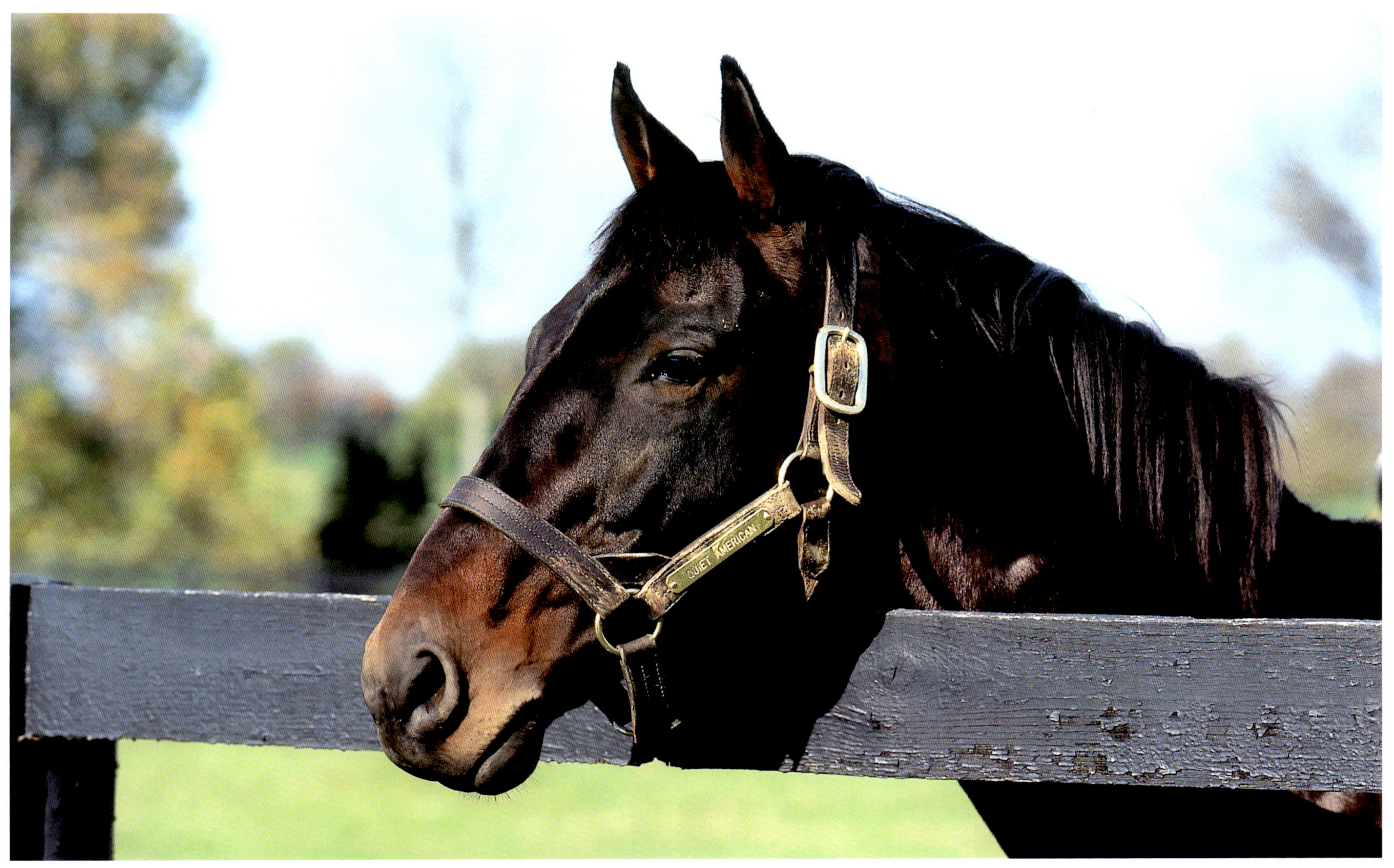

QUIET AMERICAN, SIRE OF 1998 KENTUCKY DERBY WINNER REAL QUIET

Quiet American, by Fappiano, is the sire of two Eclipse champions and twenty-six graded stakes performers. His most famous son is Real Quiet, whose crooked right front leg didn't garner much positive attention at the yearling horse sales; he was subsequently purchased for just $17,000. The colt was assigned to the stable of trainer Bob Baffert, a rising star in the industry. Baffert also trained Silver Charm, the 1997 Kentucky Derby and Preakness winner, and the next year, Real Quiet stunned the favorites in the Run for the Roses and then took the Preakness. Real Quiet raced again as a four-year-old before retiring, having finished in the money seventeen times in twenty starts and earning $3.2 million.

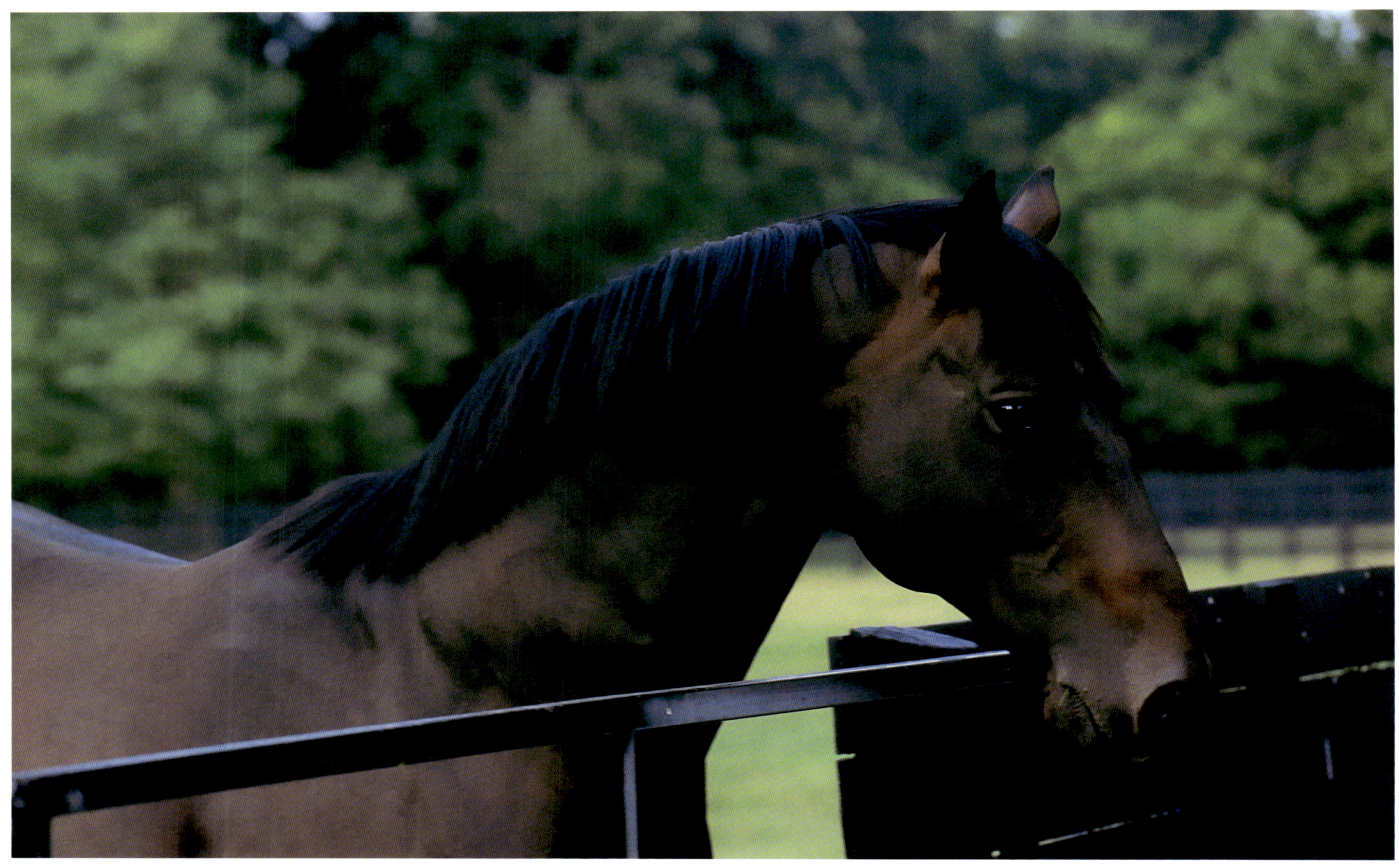

GRINDSTONE, 1996 KENTUCKY DERBY WINNER

Ridden by jockey Jerry Bailey, Grindstone—the son of 1990 Kentucky Derby victor Unbridled—was the smallest horse in a field of nineteen starters. The dark bay colt broke from post position fifteen, but after the early speed runners faded, Bailey and Grindstone made their move, catching Cavonnier in the stretch and winning by a nose at the wire. Because of an injury, Grindstone would never run again and was retired to stud at Overbrook Farm in Lexington, where he had been bred.

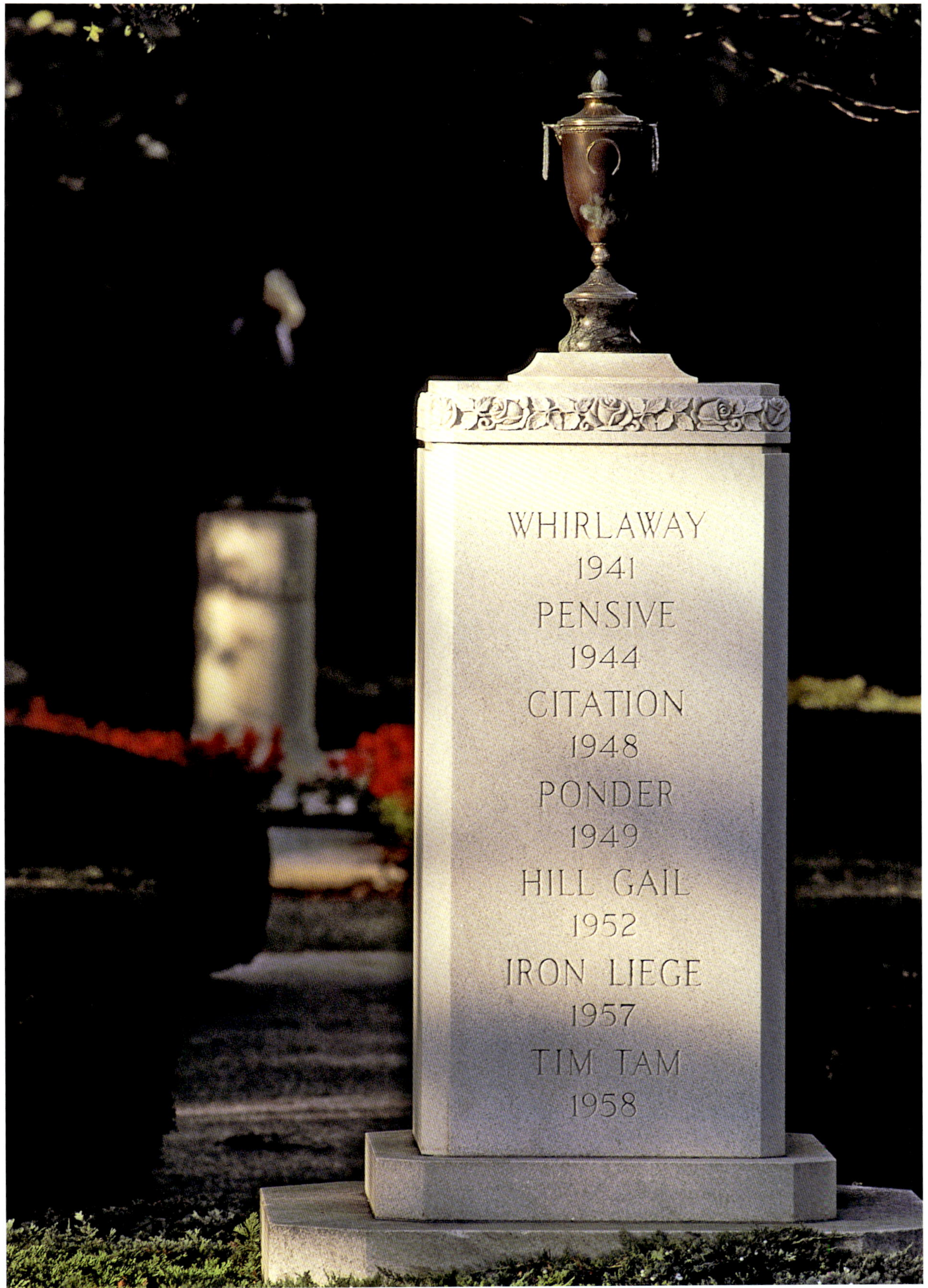

MONUMENT TO CALUMET FARM'S KENTUCKY DERBY WINNERS

Since this monument was erected in the extensive Calumet Farm Cemetery, two additional Kentucky Derby winners have been bred on the historic farm—Forward Pass in 1968 and Strike the Gold in 1991. In 1990, the body of Alydar was buried here, where it now rests alongside many of Calumet's greatest horses. The statue in the distance is of Bull Lea, the foundation sire that, under the stewardship of owner Warren Wright Sr., brought Calumet to racing glory in the 1940s and 1950s.

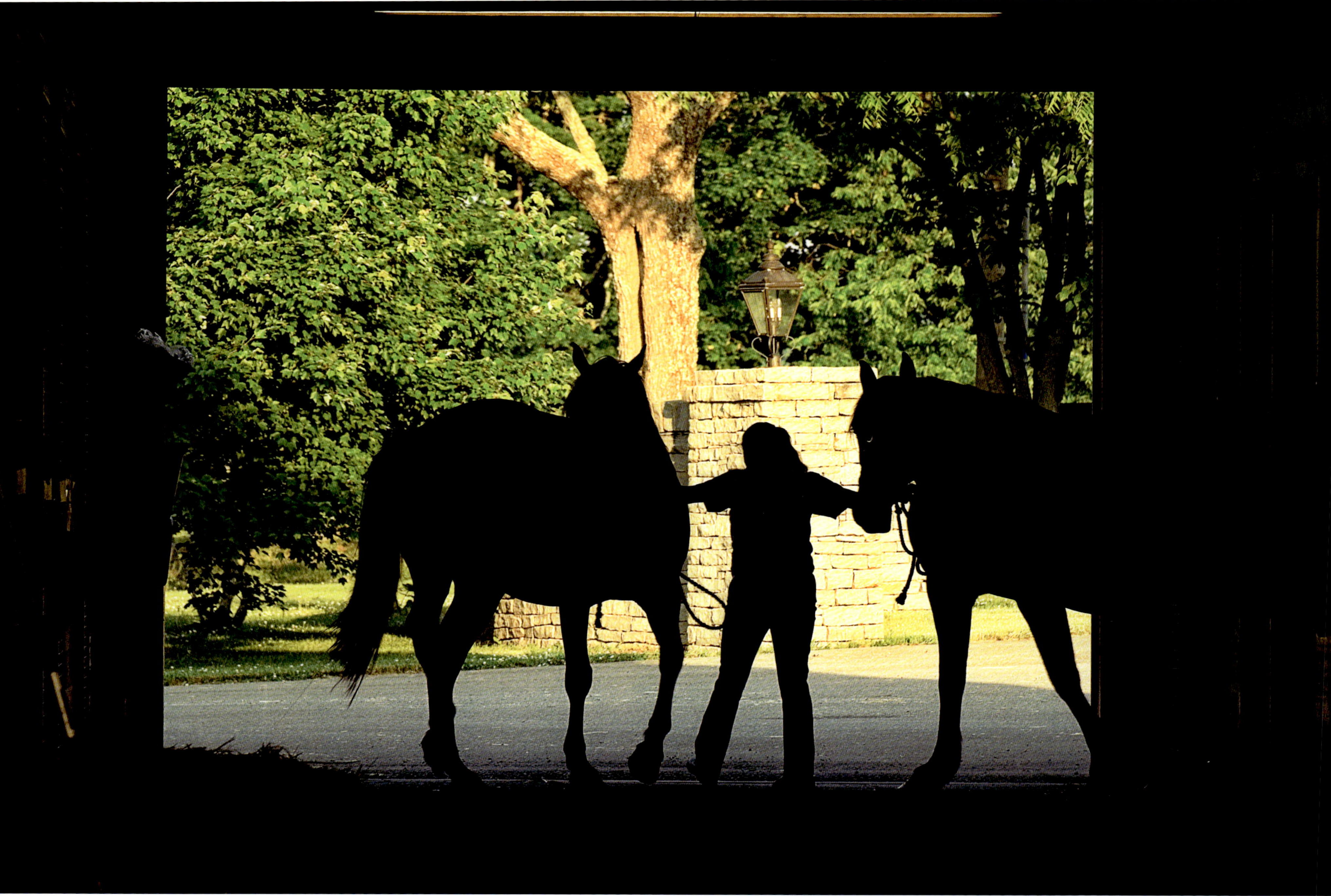

TAKING OUT THE MARES

Broodmares generally have gentle dispositions around both their own kind and their human handlers. Here, a young woman leads two mares from their stalls to the paddock. This wouldn't be possible with stallions, which are usually handled individually. While in the paddock, stallions are separated from one another by wide rows. Unless they are strictly supervised, males are prone to fight, with the potential for serious injury to horse and human alike.

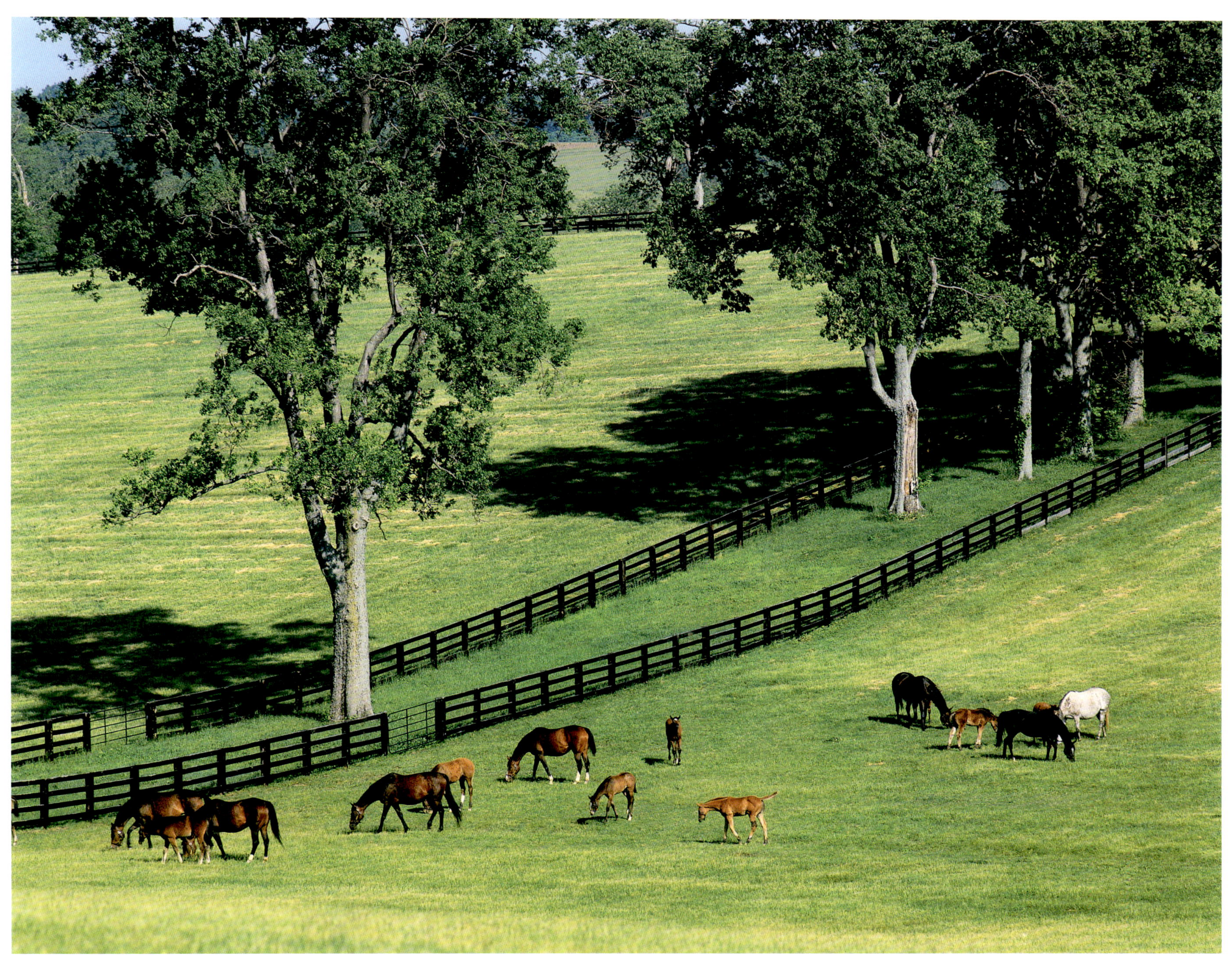

MARES AND FOALS IN MAY PASTURE

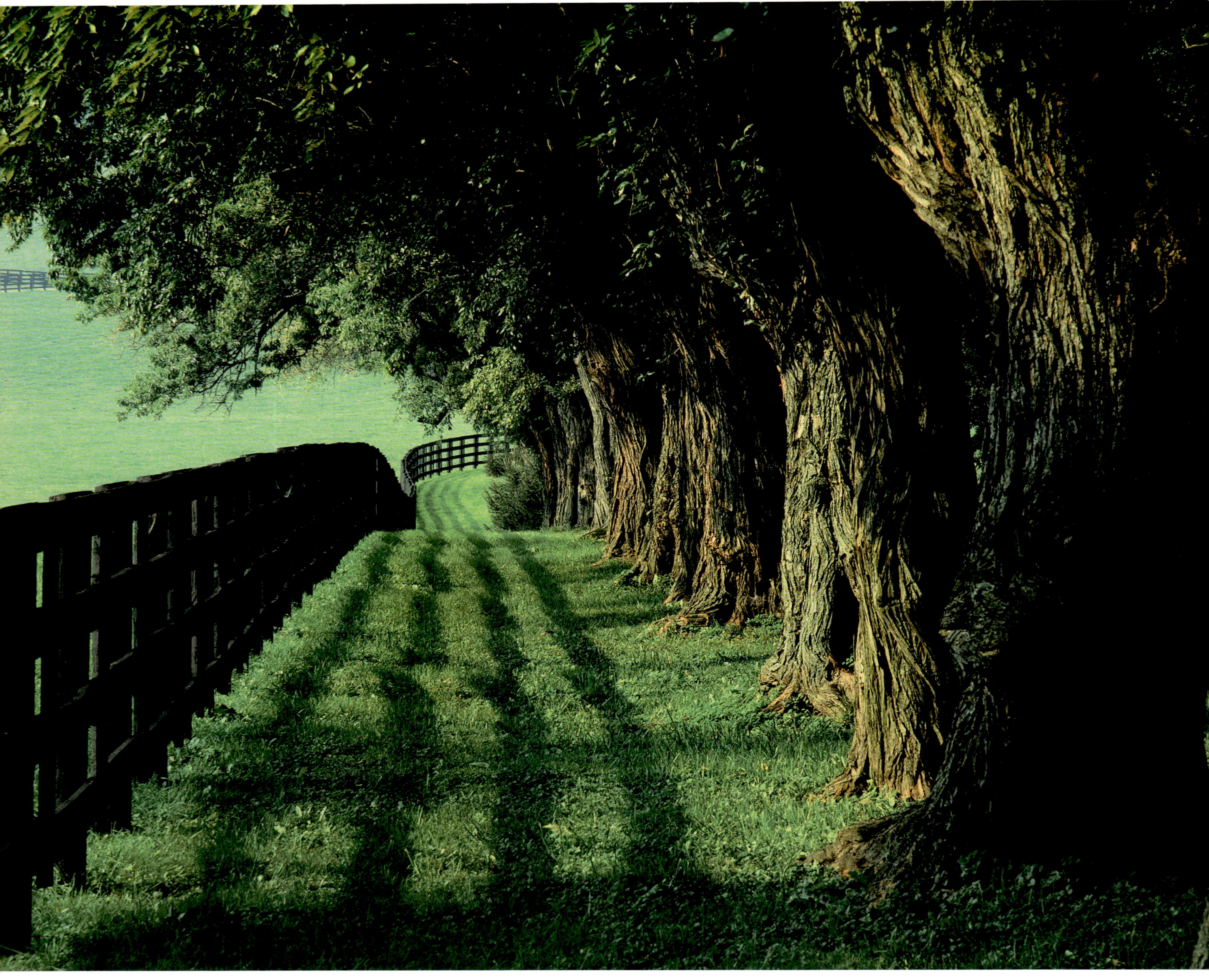

OSAGE ORANGE TREES ALONG PISGAH PIKE

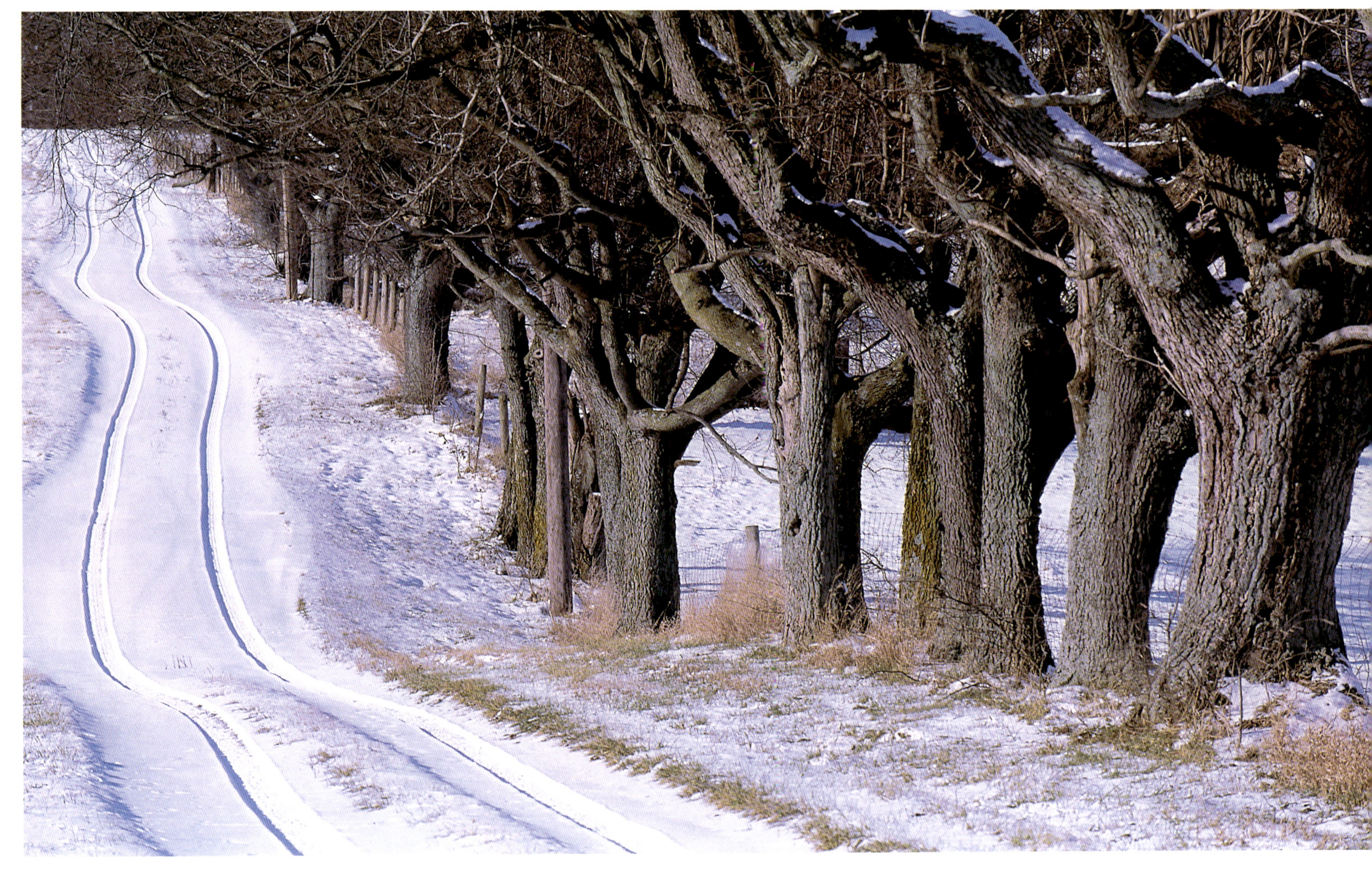

TREES BY ROAD IN WINTER

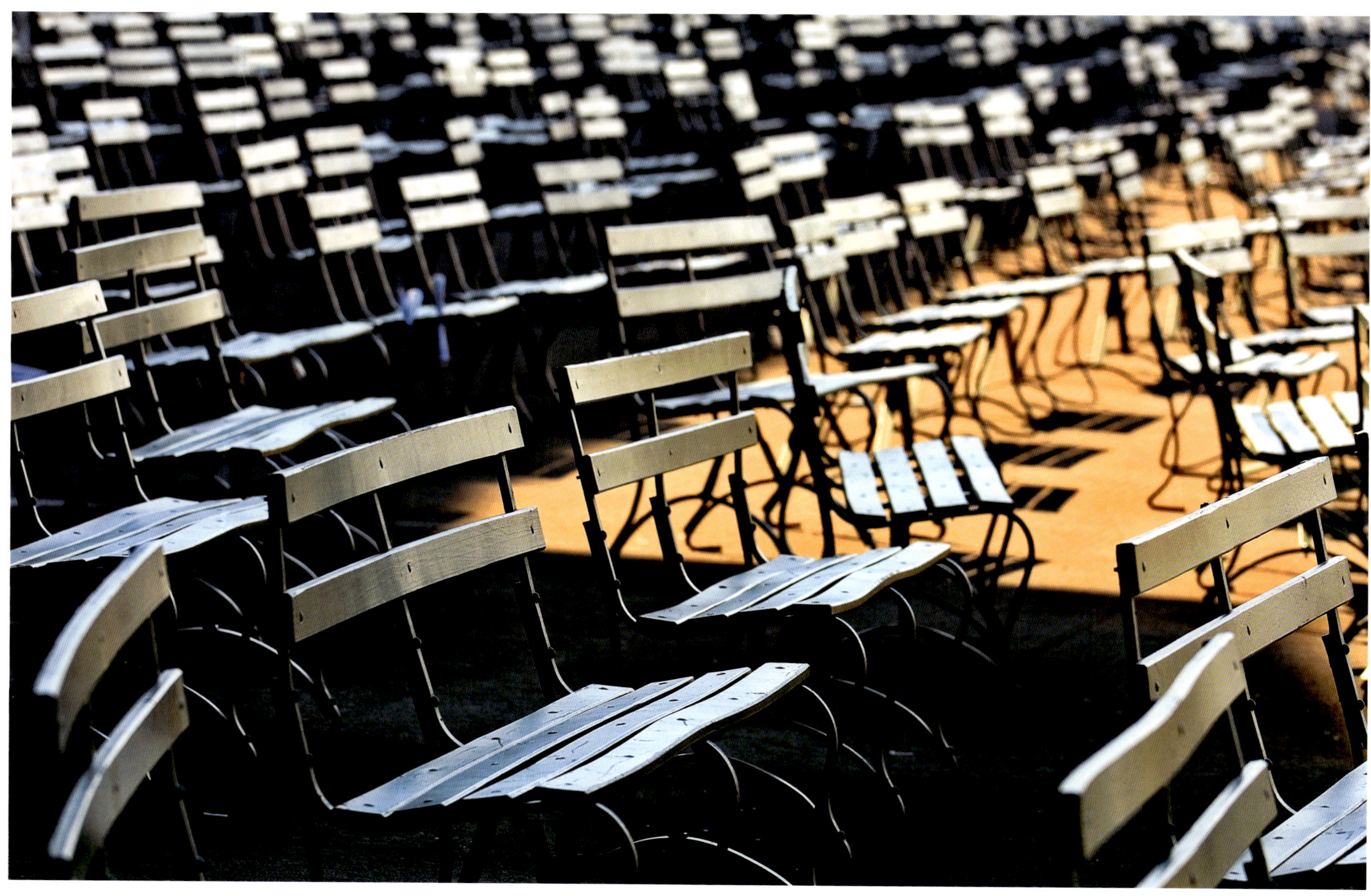

WAITING FOR RACE FANS

By post time at Keeneland, these benches will be filled by people eager to place their bets, hoping to pick some winners. Although wagering is a strong draw for fans, many people come to Keeneland to enjoy time with their friends and family, admire the beautiful horses, and sample the great food. The diverse crowds at Keeneland provide ample opportunity for another popular pastime: people watching.

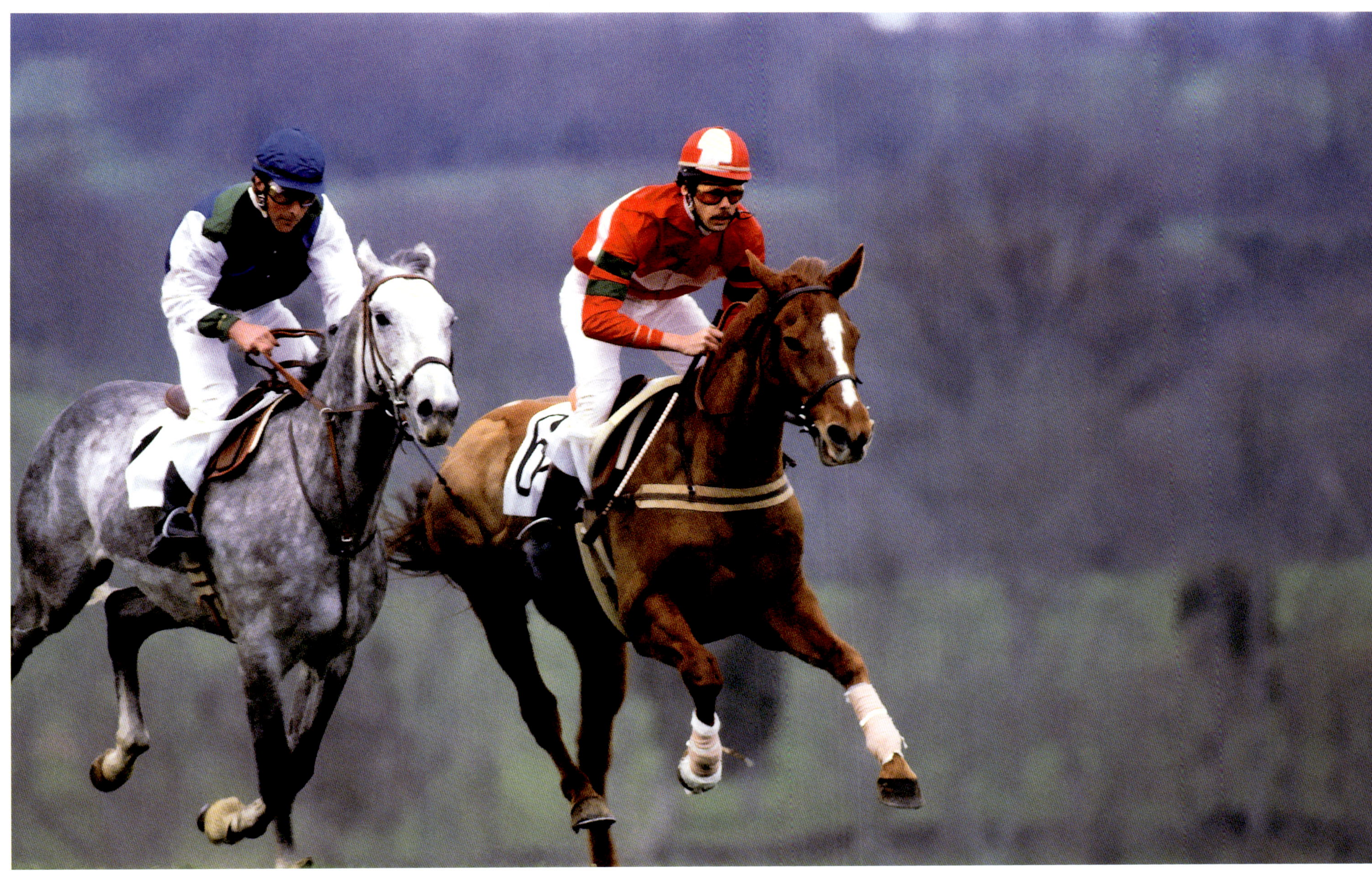

CROSS-COUNTRY STEEPLECHASE, CLARK COUNTY

The open pastures covering the hills along the Kentucky River in Clark County afford ideal conditions for long steeplechase competitions. Though beautiful to behold, much of this land is considered rough, crisscrossed by small streams and rock fences. In the months leading up to the race, a course is laid out with the cooperation of local landowners, who fence their animals and open critical gates on the day of the event. The annual race is sponsored by the Iroquois Hunt Club, which was established in 1880.

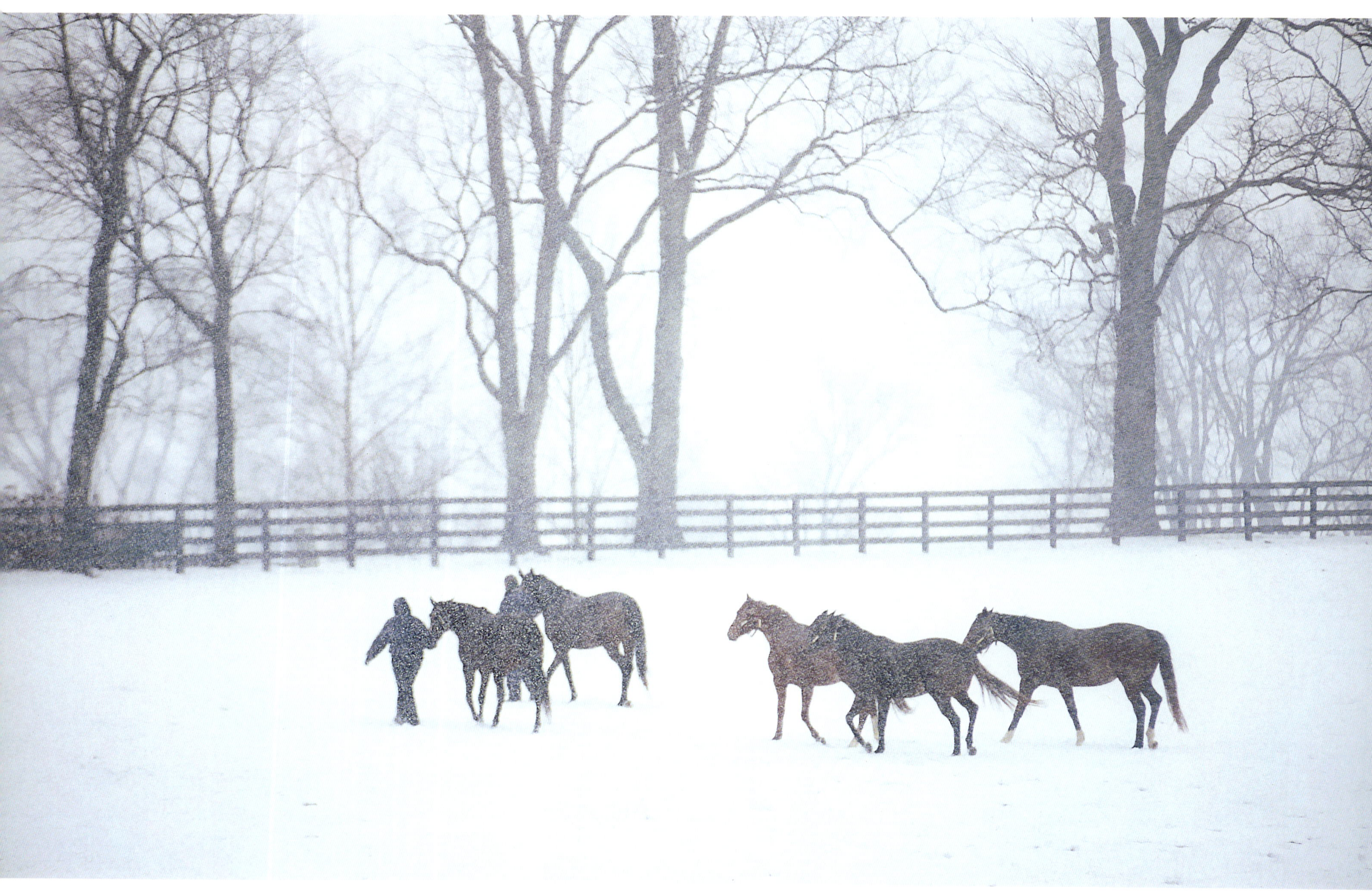

BRINGING IN THE MARES IN WINTER

There is little time for rest in the horse business. Like children, horses have to be looked after twenty-four hours a day. Unless winter storms are extremely severe, they rarely interfere with the scheduled routine. In a snowy field off Steele Road in Woodford County, Thoroughbred mares are led to their stables after a night in the paddock. Such has been the scene for nearly 200 years in the Kentucky Bluegrass.

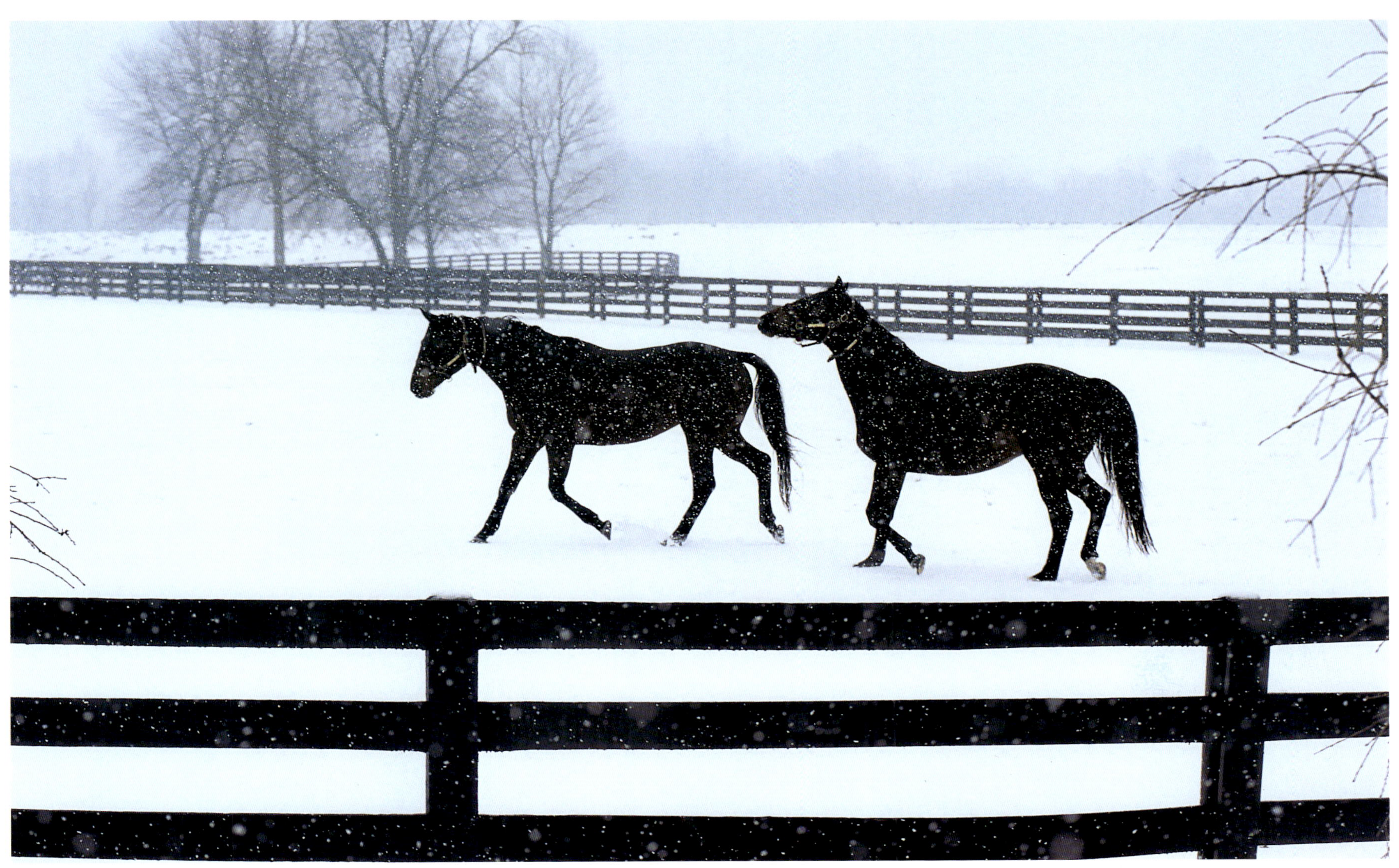

MARES PRANCING IN WINTER, RUSSELL CAVE ROAD

Horses seem to enjoy a good snowfall, which breaks the boredom of standing around in barren winter fields. At least for a time, the new snow provides a distraction, and a drive in the country bears witness to horseplay.

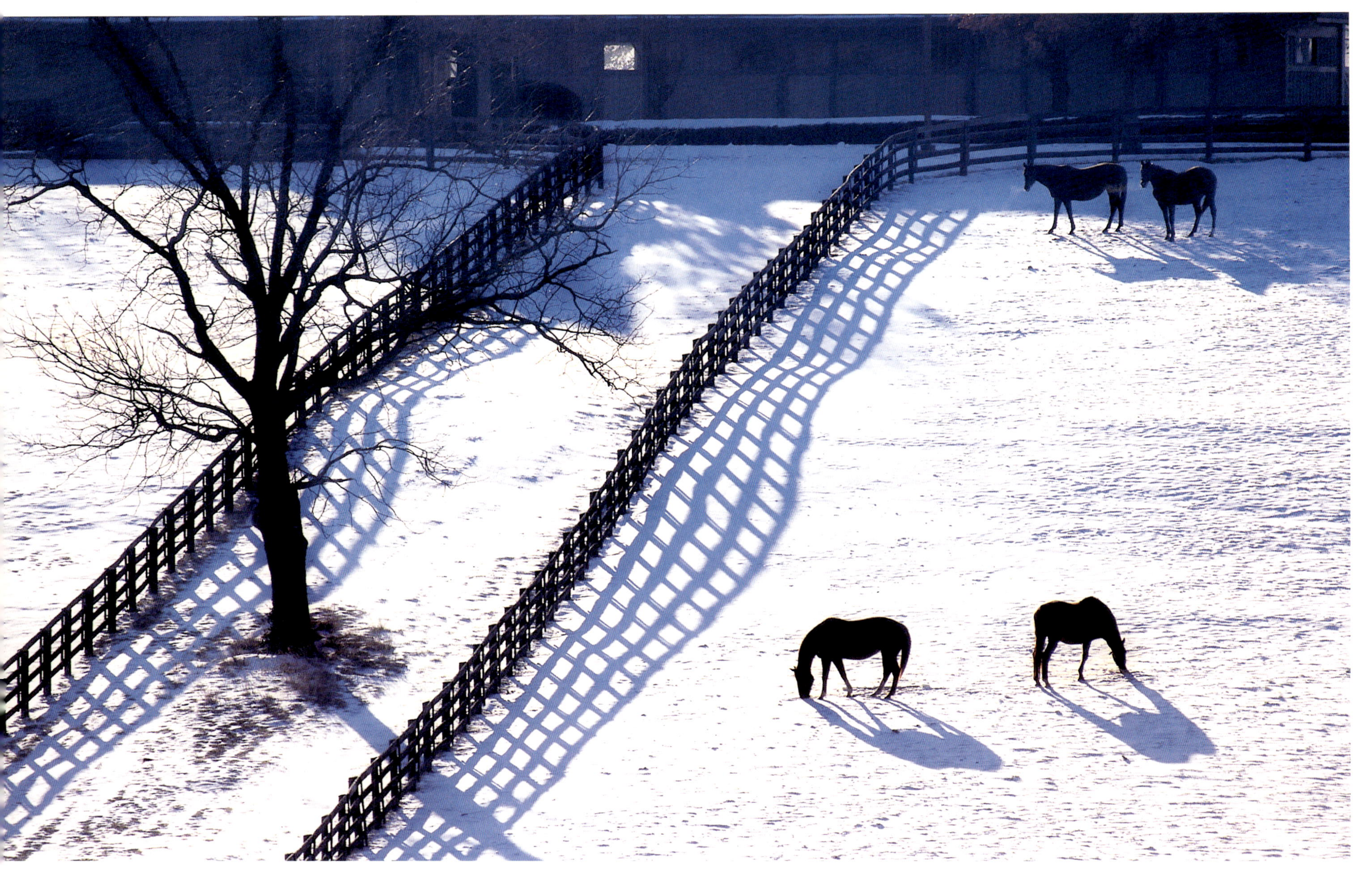

MARES GRAZING IN WINTER, GRASSY SPRINGS PIKE

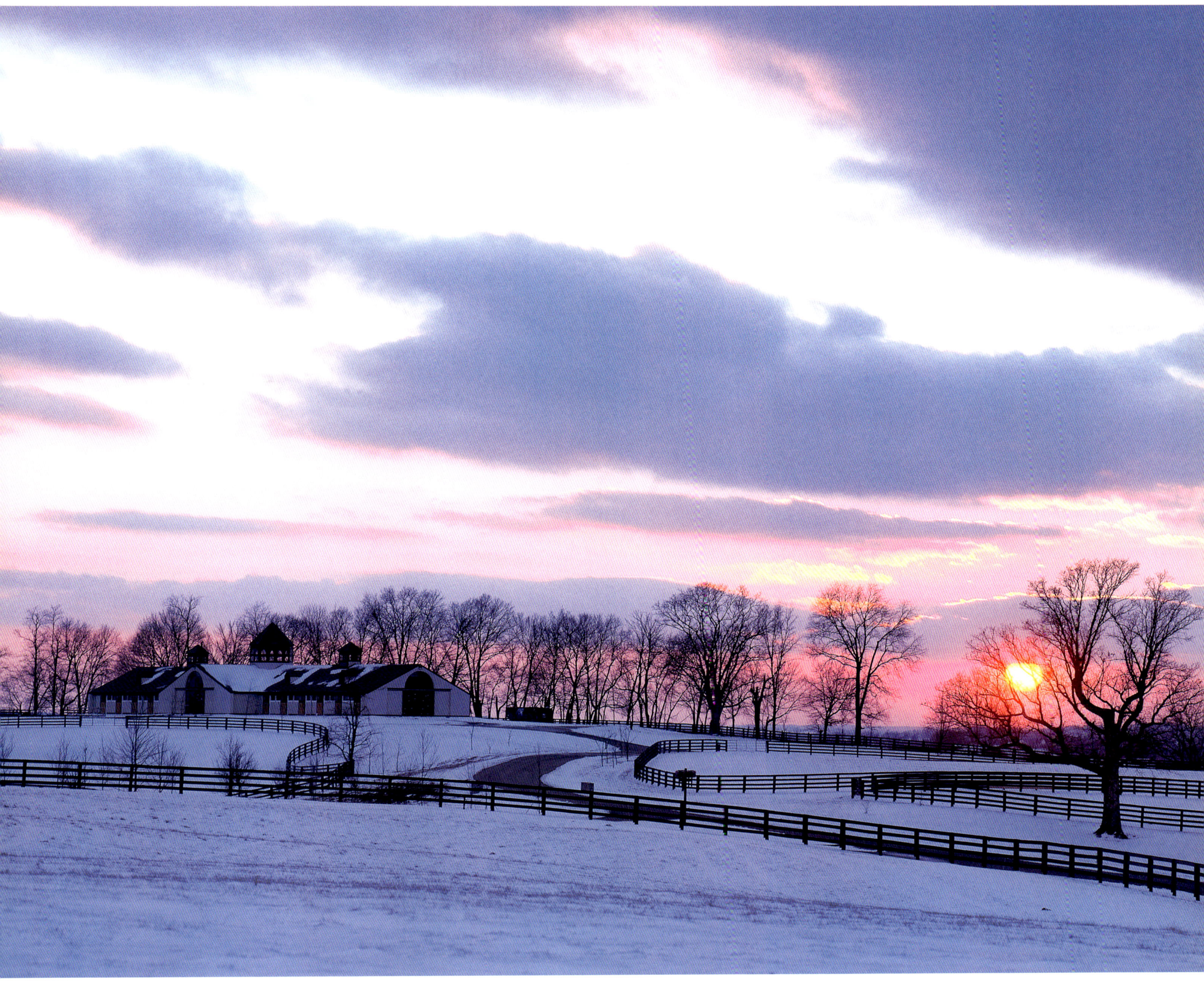

BLUEGRASS SUNSET

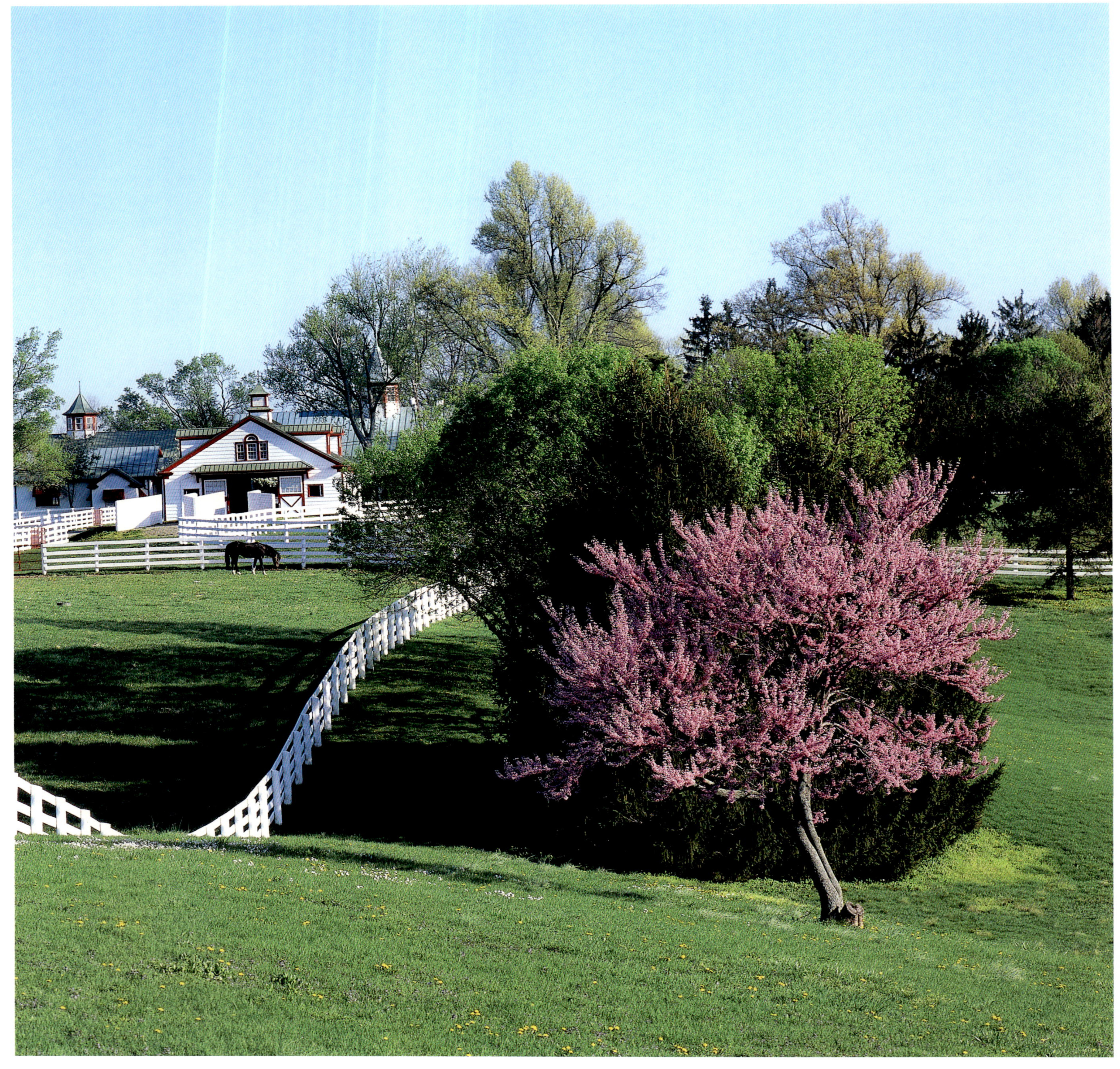

CALUMET IN SPRING FROM VERSAILLES ROAD

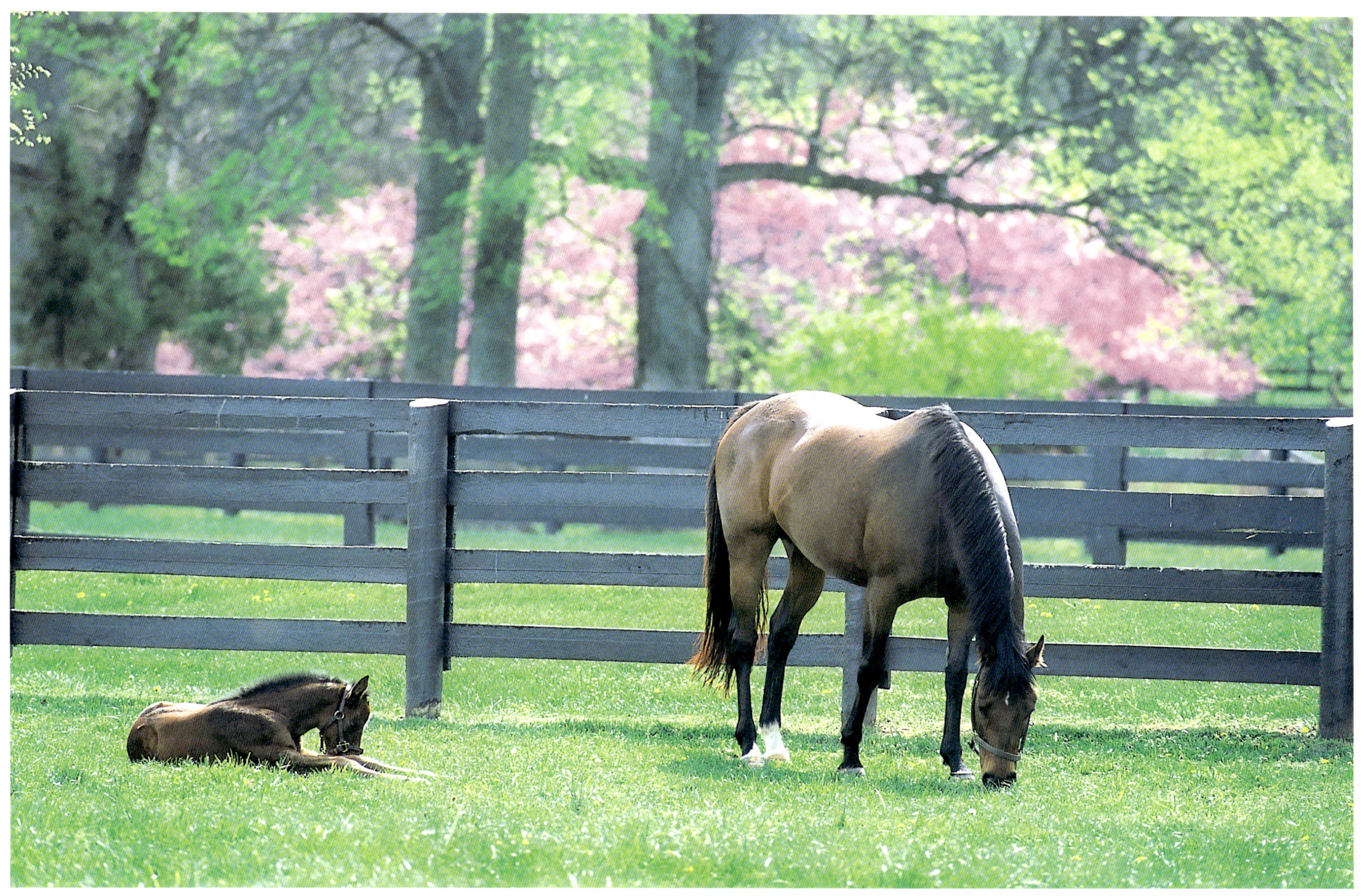

MARE AND FOAL WITH REDBUDS

In the Bluegrass, the brilliant redbud announces the arrival of spring. Kentucky's climate is perfect for this beautiful, hardy, fast-growing tree. The redbud can and does grow anywhere its seeds land, including in pastures, along fencerows, and in open woodlands, where it is the first color to appear after a dreary winter. Here, mare and foal luxuriate in the warm spring air.

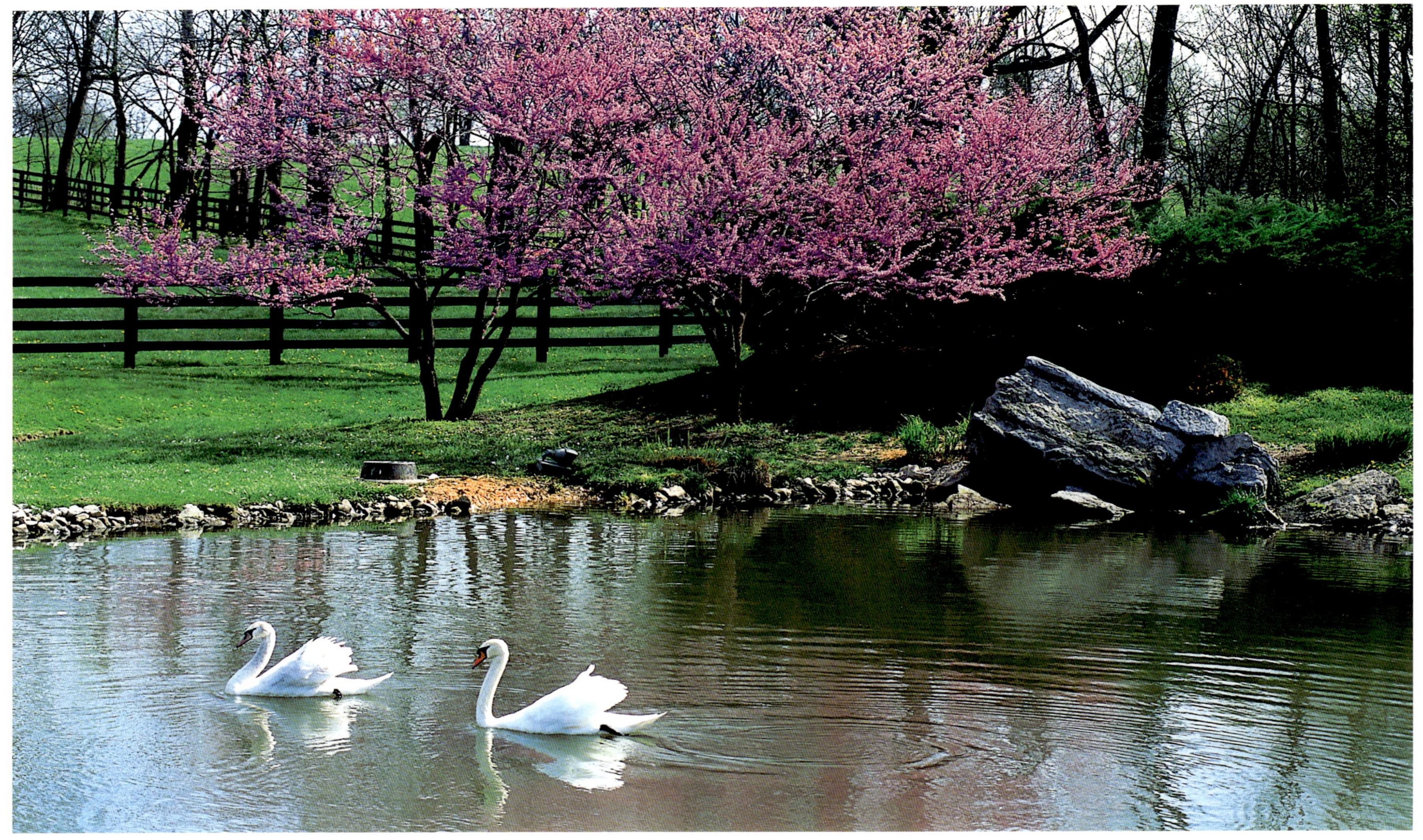

SWANS AND REDBUDS

These resident swans enjoy their private pond on a Bluegrass horse farm. Because of Kentucky's moderate winter temperatures, ponds and streams usually remain ice free, a requirement for the survival of waterfowl. As a result, many species make the Bluegrass State their permanent home. Tens of thousands of Canada geese don't bother migrating anymore, finding plenty of grass and corn—the staples of their diet.

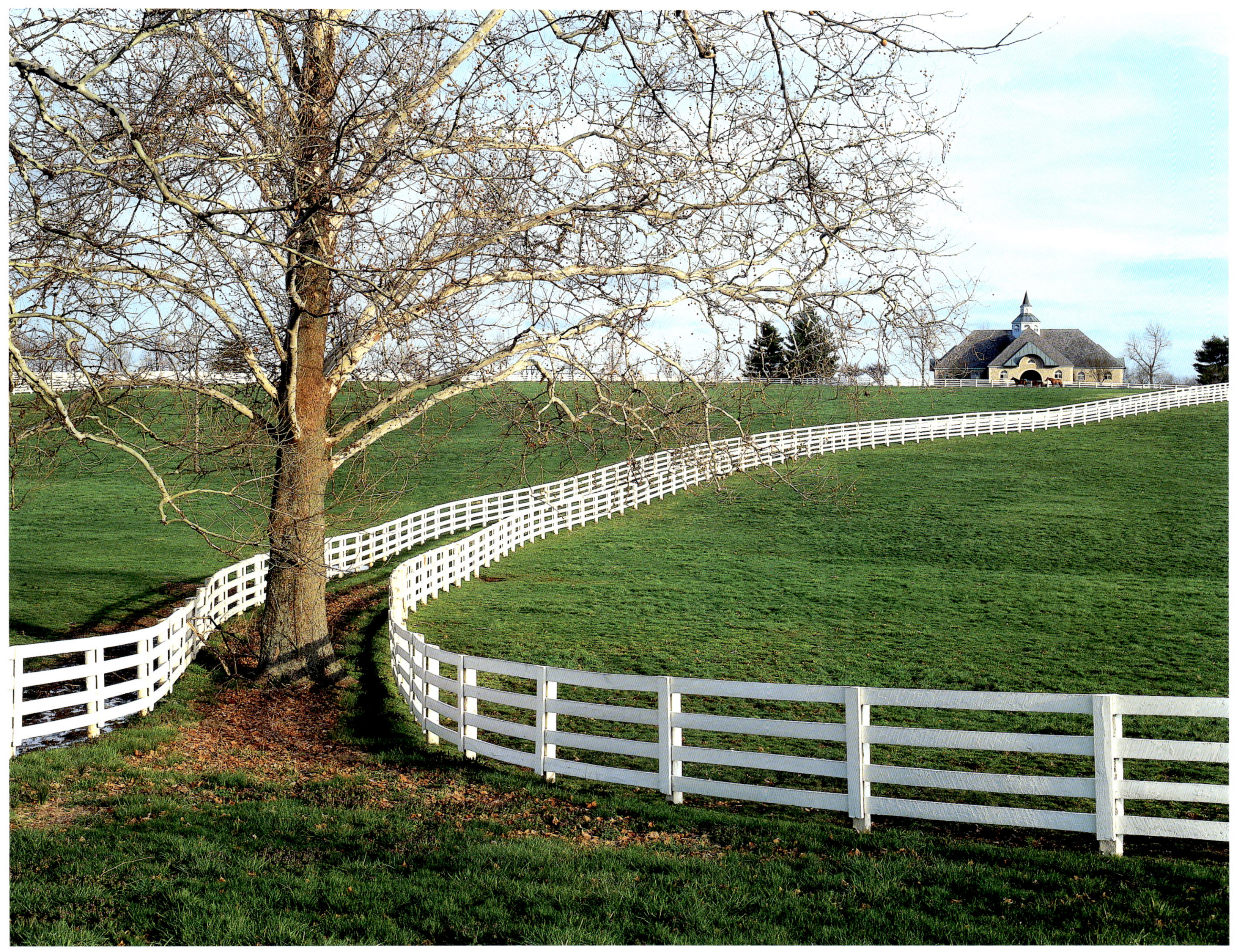

DONAMIRE FARM

Form and function matter when it comes to designing a horse farm. Considerations include the lay of the land, practical day-to-day operations, and aesthetics. At the Donamire Farm along the Old Frankfort Pike, all the barns and buildings are constructed of native stone, making it one of the most visually spectacular horse farms in the Bluegrass.

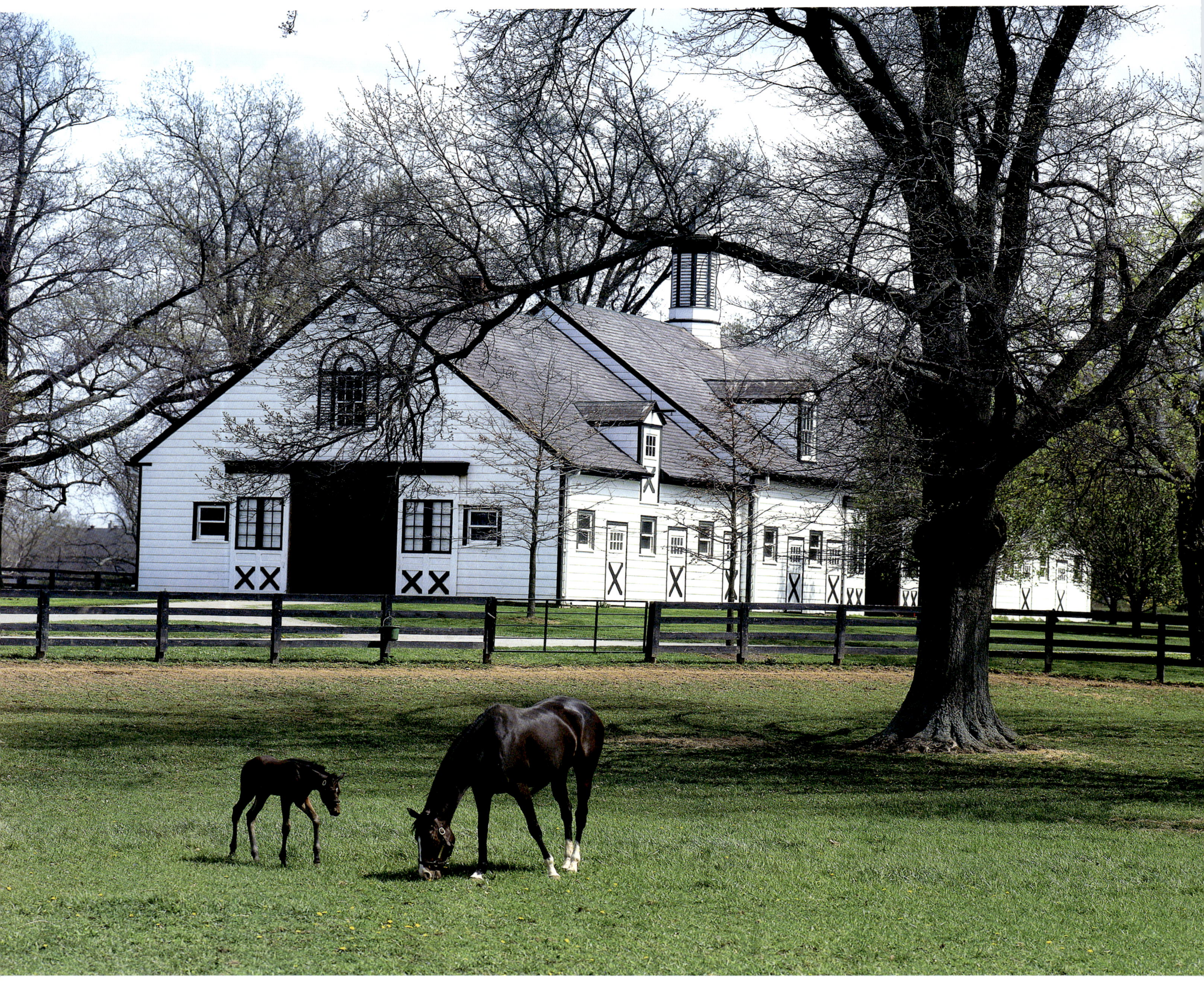

MARE AND NEWBORN FOAL ALONG KENNY LANE

Within a day or two of birth, most foals and mares are put out to pasture for part of the day. After an eleven-month gestation period, the mares seem glad to be free of the burden of carrying their foals, which can weigh up to 135 pounds at birth. Bonded together, mare and foal will be at each other's side during the four- to six-month nursing period. Healthy broodmares with good pedigrees are bred again and again, often up to age fifteen or twenty.

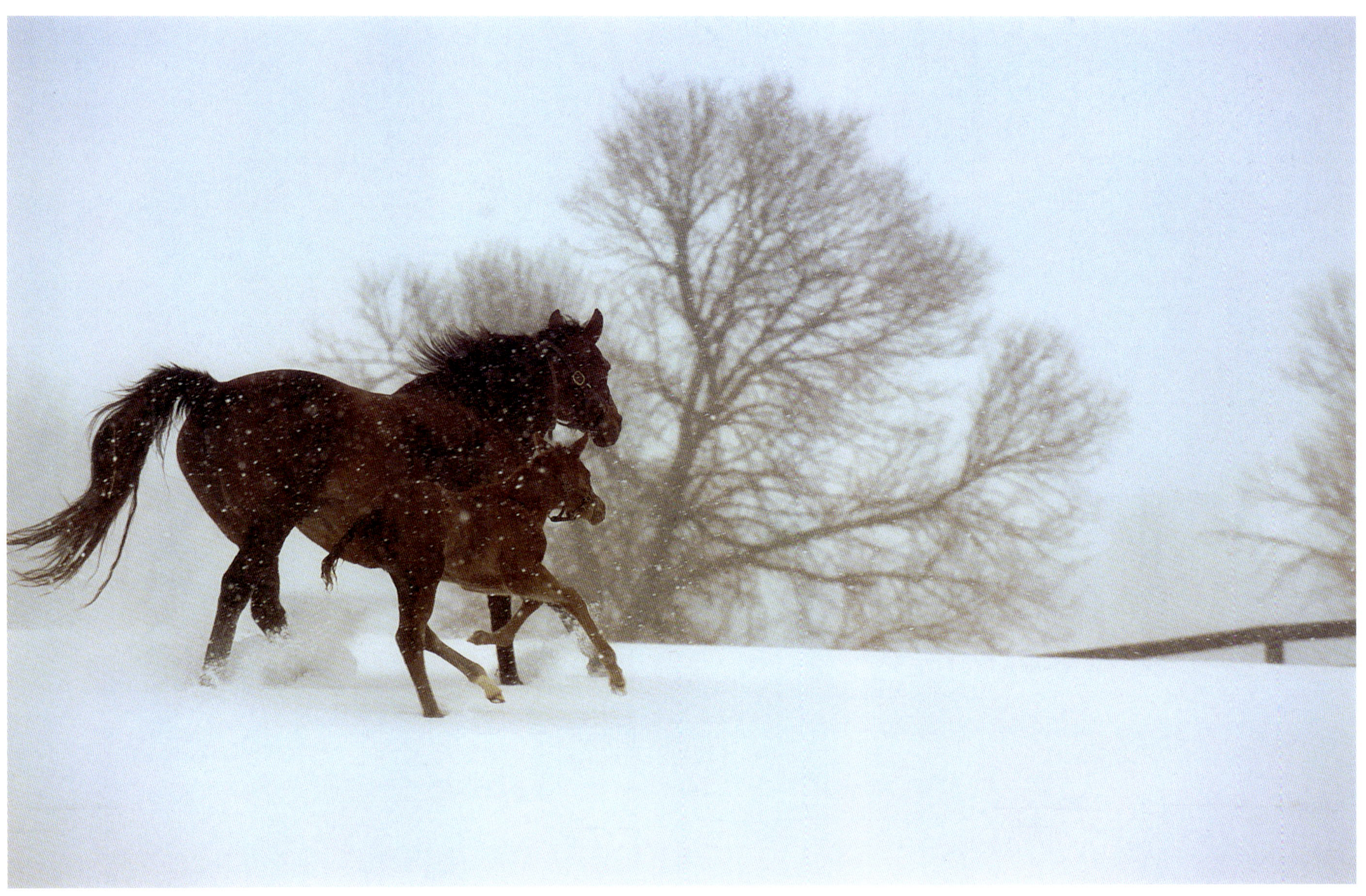

FOAL AND MARE RUNNING IN WINTER

In 1775, Daniel Boone and a small party of pioneers crossed the Cumberland Gap and established Fort Boonesborough on the Kentucky River near present-day Lexington. Just twenty-two years later, Benjamin Wharton brought a Thoroughbred named Blaze through that same gap from Virginia to Scott County and advertised his stud fee ($12) in the *Kentucky Gazette* on 9 December 1797. Part of the advertisement read: "BLAZE is a beautiful bay, near seventeen hands high, nicely marked, of uncommon great strength and activity; his figure is given up to be unexceptionable."

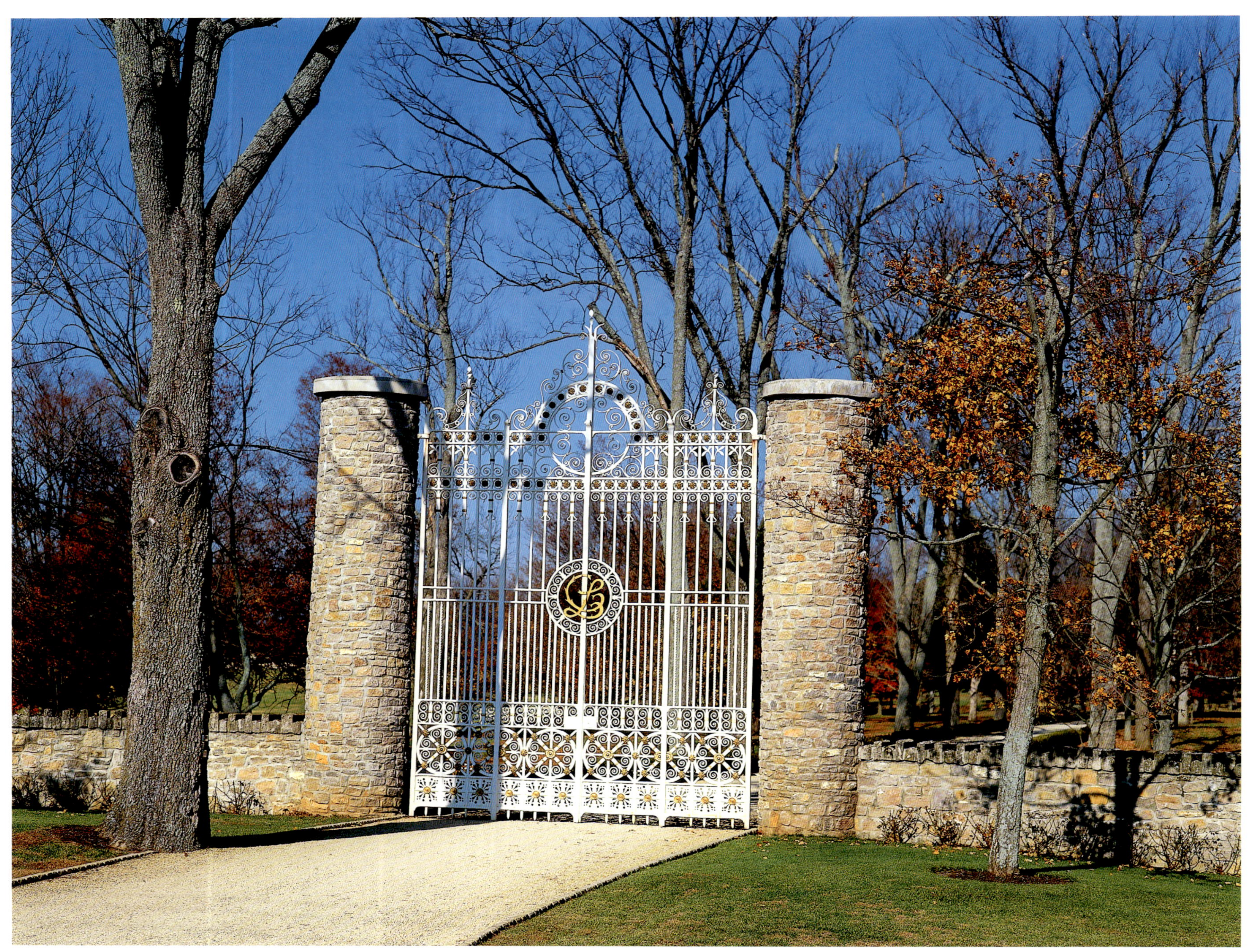

FARM GATE ALONG IRON WORKS PIKE

While most horse farms have modest signs and functional gates at their entrances, there is an occasional show of opulence. Some farms spare no cost when it comes to their front doors. This gate at the Castleton Lyons complex on the Iron Works Pike in Fayette County is such an example.

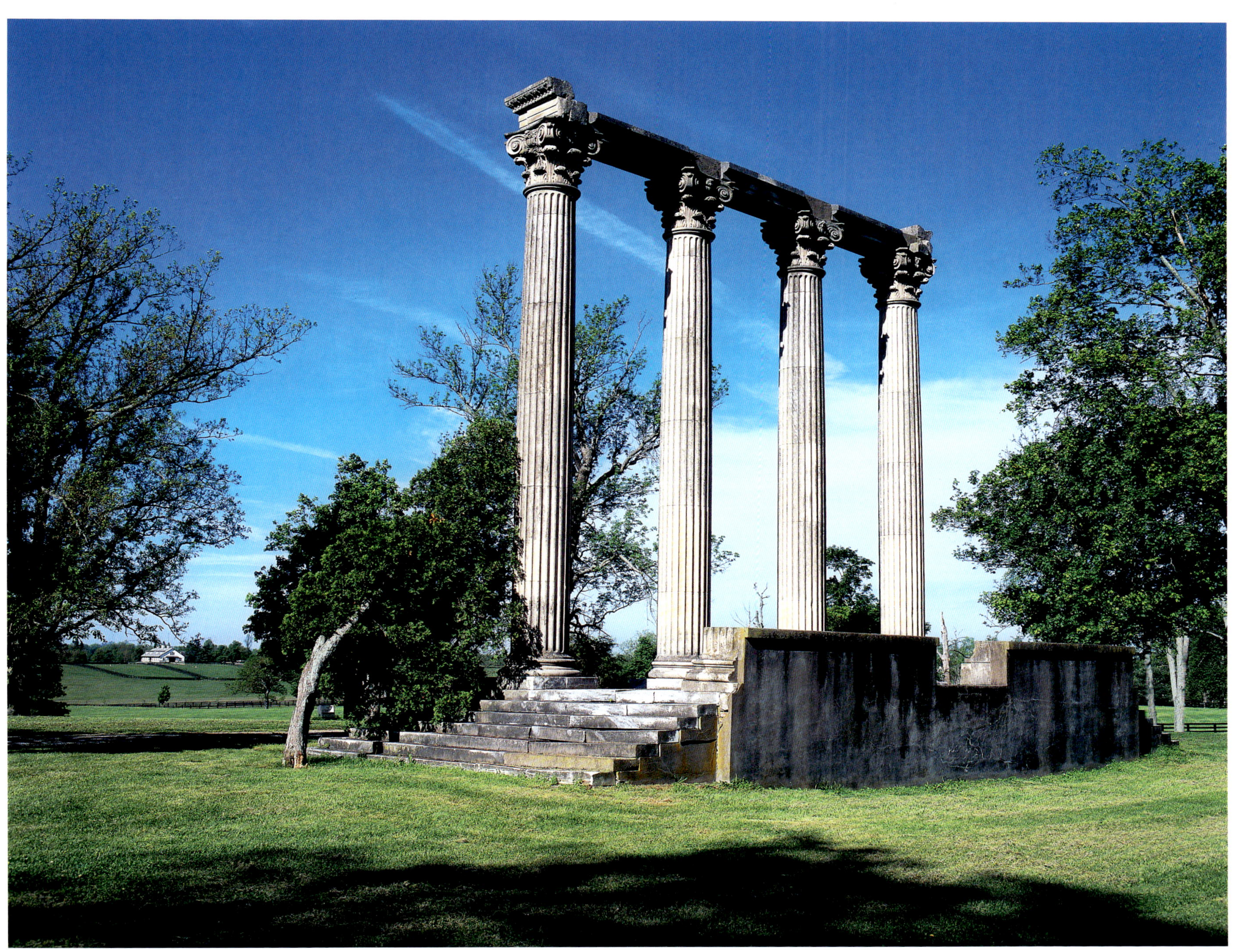

COLUMNS OF GREEN HILLS MANSION, ELMENDORF FARM

These imposing columns are all that remain of the forty-room Green Hills mansion, built in 1897 by horseman James Ben Ali Haggin on his Elmendorf Farm, located along Paris Pike north of Lexington. The marble mansion cost $1 million—a prohibitive sum at the time. Having made a fortune in gold and silver mines in the West, Haggin proceeded to accumulate 8,000 acres of land that he added to the Elmendorf holdings. At one time, the farm had more than 300 mares and bred many notable stakes winners. After Haggins's death, the mansion and a portion of the original Elmendorf Farm were purchased by Joseph E. Widener, who continued the farm's rich tradition of Thoroughbred excellence. The mansion was later razed by Widener.

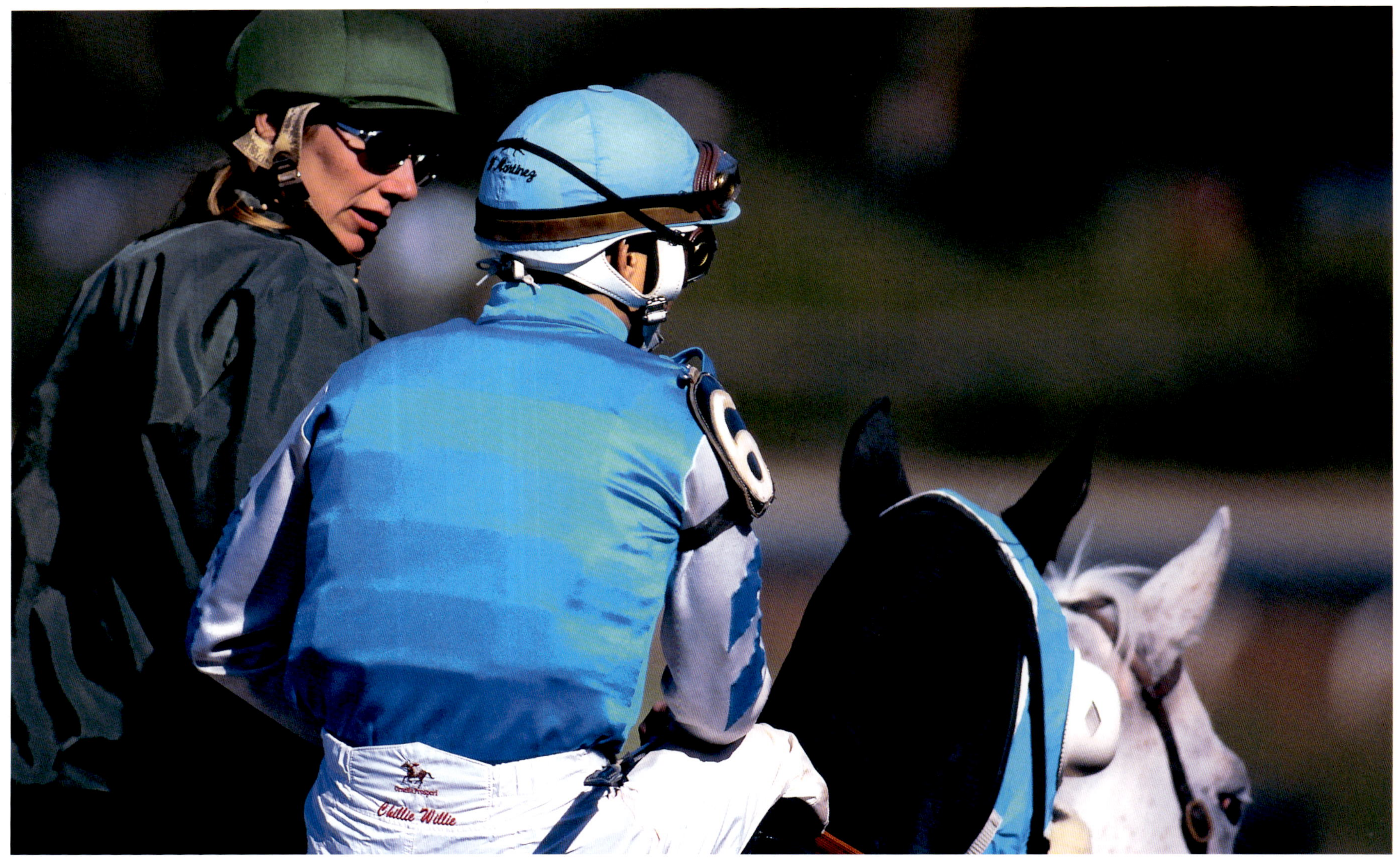

LEAD PONY AND JOCKEY AT KEENELAND

A lead pony rider chats with No. 6 as she escorts him and his mount to the post before a race at Keeneland. The practice of using lead ponies (actually horses) is believed to settle and relax the runners in the minutes prior to entering the starting gate. Some jockeys stay with their lead ponies during the procession, while others prefer to trot off for some gentle last-minute exercise.

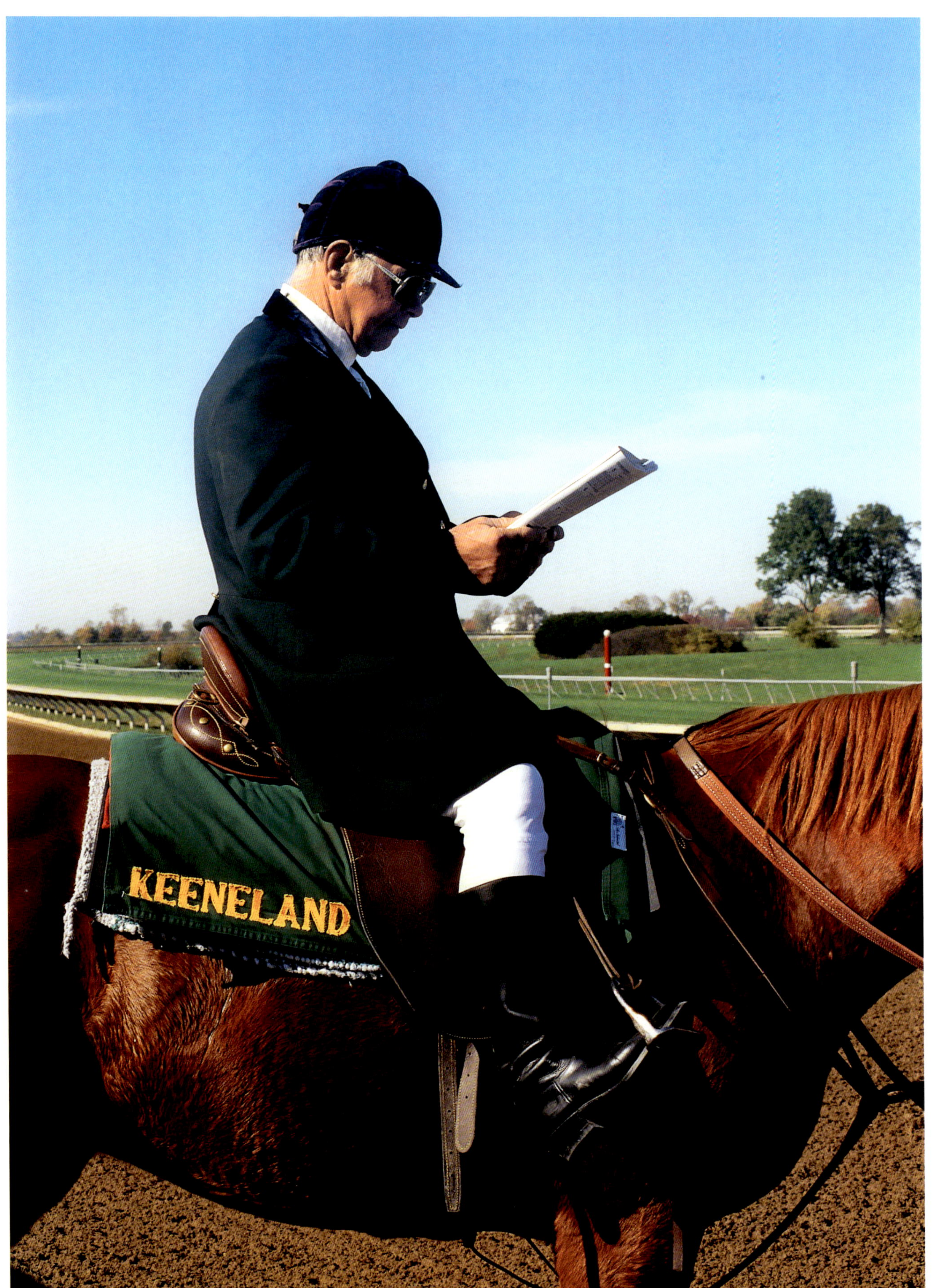

BETWEEN RACES

At the Keeneland Race Course, a track official called an outrider checks his program while waiting for the start of the next race. His job includes leading the parade to the post, making sure that each race starts on time, and assisting horses and jockeys in the event of an accident during a race. Outriders are accomplished horsemen who usually live in the area and return to work at Keeneland year after year for the love of horses and racing.

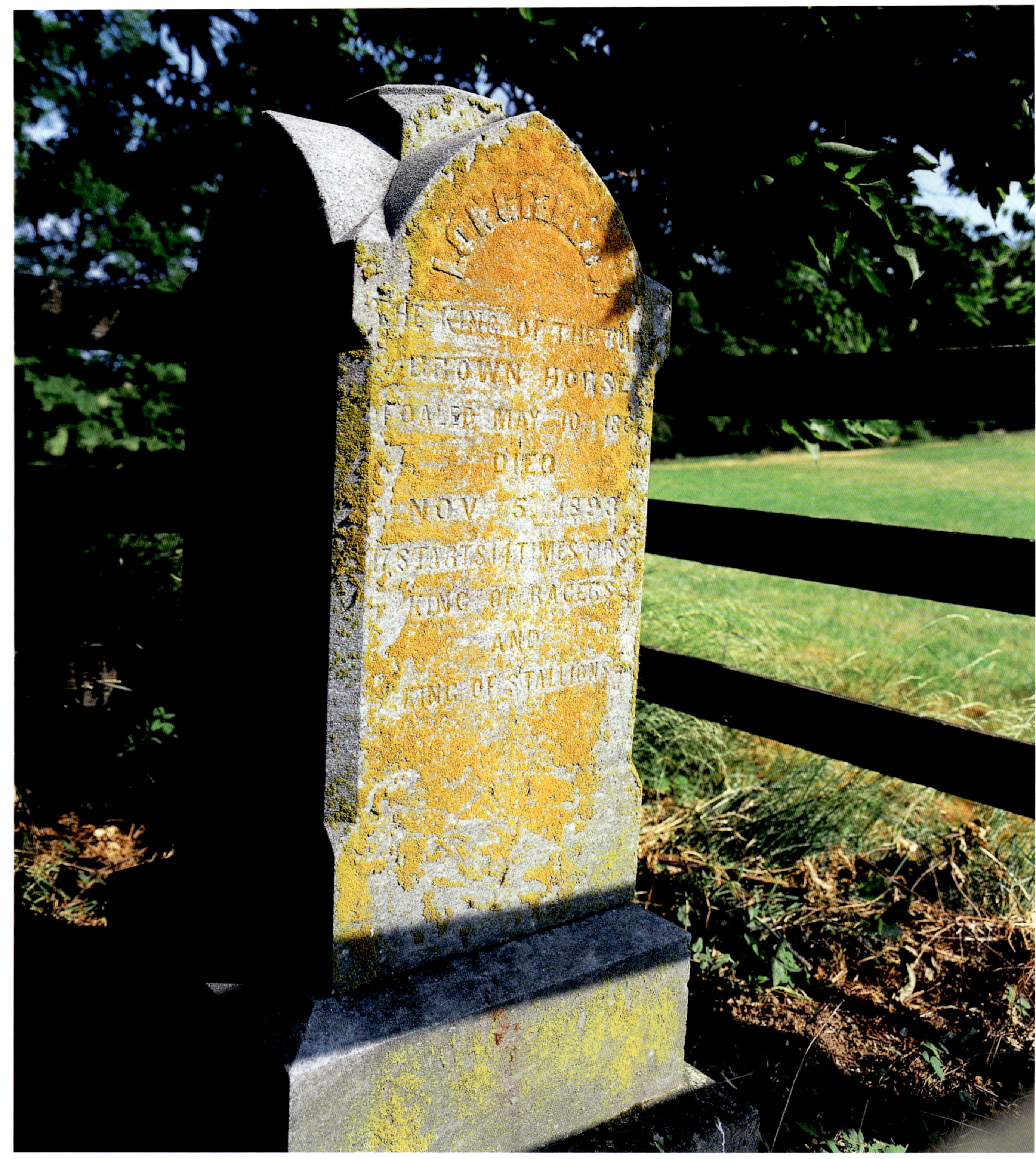

GRAVE OF LONGFELLOW

Longfellow was one of the most popular racers of the 1870s. While winning fourteen of his seventeen starts, the big brown colt defeated some of the best horses of his time, including Kingfisher, Harry Bassett, and Preakness. Longfellow was a son of Leamington, who stood at Bosque Bonita, the Woodford County stud farm of Confederate general Abe Buford. The grave rests next to that of Ten Broeck, another great racer of that period. The site was once part of Nantura Farm, owned by John Harper, the breeder of both horses. Although still called Nantura, it is no longer a horse farm.

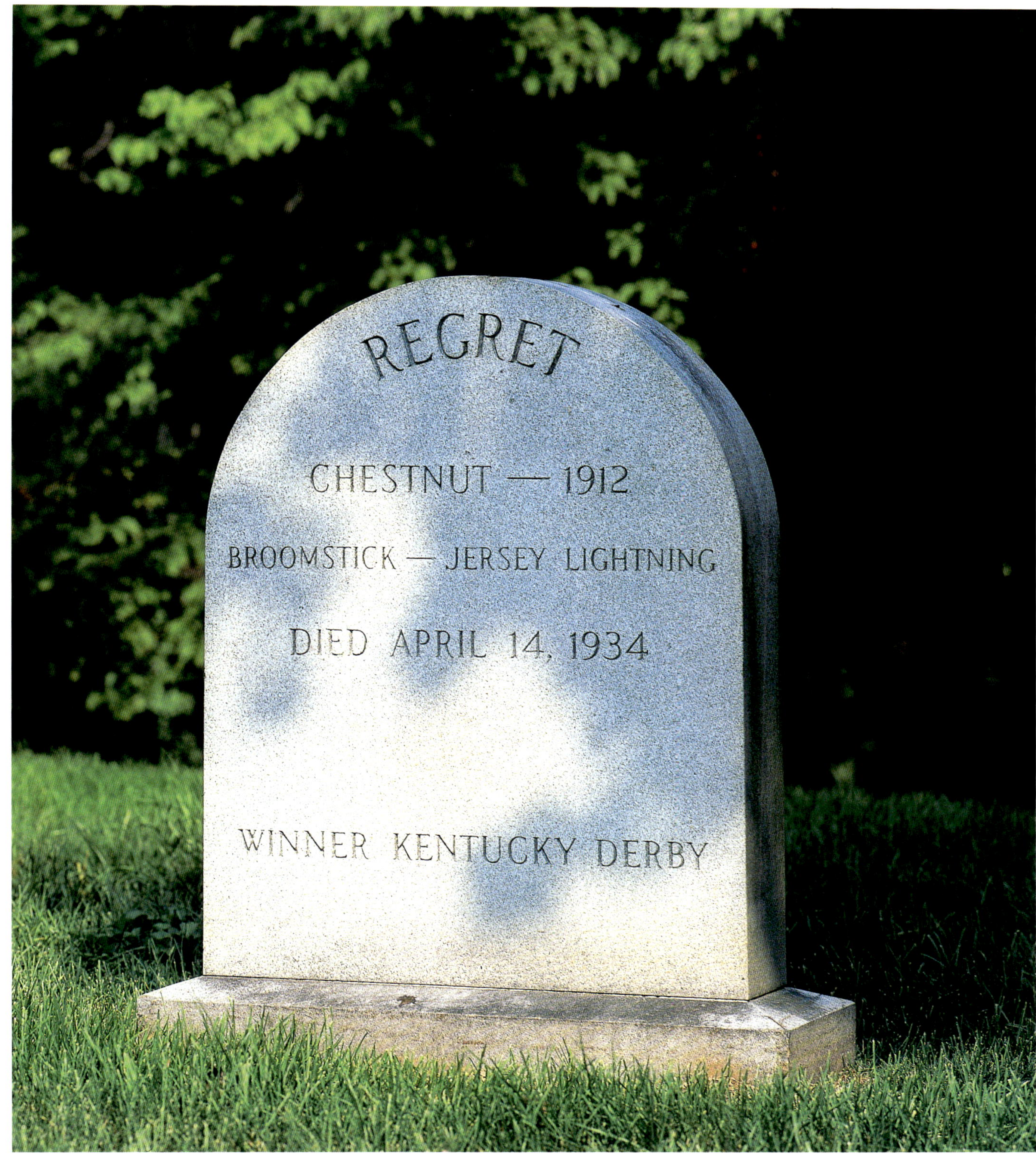

GRAVE OF REGRET, FIRST FILLY TO WIN THE KENTUCKY DERBY

Like many long-established horse farms in the Bluegrass, Gainesway Farm on the Paris Pike pays homage to past champions. On a hilltop overlooking green pastures are the graves and headstones of the horses that helped make the farm famous. Here, the headstone of Regret honors the first filly (one of only three) to win the Kentucky Derby (1915). This portion of Gainesway was owned by the Whitney family at the time of Regret's victory. Gainesway's former owner, John Gaines, was the driving force behind the establishment of the annual Breeders' Cup Races, where leading horses go head-to-head for big purses and greater fame. Gainesway is now owned by Graham Beck.

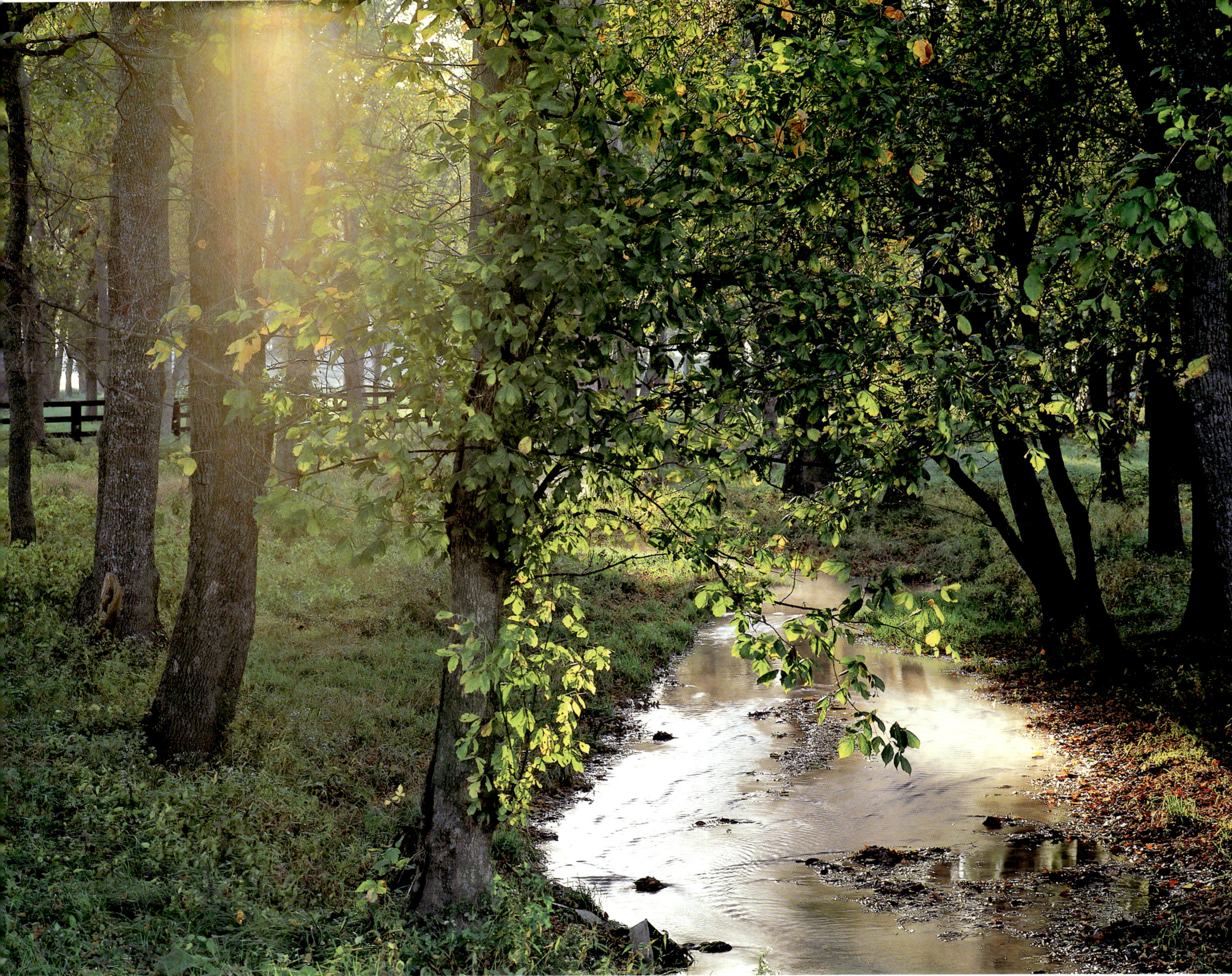

ELKHORN CREEK TRIBUTARY

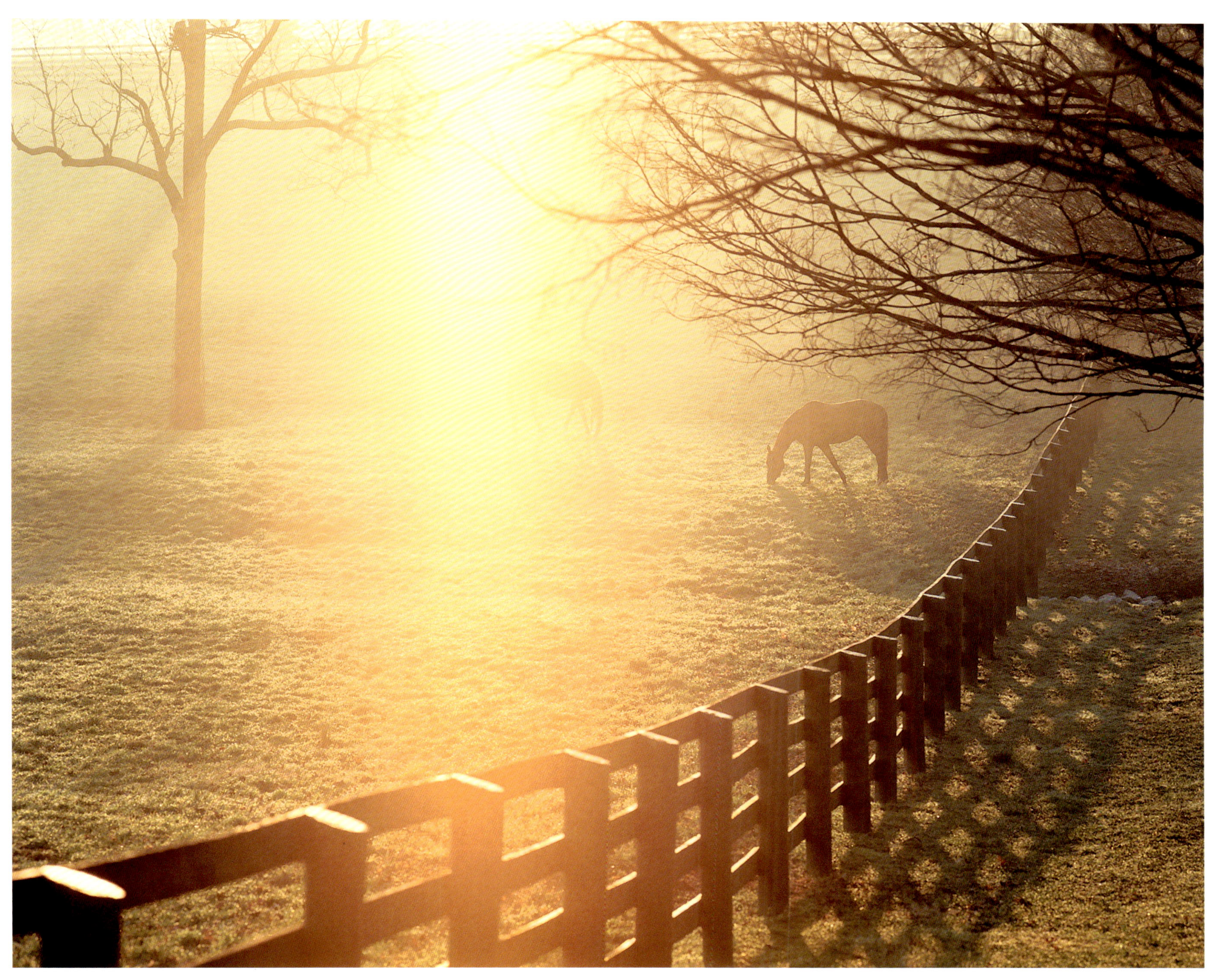

LIFTING FOG ALONG LEESBURG-NEWTOWN ROAD

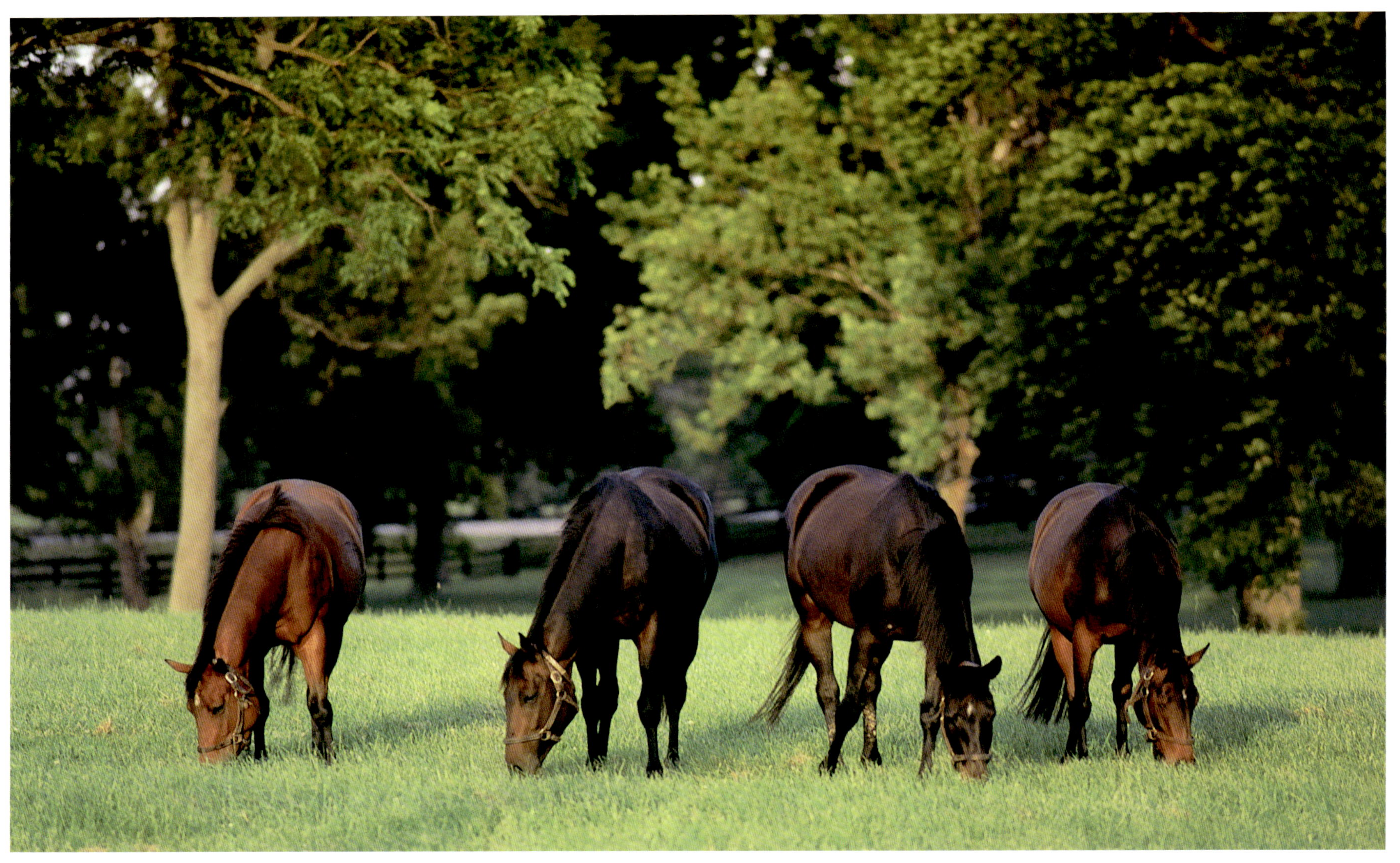

MARES IN SUMMER

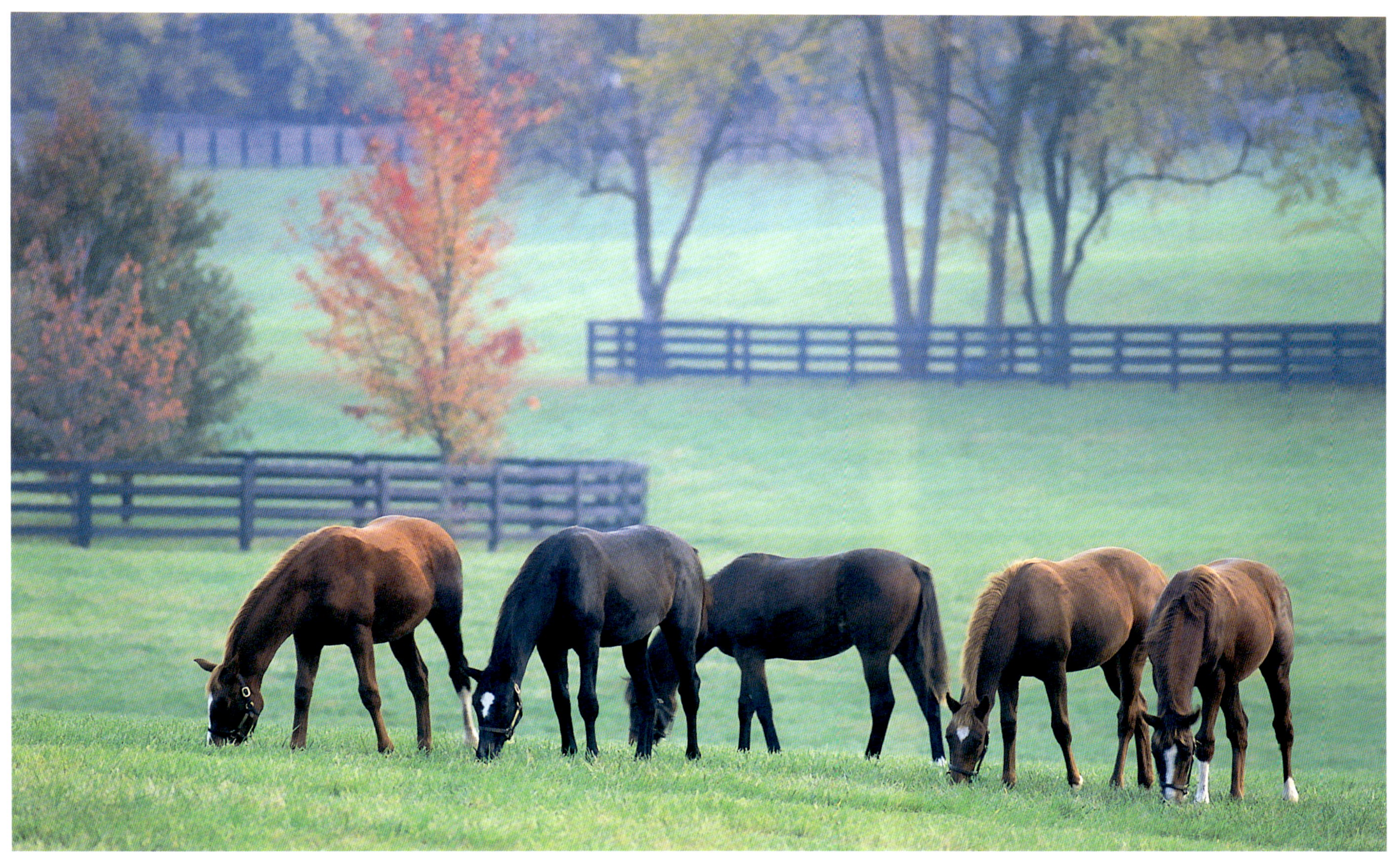

MARES IN AUTUMN

MARES AT FARES FARM

On any given day, there are tens of thousands of horses of all breeds grazing on central Kentucky grassland, like these mares crossing a rolling pasture. Early settlers of the Bluegrass recognized the richness and fertility of the soil, along with something else they couldn't quite explain. That something else is limestone, deposited over tens of millions of years. It is said that the limestone in the soil imparts nutrients to the grass that help build strong bones. Thus, the Bluegrass soil is at least partially responsible for producing some of the world's best horses.

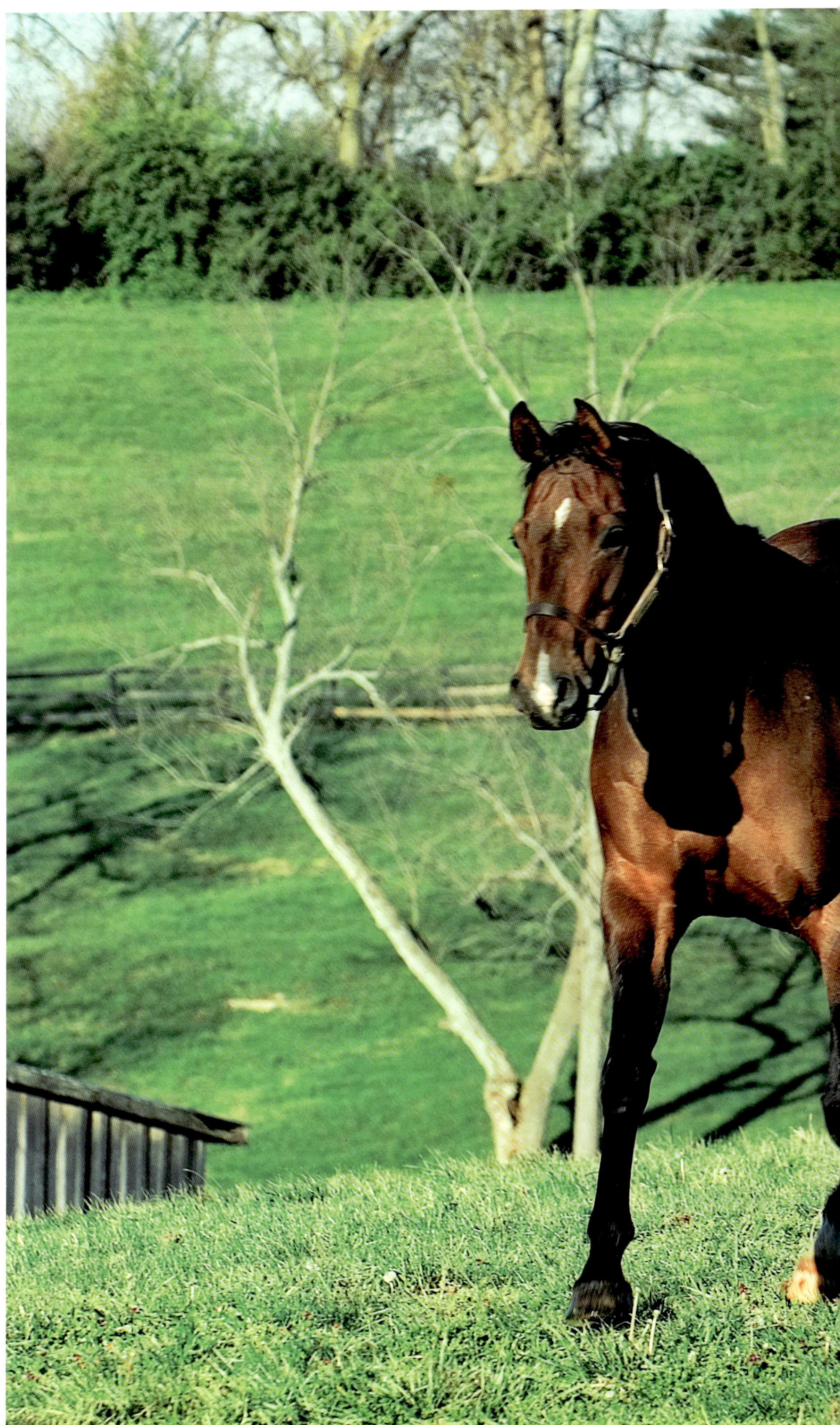

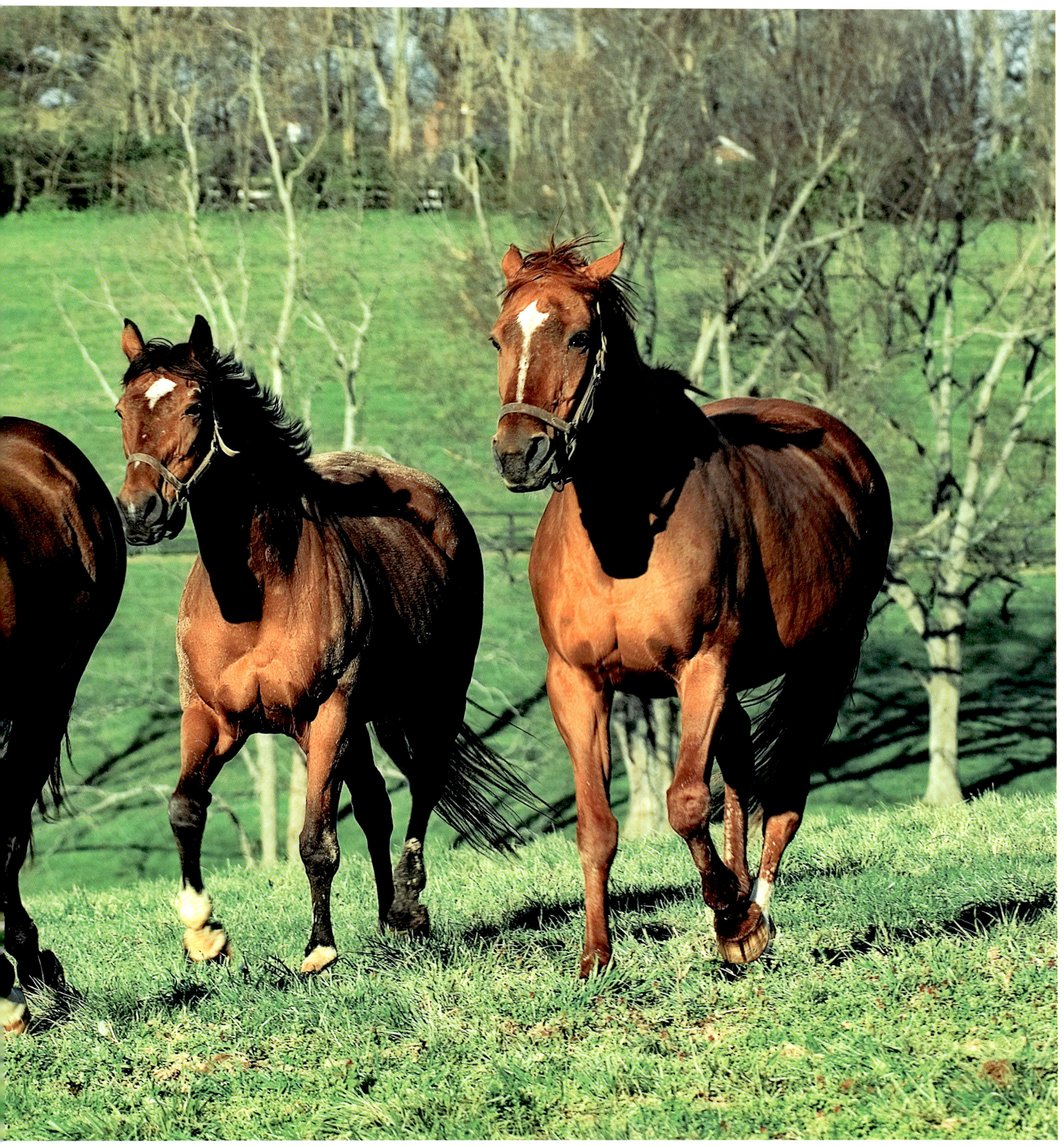

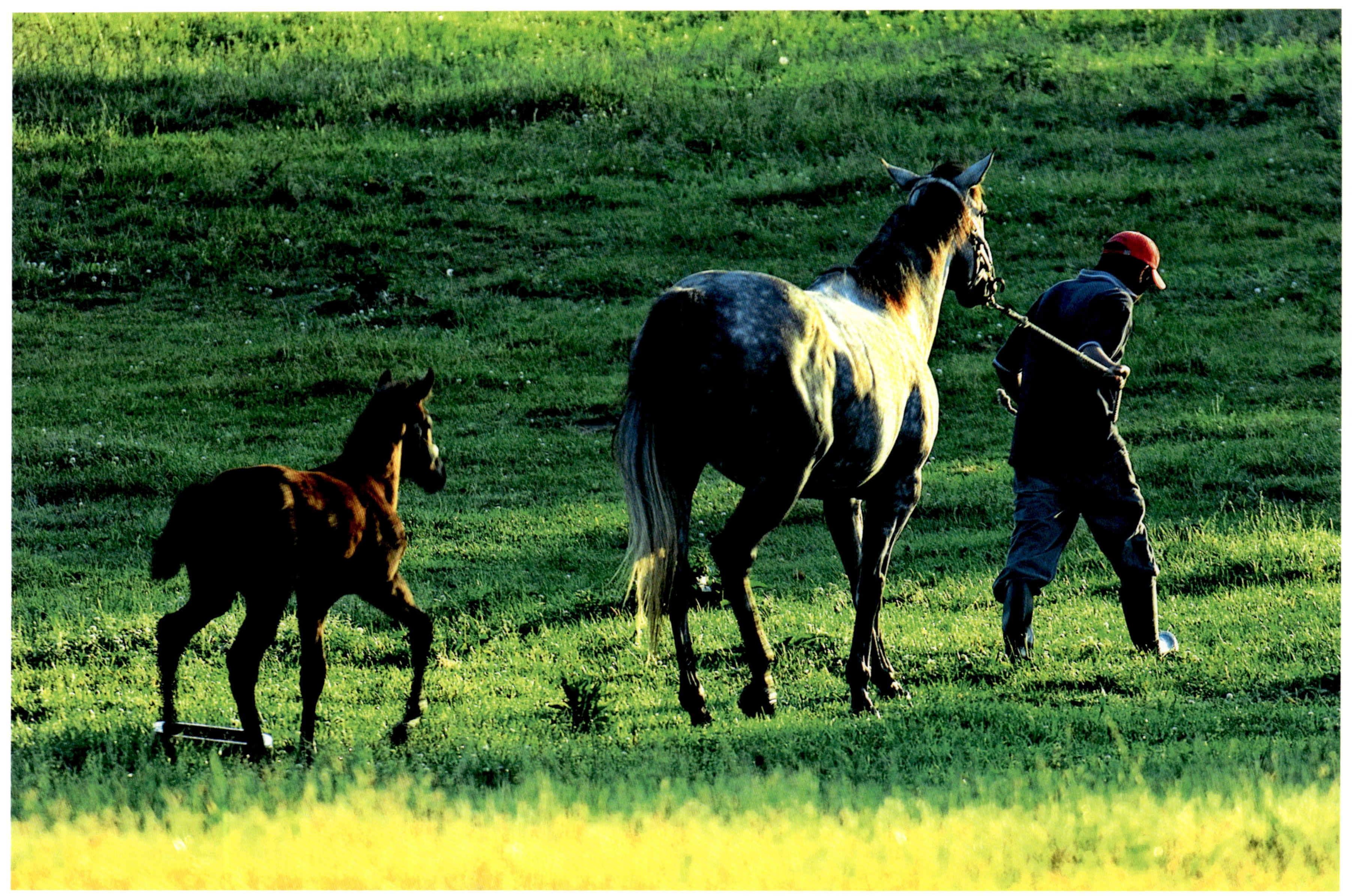

HEADED TO THE STABLE

Morning light filters through the trees bordering a paddock as a mare and her foal are led to the barn after a night in the fields. This healthy broodmare will nurture her foal for several months before the youngster is tested as a potential racer. The question of what to do with horses that are no longer needed for racing or breeding purposes is now being addressed. Many retired racers and broodmares are used for pleasure riding. Public and private organizations and individuals are establishing farms to care for retired racehorses. The Blackburn Correctional Complex near Lexington has instituted such a program for its inmates.

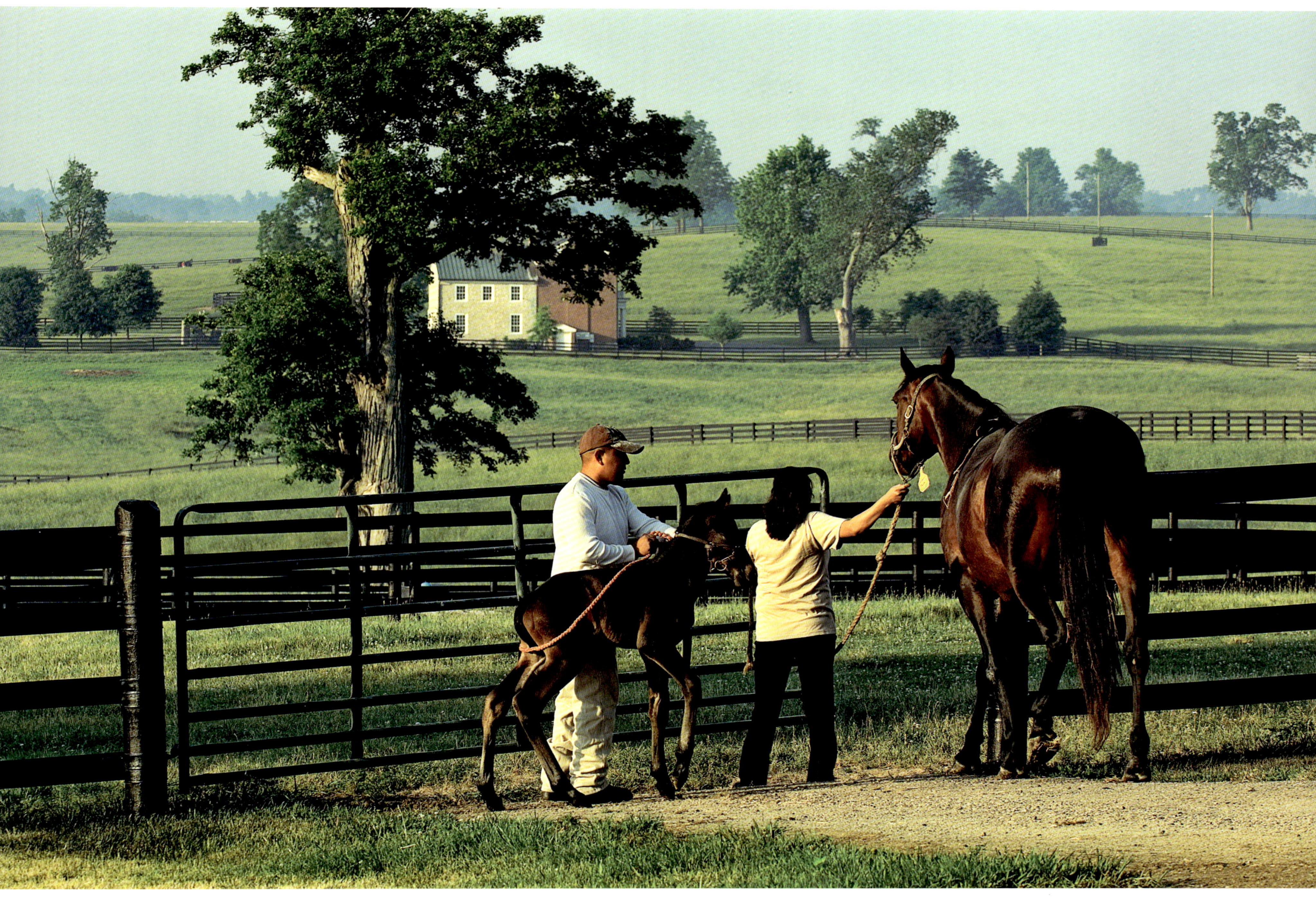

BEING LED TO THE PADDOCK

A Standardbred mare and her youngster are led to a paddock after a night in the stable on the Kentuckiana Farm in Scott County. Although the Thoroughbred has the highest profile of the many breeds of Bluegrass horses, the Standardbred is a strong second in the pastures of central Kentucky. Standardbreds are trotters and pacers; they race harnessed to sulkies piloted by drivers. Lexington's Red Mile is one of the premier harness racing tracks in the country. Many of the Standardbreds foaled in the Bluegrass are sold to interests in Europe, where harness racing has a large following.

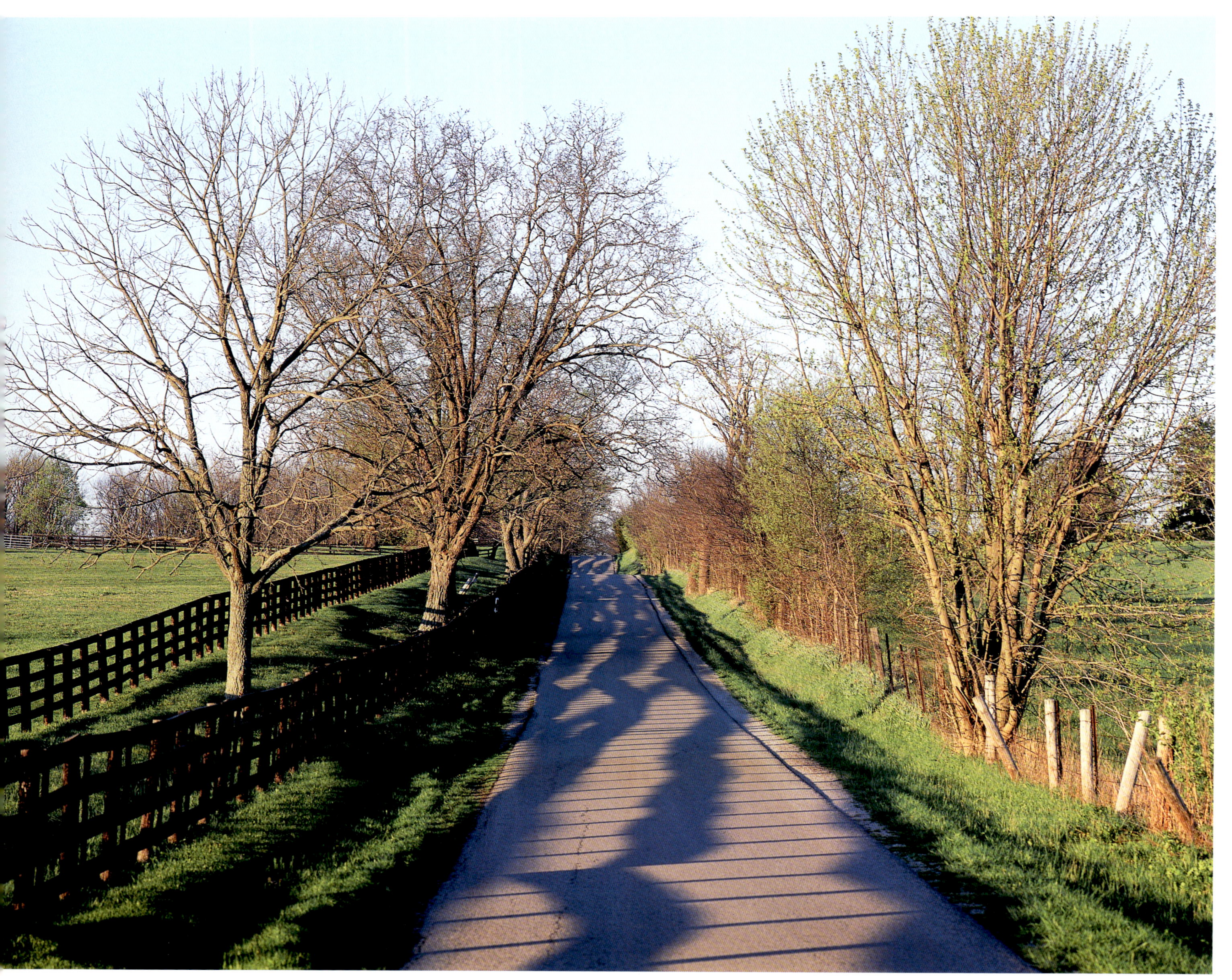

BACK ROAD IN EARLY SPRING

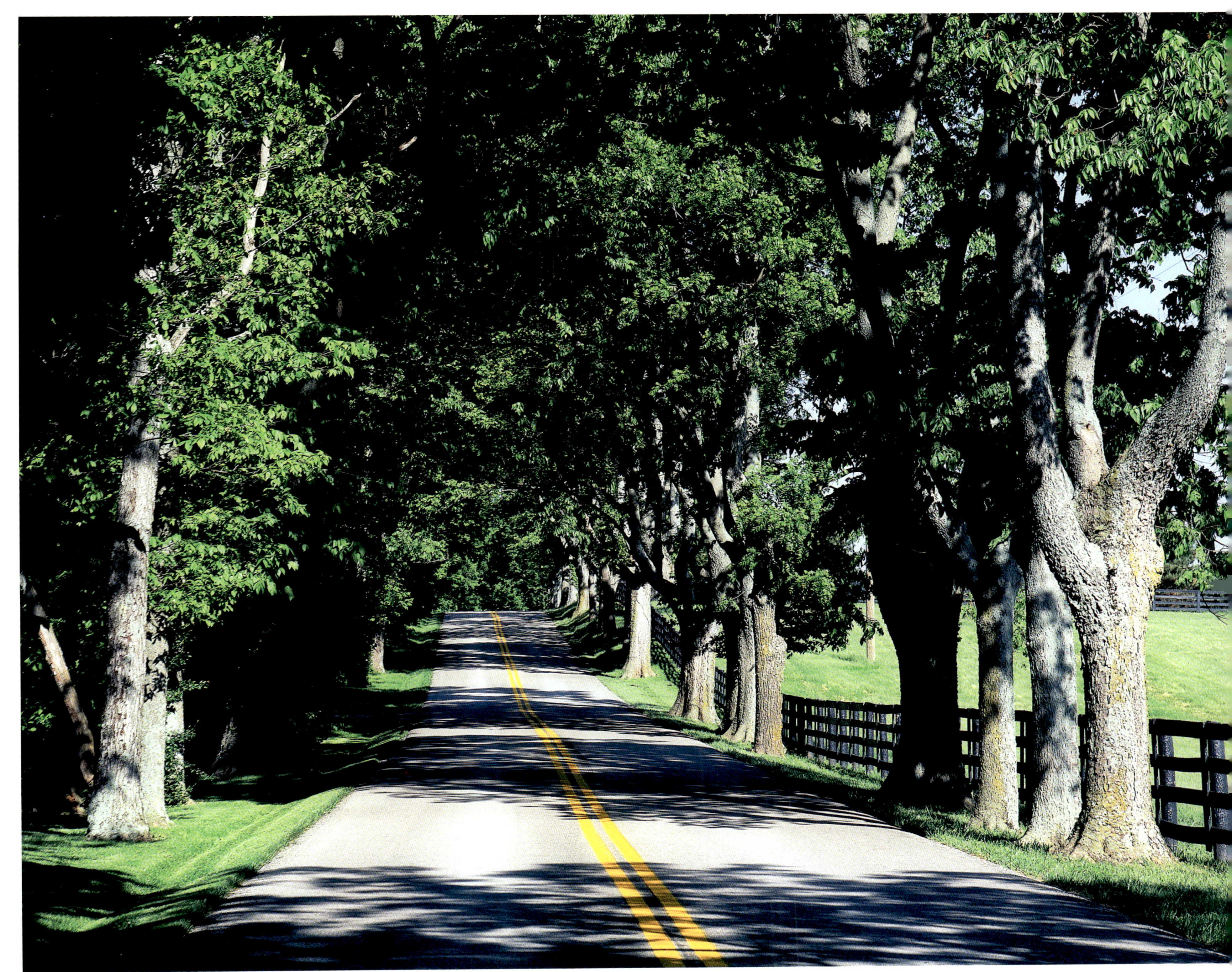

OLD FRANKFORT PIKE IN SUMMER

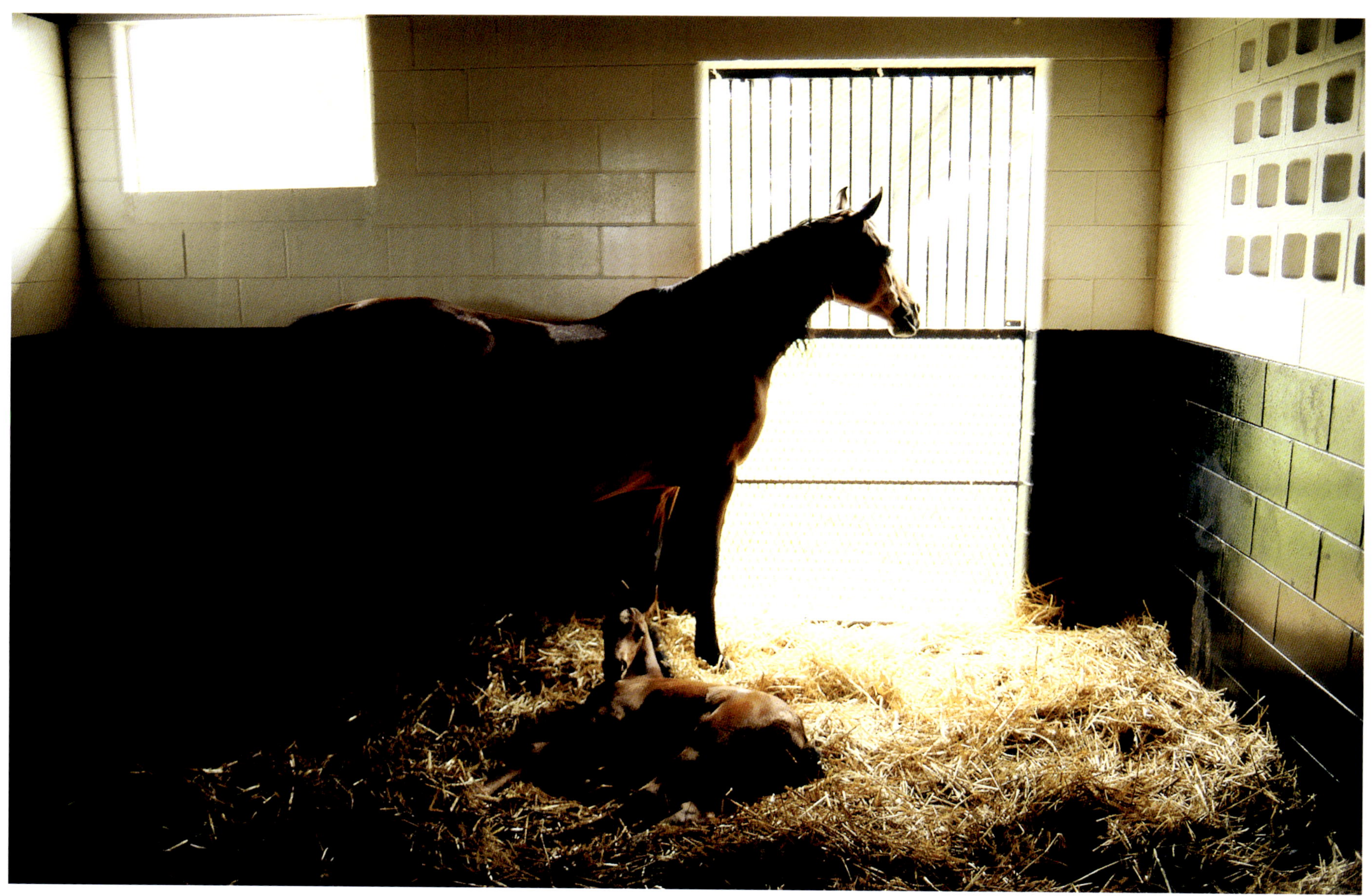

ARABIAN MARE AND NEWBORN FOAL

The Arabian is considered the oldest breed of horse. Having originated in the desert environment of North Africa and the Middle East, these horses are able to travel long distances in the harshest conditions. Many modern breeds can trace their bloodlines to the Arabian, including the Thoroughbred and, through further crossbreeding, the Standardbred.

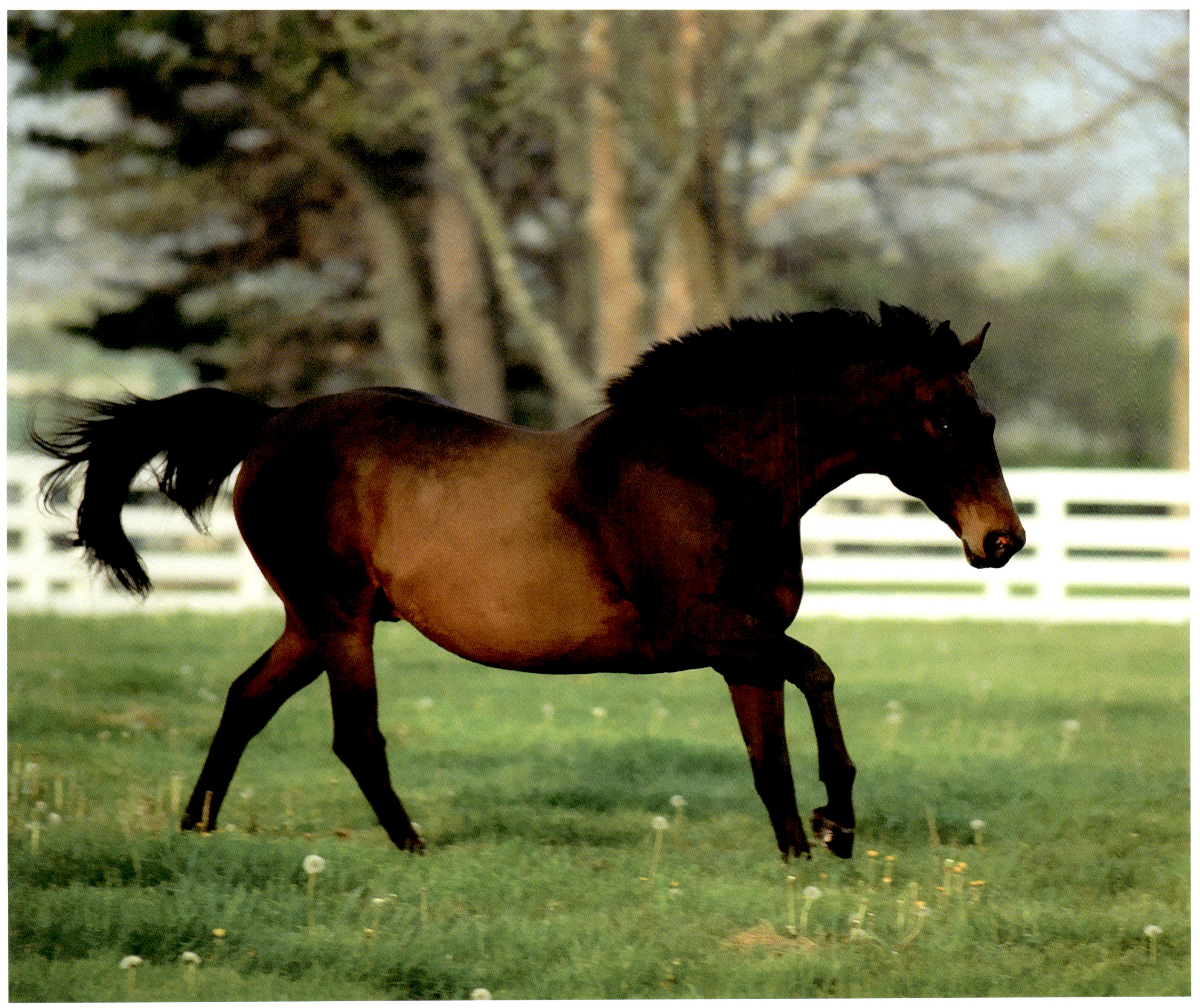

JOHN HENRY, THE LITTLE GELDING THAT WOULDN'T QUIT

By any reasonable standard, John Henry shouldn't have had a great racing career. Early on, he was called "scrawny" and "headstrong," and because of his bad temper, the colt was gelded. After that, John Henry gave his huge heart and determination to racing. Foaled at Golden Chance Farm in Bourbon County, Kentucky, John Henry won thirty-nine of eighty-three starts in a career spanning eight years. He amassed winnings of nearly $7 million. He was retired at the Kentucky Horse Park in Lexington and died in October 2007, shortly after his thirty-second birthday.

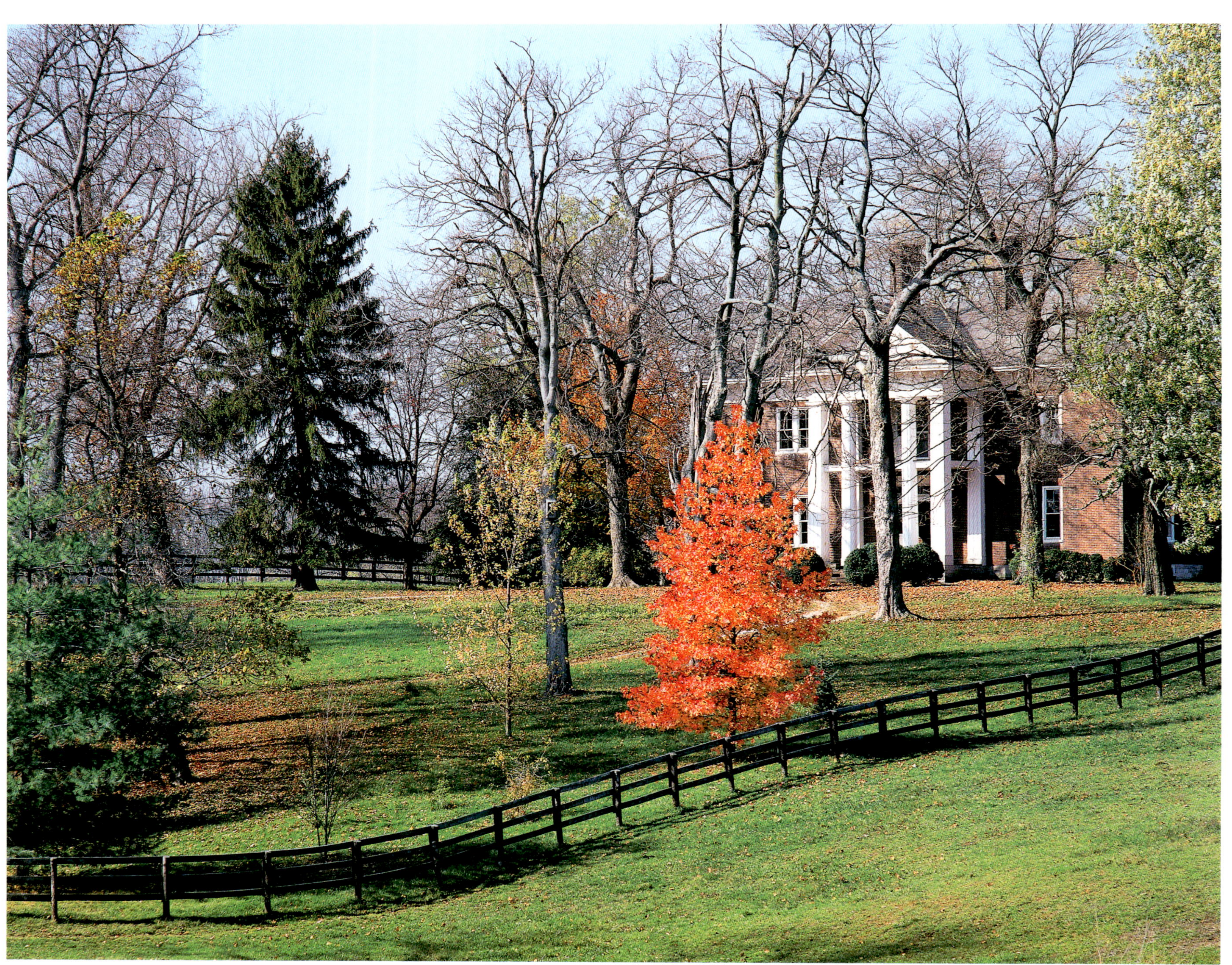

BLUEGRASS ARCHITECTURE

Kentucky was the first western frontier in America, and the Bluegrass was its prime region. Because of its early settlement, Bluegrass architecture dates to the late 1700s. During the antebellum period and through the nineteenth century, the area became known for its Federal and Greek Revival styles. Many of the mansions of the period were built on the farms of wealthy planters and horse breeders. The cost of maintaining these large homes can be staggering, and some of them have been turned over to public institutions and private foundations that preserve the structures in the interest of history and offer public tours.

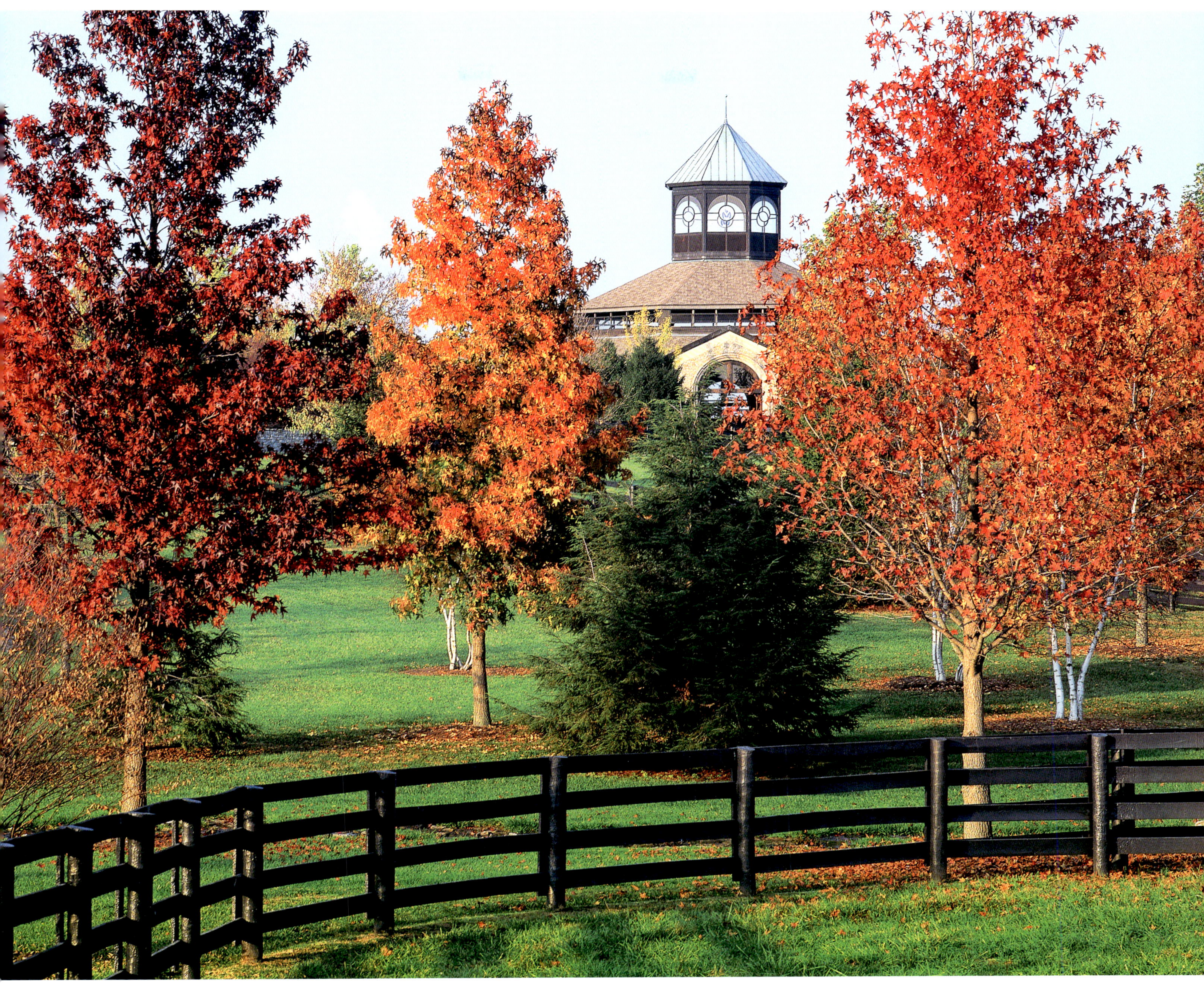

STALLION BARN, DARLEY'S GAINSBOROUGH FARM, WOODFORD COUNTY

Owned by His Highness Sheikh Mohammed bin Rashid al Maktoum, ruler of Dubai, the multimillion-dollar stallion complex at Darley's Gainsborough Farm is one of the most lavish barn complexes in the Bluegrass. It consists of three separate structures built of native limestone. Inside, each building is paneled in rich wood and finished with heavy brass and iron fittings.

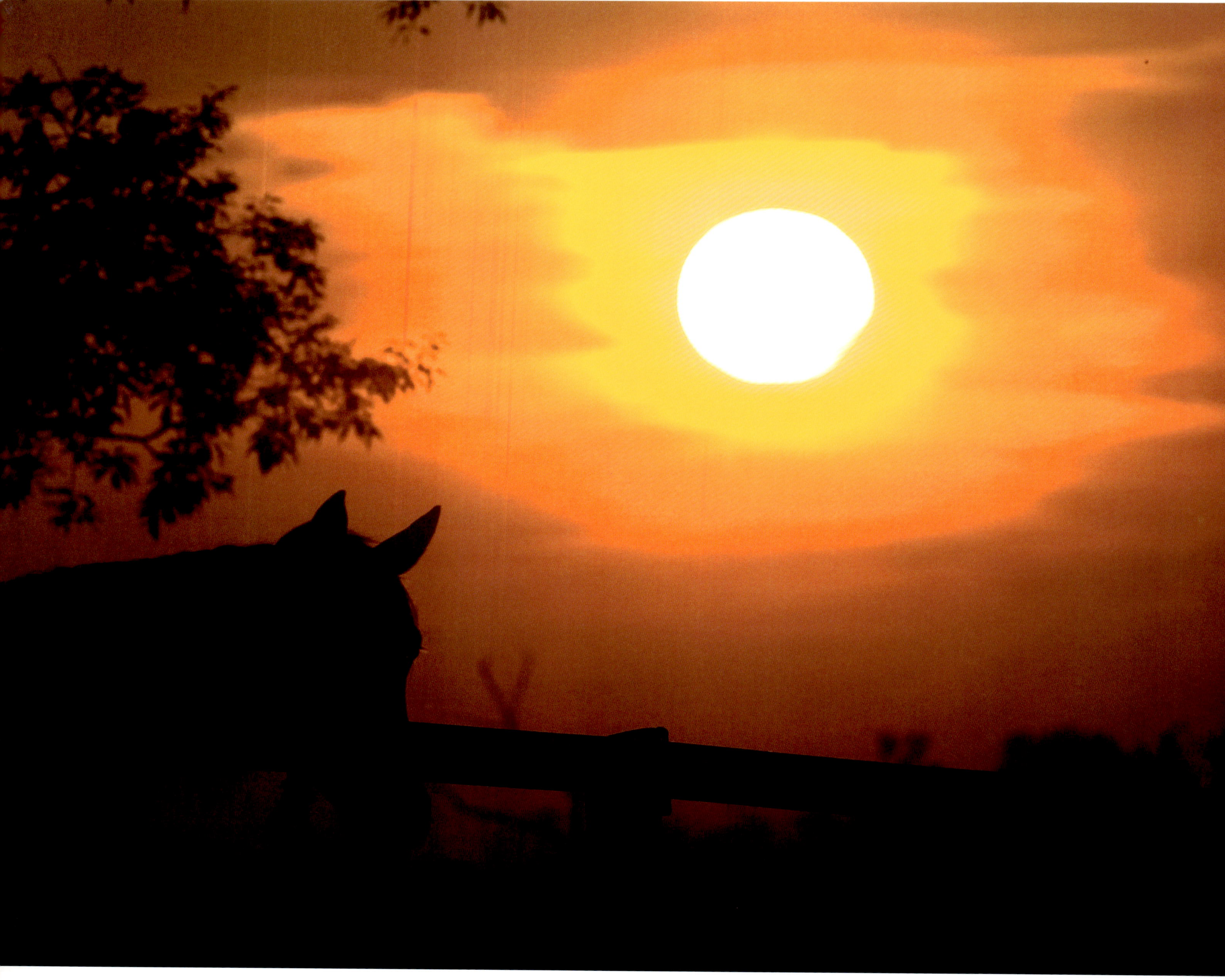

MARE AT SUNRISE

Many horses spend their nights in the pastures, and what they do out there is anybody's guess. On the larger farms, employees on night watch monitor the horses every few hours, slowly driving pickup trucks or four-wheelers through the fields, and sometimes getting out on foot with flashlights to check on groups or individuals. They look for signs of sickness or injury, and during the foaling season, they want to know if a mare has unexpectedly delivered her foal in the darkness.

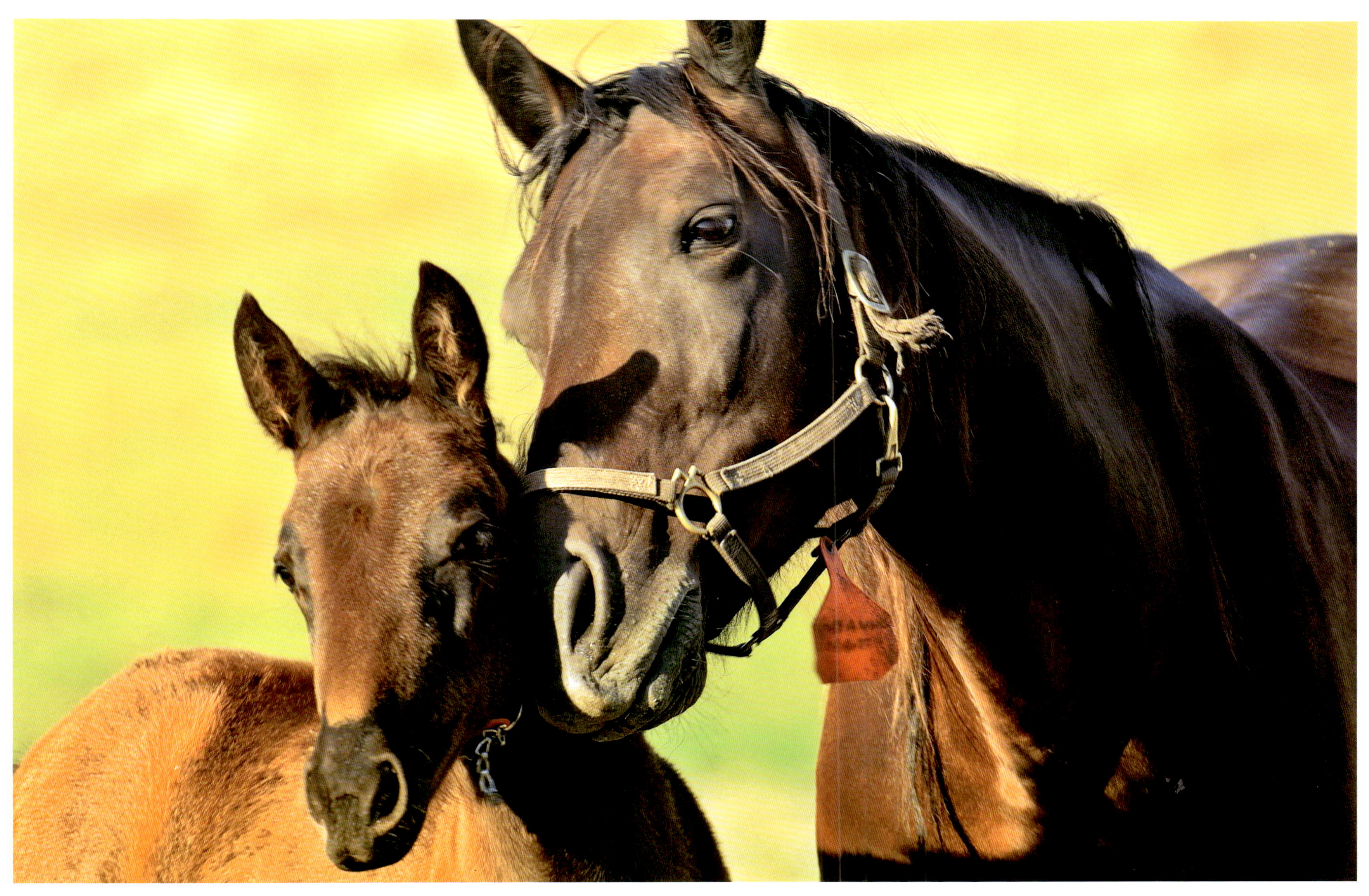

NUDGING HER FOAL

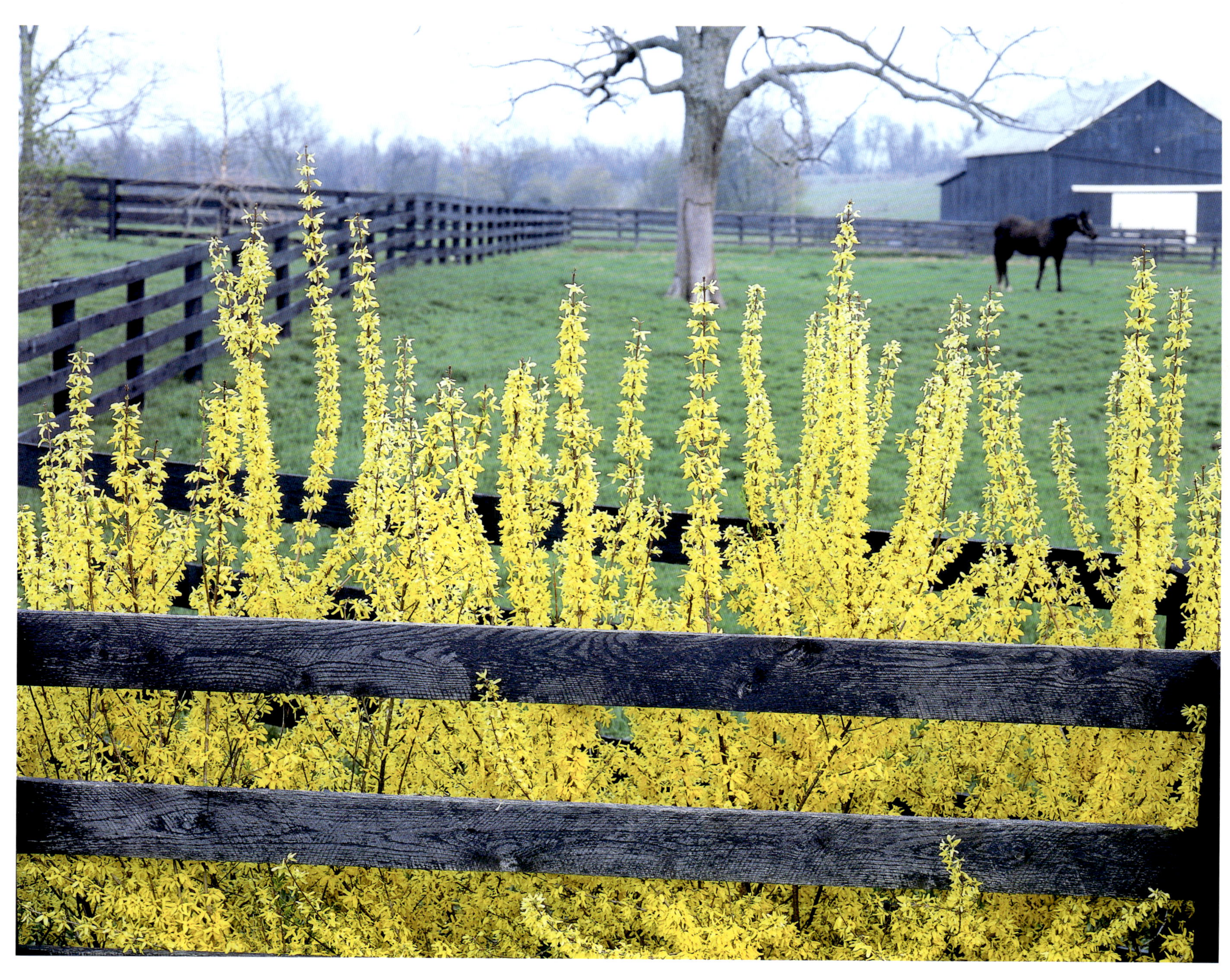

FORSYTHIA AND THOROUGHBRED STALLION, PARIS PIKE

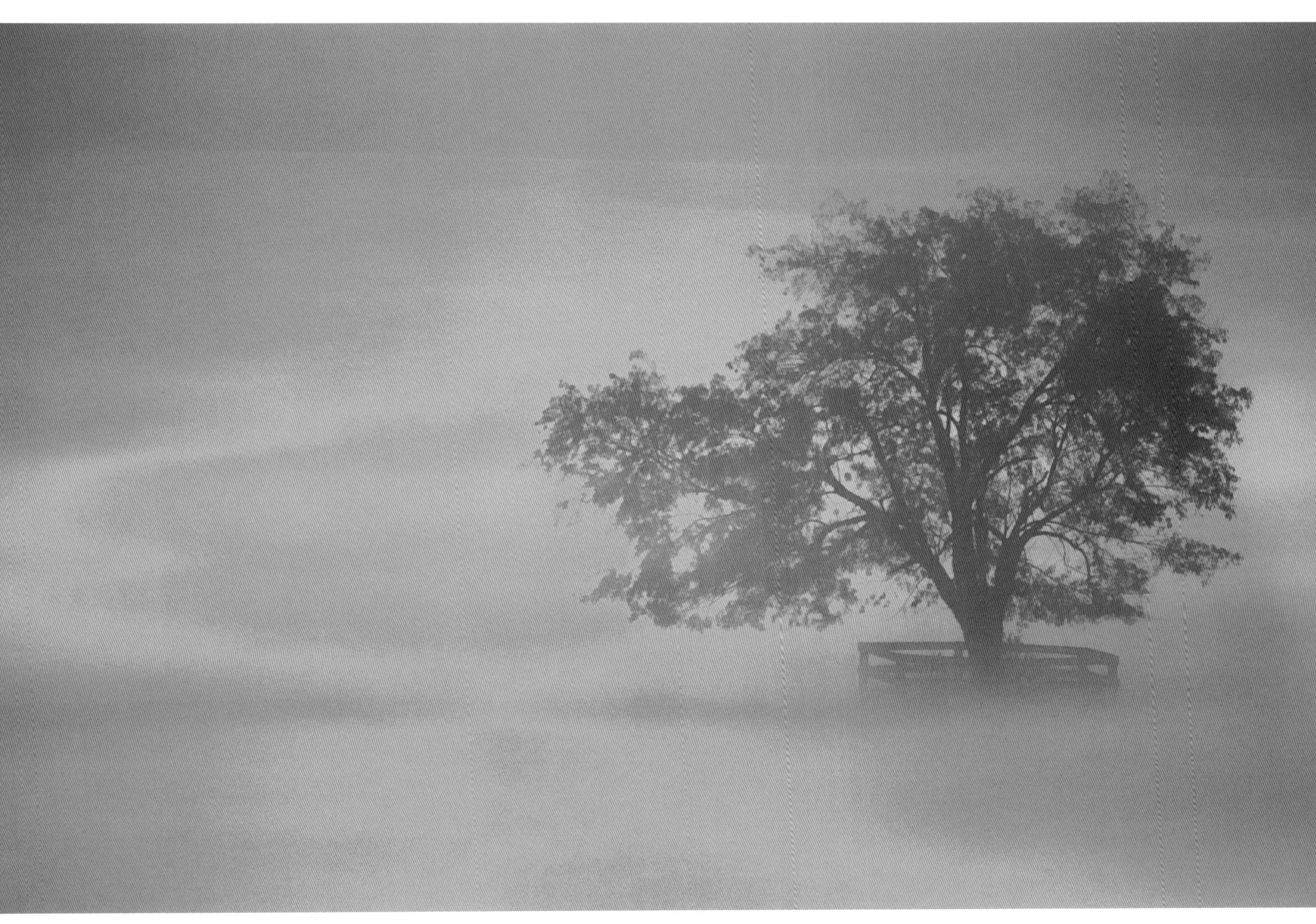

TREE AT SUNRISE, BOURBON COUNTY

Sunrise casts an eerie glow over a fog-shrouded horse farm just outside Paris. In spring and fall, Kentucky landscapes are often blanketed in a low-lying, early-morning fog that quickly burns off after daybreak. The fence surrounding the tree is intended to protect the trunk from the ravages of bored, bark-chewing horses. With nearly 100 horse farms, Bourbon County ranks third in equine sales in Kentucky.

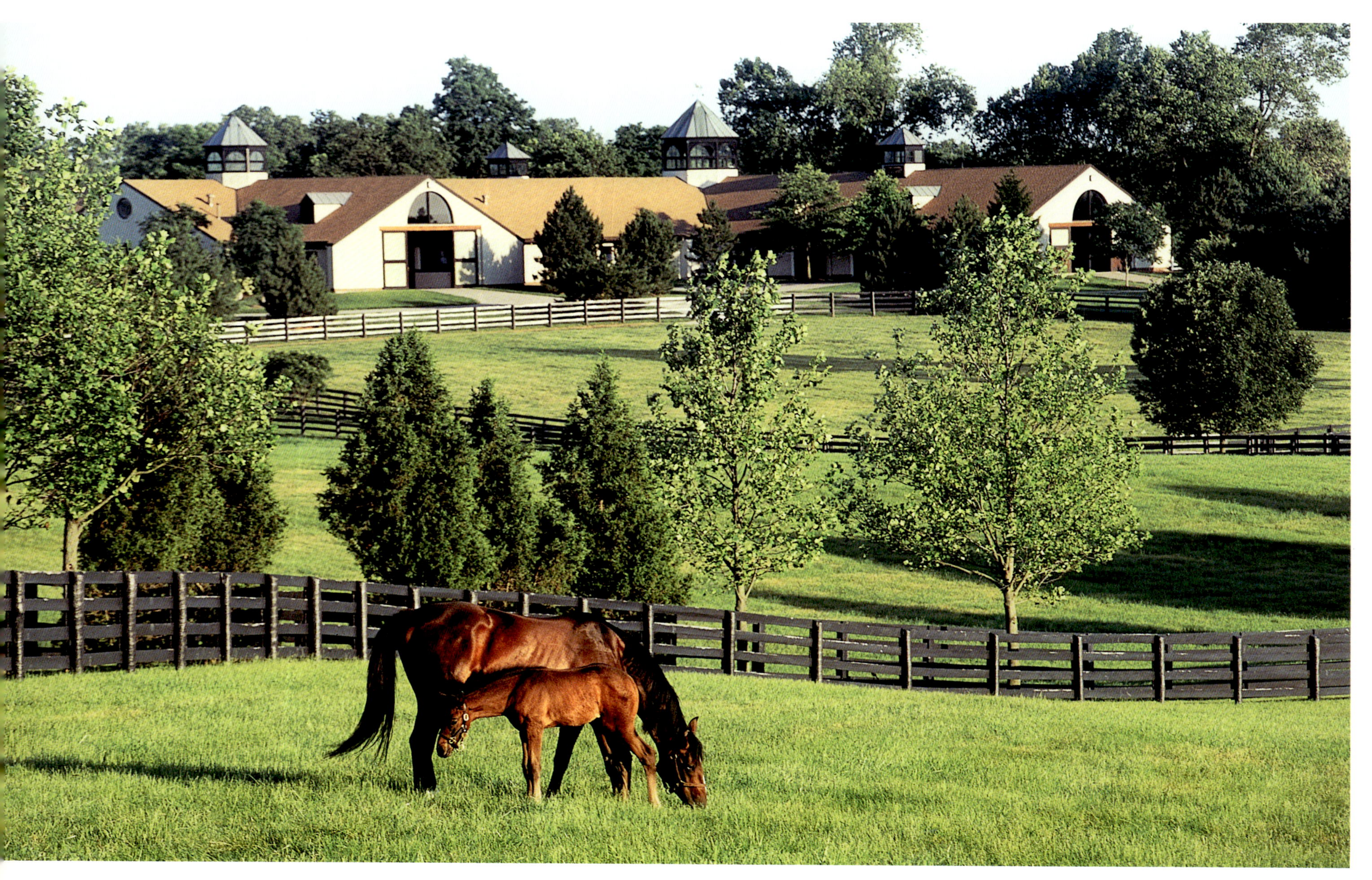

MARE AND FOAL GRAZING, WOODFORD COUNTY

Darley's Gainsborough Farm in Woodford County is one of the largest horse farms in Kentucky. Rich fields of bluegrass roll endlessly from horizon to horizon on the 2,000-acre tract. The operation is owned by His Highness Sheikh Mohammed bin Rashid al Maktoum, ruler of Dubai and one of the leading horsemen in the world. Among the many beautiful barns is the stallion complex, one of the most impressive in the entire Bluegrass. Successful stallions standing at stud here (now at Darley at Jonabell) include Elusive Quality and Quiet American, sires of Kentucky Derby winners Smarty Jones (2004) and Real Quiet (1998), respectively.

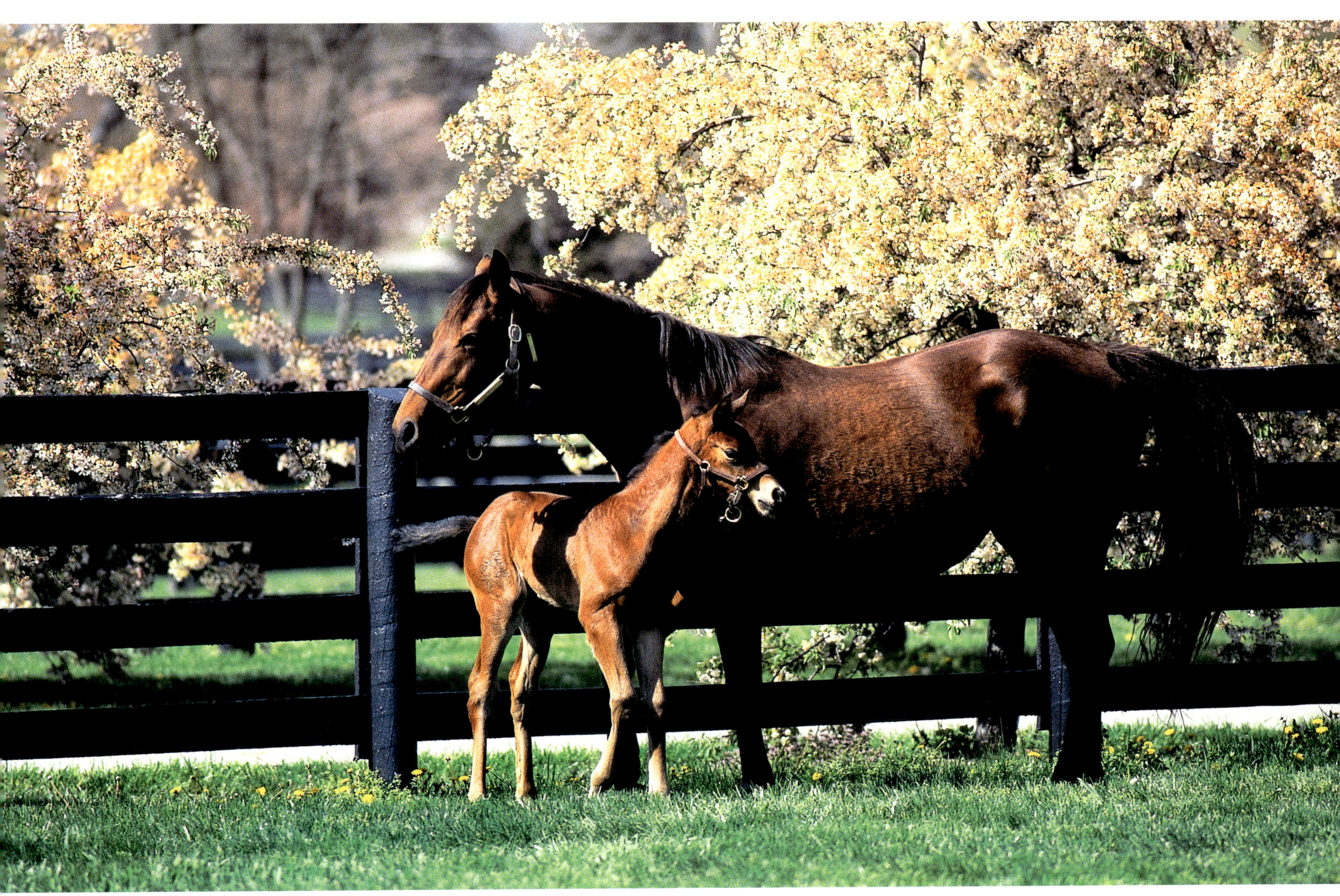

MARE AND FOAL WITH FLOWERING CRAB APPLE

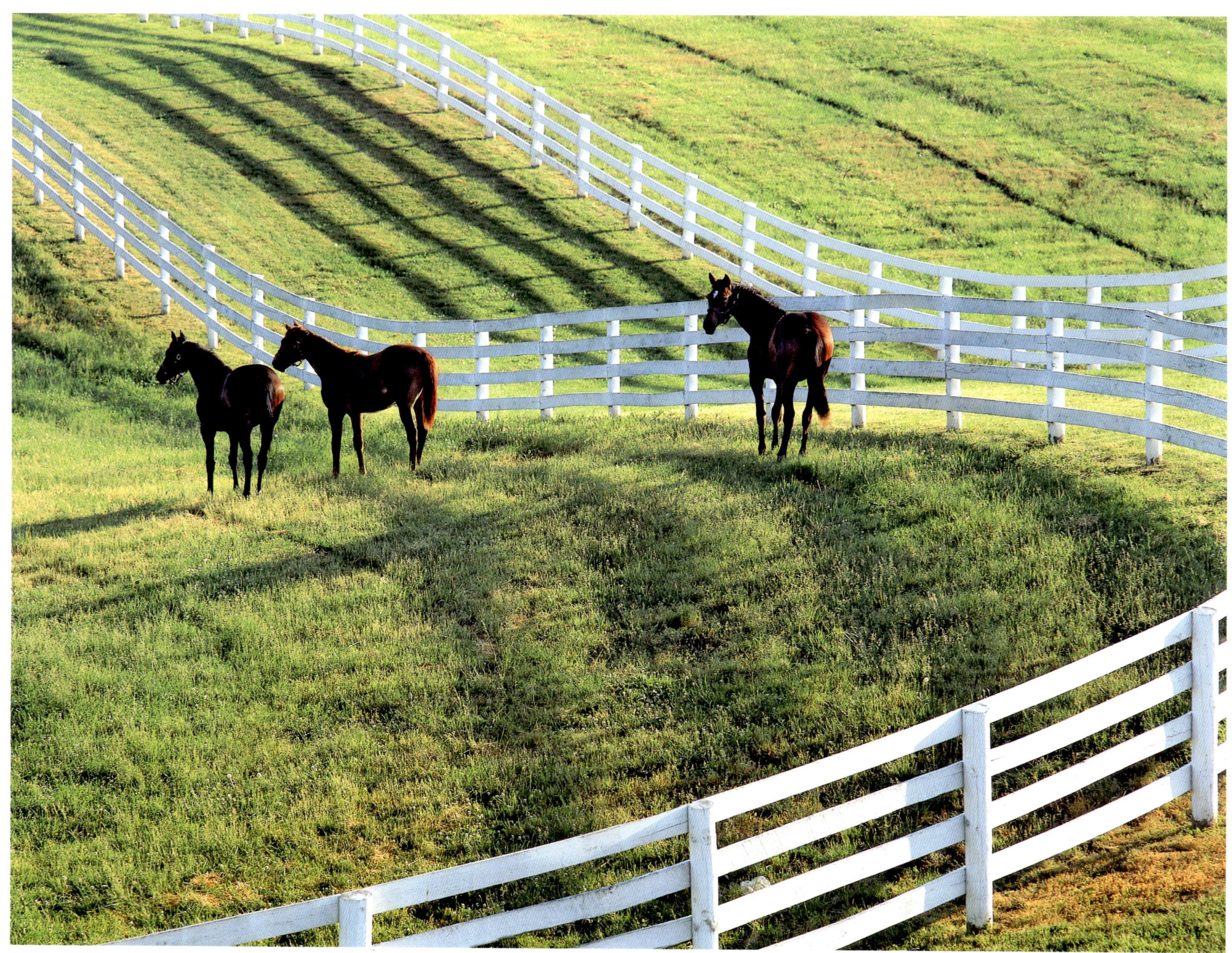

YEARLINGS ALONG VERSAILLES ROAD

The yearling period is the most carefree time in a horse's life. A horse's maturation is immensely compressed compared with that of humans, so yearlings are somewhat like adolescents. They have little responsibility, and for a few months, all they have to do is eat and grow.

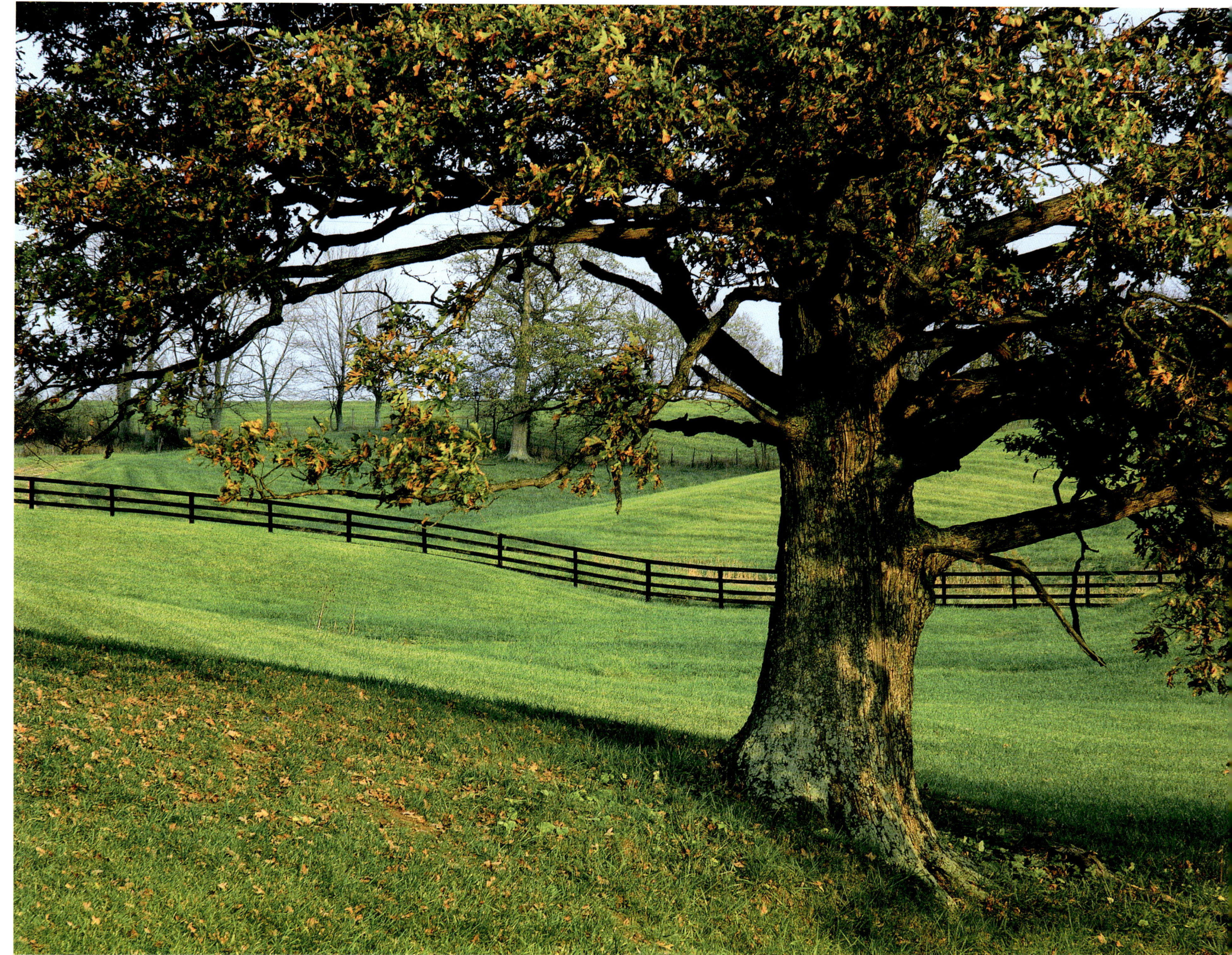

BUR OAK IN PASTURE

This bur oak has been the monarch of these fields for more than 300 years. Just a seedling in the century before European settlement, this tree has "watched" the natural savanna grasslands give way to pioneer farms and then to pastures of bluegrass. The original landscape, consisting of thousands of acres of native grasses interspersed with giant oaks, ashes, and walnuts, is gone. But many of the individual trees remain as reminders of the past.

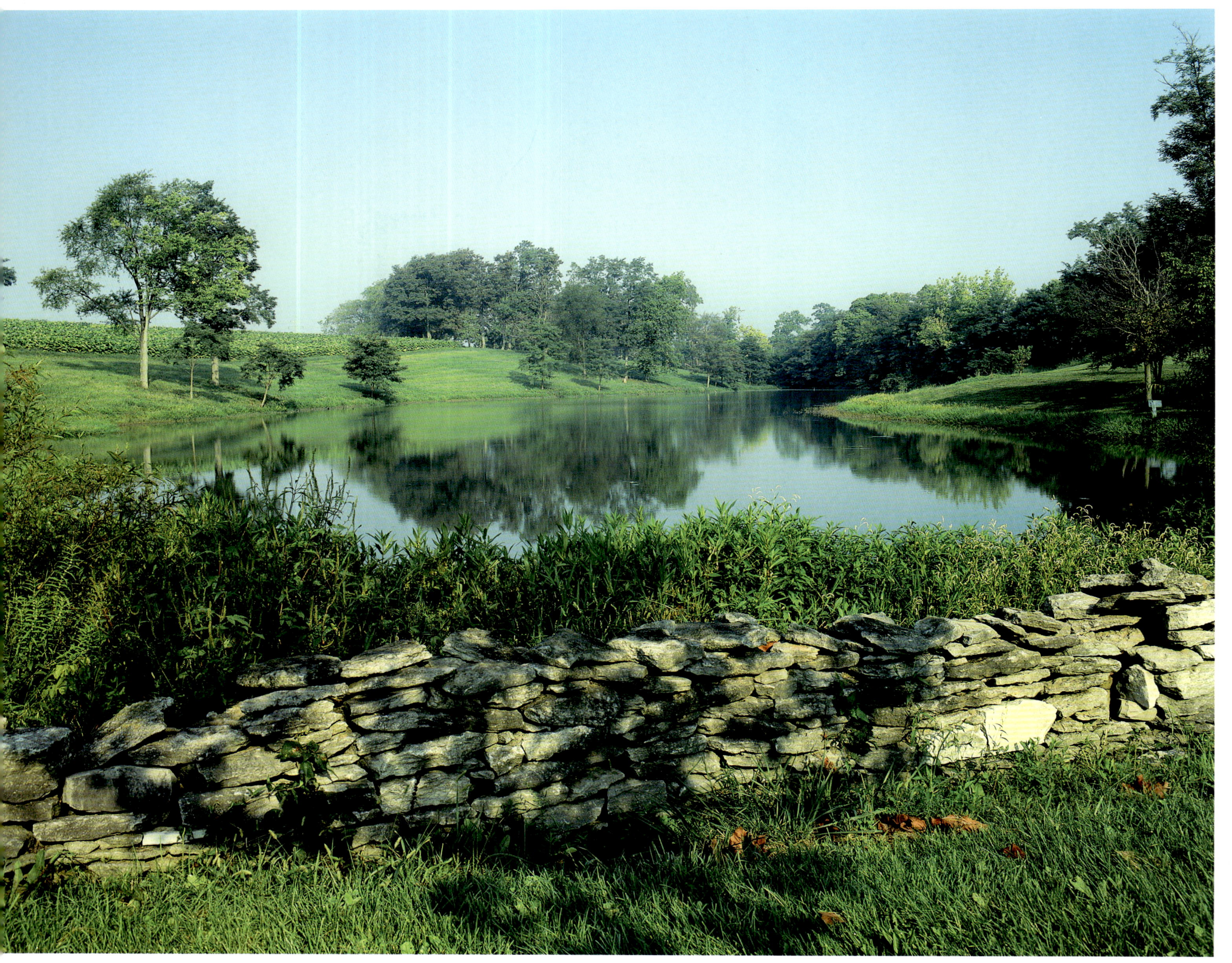

LIMESTONE FENCE AND POND

The unique geology of the Bluegrass region gives rise to thousands of natural springs, allowing the creation of ponds and small lakes for the watering of horses and livestock. The abundant natural limestone provided the earliest fencing material. Miles and miles of rock walls, some more than 200 years old, are a symbol of the Bluegrass country and its pastoral elegance.

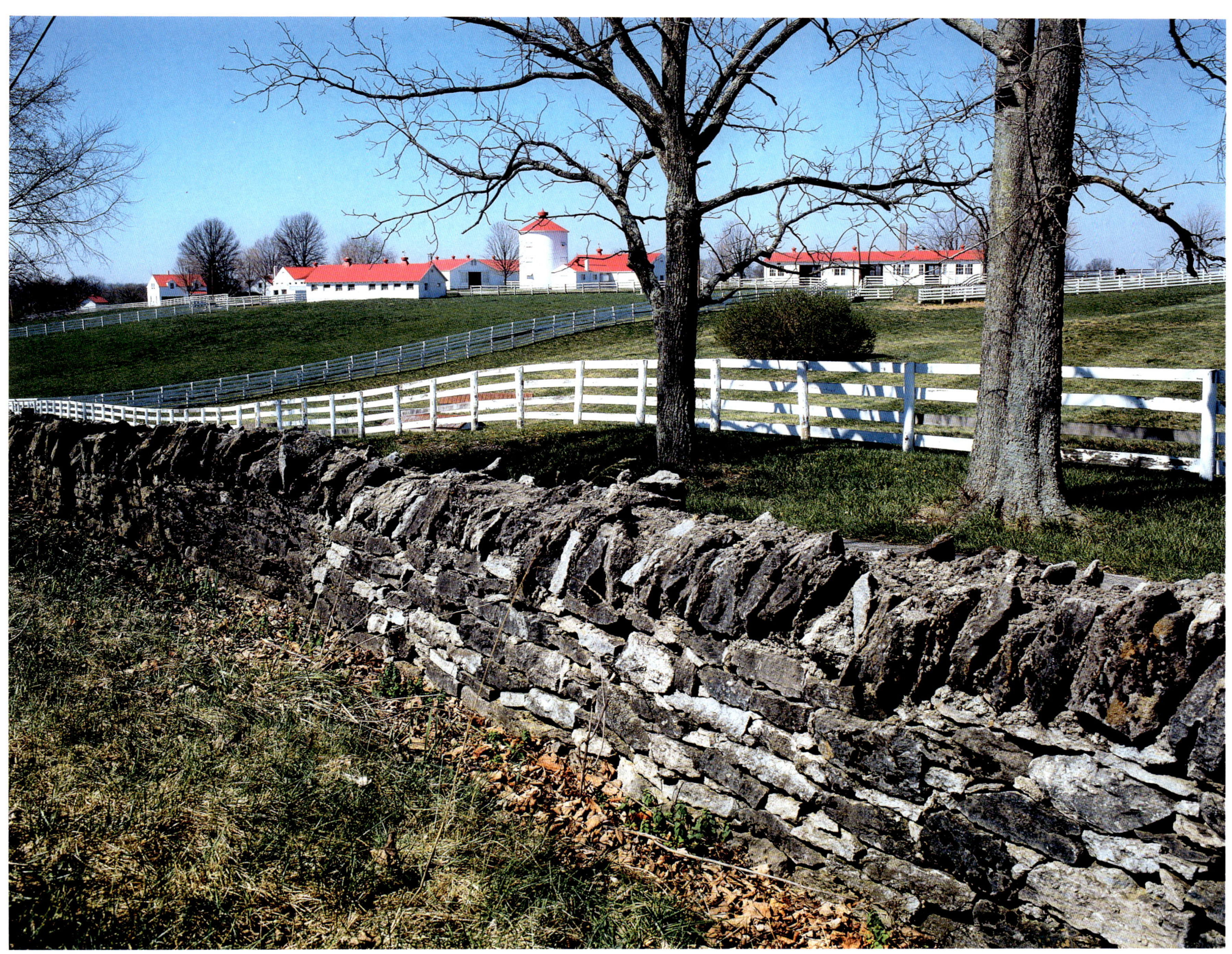

BIRTHPLACE OF JOHN HENRY, 1975

Golden Chance Farm lies along the banks of Stoner Creek in Bourbon County. Robert E. Lehmann owned the farm in 1970 when he entered the colt Dust Commander in the ninety-sixth running of the Kentucky Derby. Against odds of thirty-five to one, the little chestnut thrilled his backers by winning the race by five lengths. Under the guidance of Lehmann's widow, Verna, Golden Chance would be associated with even greater equine fame when in 1975 the farm produced a foal named John Henry, one of the greatest Thoroughbred racers of all time.

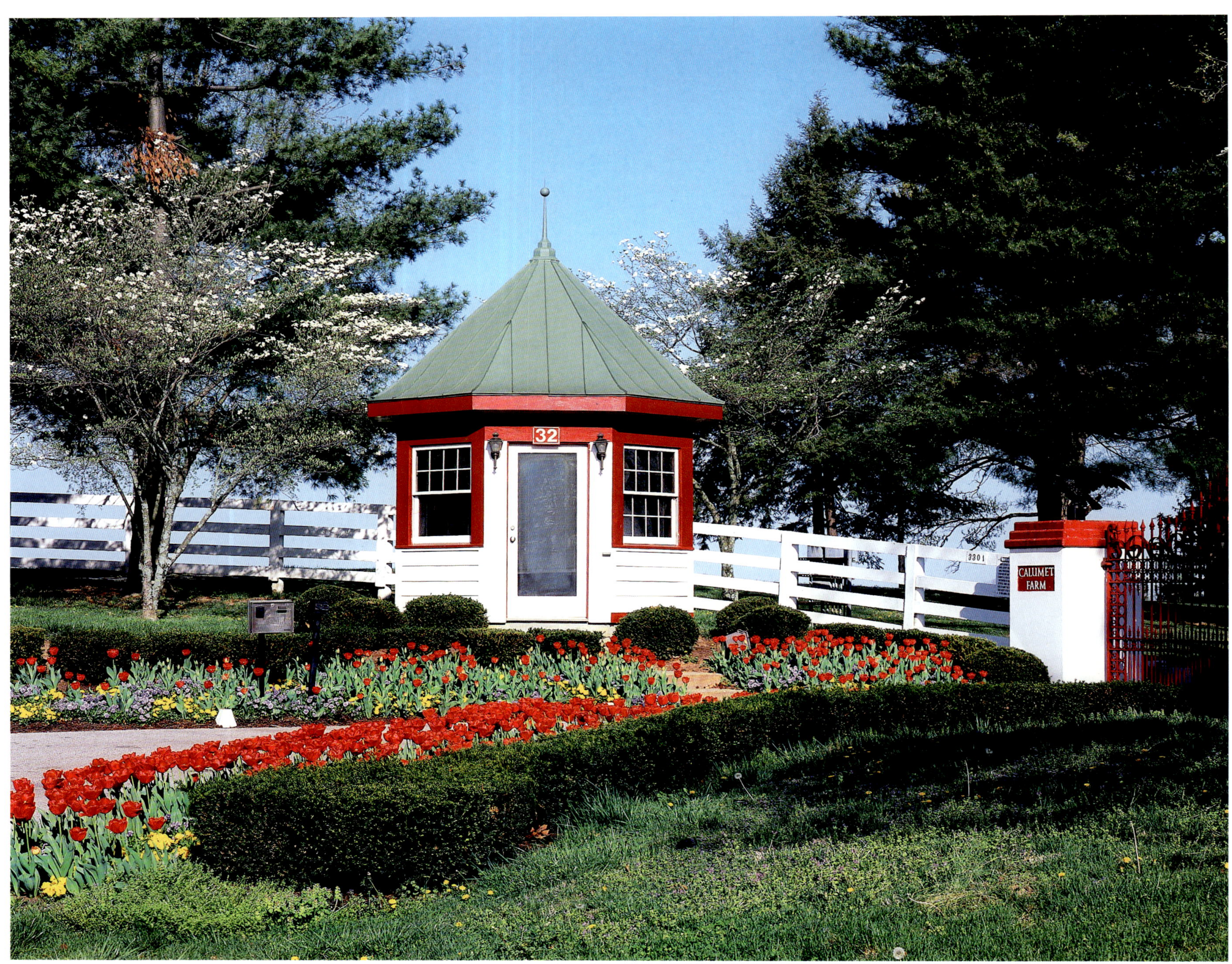

ENTRANCE TO CALUMET FARM

Many of the most prominent farms in the Bluegrass like to show off with an elaborate front door. Here, the main entrance to Calumet Farm welcomes visitors to its 850 acres of Bluegrass history and splendor. Within these gates, such famous horses as Whirlaway, Hill Gail, and Tim Tam have walked, and nine Kentucky Derby winners have been bred here. The greatest was Citation, who won the Triple Crown and was named 1948 Horse of the Year. His astounding record included thirty-two wins, ten seconds, and two thirds in forty-five starts.

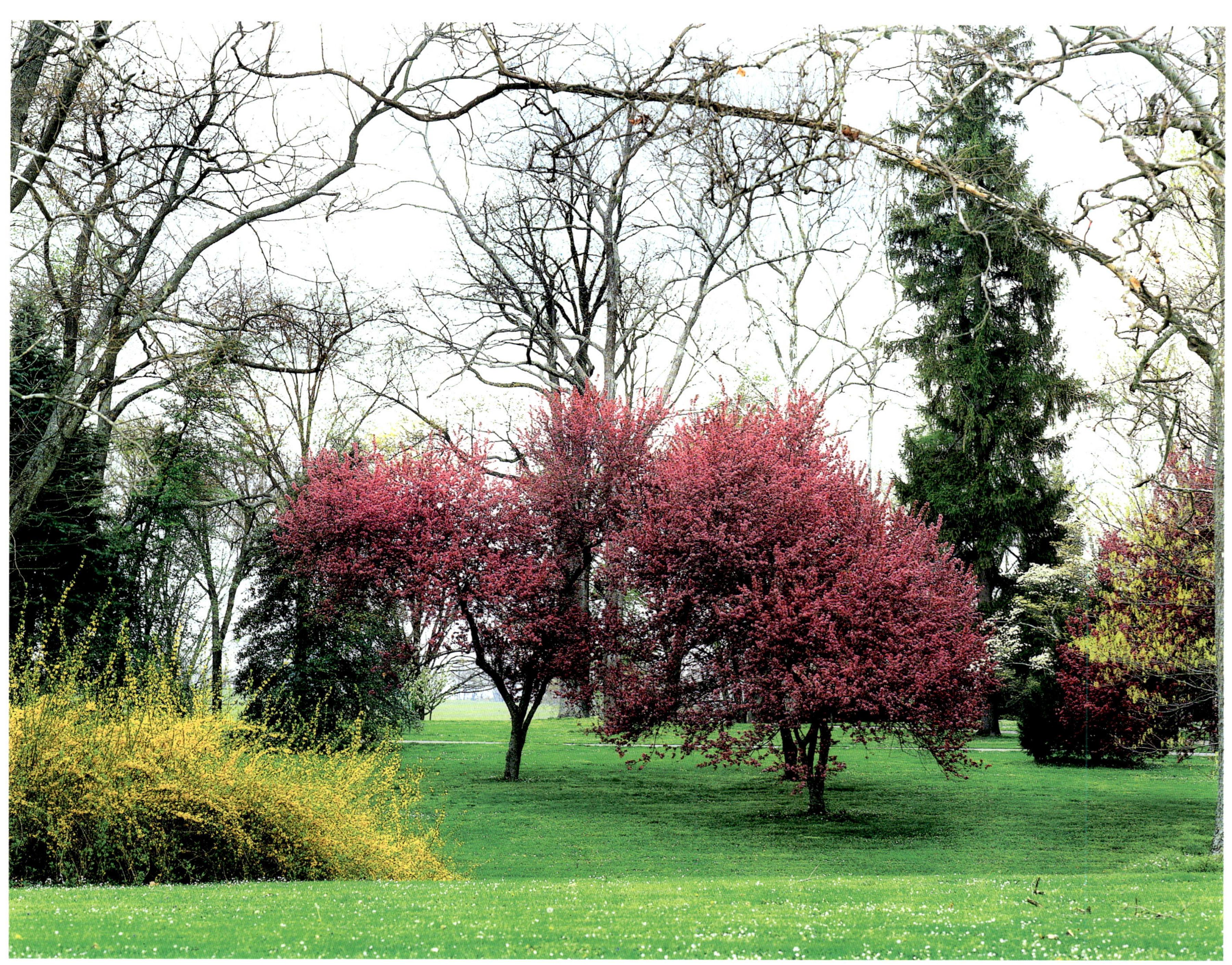

FLOWERING TREES

The Bluegrass region of Kentucky is a veritable garden of Eden. Few places on earth harbor such a diversity of trees, shrubs, and wildflowers. The moderate climate and abundant rainfall are perfect for the growth of both northern and southern species. The earliest explorers of the region recognized the richness of the land, and the first settlers were eager to claim their piece of heaven on earth.

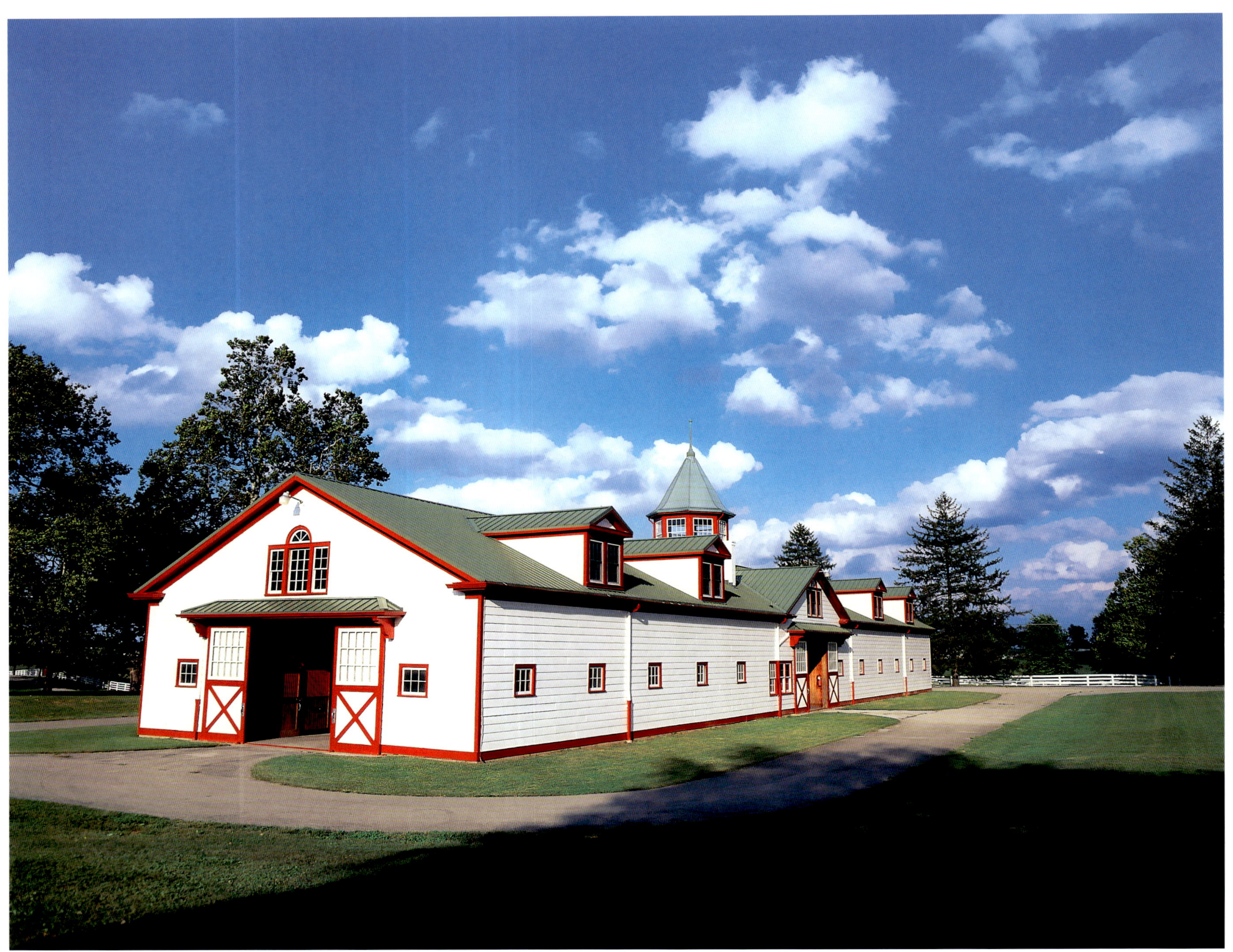

BARN AT CALUMET FARM

When flying into Lexington, the final approach is almost invariably directly over Calumet Farm, with its white plank fencing and signature red and white buildings. The farm represents a first and lasting impression of Lexington and the Bluegrass.

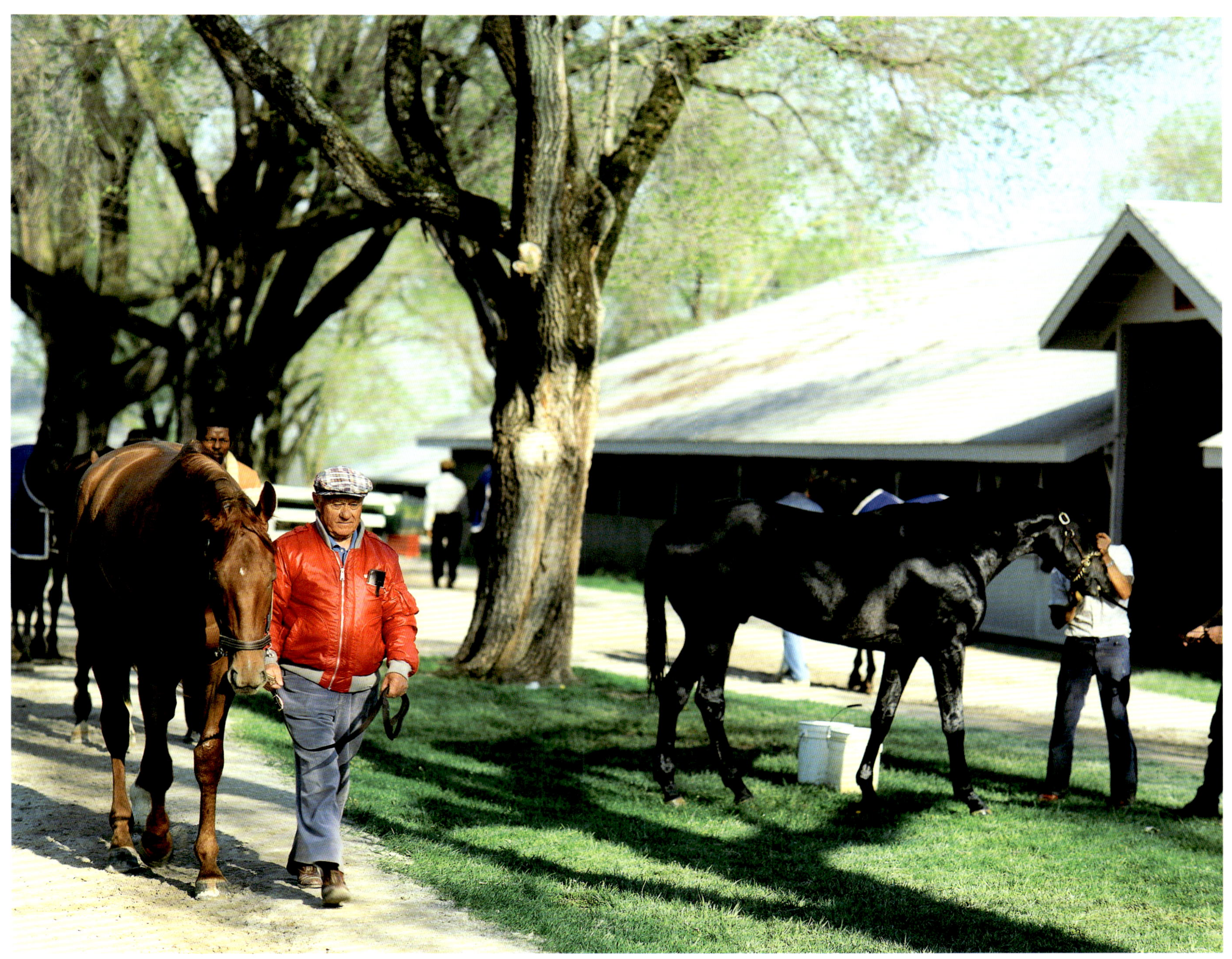

SECRETARIAT'S TRAINER LUCIEN LAUREN AT KEENELAND

Most horse trainers know their charges better than anyone and are not afraid to get their hands dirty. Here, Lucien Lauren, famed trainer of 1973 Triple Crown winner Secretariat, walks one of his colts in the barn area of Keeneland Race Course during a spring meet. Trainers are among the first to arrive at the stables at dawn and the last to leave at night. Lauren also trained 1972 Kentucky Derby victor Riva Ridge.

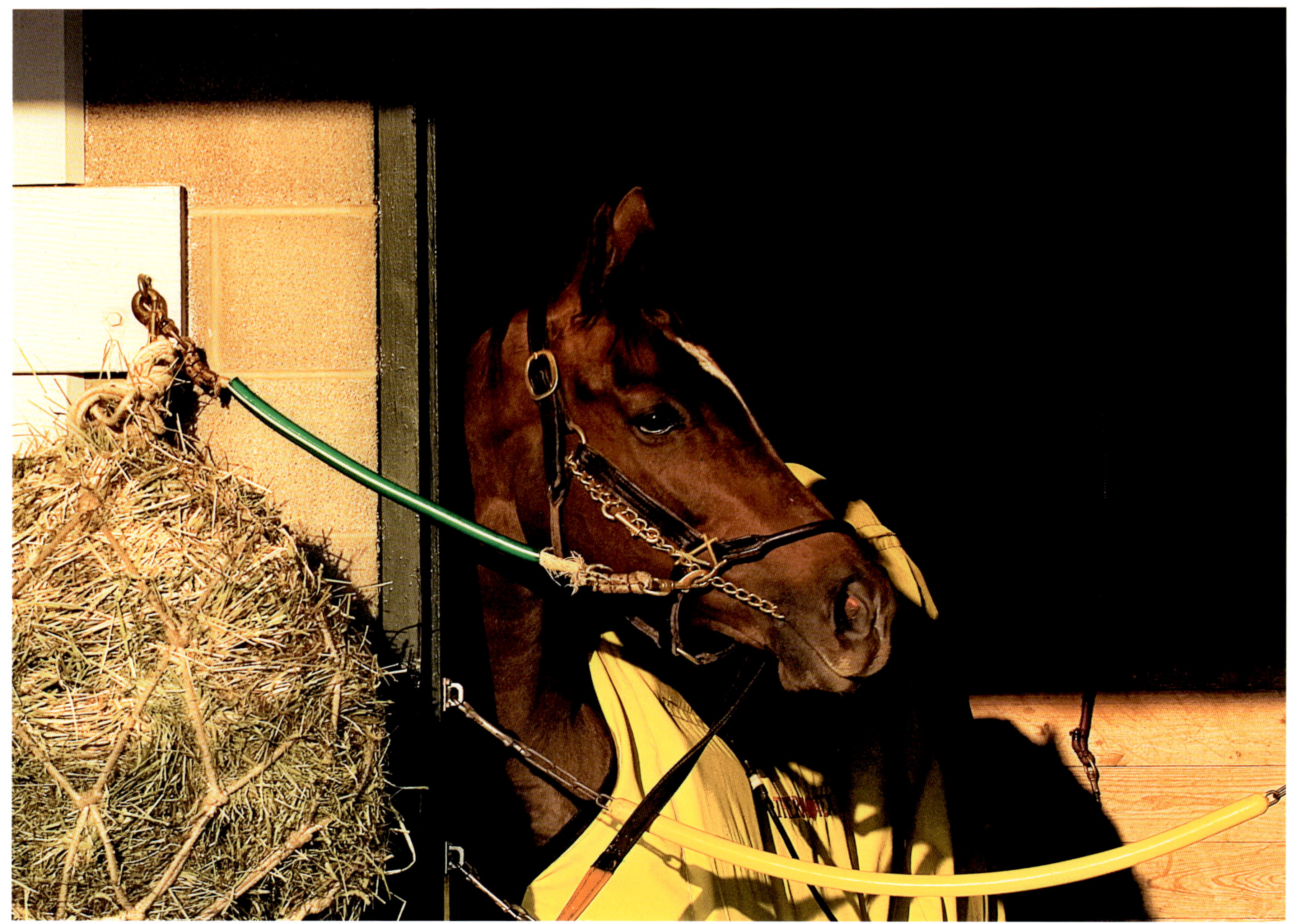

STABLE AT KEENELAND

Having completed his morning workout, a blanketed Thoroughbred watches the comings and goings from his stall in the barn area behind Keeneland. Owners and trainers house their horses here during the spring and fall racing meets. Most bring along a contingent of exercise riders, grooms, and other stable hands, who perform the specialized functions required to keep the horses in top condition. The barn area is a veritable city of people who work from before sunup to well after the last race is over.

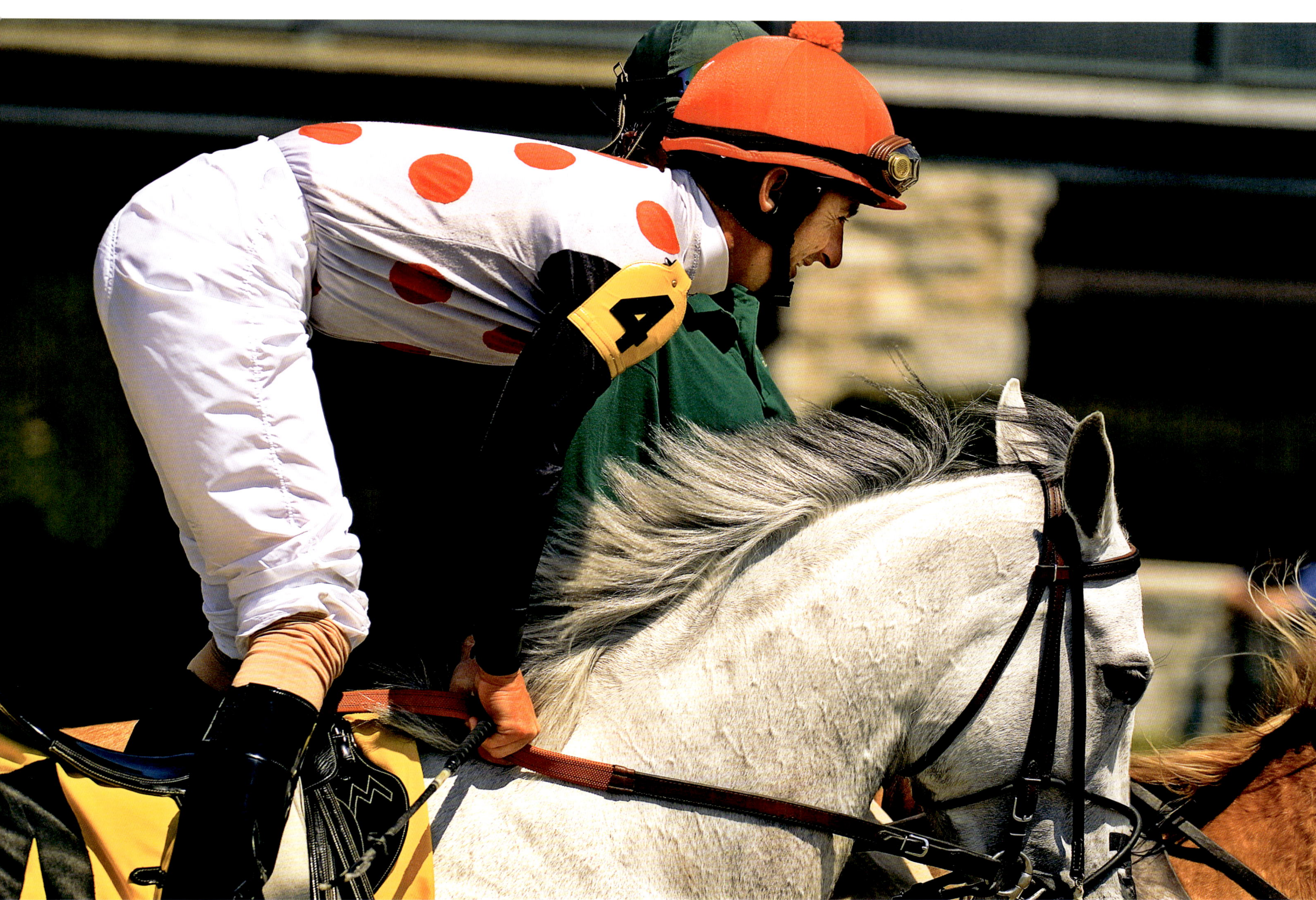

WINNING JOCKEY AT KEENELAND

With a smile on his face, a jockey and his mount are led to the winner's circle at the Keeneland Race Course. Jockeys are athletes, and they require such attributes as intuition, patience, and quick thinking, along with rigorous weight control and physical fitness. Only a handful of jockeys receive national recognition, but the profession numbers in the thousands.

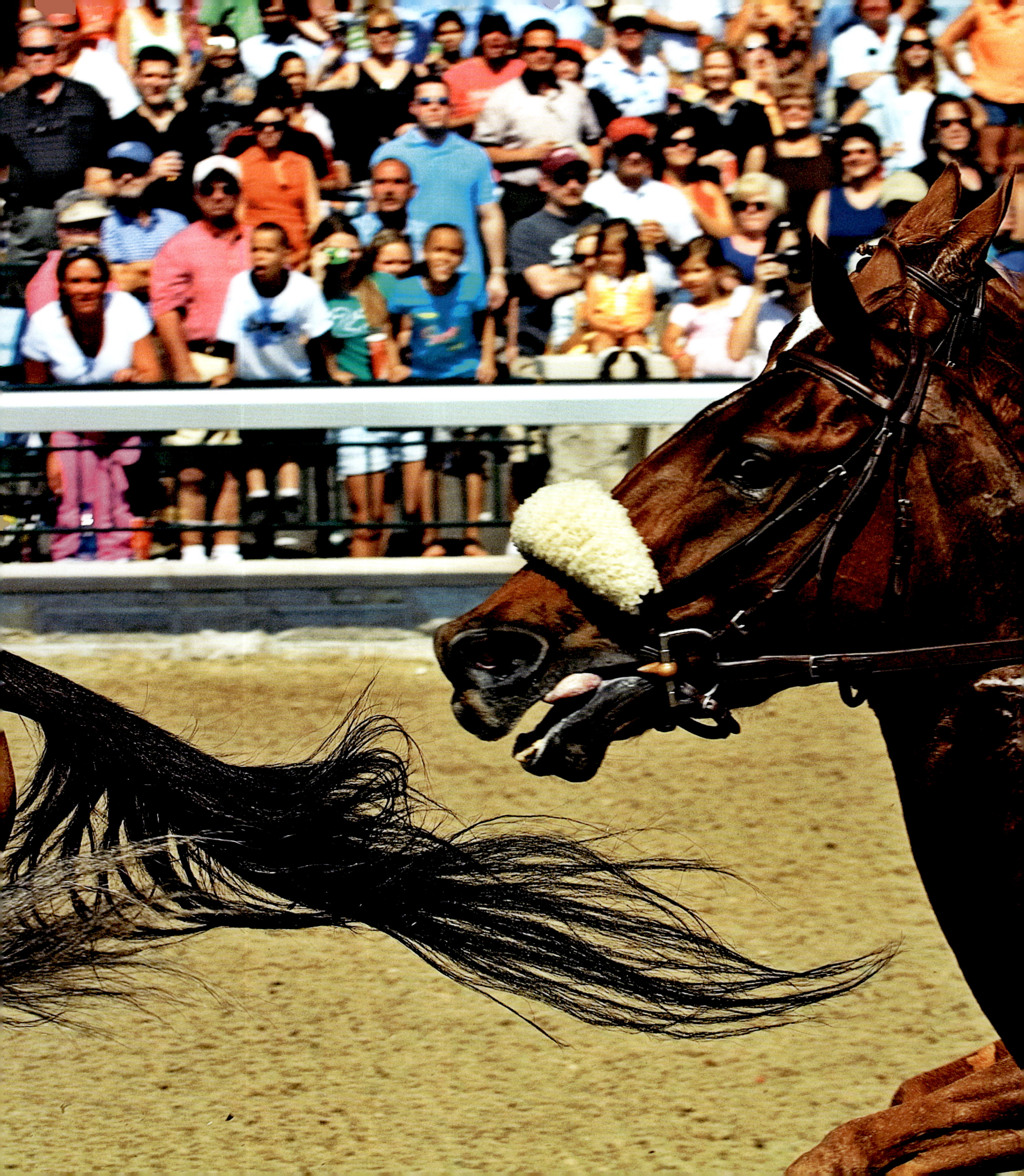

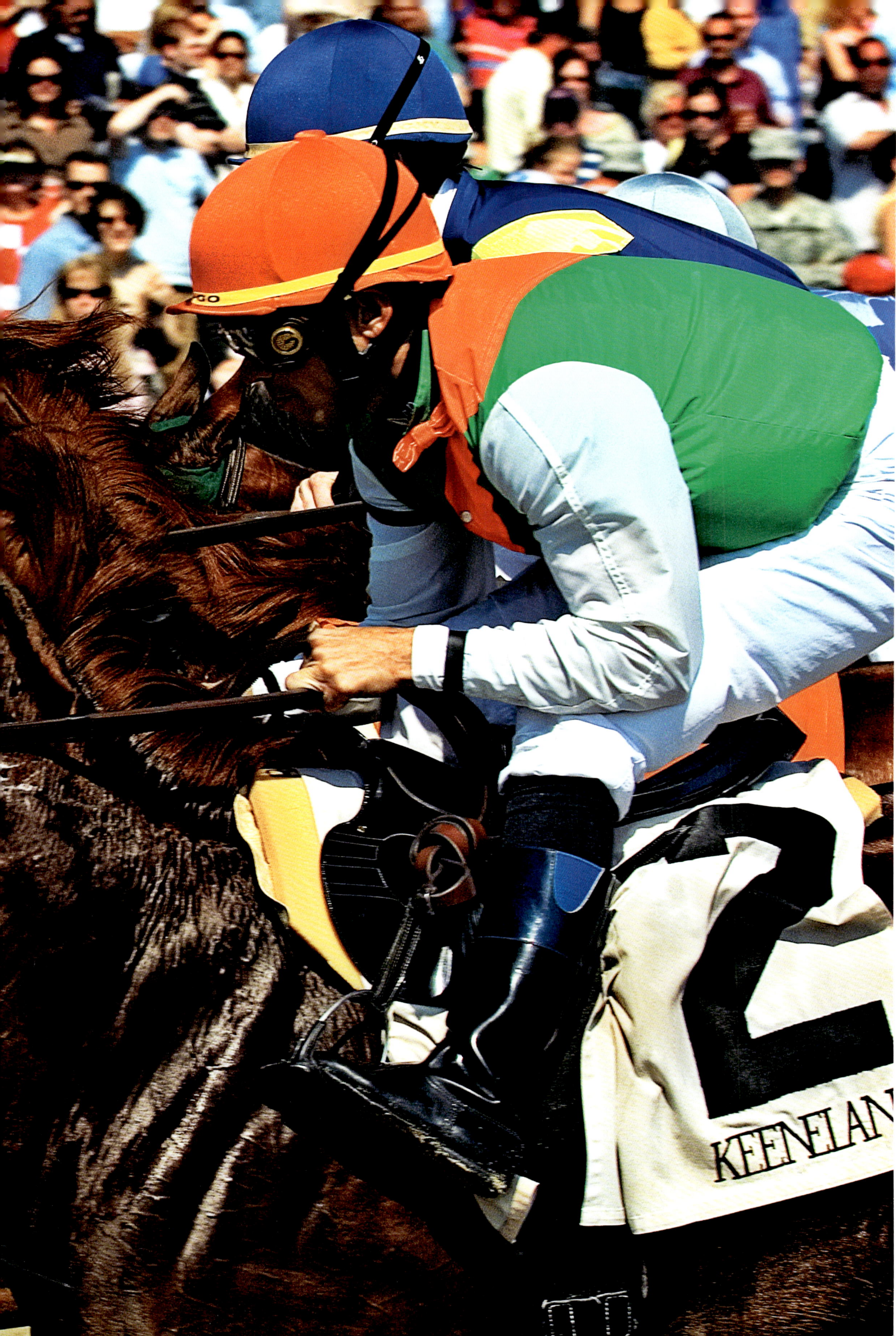

IN FRONT OF THE GRANDSTAND AT KEENELAND

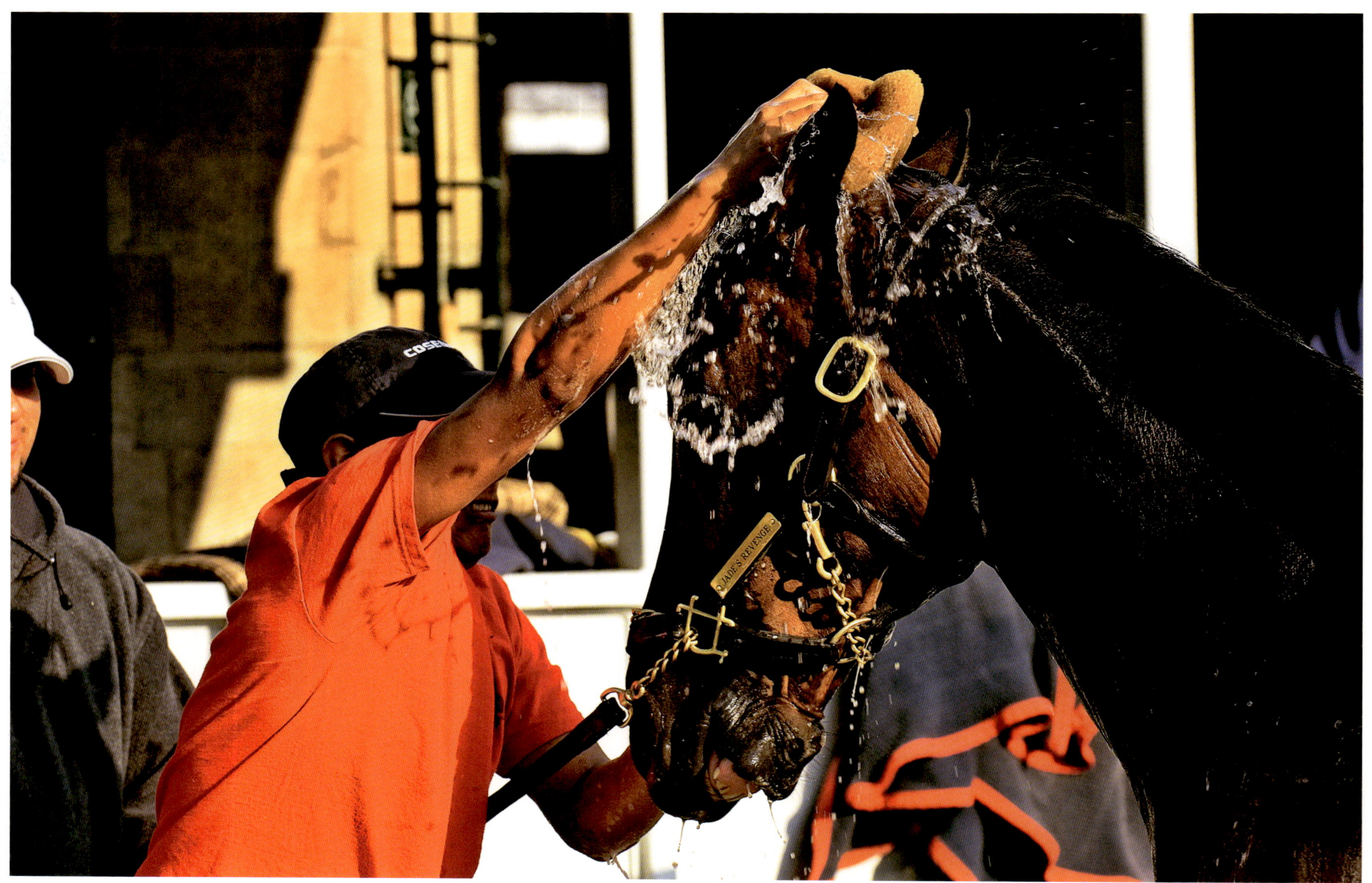

WORKOUT'S REWARD

After strenuous morning exercise, racehorses are cooled down with a few walks around the barn area, followed by a bath. They are hosed and soaped from top to bottom, then vigorously dried. In cool weather, a blanket is placed on the animal before it is put in its stall for the day, where a bucket of oats might be waiting.

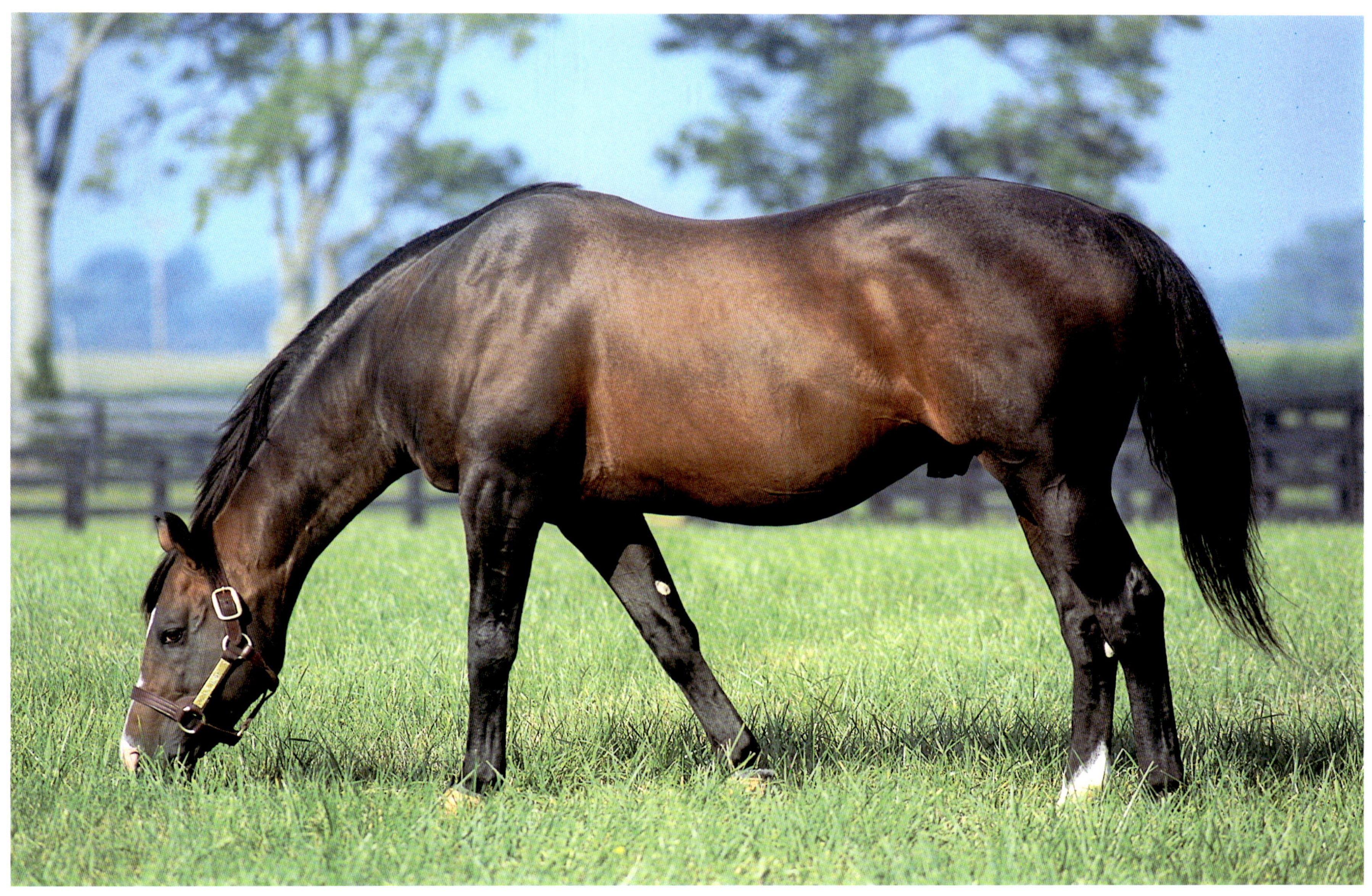

A. P. INDY

A. P. Indy took home the Belmont Stakes in 1992. Fifteen years later, his daughter Rags to Riches won the same prize, becoming the third filly to win the mile-and-a-half test and the first since 1905. In a blazingly fast stretch duel, Rags to Riches held off Preakness winner Curlin by a head. A. P. Indy is a son of Triple Crown winner Seattle Slew and stands at stud at Lane's End Farm in Versailles. In his racing career, he won eight of eleven starts and earned nearly $3 million. He is considered one of the greatest sires of his time.

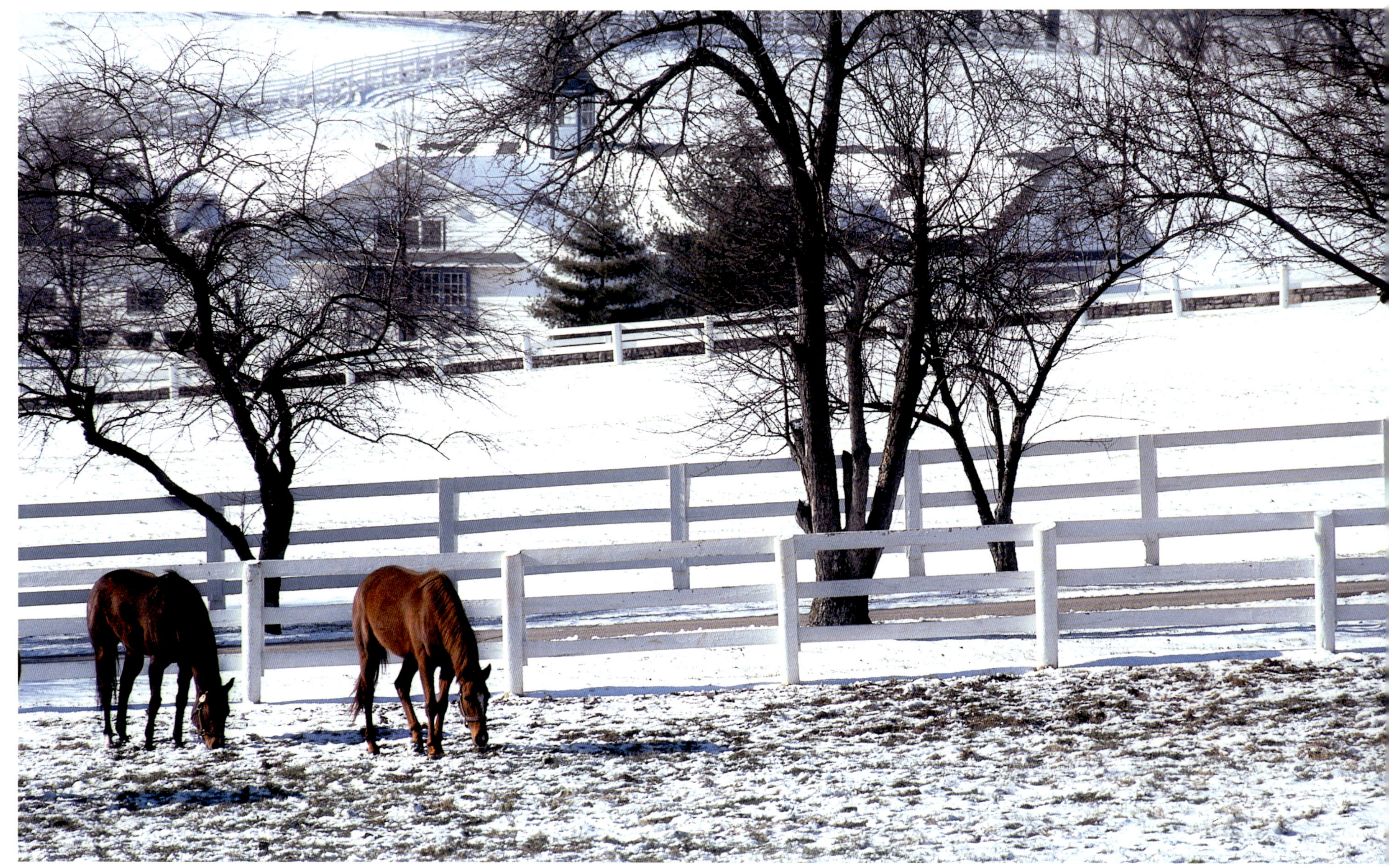

MARES IN WINTER ALONG ELKCHESTER ROAD

An overnight snow covers the grassy hills along Elkchester Road behind the Keeneland Race Course in Lexington. Light snowfalls like this are the norm in the Bluegrass, and any accumulation is often melted by the next day. Although a few owners and trainers choose to keep their charges in the barns during harsh weather, most put their horses out every day, except in the most bitter cold or oppressive heat.

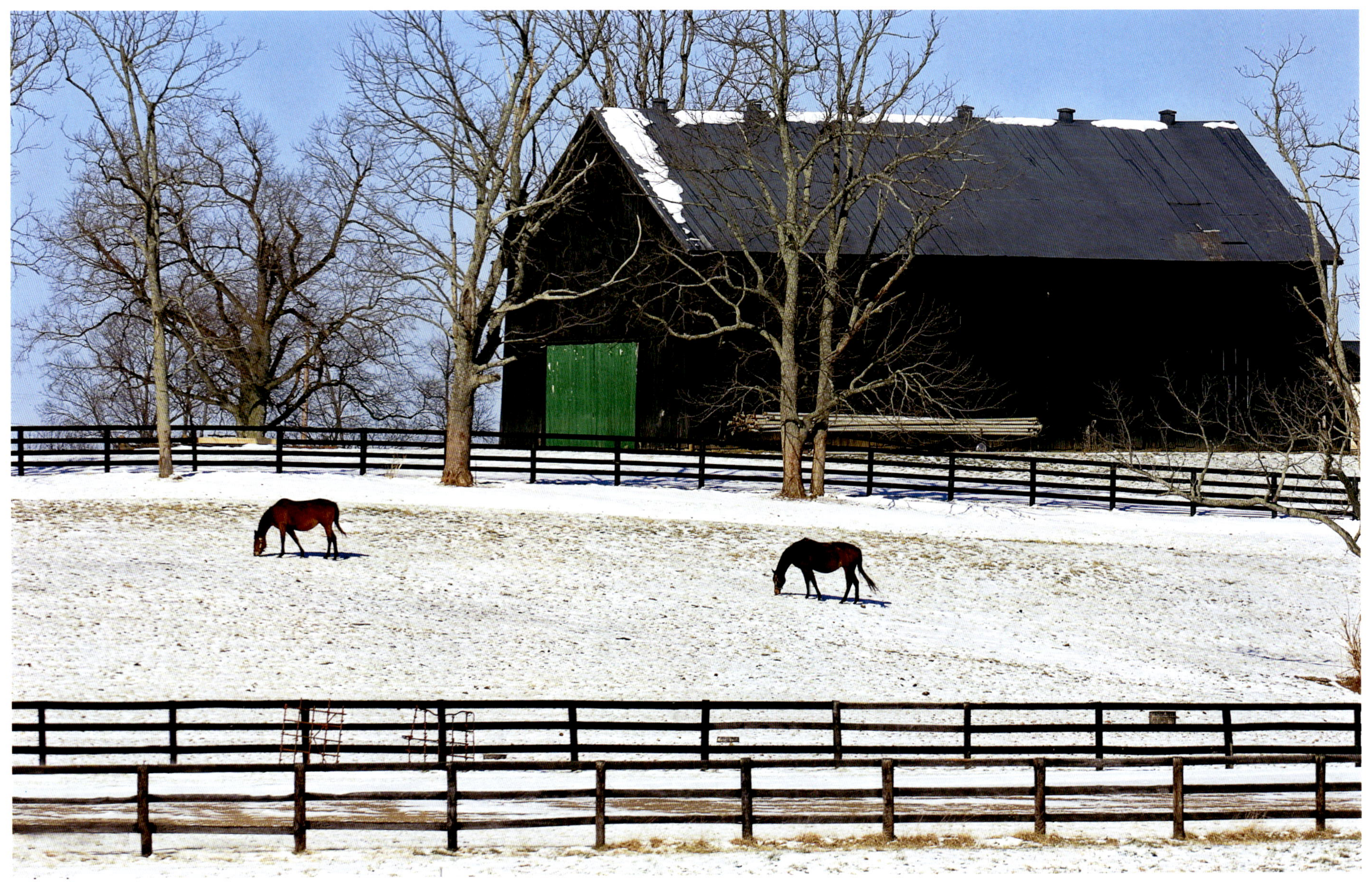

WINTER PASTURE, FULL CIRCLE FARM, FAYETTE COUNTY

A tobacco barn dominates a hillside pasture on a winter morning. Traditional agriculture plays a significant role in the economy of central Kentucky. Many farms divide their interests between raising horses and producing crops, traditionally tobacco, corn, and soybeans. Raising cattle is big business too, and they often graze side by side with horses. Vegetable production is also on the rise, spurred by the existence of farmers' markets in nearly every small town. These markets help farmers supplement their income and provide fresh, locally grown produce to the public.

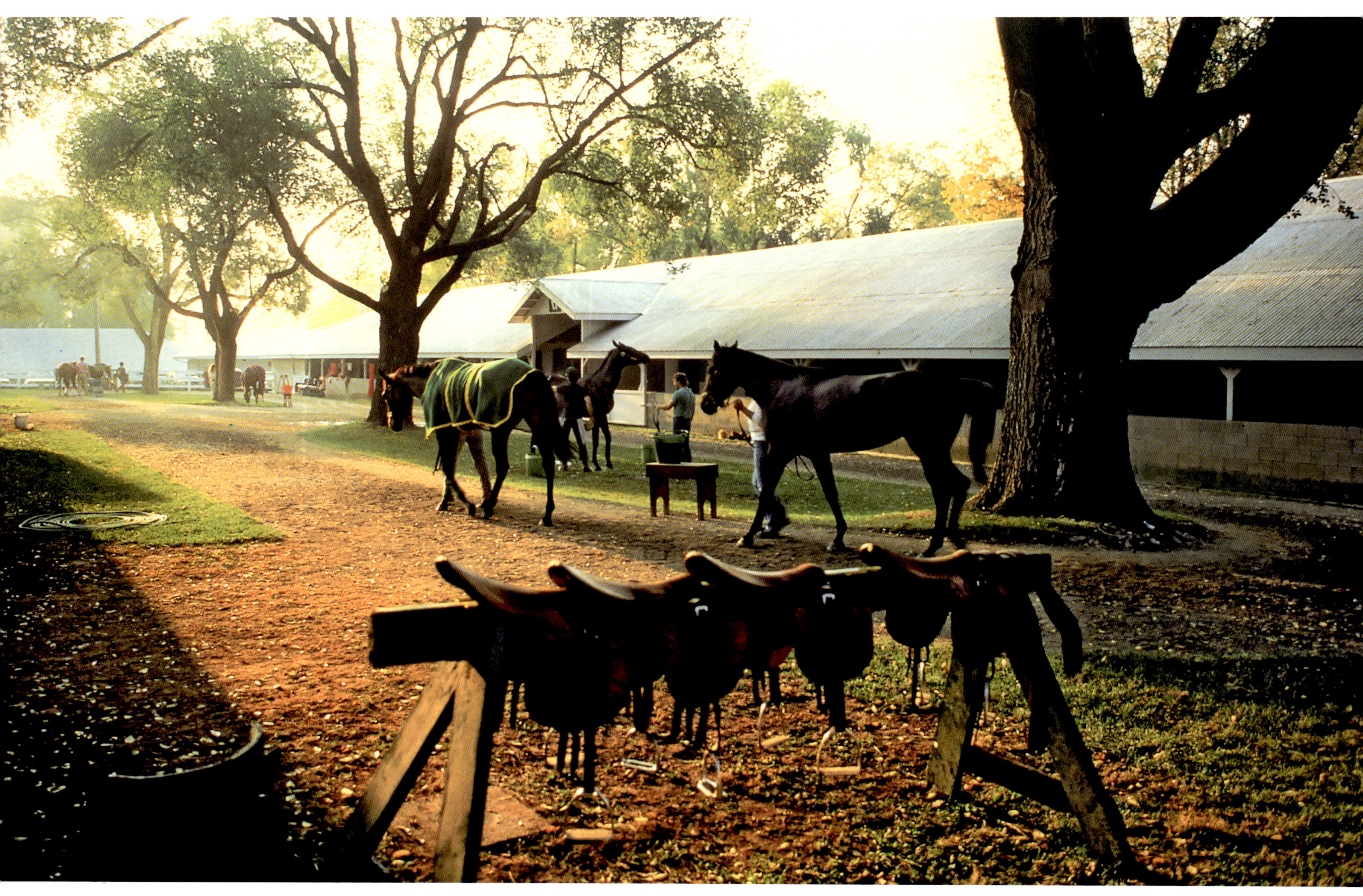

RACING SADDLES AT KEENELAND

Unlike the heavy saddles associated with cowboys, racing saddles are lightweight (weighing only a few pounds) and are built for strength and speed. They must be able to carry a jockey securely through the rigors of a race. Since the turn of the twentieth century, the technique or style of riding a racehorse has changed dramatically. Back then, jockeys would sit on the saddle with their feet in long stirrups during the race. Now they ride with their boots in raised stirrups and their bodies high above the backs of the horses.

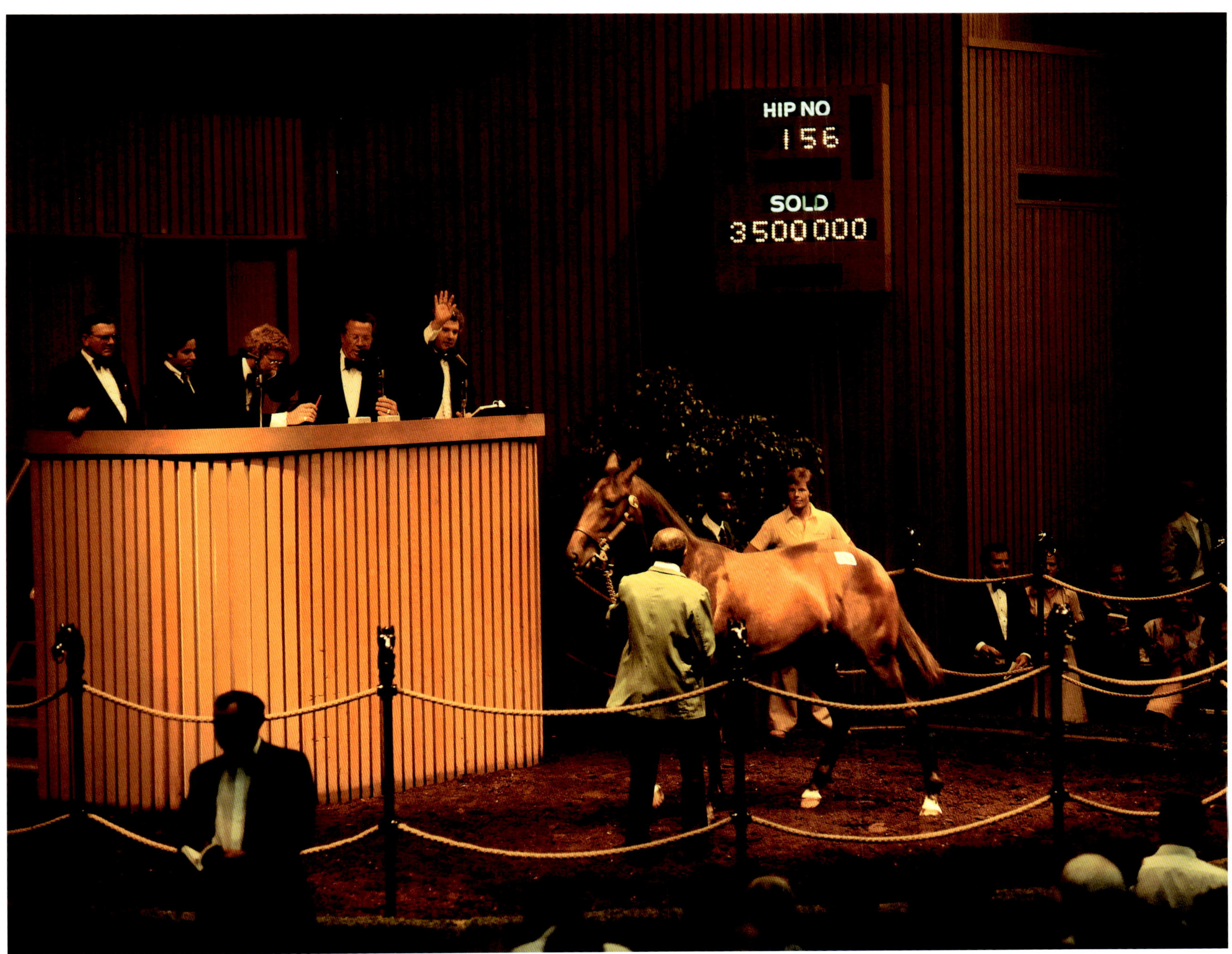

THOROUGHBRED HORSE SALES AT KEENELAND

For decades, the annual Thoroughbred horse sales at Keeneland have attracted the world's richest and most influential buyers. Many of the best equine pedigrees are consigned through Keeneland. During the September yearling sale, young, untested colts regularly sell for hundreds of thousands to millions of dollars. A yearling colt by Nijinsky II out of My Charmer in 1985 sold for $13.1 million, a world record. The November breeding stock sales at Keeneland also attract large numbers of buyers. In addition, Fasig-Tipton on Newtown Pike hosts several Thoroughbred yearling and selected mixed sales during the year.

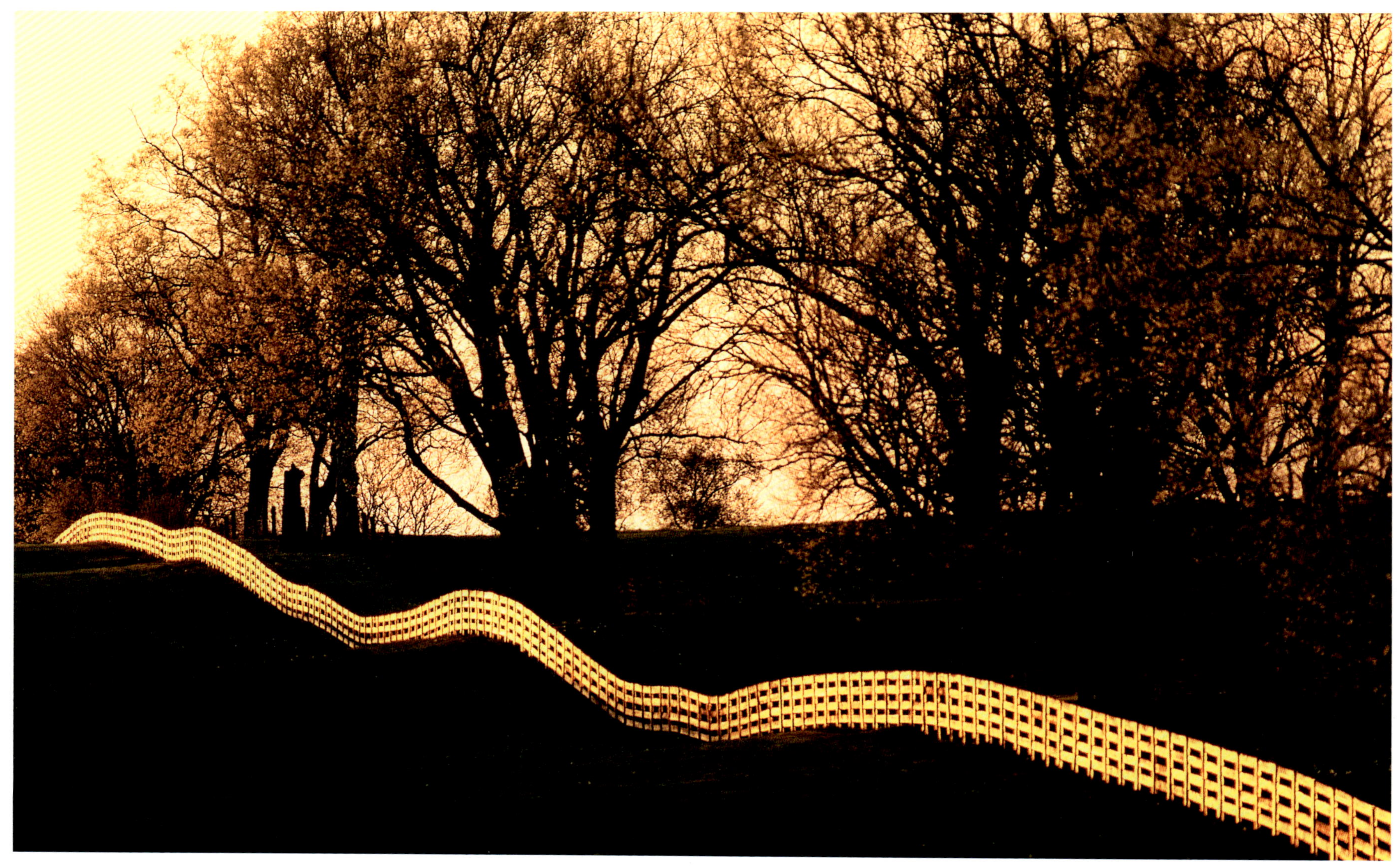

FENCE AT EVENING

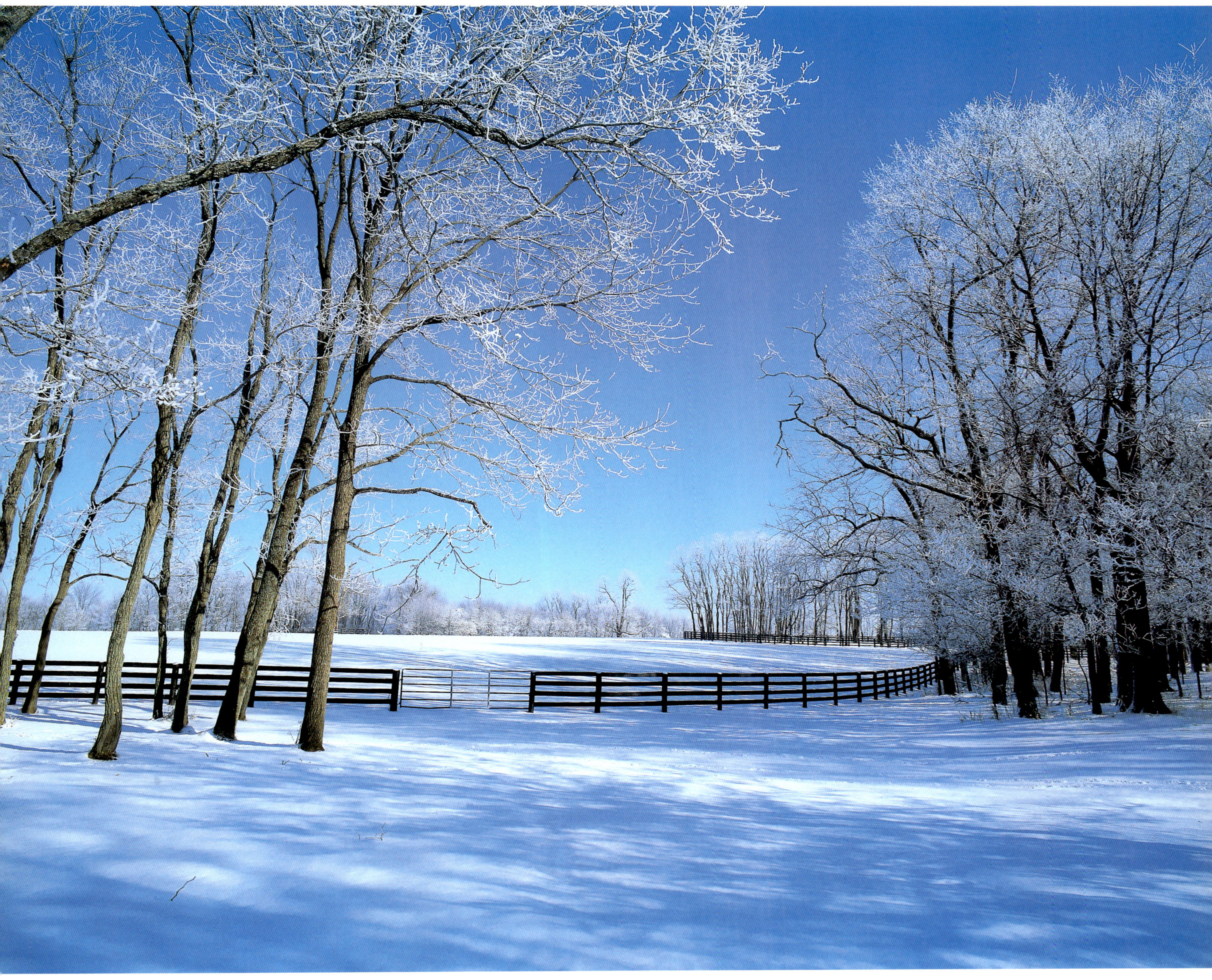

WINTER MORNING, WOODFORD COUNTY

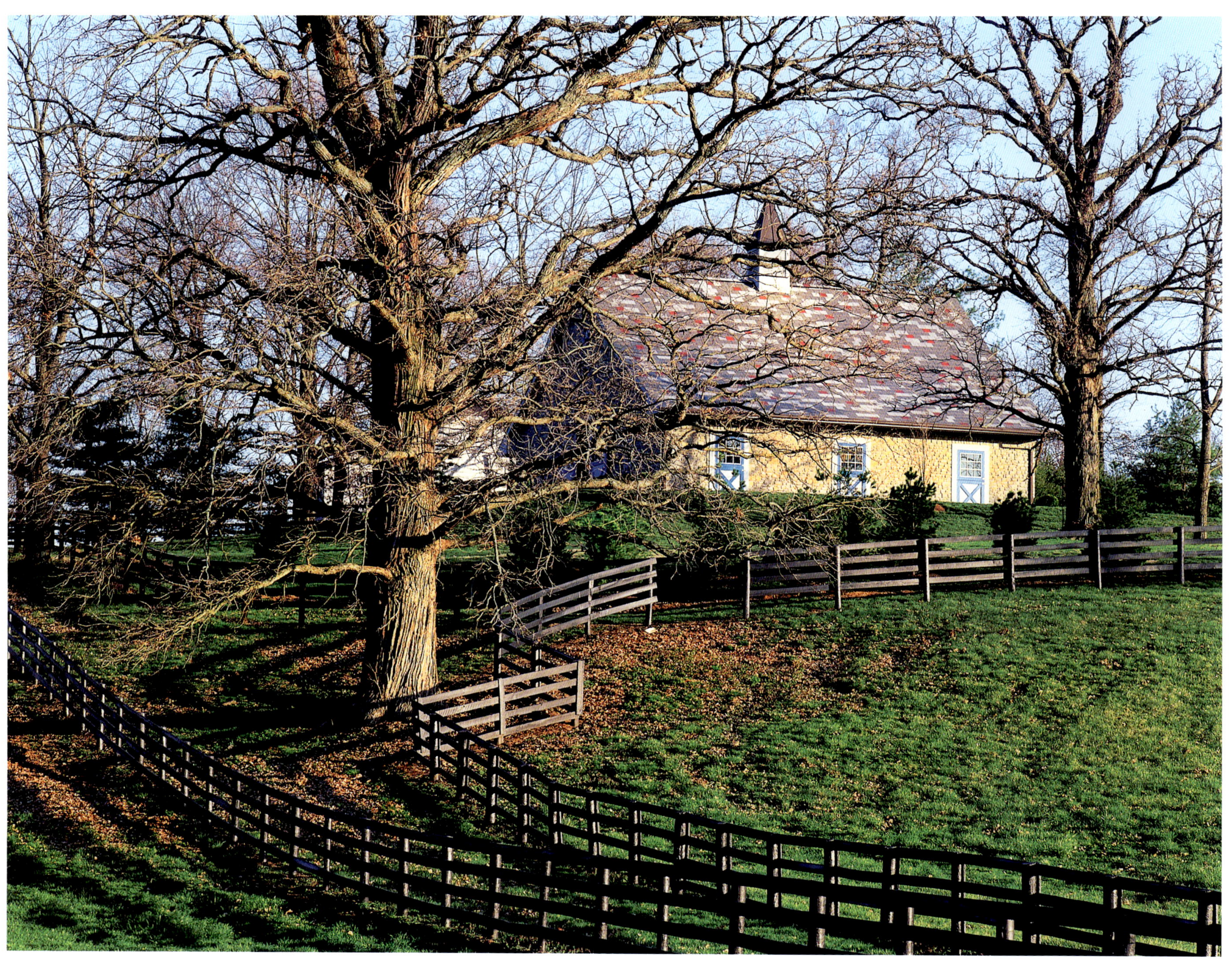

BARN AT ASHFORD STUD

Along the road between Versailles and Frankfort are several of the largest horse farms in Kentucky. The size of a single farm can exceed 2,000 acres. The Ashford Stud is set among rolling hills and is known for its beautiful landscapes and architecturally unique barns and buildings in a European style.

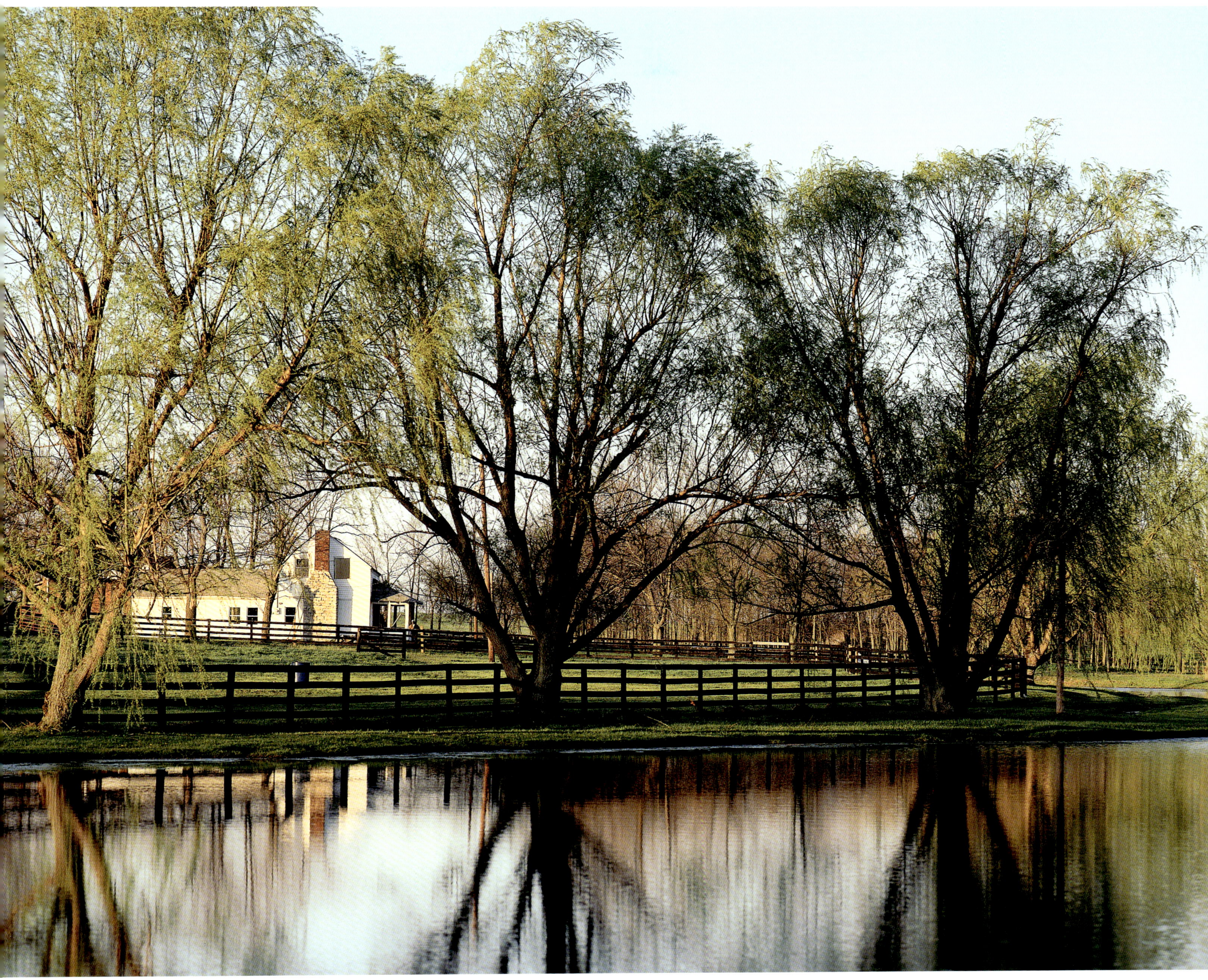

HOUSE ALONG CARRICK PIKE

This old house beside a pond along Carrick Pike in Scott County is emblematic of how life in the Bluegrass is changing. Until recently, this small piece of land, with a modest home and a barn or two, could easily support a family. But property values in the region have soared in recent years, and shortly after this photograph was taken, the acreage was sold, the house torn down, and the land consolidated into a large horse farm operation.

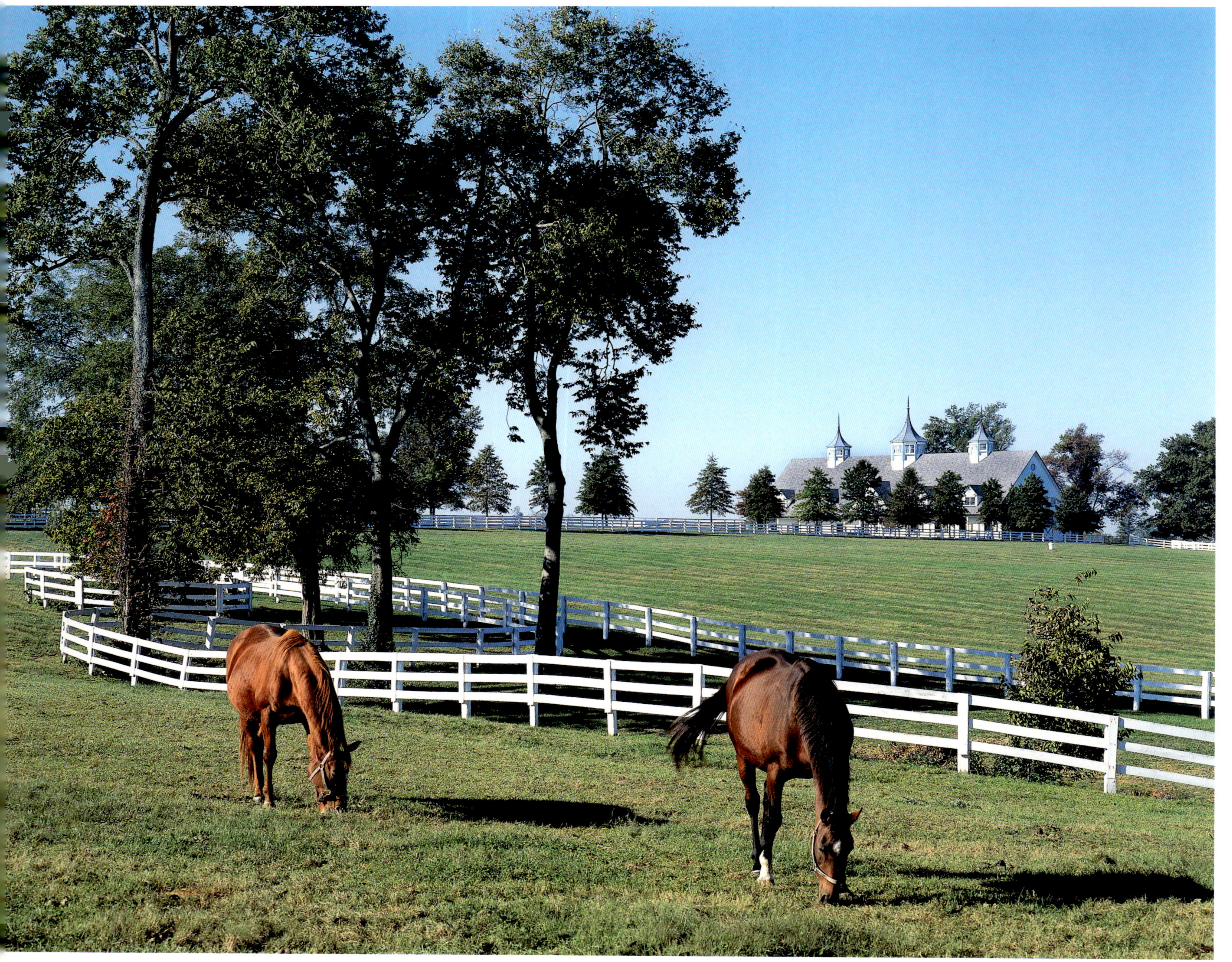

MARES AND BARN AT MANCHESTER FARM

People who visit the Bluegrass are often amazed by the luxurious accommodations provided for the horses. In recent years, the influx of foreign investment in the horse business has seen the construction of horse barns valued at millions of dollars. This barn on the Manchester Farm dominates the ridge behind Keeneland Race Course. Close to Lexington and accessible by public roads, this barn is arguably the most photographed horse barn in Kentucky.

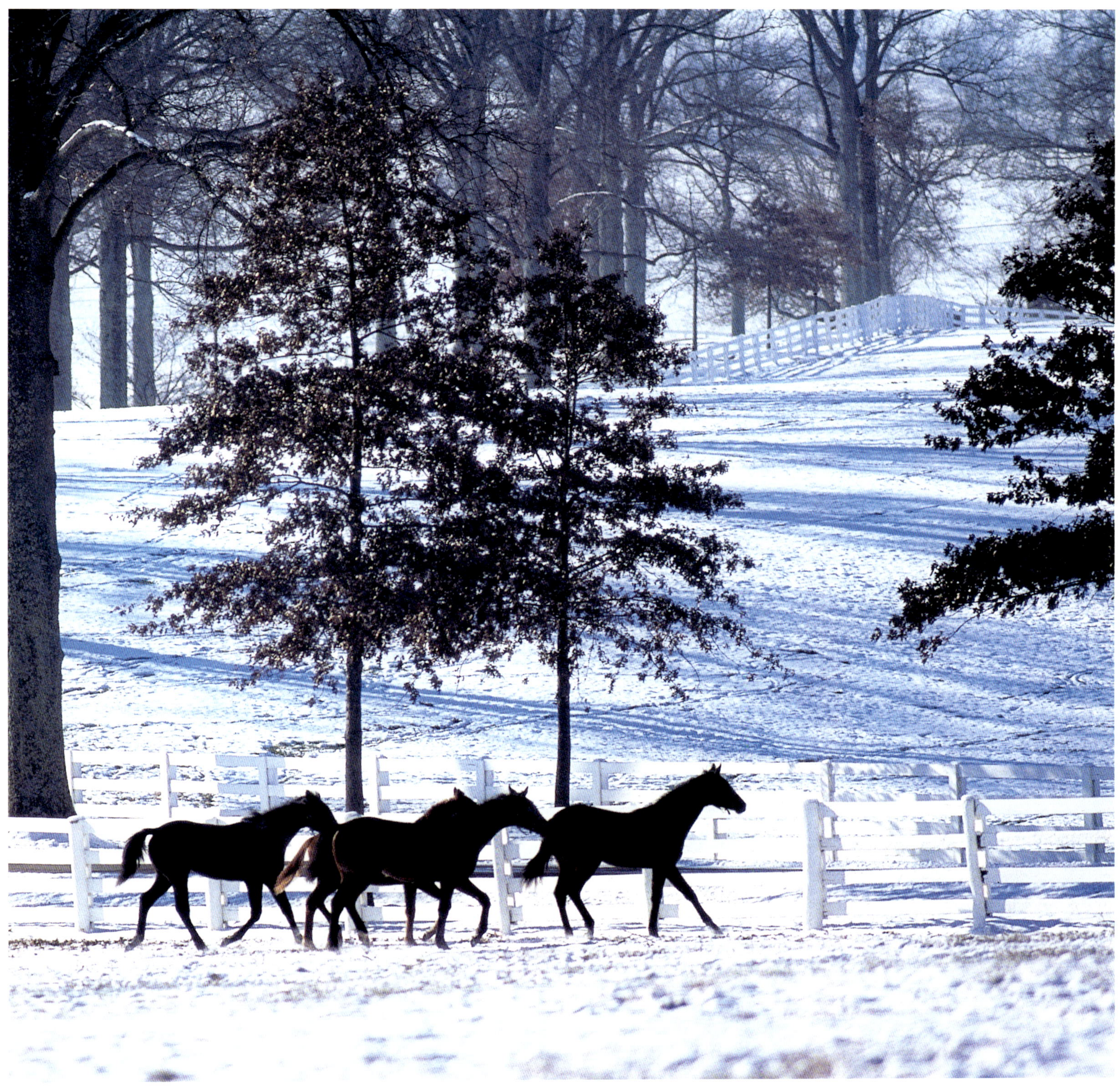

YEARLINGS IN SNOW AT DARBY DAN FARM

Darby Dan Farm on the Old Frankfort Pike has a long history as a producer of champion Thoroughbreds. The farm was once part of Colonel E. R. Bradley's Idle Hour Stock Farm, which produced four Kentucky Derby winners in the 1920s and 1930s. John Galbreath purchased Darby Dan in the late 1950s and continued its legacy as the home of racing's elite. Darby Dan's stars included Kentucky Derby winners Chateaugay (1963) and Proud Clarion (1967); the major sire Graustark; and Roberto, winner of the Epsom Derby in 1972. Roberto was named for baseball star Roberto Clemente, whose team, the Pittsburgh Pirates, was owned by Galbreath.

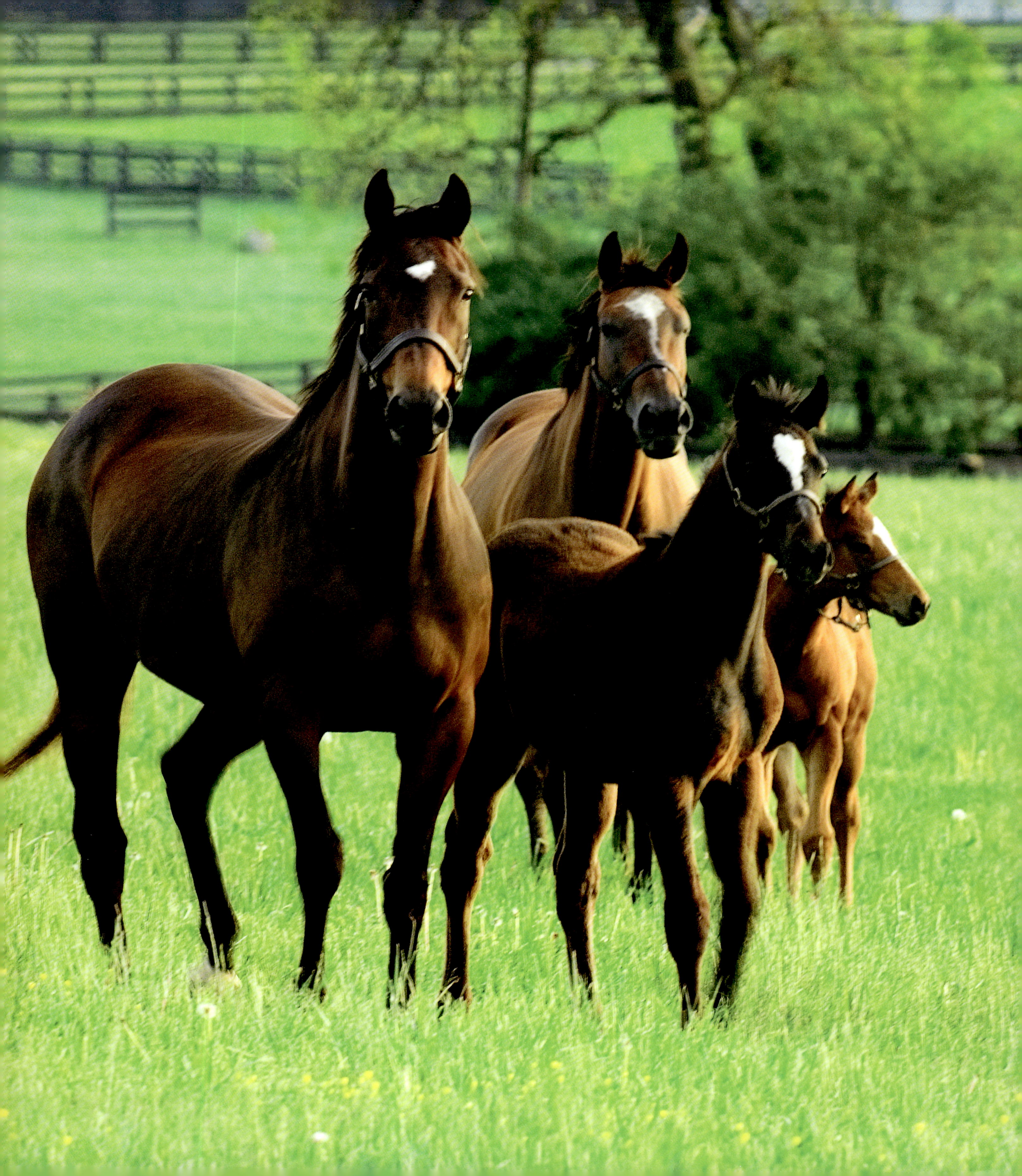

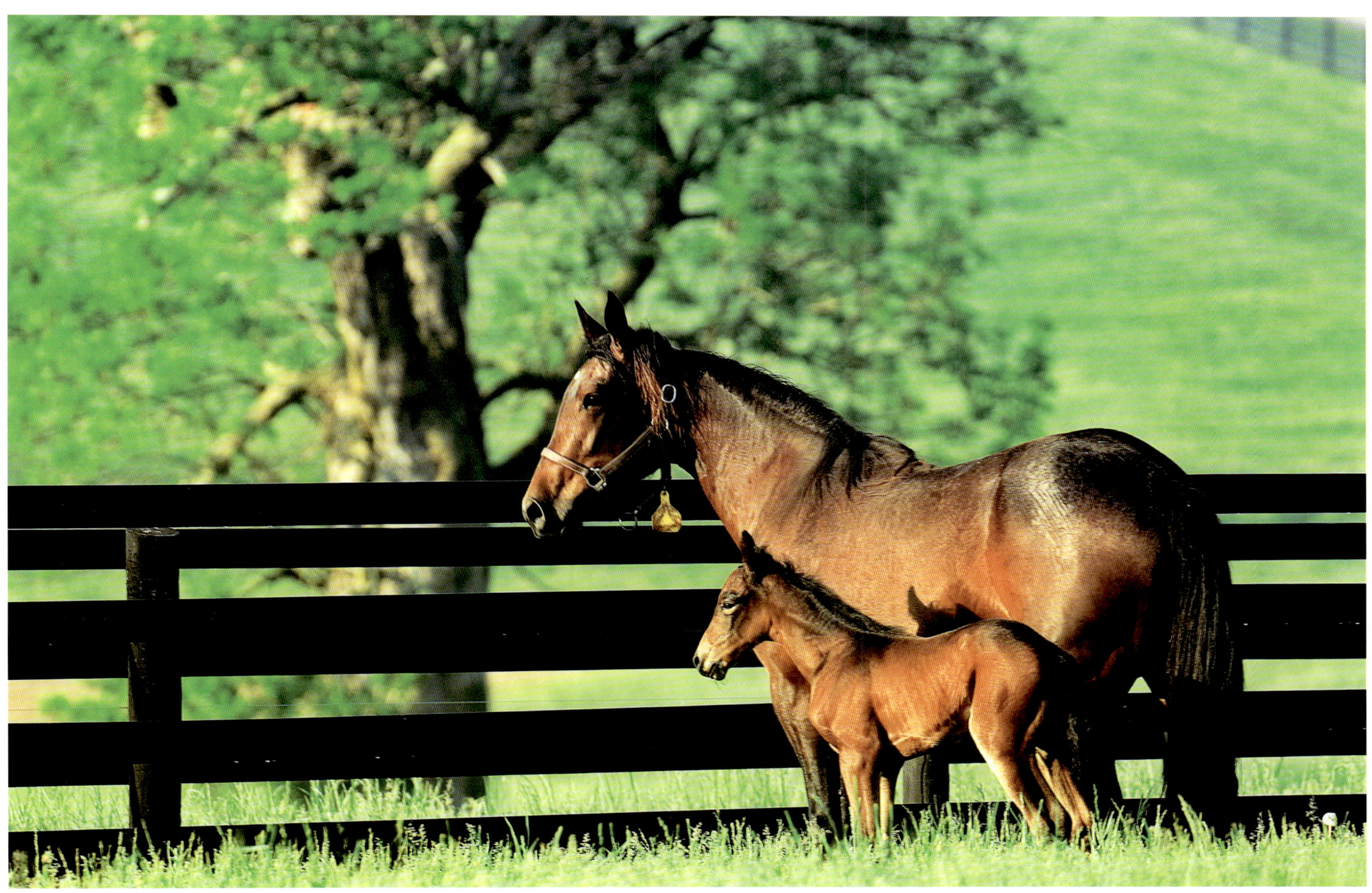

Facing: MARES AND THEIR FOALS, EARLY SPRING

Between January and June, the Bluegrass comes alive with the birthing of foals. The first day of the year is the common birthday for all Thoroughbred and Standardbred horses. Thus, whether a horse is born in January, March, or June, it is considered a one-year-old on 1 January of the following year. This means that a "one-year-old" foal born in January is older and physically more mature than one born in June. Whether this makes a difference on the track when the horses become two- and three-year-olds is open to debate. Because of its size, the near foal in this photograph was probably an early January baby.

Above: MARE AND FOAL WITH BUR OAK

Night turns to day on this Scott County Standardbred farm as mare and foal stand in their paddock near an old bur oak. Many of these trees were alive before the European settlers arrived. The Bluegrass region of Kentucky was covered in a predominantly savanna-like grassland along with large, widely spaced trees. Stands of cane ran alongside the creeks. Most of the native grasses have been replaced by bluegrass, but many of the original trees remain.

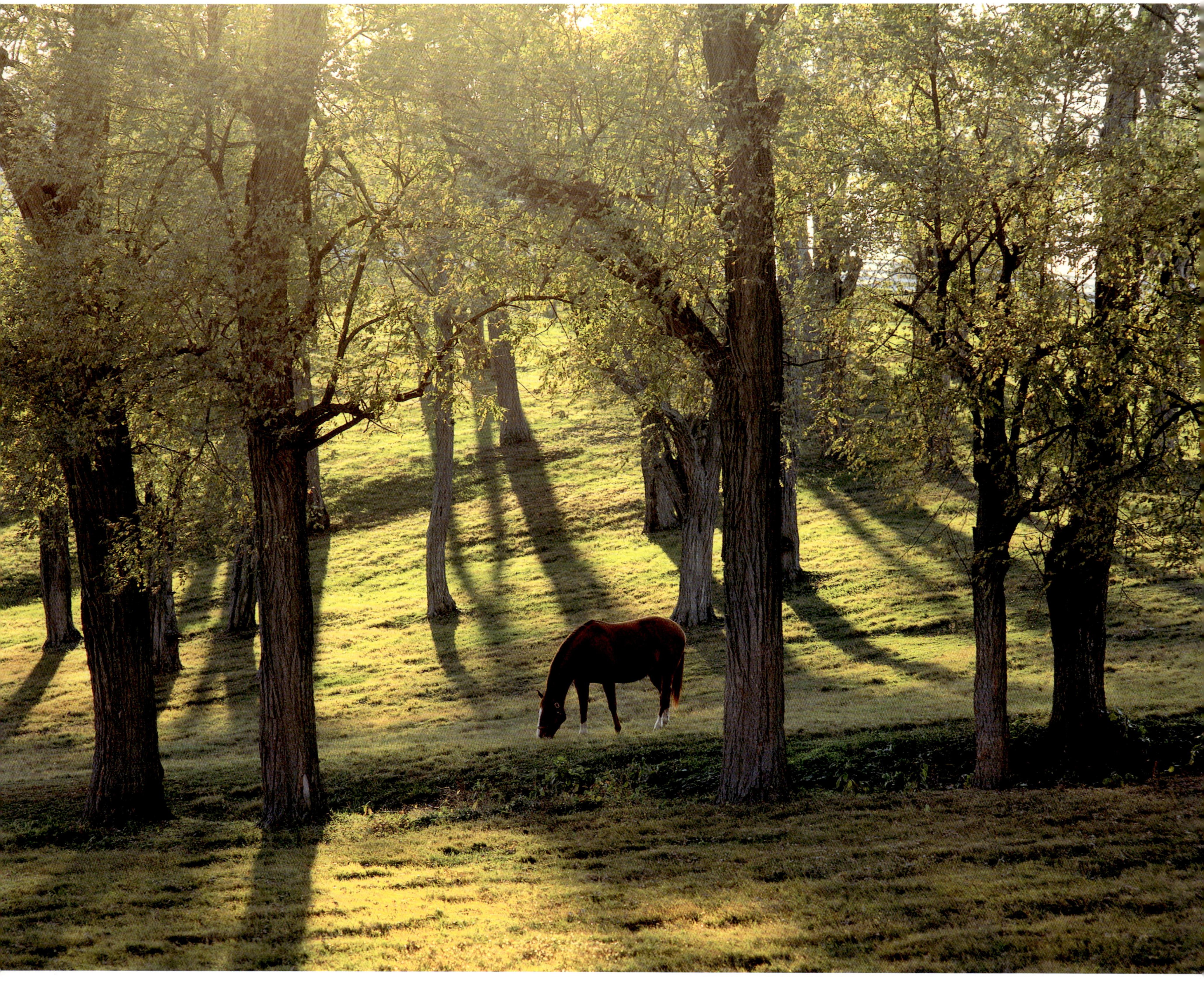

THOROUGHBRED MARE IN GROVE OF LOCUSTS

Because of the scarcity of trees in the Bluegrass, it is rare to see horses grazing among them. This stand of mature locusts affords some shade while still allowing plenty of light for the grass to prosper.

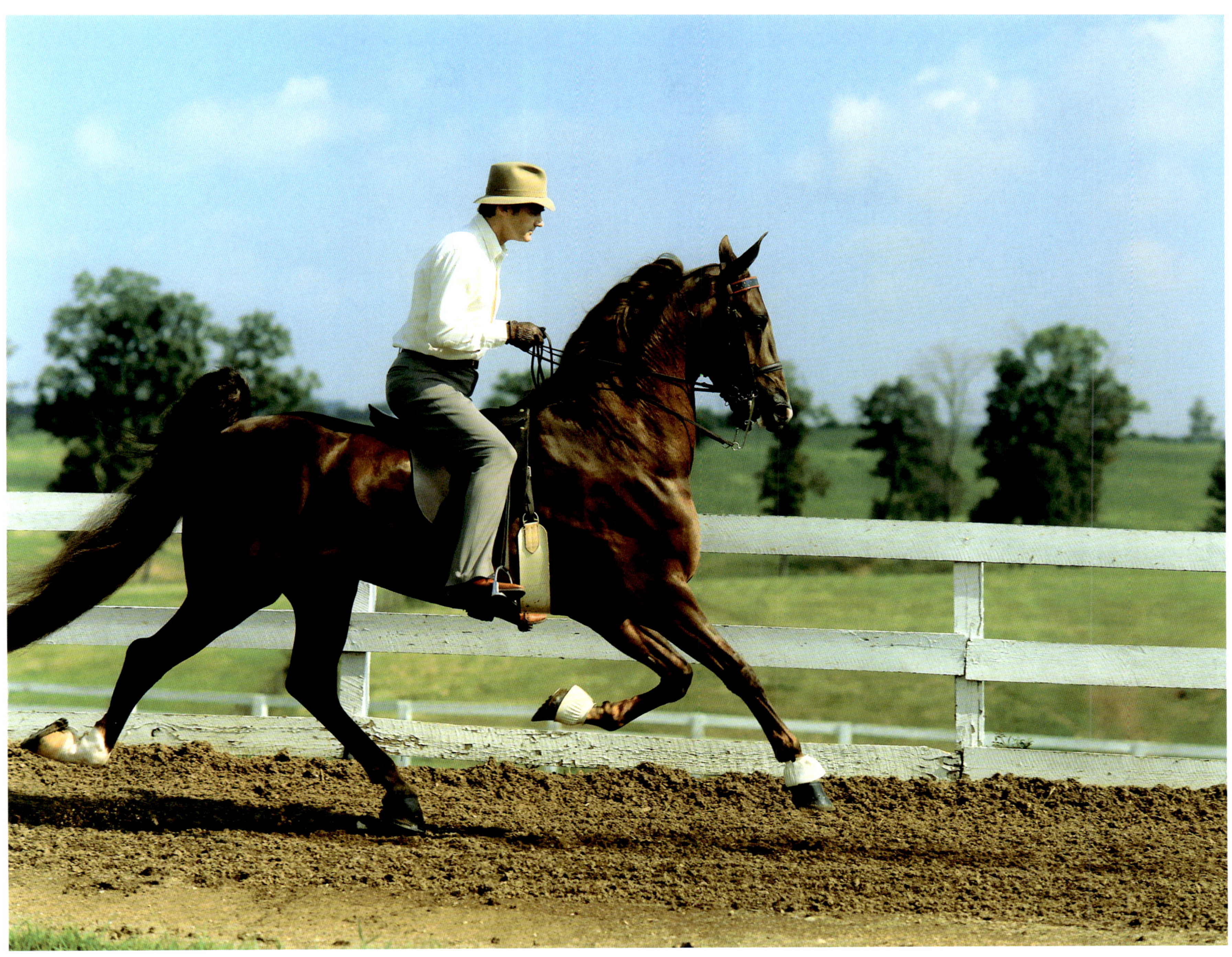

IMPERATOR, WORLD CHAMPION SADDLEBRED

The American Saddlebred may be the most handsome and elegant of all the horse breeds that walk Bluegrass fields. These high-spirited horses, exhibiting great strength and stamina, were bred by early Kentucky horsemen who meticulously combined specific breeds with desirable characteristics to create these beautiful animals. Central Kentucky is still home to many Saddlebred farms, and Lexington plays host to the annual world-renowned Junior League Horse Show. During the 1970s and early 1980s, Imperator was four-time, five-gaited World Grand Champion. He was retired at the Kentucky Horse Park.

Overleaf: **TESTING ITS LEGS**

Morning fog surrounds the paddock as this mare and her newborn are released from the stable for the day. The mare seems to be ignoring her baby for the moment, but she will see plenty of antics over the next several months. Young foals love to feel their legs under them; they run until they tire out, and then they run some more. It's what they were born to do.

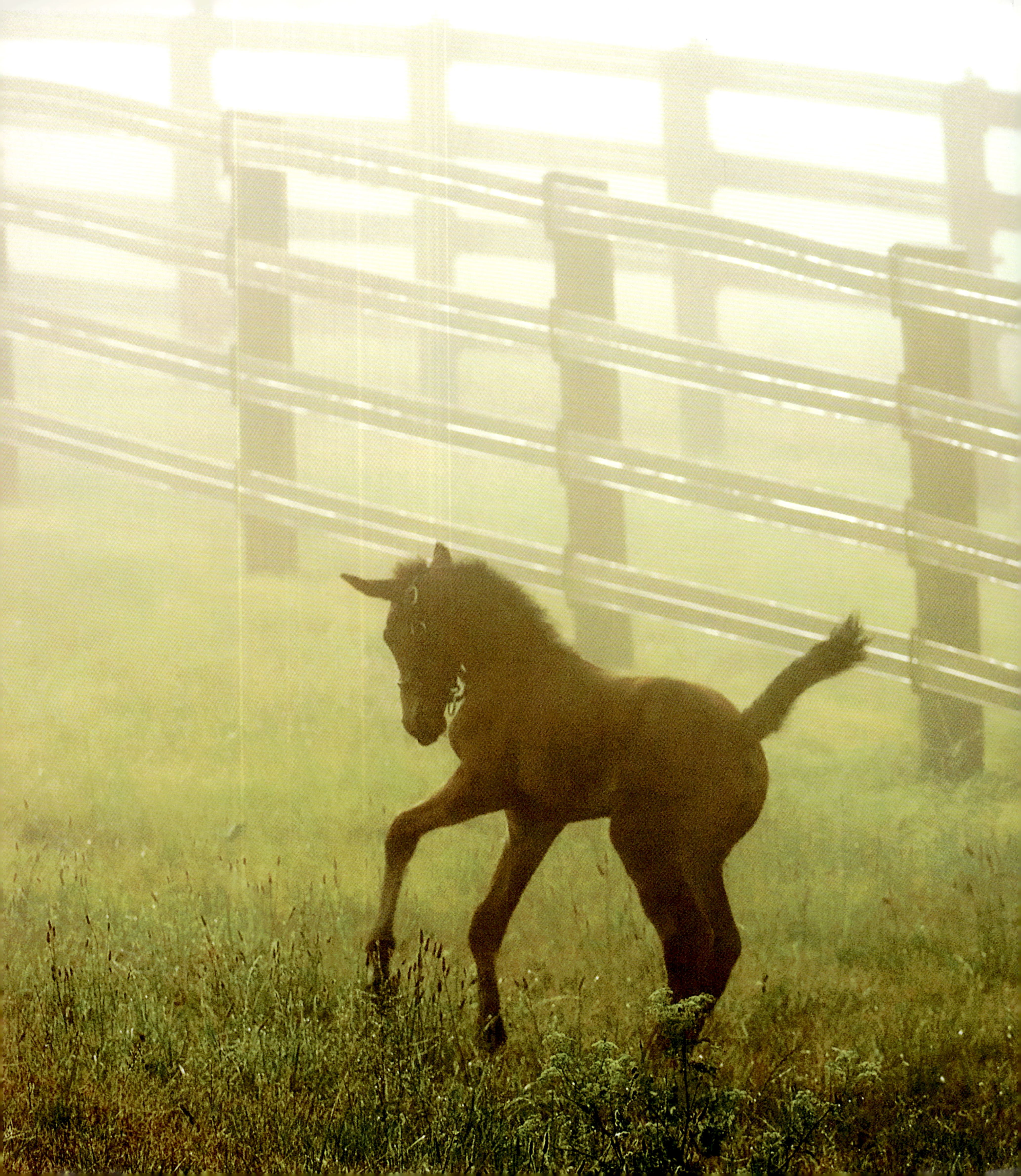

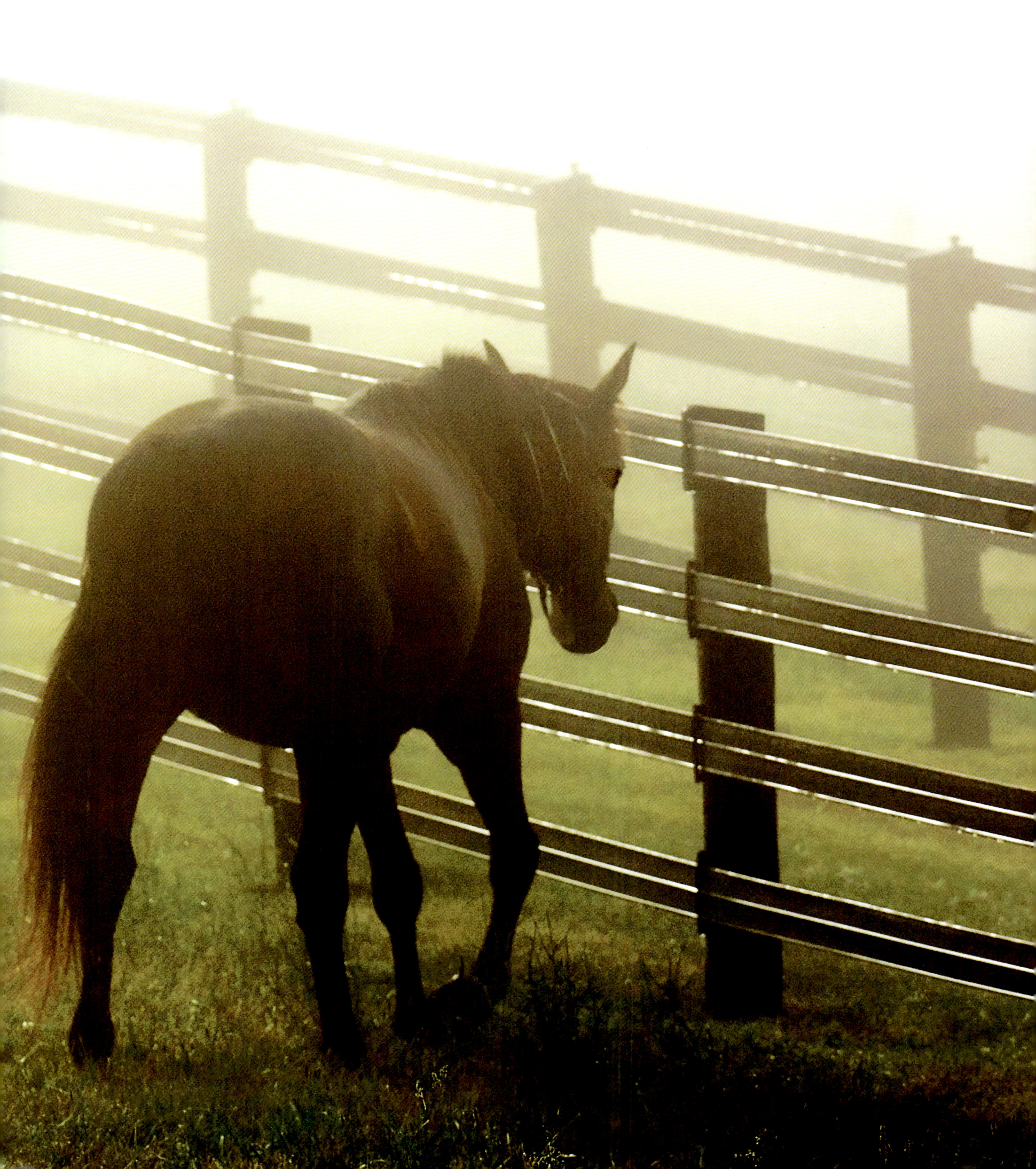

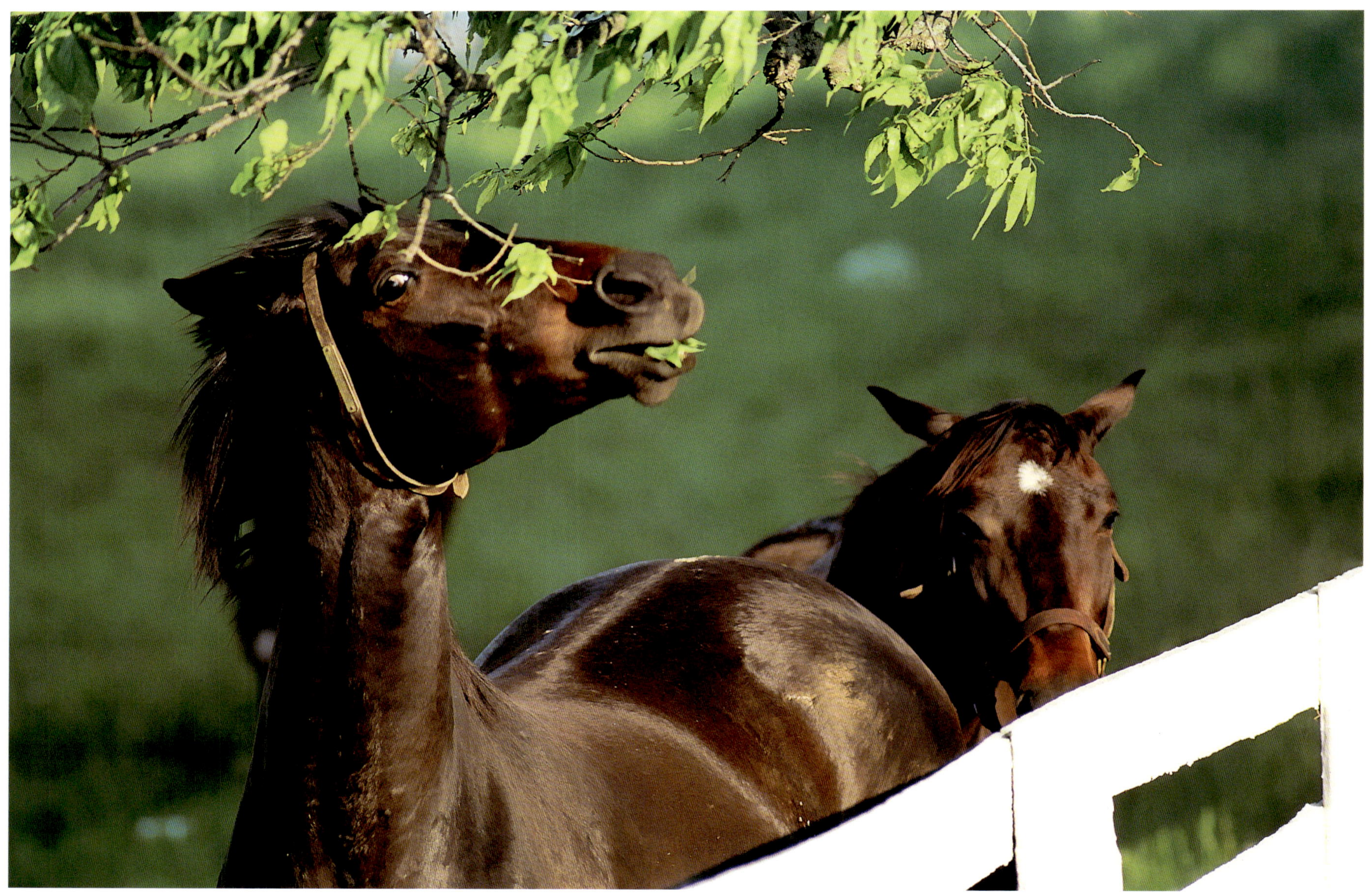

MISCHIEF

Like young children, yearlings will eat just about anything, including fences and tree branches. Here, a leafy morsel becomes the forbidden fruit—note the somewhat guilty stare directed at the photographer.